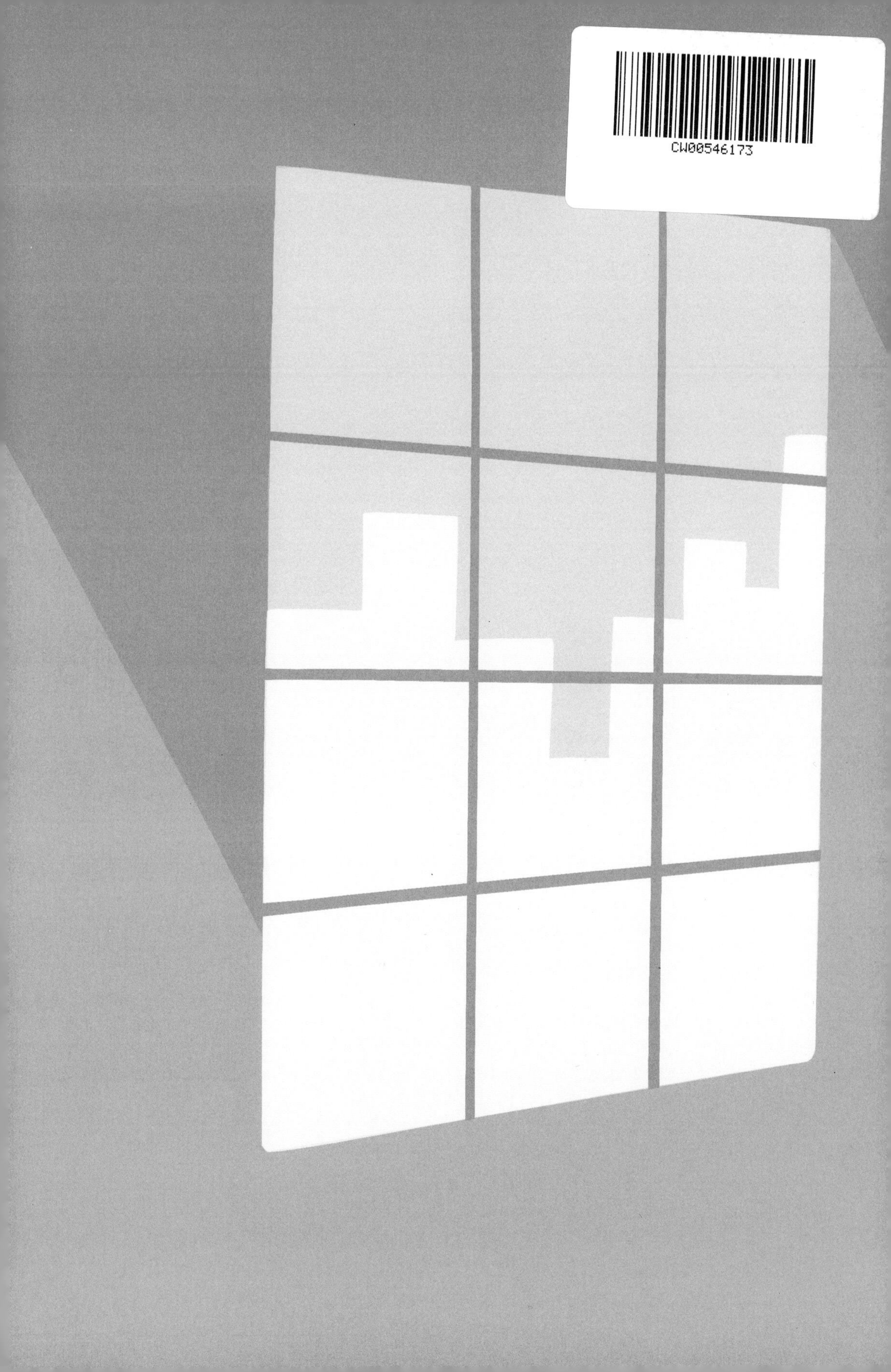

FLUNG OUT OF SPACE

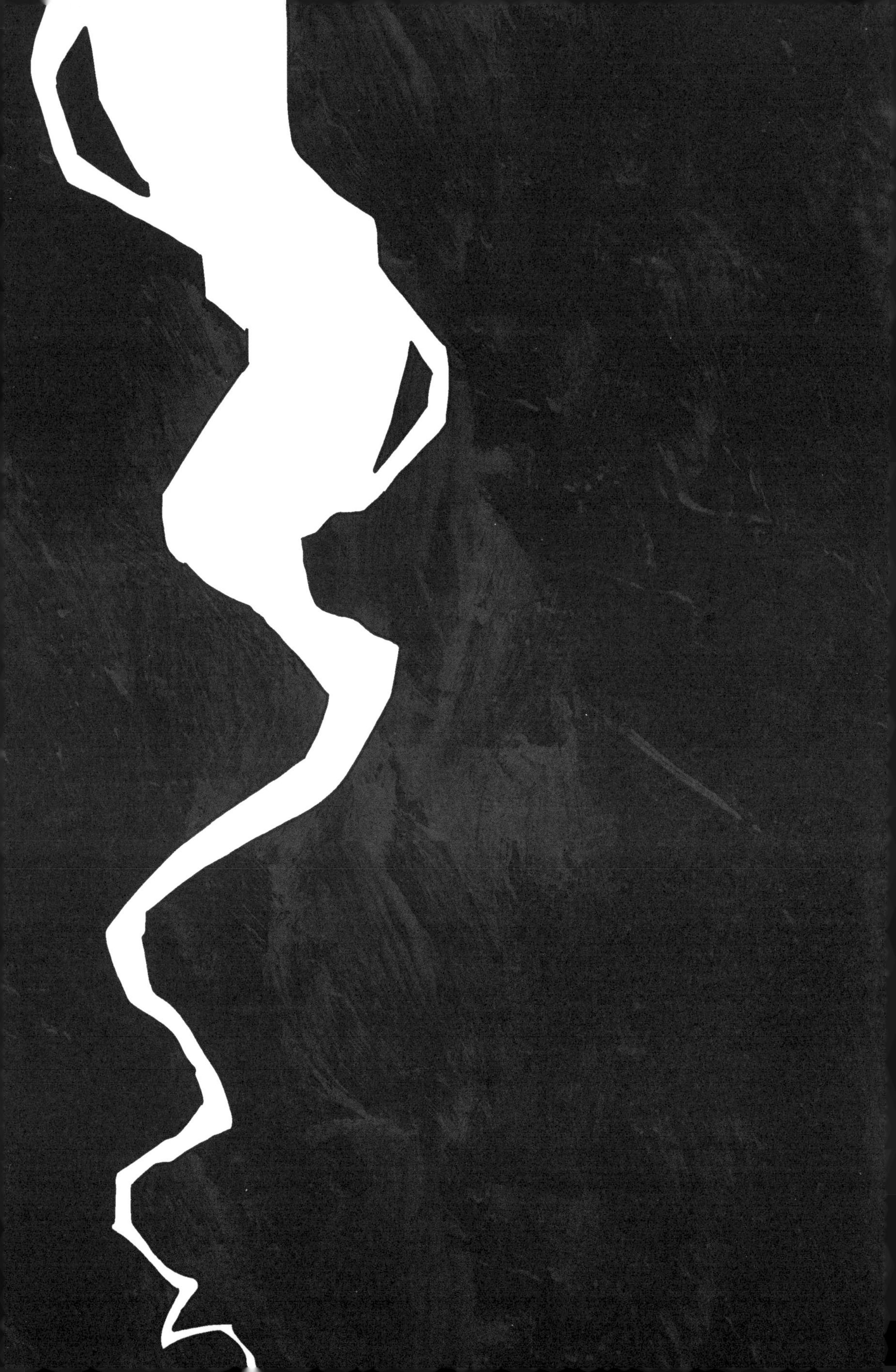

FLUNG OUT OF SPACE

INSPIRED BY THE INDECENT ADVENTURES OF PATRICIA HIGHSMITH

BY GRACE ELLIS
AND HANNAH TEMPLER

Abrams ComicArts SURELY, New York

SURELY publishes LGBTQIA+ stories by LGBTQIA+ creators, with a focus on new stories, new voices, and untold histories, in works that span fiction and nonfiction, including memoir, horror, comedy, and fantasy. Surely aims to publish books for teens and adults that lend context and perspective to our current struggles and victories, and to support those creators underrepresented in the current publishing world. We are bold, brave, loud, unexpected, daring, unique.

Surely Curator: Mariko Tamaki
Editor: Charlotte Greenbaum
Designers: Andrea Miller & Kay Petronio
Managing Editor: Marie Oishi
Production Manager: Alison Gervais

Library of Congress Control Number 2021933727

ISBN 978-1-4197-4433-4

Printed and bound in China
10 9 8 7 6 5 4 3 2 1

Abrams ComicArts books are available at special discounts
when purchased in quantity for premiums and promotions
as well as fundraising or educational use.
Special editions can also be created to specification.
For details, contact specialsales@abramsbooks.com or the address below.

Abrams ComicArts® is a registered trademark of Harry N. Abrams, Inc.
SURELY™ is a trademark of Mariko Tamaki and Harry N. Abrams, Inc.

ABRAMS The Art of Books
195 Broadway, New York, NY 10007
abramsbooks.com

AUTHOR'S NOTE

PATRICIA HIGHSMITH (1921–1995) was a bestselling American author who is most famous for what she described as "suspense novels," although even that categorization feels limiting. I think I would call them "psychological thriller romps." Twisted and unsettling? Undoubtedly. But a fun romp? Absolutely, and I think that's an important part of what makes them works of art. Highsmith believed that everyone feels the tug of dark impulses from time to time, and she played on those impulses to elicit the sick glee of identifying with liars, criminals, and murderers. The suspense in her work doesn't come from asking, "Whodunit?" but from asking, "Will they get away with it?" followed by a furtive "I hope so."

All of Pat's novels are like this, with one notable exception: *The Price of Salt*, later retitled *Carol*. To say that *Carol* found its audience would be an understatement; its audience sought it out, and it remains one of the most fundamental and beloved works of lesbian fiction to this day. Even as this audacious book stands alone in her canon, *Carol* is in many ways a very classically Highsmithian story, especially considering Pat's ability to connect the passion of murder to the passion of love. Will Carol and Therese get away with it? I hope so.

Pat's biographer, Joan Schenkar, who had planned to write an afterword for *Flung Out of Space* but who sadly passed away suddenly, described this book you're holding as a "fantasia," which I think is apt. This is a fictionalized, narrative version of a true story. I think of it as the version you would tell around a campfire. The timeline is condensed, the conversations are imagined, some of the characters are composites of multiple real people, but the most interesting facts and events are true.

This is a story I believe is worth telling. That being said, I want to be clear: The protagonist of this story is not a good person. In fact, Patricia Highsmith was an appalling person. She was deeply anti-Semetic, racist, and misogynistic, even by the standards of her time. I am not being hyperbolic when I say that many of her beliefs were nothing short of evil, and I know I speak for Hannah and the rest of this book's team when I say that we condemn these beliefs as vehemently as possible.

Although this is not a story directly about her prejudices, this book contains instances of Pat's bigotry. We made the informed choice to include them because her hatefulness is an important piece in understanding who she was as a person, and it's something you should be aware of as you're reading. I take no pleasure in writing about her prejudices; I do not expect you to take pleasure in reading about them. If you're interested in learning more, I recommend the books that are listed as sources at the end of this book. As I write this note, there are plans to publish Pat's diaries, which I'm sure will add new depth this conversation as well.

By all accounts, Pat had a magnetic personality and could be charming when she wanted to be, and in that way, she closely resembles the characters she's most famous for writing: charismatic sociopaths who are worryingly easy to root for. The fact that she was a terrible person contributed to her success.

History is populated by complicated and destructive human beings. I think it's important that we reckon with that. Not every influential or important figure deserves to be put on a pedestal, including women and LGBTQ people. Simplified hagiographies have their purposes, but I think they ultimately do us all a disservice by flattening real people into heroes and villains when the truth is almost always richer and more complicated. Patricia Highsmith is not a hero, and she had a huge, positive impact on LGBTQ literature, not to mention American literature in general, and because of that, her story is a fundamental part of our history.

I love and admire Patricia Highsmith's writing. I'm sure that many of you do, too. My goal is not to dissuade you from your love but to simply tell you the story of an iconic book's unconventional (and in some ways, surprising) origins.

If you read this book and end up conflicted about Highsmith and her legacy: good.

Grace Ellis, 2022

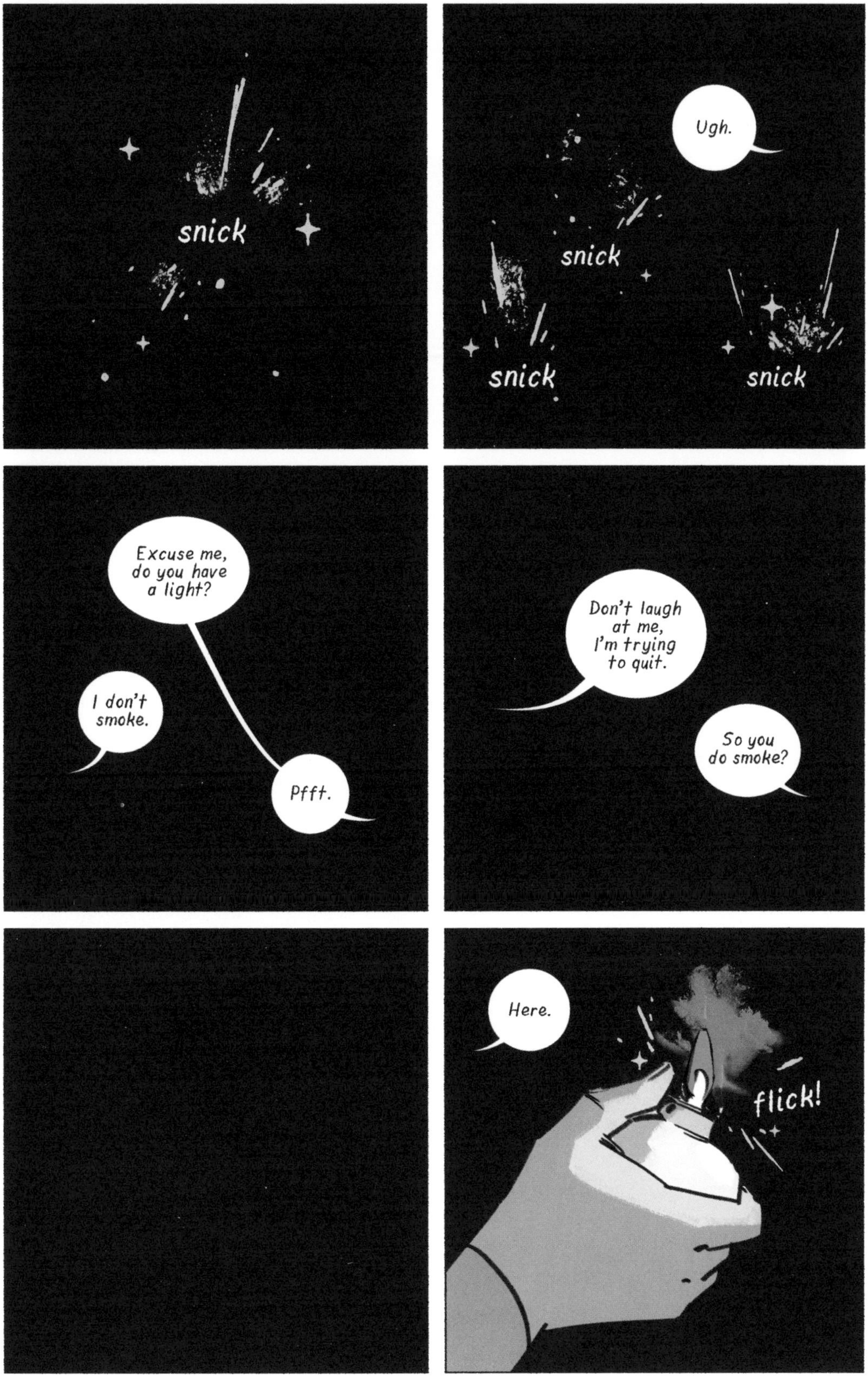
snick
Ugh.
snick
snick
snick
Excuse me, do you have a light?
I don't smoke.
Pfft.
Don't laugh at me, I'm trying to quit.
So you do smoke?
Here.
flick!

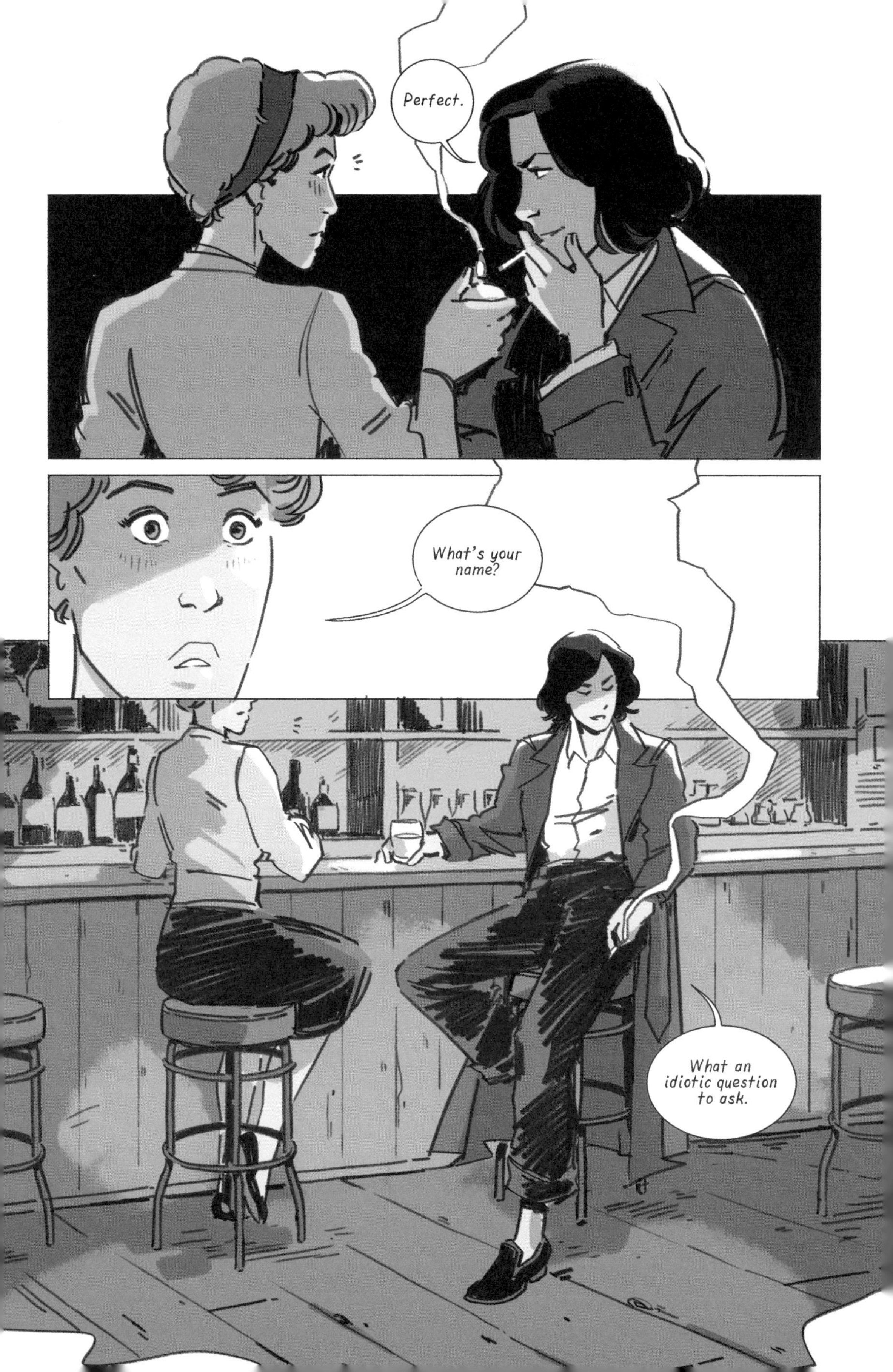
Perfect.
What's your name?
What an idiotic question to ask.

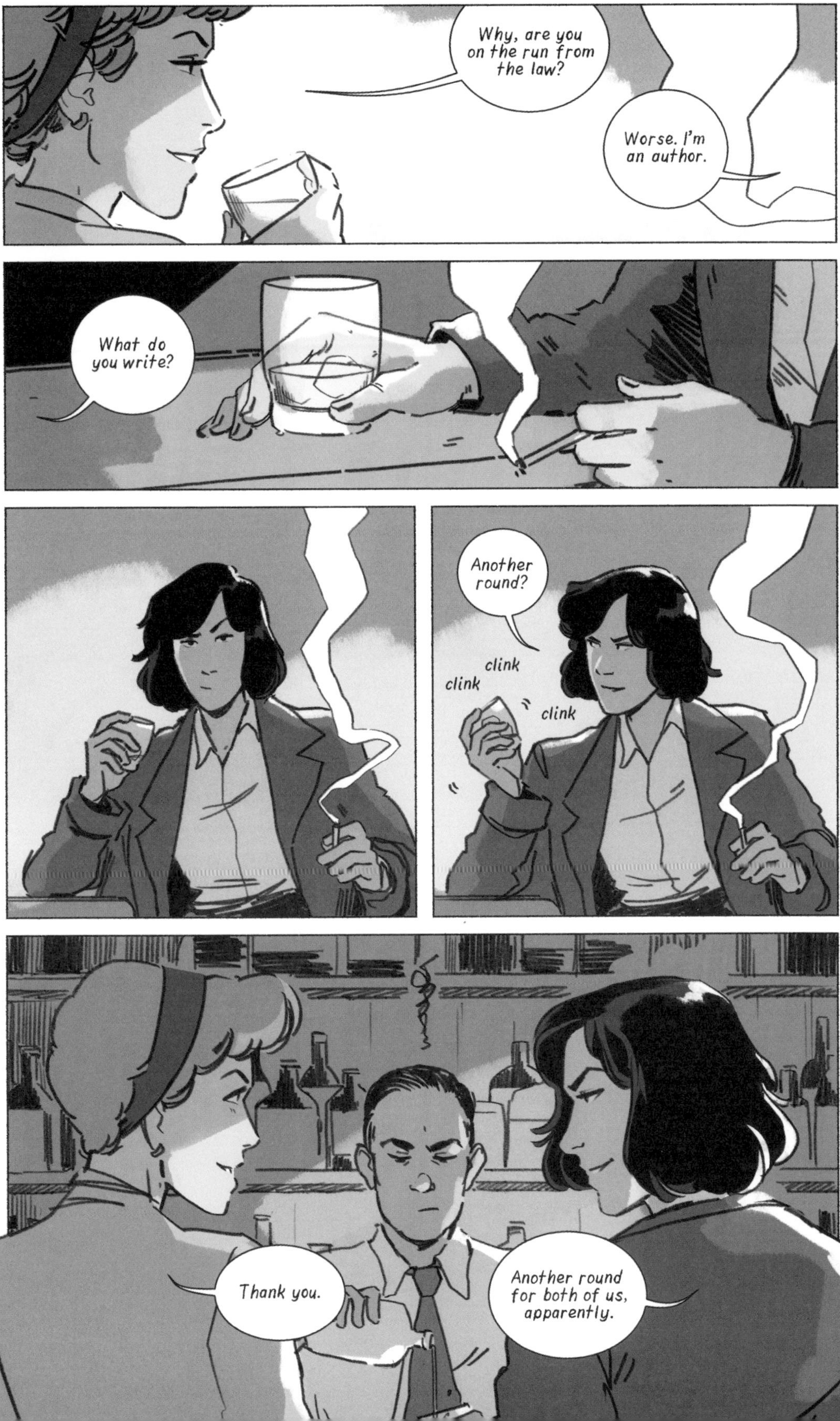
Why, are you on the run from the law?
Worse. I'm an author.
What do you write?
Another round?
clink
clink
clink
Thank you.
Another round for both of us, apparently.

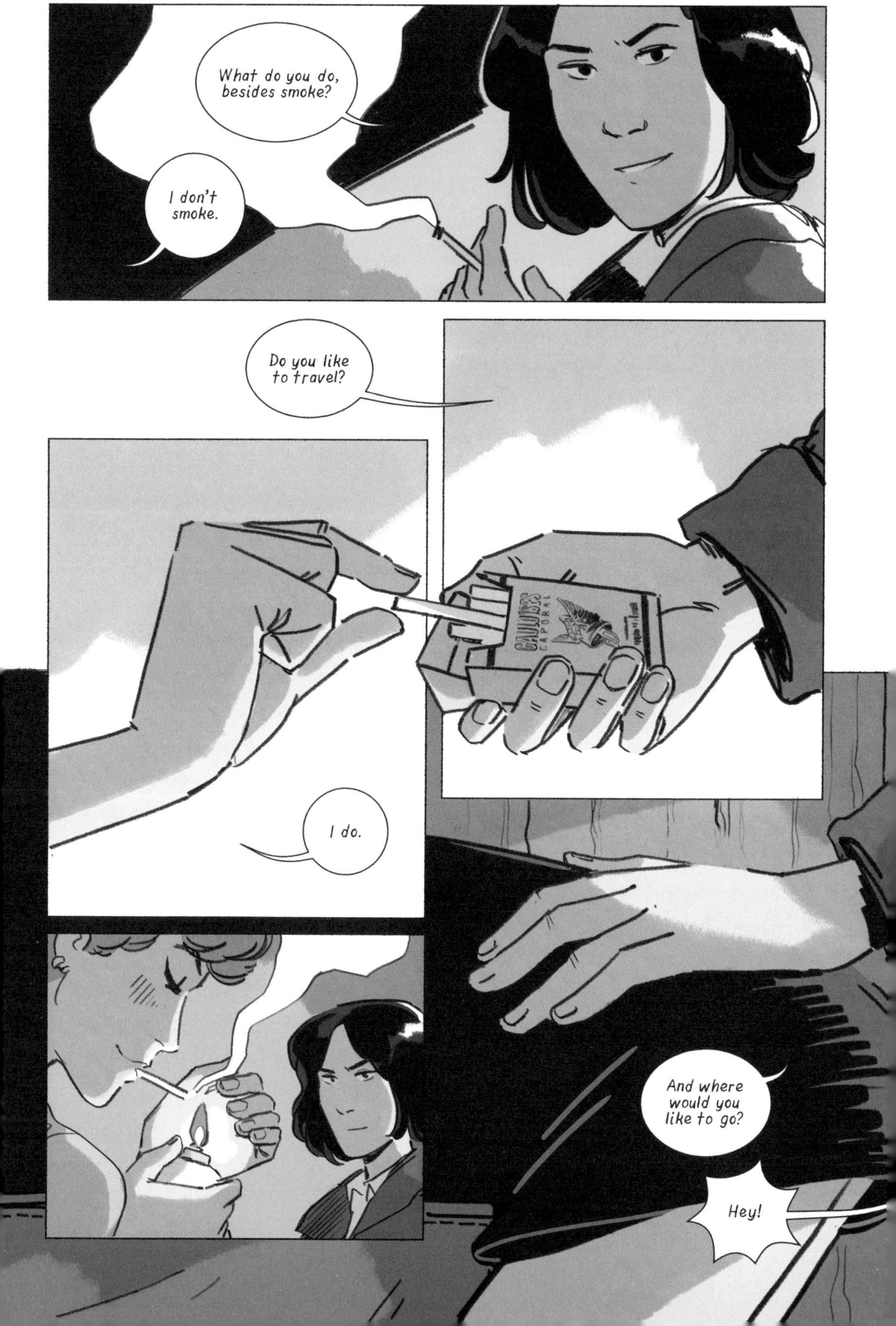
What do you do, besides smoke?
I don't smoke.
Do you like to travel?
I do.
And where would you like to go?
Hey!

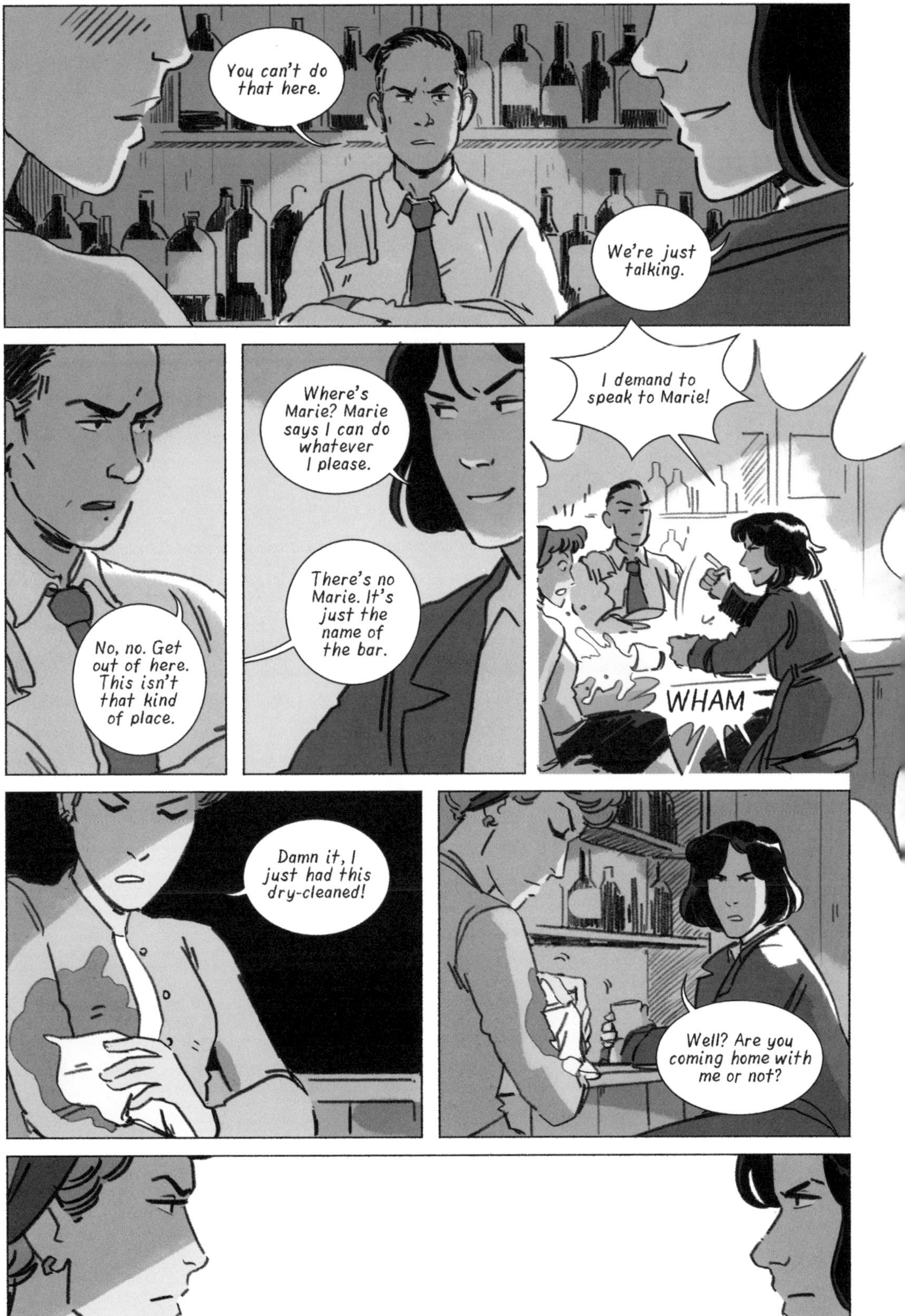

You can't do that here.
We're just talking.
No, no. Get out of here. This isn't that kind of place.
Where's Marie? Marie says I can do whatever I please.
There's no Marie. It's just the name of the bar.
I demand to speak to Marie!
WHAM
Damn it, I just had this dry-cleaned!
Well? Are you coming home with me or not?

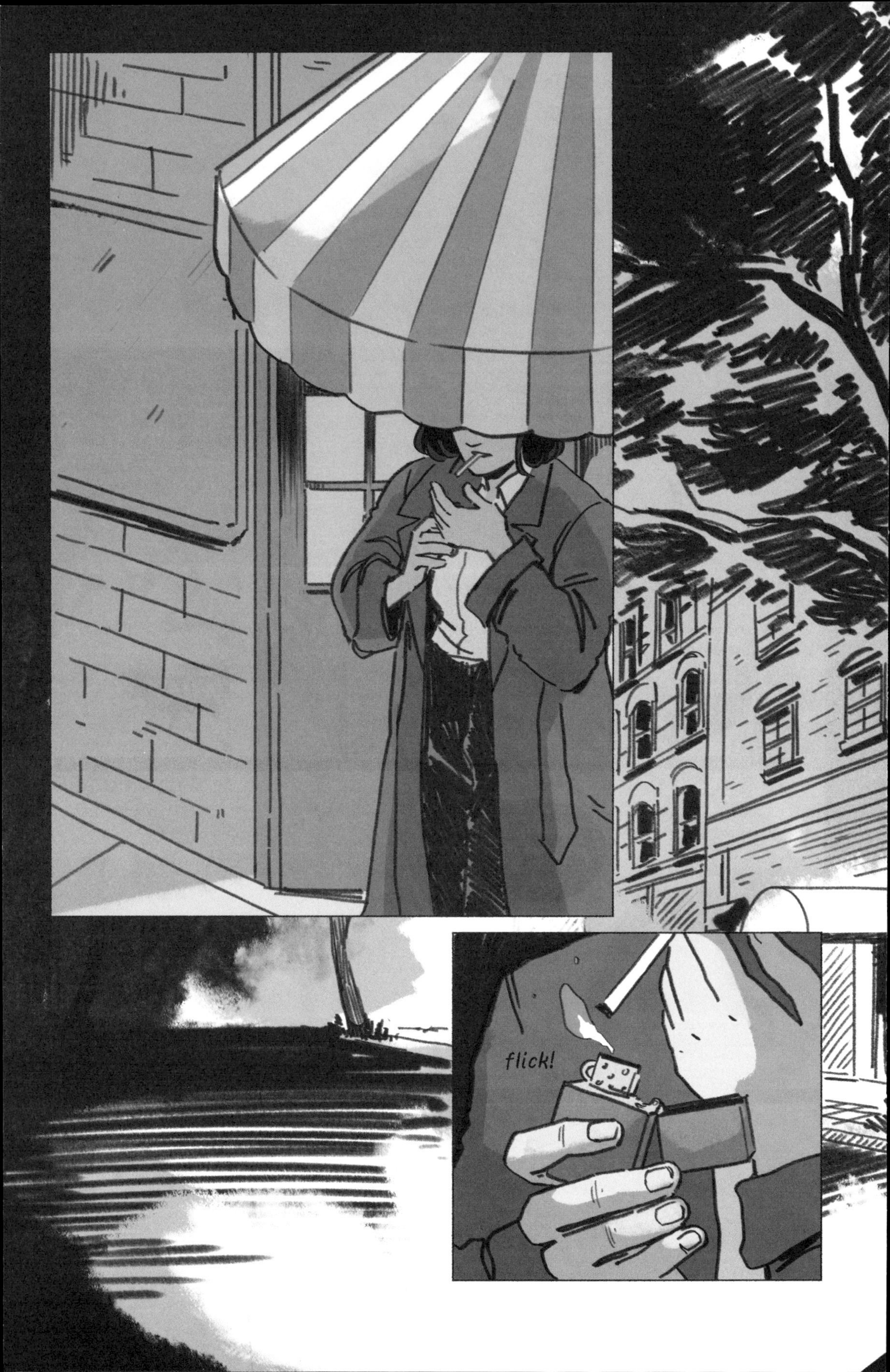
flick!

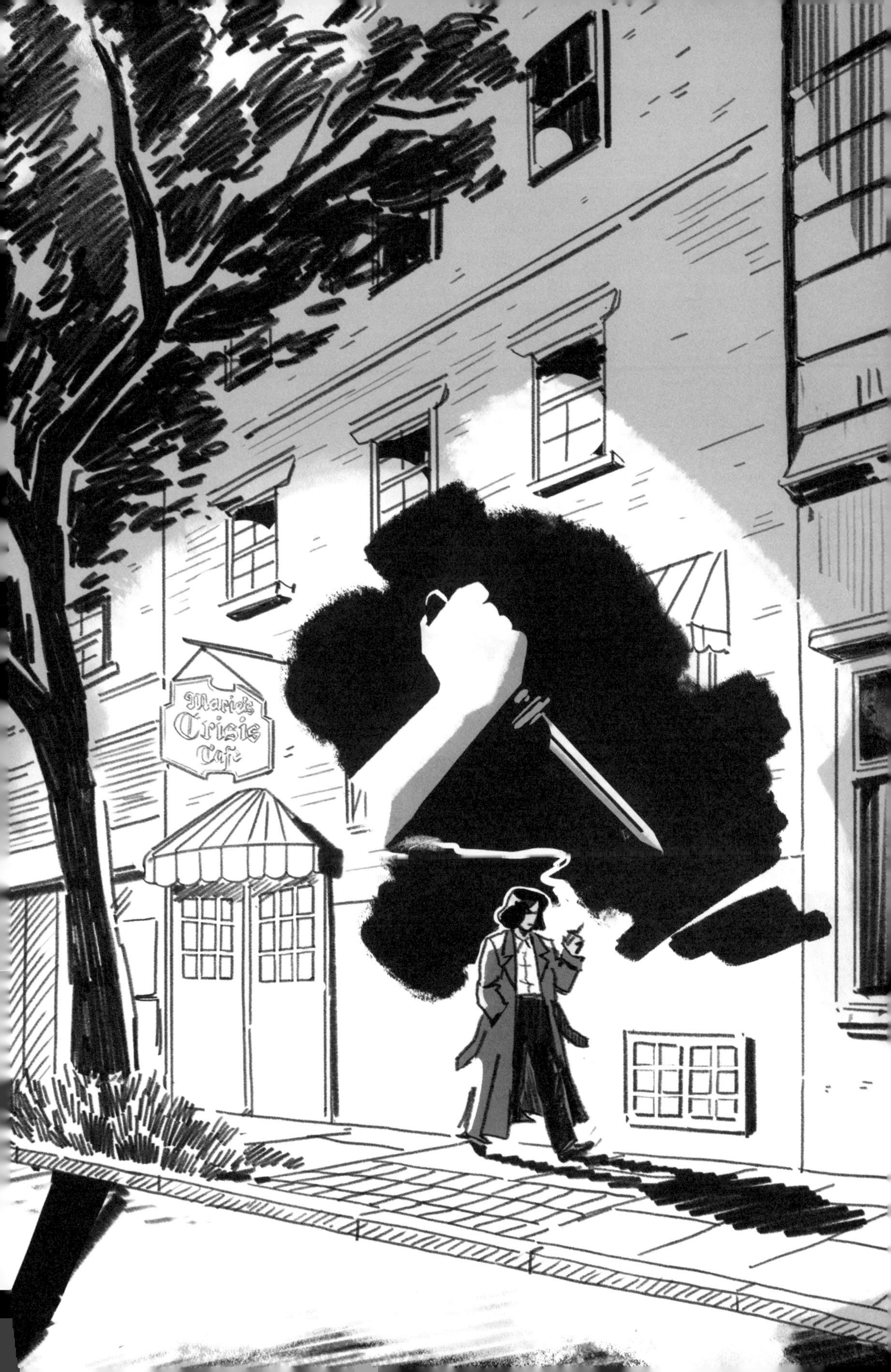
Marie's Crisis Café

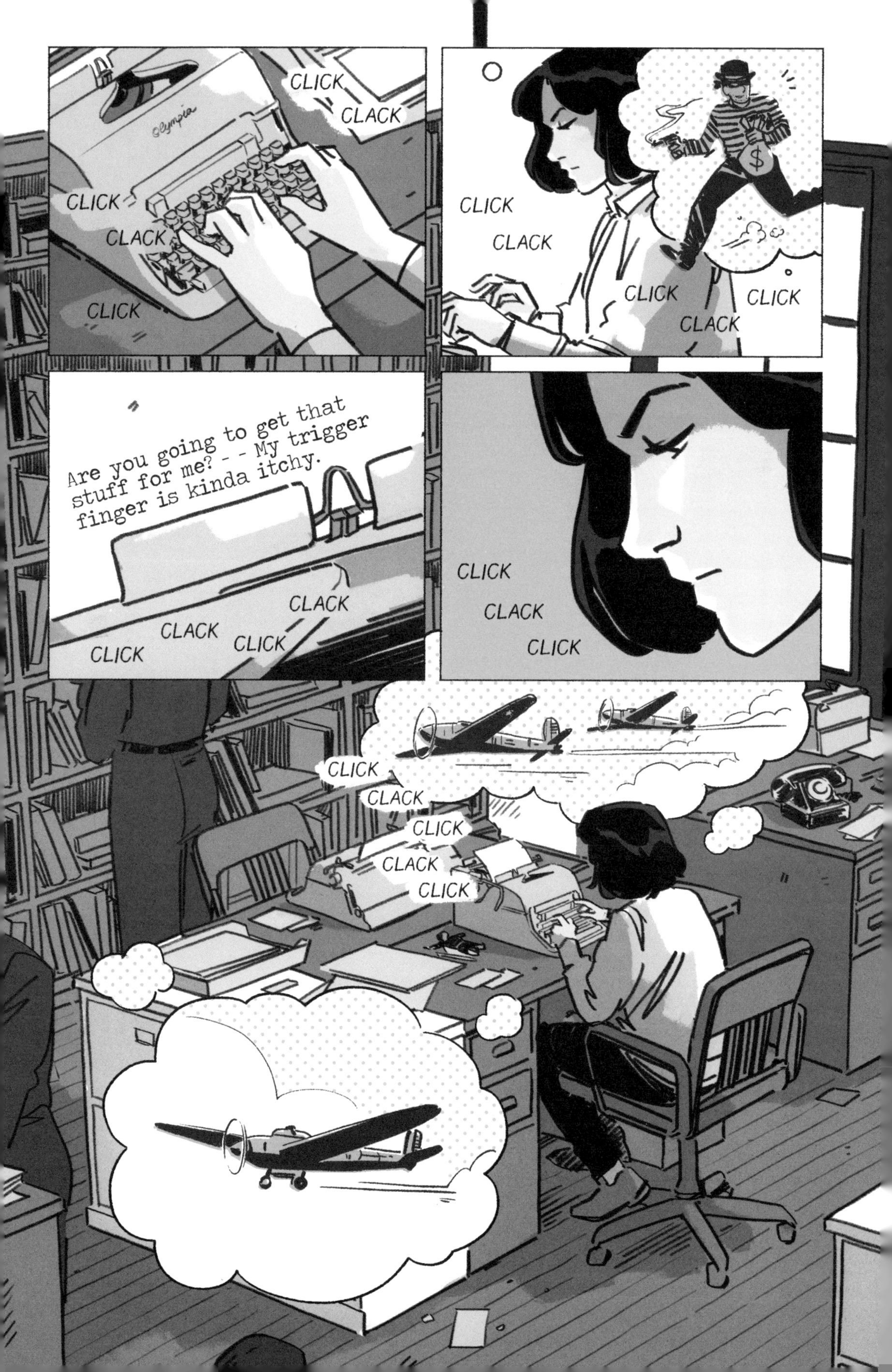

Olympia
CLICK
CLACK
CLICK
CLACK
CLICK
CLICK
CLACK
CLICK
CLACK
CLICK
Are you going to get that stuff for me? - - My trigger finger is kinda itchy.
CLICK
CLACK
CLICK
CLACK
CLICK
CLACK
CLICK
CLICK
CLACK
CLICK
CLACK
CLICK

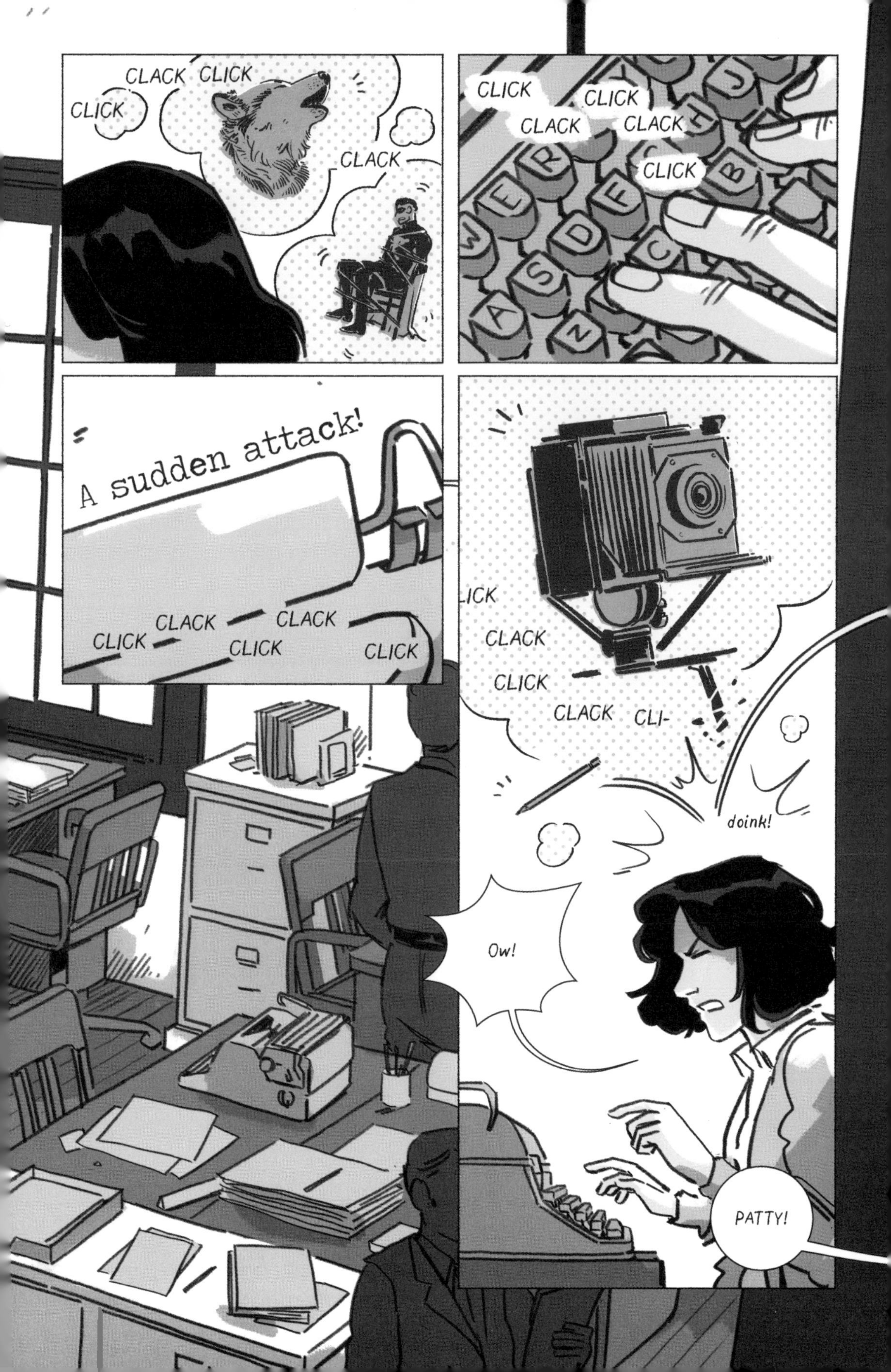

CLICK
CLACK CLICK
CLACK
CLICK
CLACK
CLICK
CLACK
CLICK
A sudden attack!
CLICK
CLACK
CLICK
CLACK
CLICK
LICK
CLACK
CLICK
CLACK
CLI-
doink!
Ow!
PATTY!

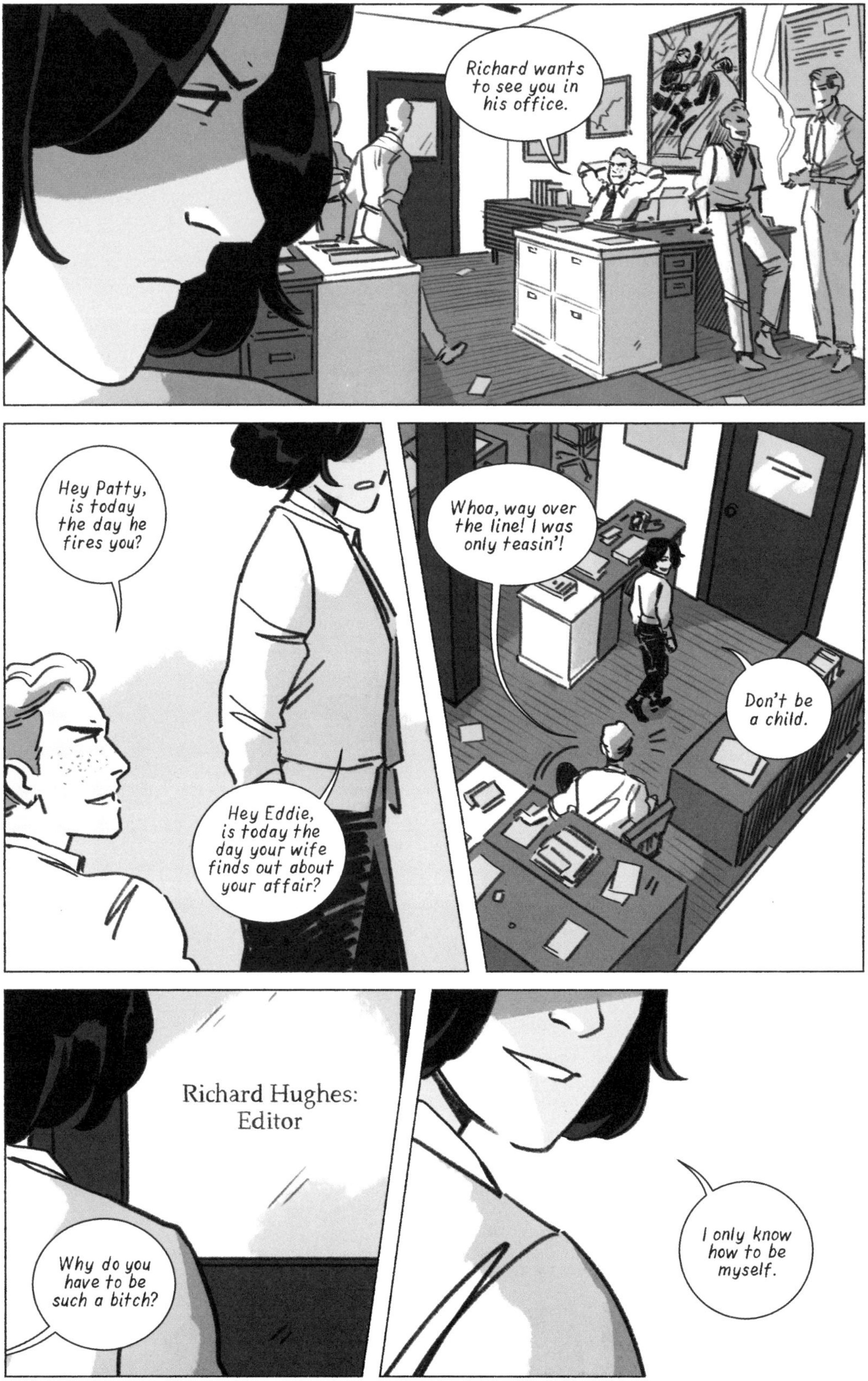

Richard wants to see you in his office.
Hey Patty, is today the day he fires you?
Hey Eddie, is today the day your wife finds out about your affair?
Whoa, way over the line! I was only teasin'!
Don't be a child.
Richard Hughes: Editor
Why do you have to be such a bitch?
I only know how to be myself.

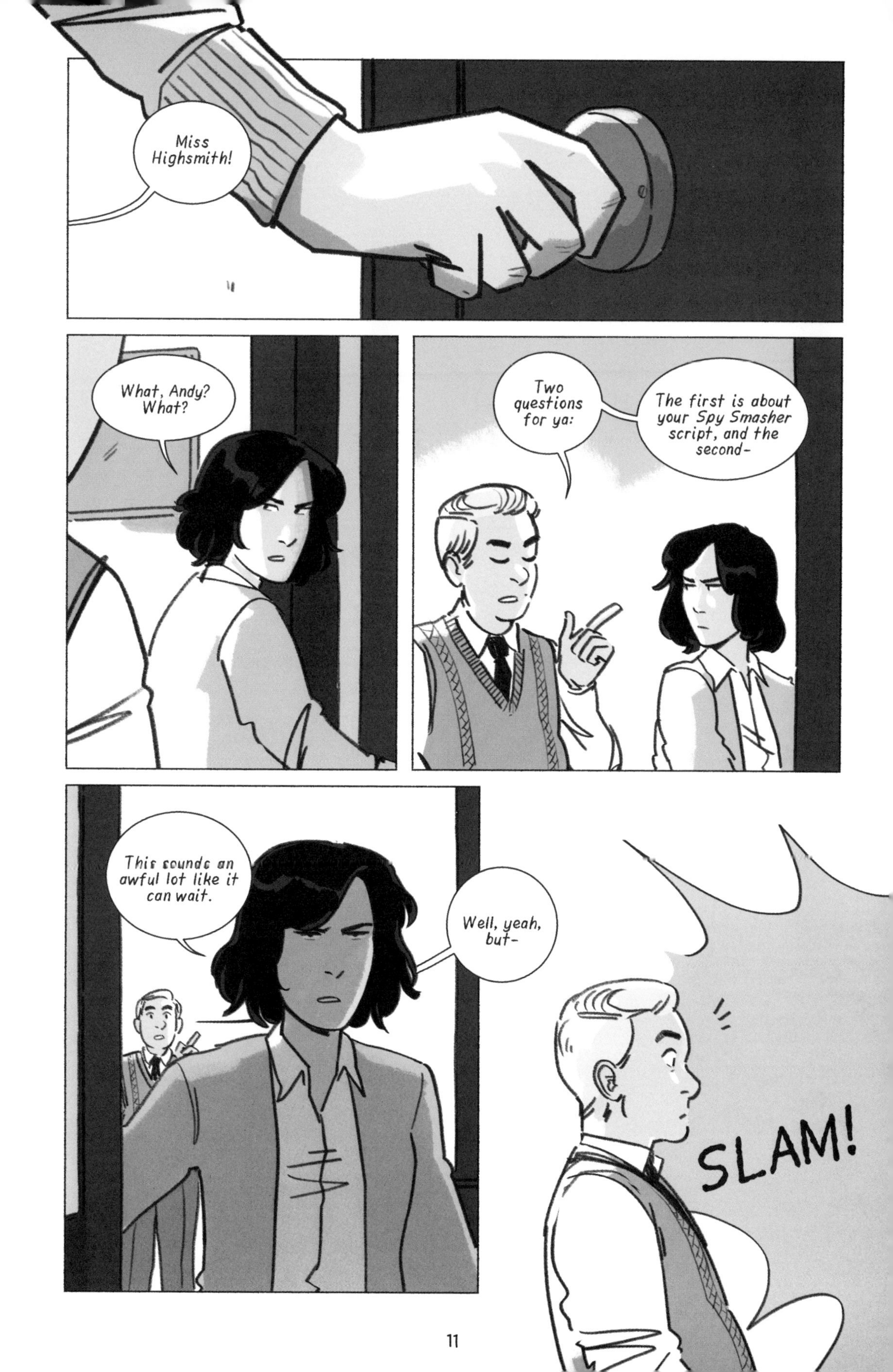
Miss Highsmith!
What, Andy? What?
Two questions for ya:
The first is about your *Spy Smasher* script, and the second-
This sounds an awful lot like it can wait.
Well, yeah, but-
SLAM!

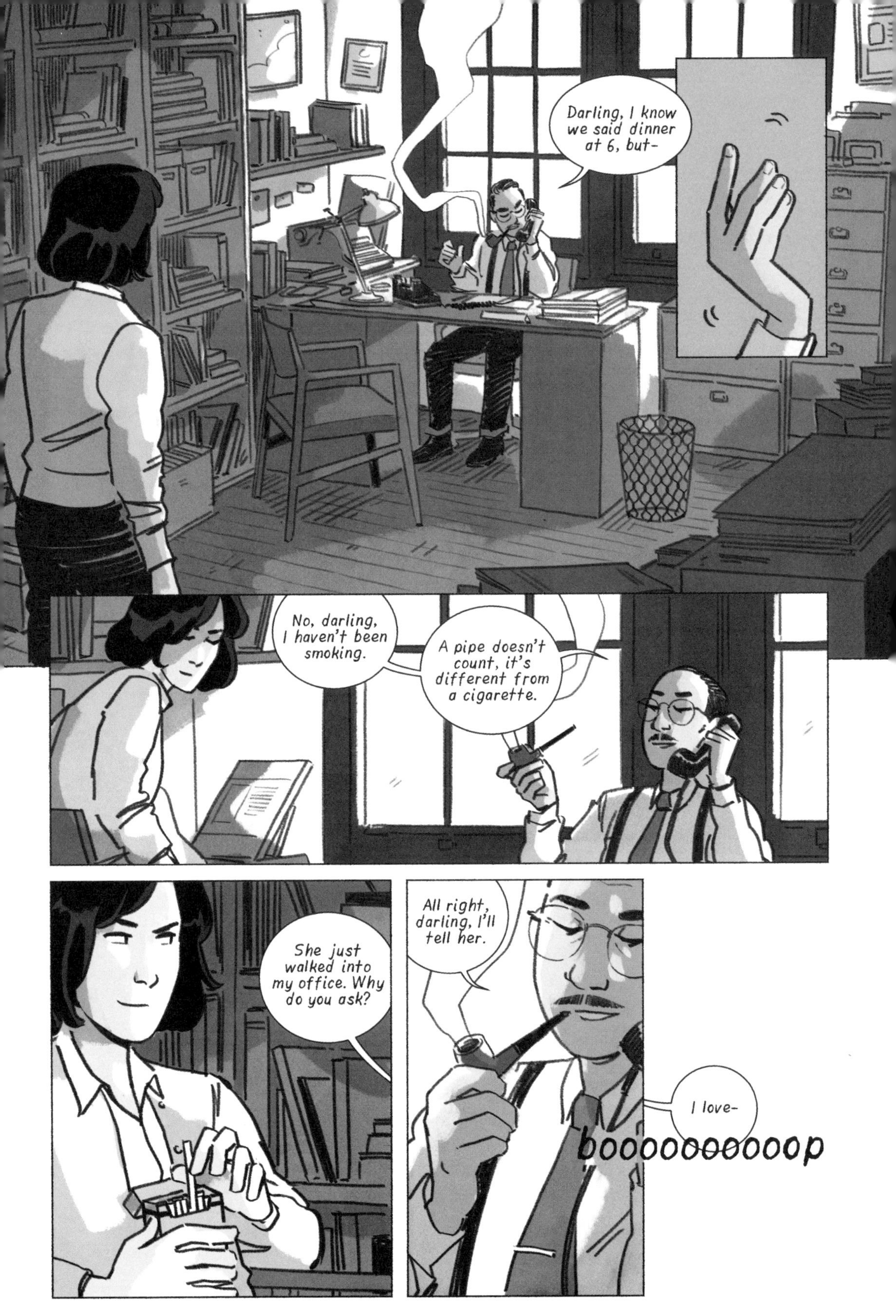

Darling, I know we said dinner at 6, but-
No, darling, I haven't been smoking.
A pipe doesn't count, it's different from a cigarette.
She just walked into my office. Why do you ask?
All right, darling, I'll tell her.
I love-
boooooooooop

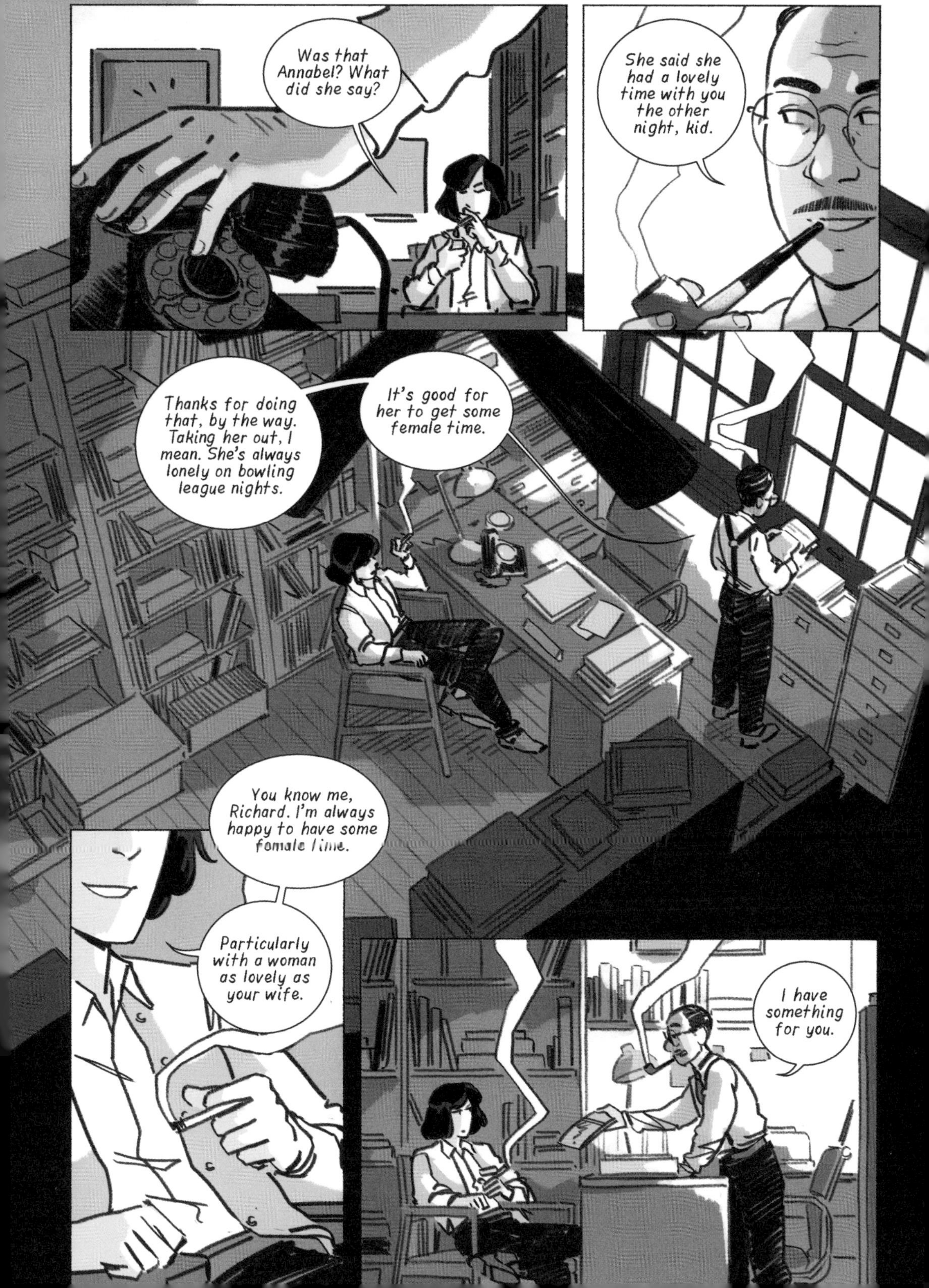
Was that Annabel? What did she say?
She said she had a lovely time with you the other night, kid.
Thanks for doing that, by the way. Taking her out, I mean. She's always lonely on bowling league nights.
It's good for her to get some female time.
You know me, Richard. I'm always happy to have some female time.
Particularly with a woman as lovely as your wife.
I have something for you.

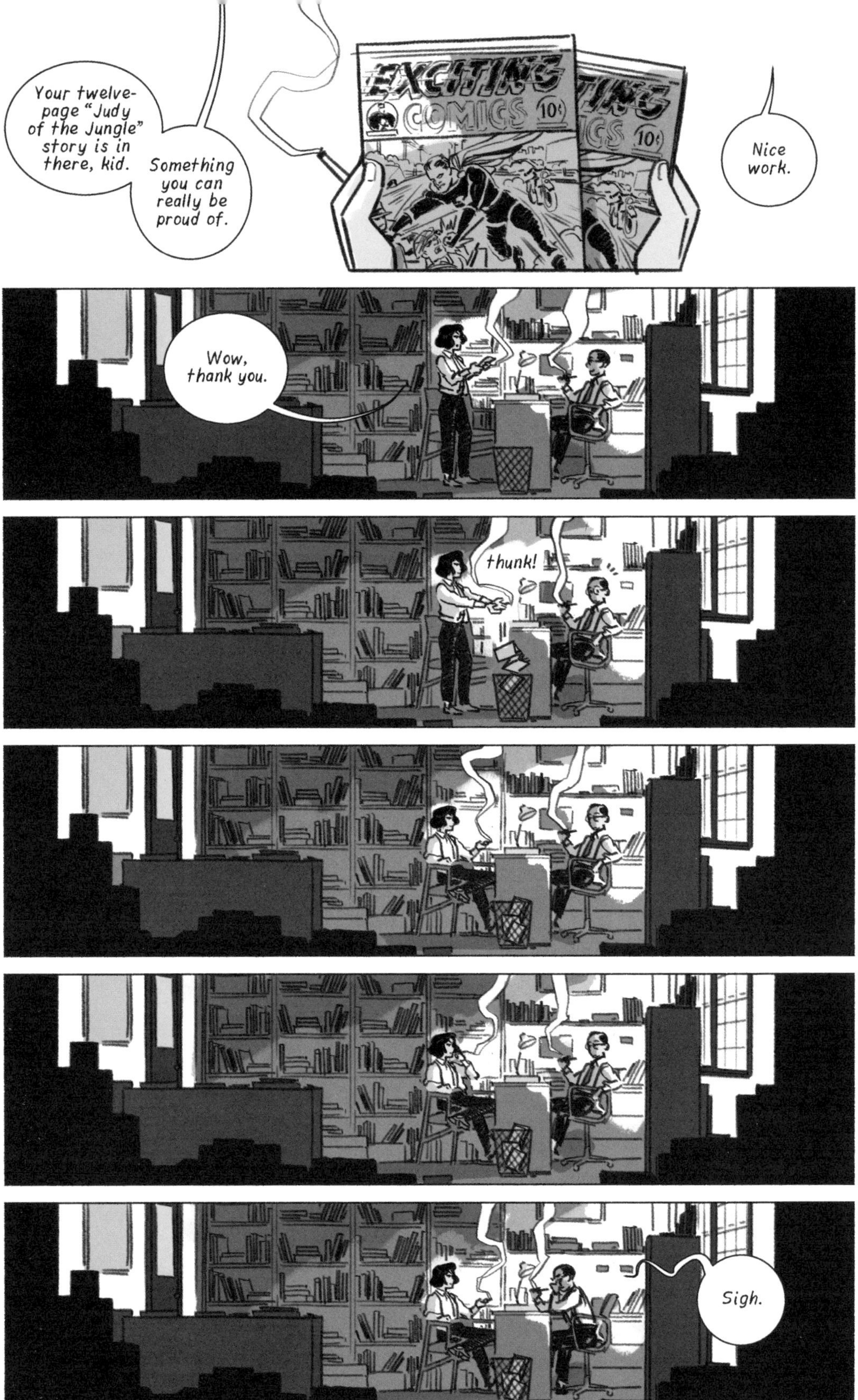
Your twelve-page "Judy of the Jungle" story is in there, kid.
Something you can really be proud of.
EXCITING COMICS 10¢
Nice work.
Wow, thank you.
thunk!
Sigh.

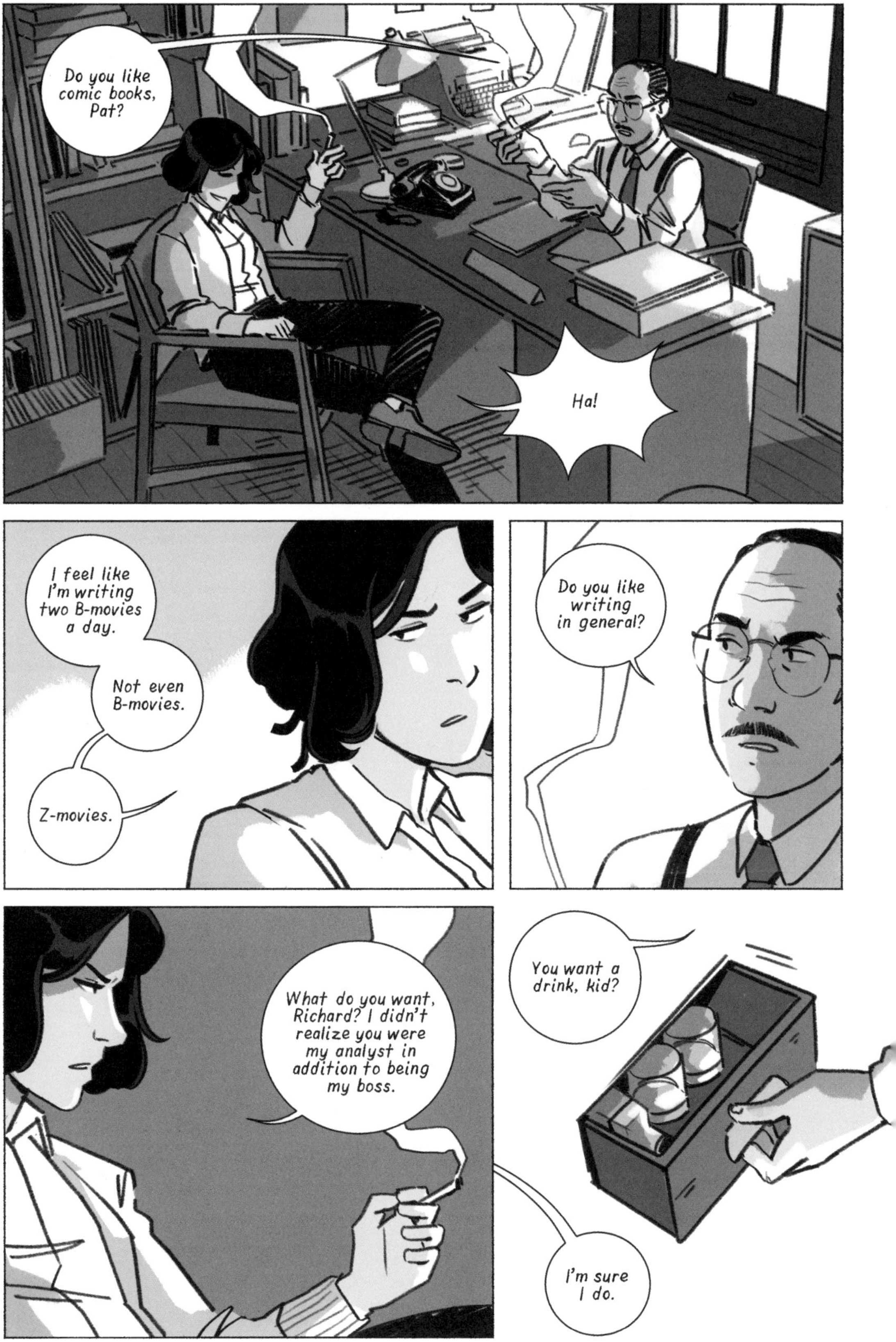
Do you like comic books, Pat?
Ha!
I feel like I'm writing two B-movies a day.
Not even B-movies.
Z-movies.
Do you like writing in general?
What do you want, Richard? I didn't realize you were my analyst in addition to being my boss.
You want a drink, kid?
I'm sure I do.

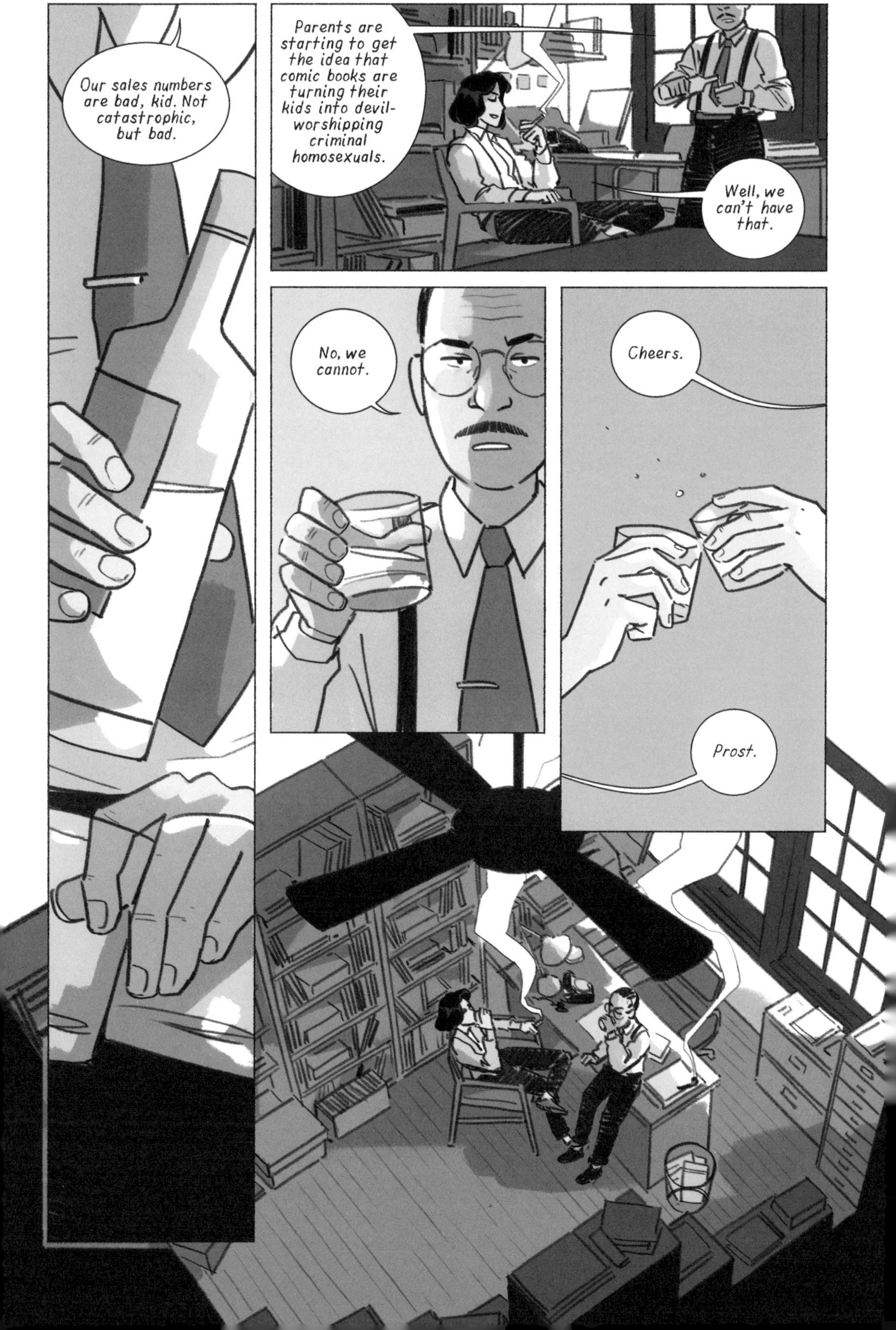
Our sales numbers are bad, kid. Not catastrophic, but bad.
Parents are starting to get the idea that comic books are turning their kids into devil-worshipping criminal homosexuals.
Well, we can't have that.
No, we cannot.
Cheers.
Prost.

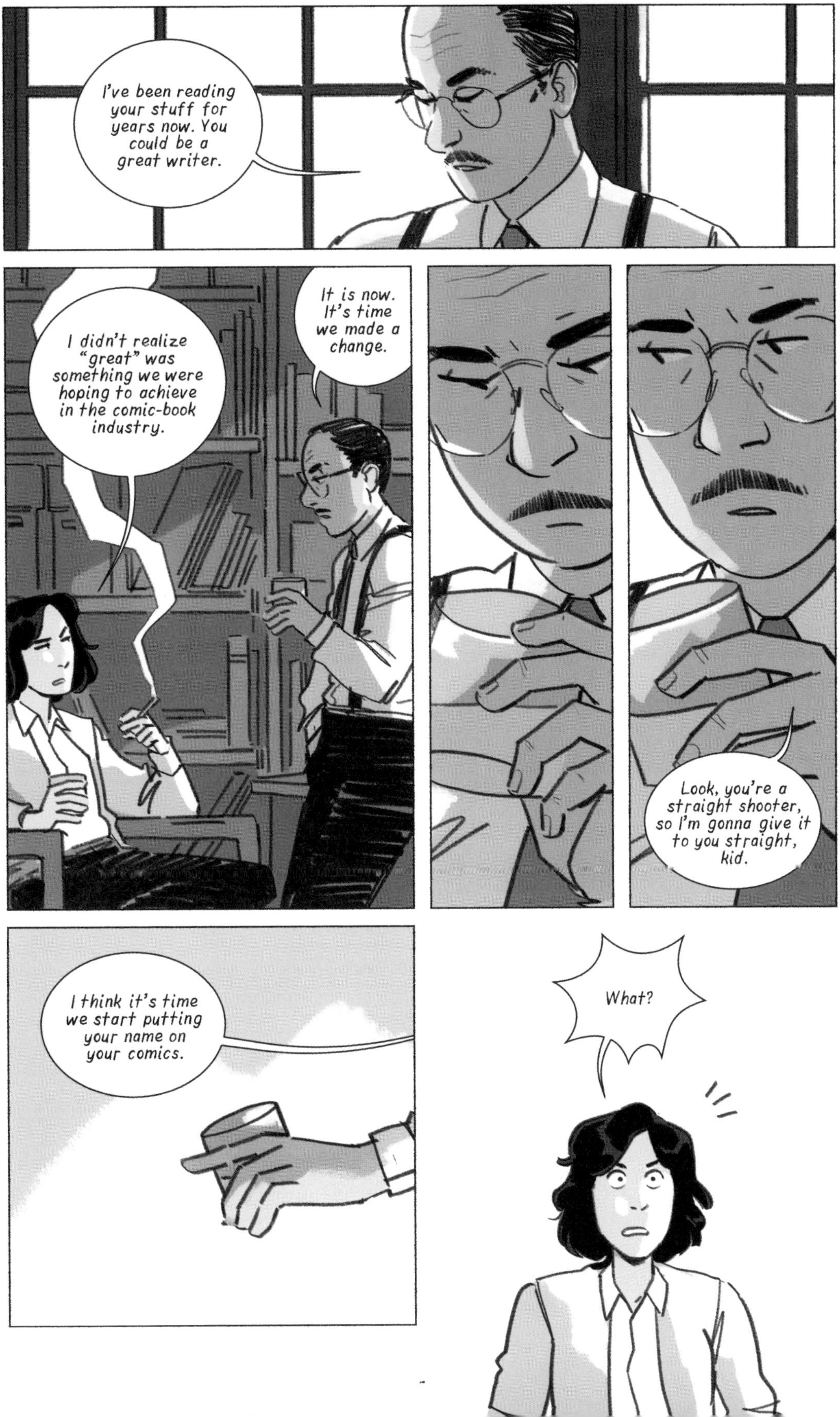

I've been reading your stuff for years now. You could be a great writer.
I didn't realize "great" was something we were hoping to achieve in the comic-book industry.
It is now. It's time we made a change.
Look, you're a straight shooter, so I'm gonna give it to you straight, kid.
I think it's time we start putting your name on your comics.
What?

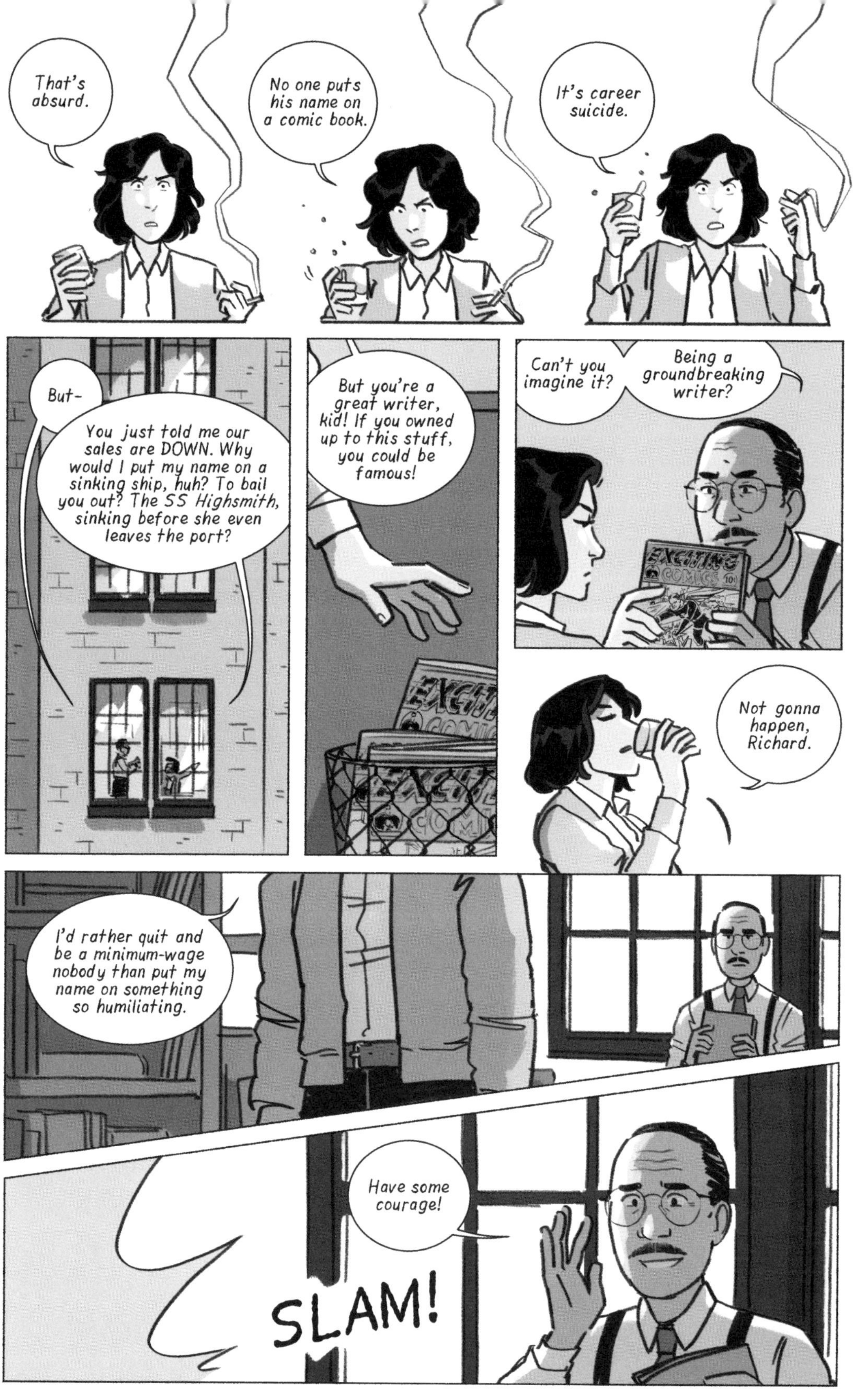
That's absurd.
No one puts his name on a comic book.
It's career suicide.
But-
You just told me our sales are DOWN. Why would I put my name on a sinking ship, huh? To bail you out? The SS Highsmith, sinking before she even leaves the port?
But you're a great writer, kid! If you owned up to this stuff, you could be famous!
Can't you imagine it?
Being a groundbreaking writer?
EXCITING COMICS
Not gonna happen, Richard.
I'd rather quit and be a minimum-wage nobody than put my name on something so humiliating.
Have some courage!
SLAM!

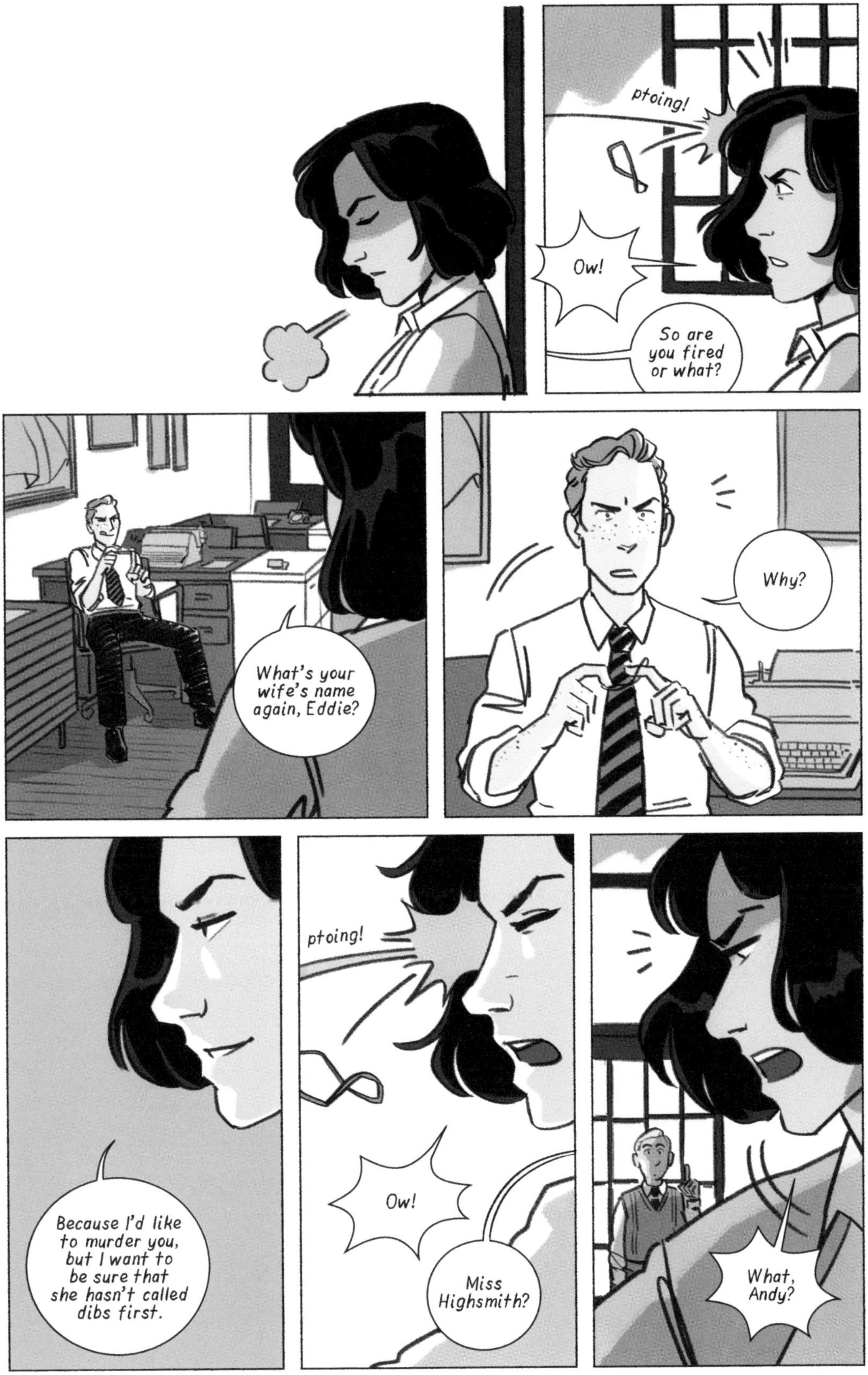
ptoing!
Ow!
So are you fired or what?
What's your wife's name again, Eddie?
Why?
Because I'd like to murder you, but I want to be sure that she hasn't called dibs first.
ptoing!
Ow!
Miss Highsmith?
What, Andy?

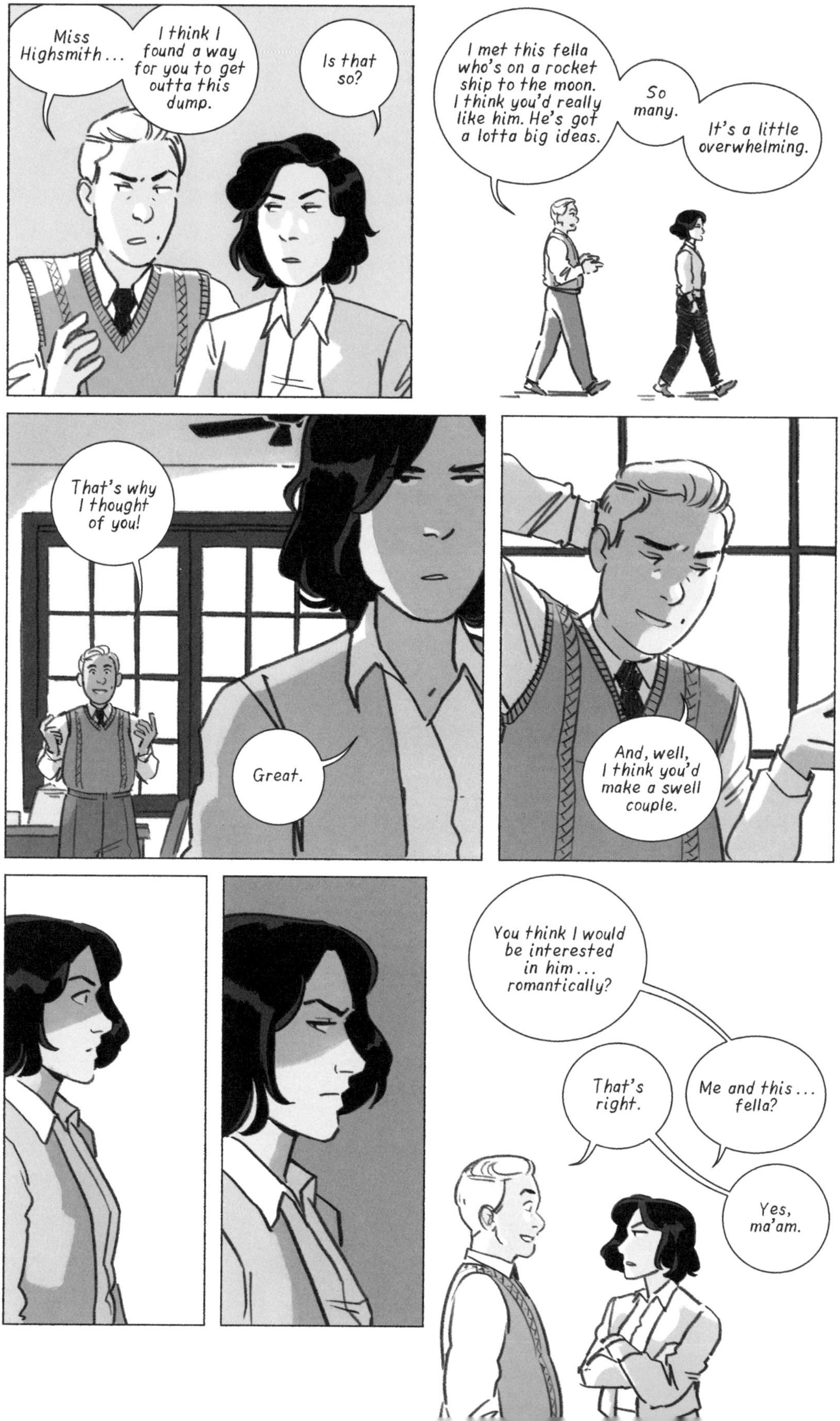
Miss Highsmith...
I think I found a way for you to get outta this dump.
Is that so?
I met this fella who's on a rocket ship to the moon. I think you'd really like him. He's got a lotta big ideas.
So many.
It's a little overwhelming.
That's why I thought of you!
Great.
And, well, I think you'd make a swell couple.
You think I would be interested in him... romantically?
That's right.
Me and this... fella?
Yes, ma'am.

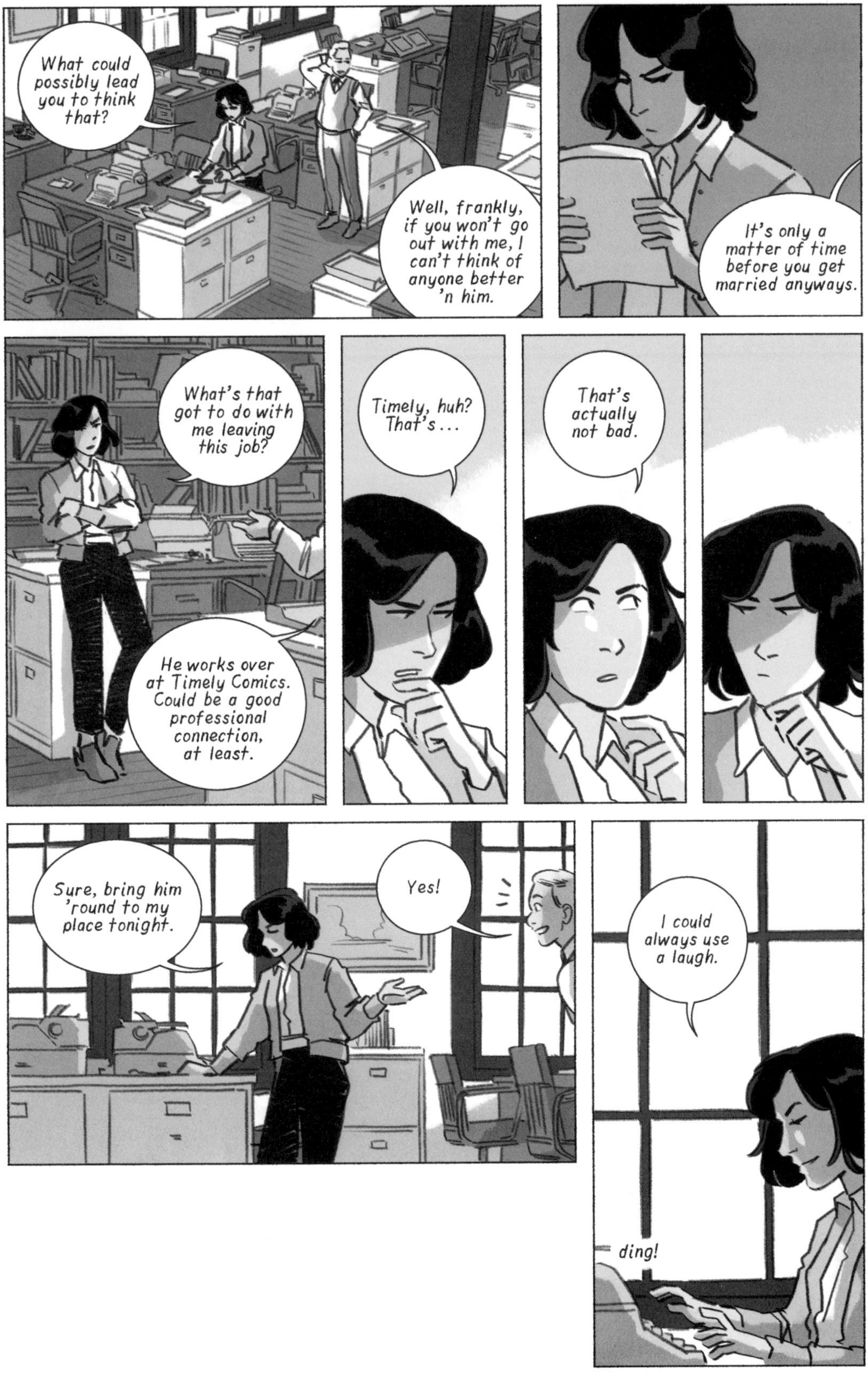
What could possibly lead you to think that?
Well, frankly, if you won't go out with me, I can't think of anyone better 'n him.
It's only a matter of time before you get married anyways.
What's that got to do with me leaving this job?
He works over at Timely Comics. Could be a good professional connection, at least.
Timely, huh? That's...
That's actually not bad.
Sure, bring him 'round to my place tonight.
Yes!
I could always use a laugh.
ding!

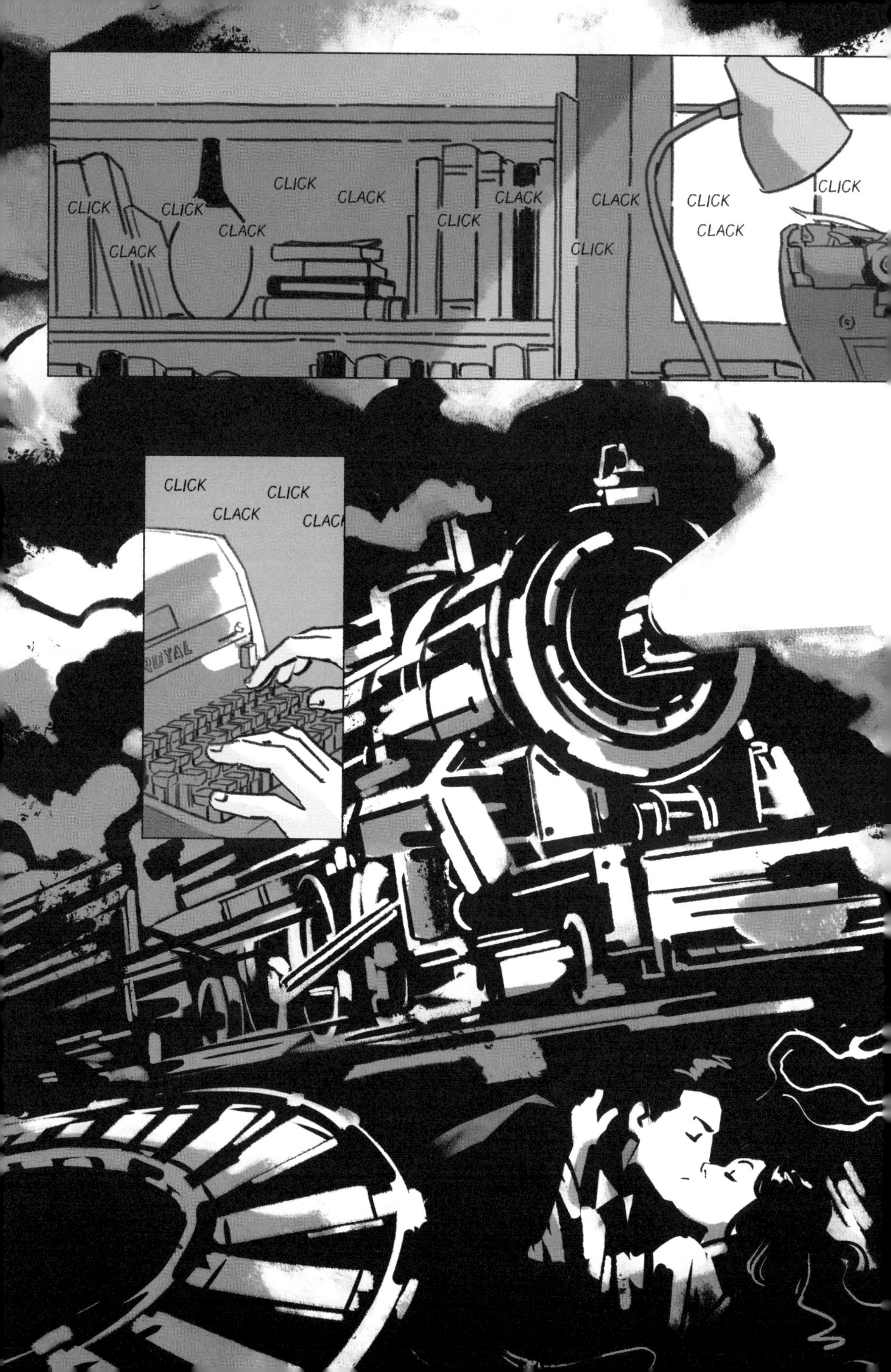
CLICK
CLACK
CLICK
CLACK
CLICK
CLACK
CLICK
CLACK
CLACK
CLICK
CLICK
CLACK
CLICK
CLICK
CLACK
CLICK
CLACK
CLICK
CLAC
ROYAL

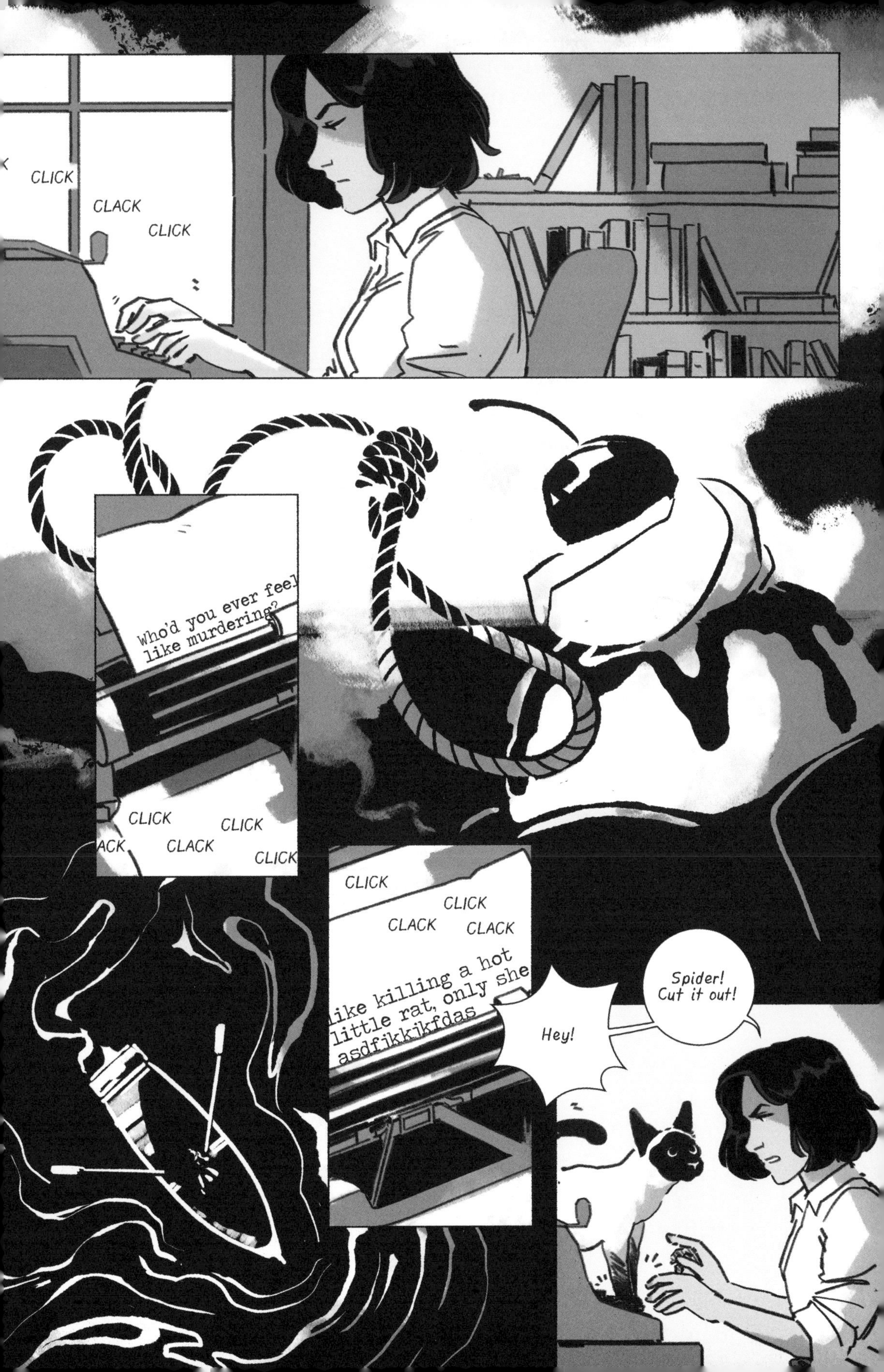

CLICK
CLACK
CLICK
Who'd you ever feel
like murdering?
CLICK
CLICK
ACK
CLACK
CLICK
CLICK
CLICK
CLACK
CLACK
like killing a hot
little rat, only she
asdfikkikfdas
Hey!
Spider!
Cut it out!

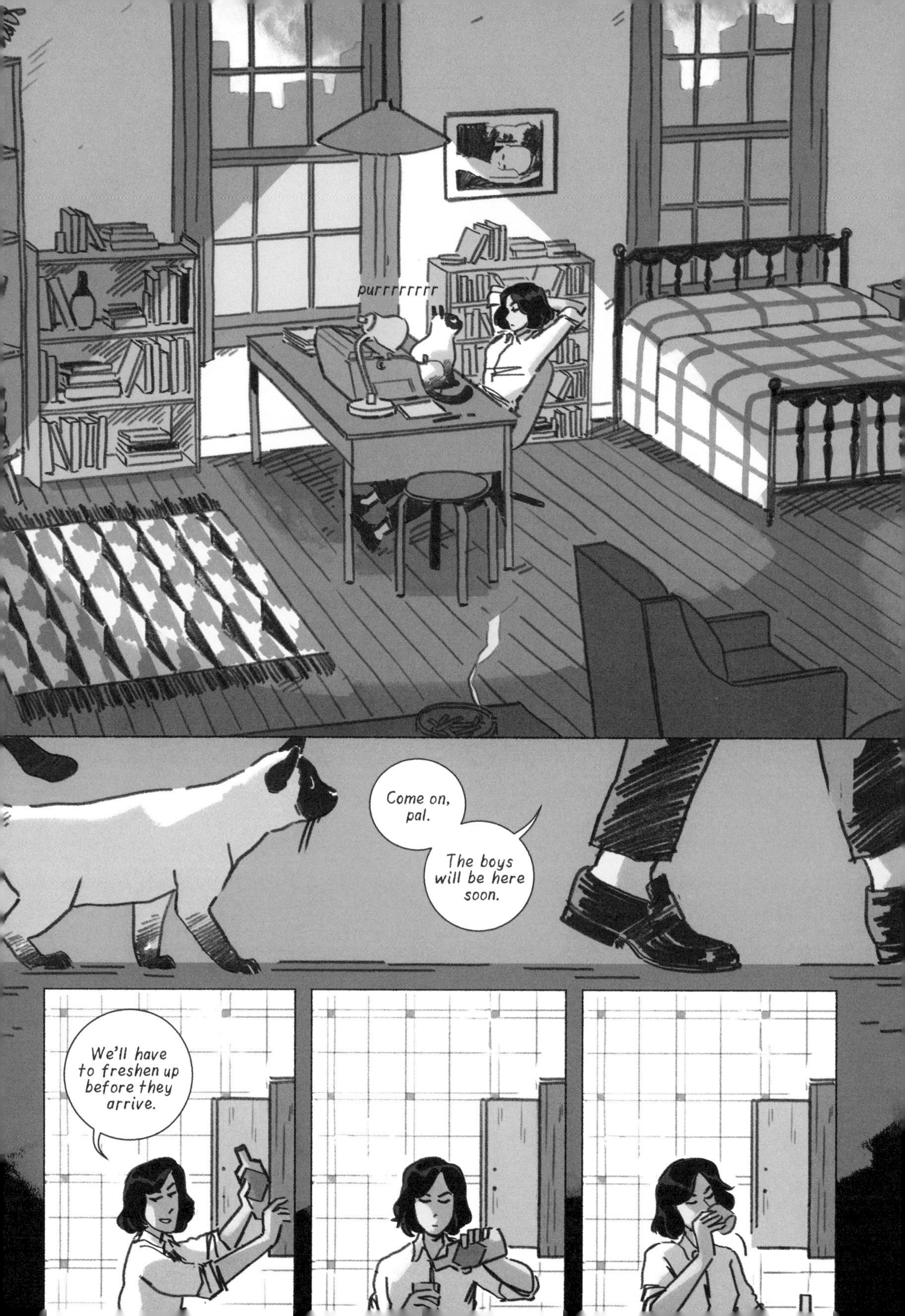
purrrrrrrr
Come on, pal.
The boys will be here soon.
We'll have to freshen up before they arrive.

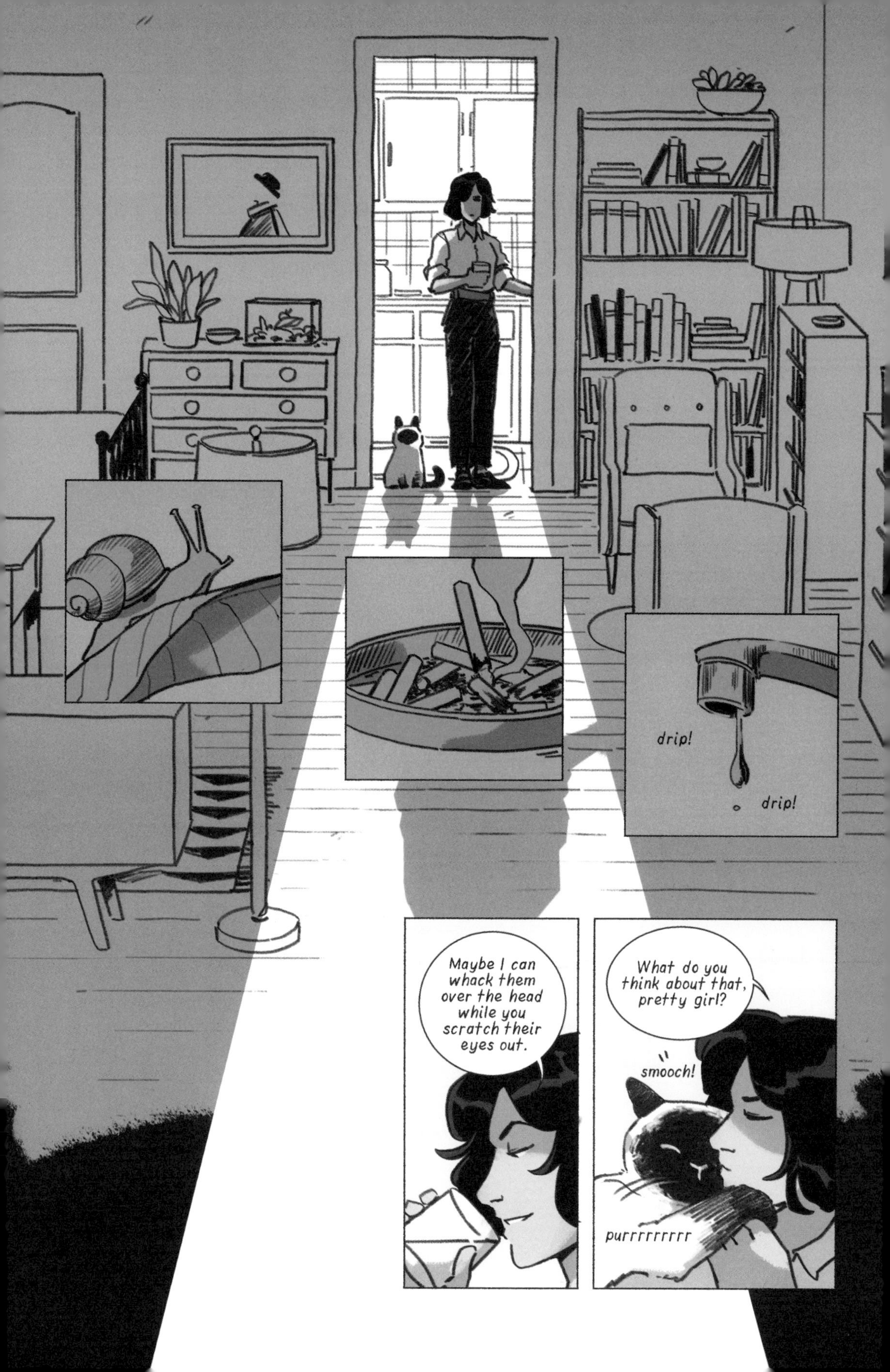
drip!
drip!
Maybe I can whack them over the head while you scratch their eyes out.
What do you think about that, pretty girl?
smooch!
purrrrrrrrr

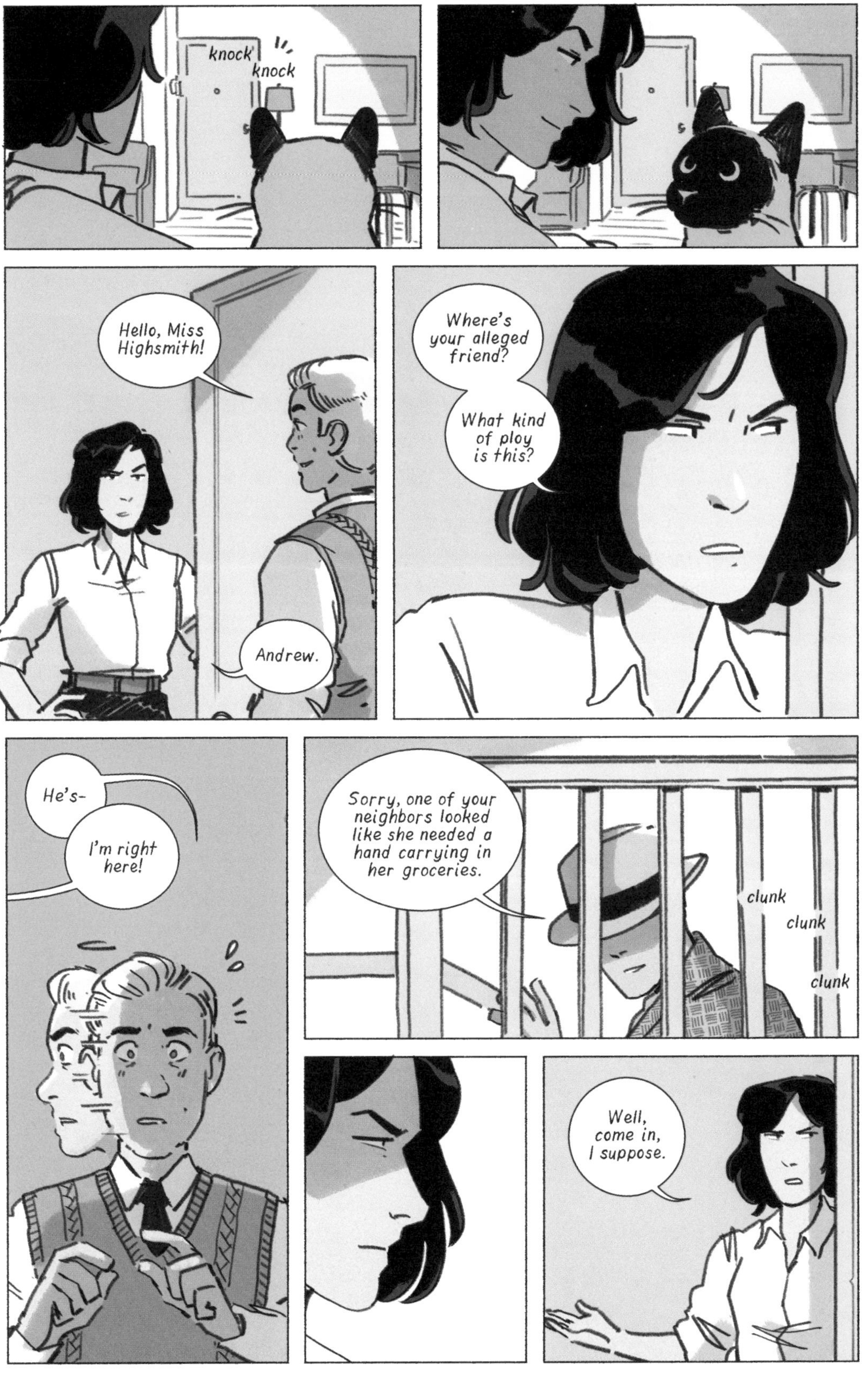
knock
knock
Hello, Miss Highsmith!
Andrew.
Where's your alleged friend?
What kind of ploy is this?
He's-
I'm right here!
Sorry, one of your neighbors looked like she needed a hand carrying in her groceries.
clunk
clunk
clunk
Well, come in, I suppose.

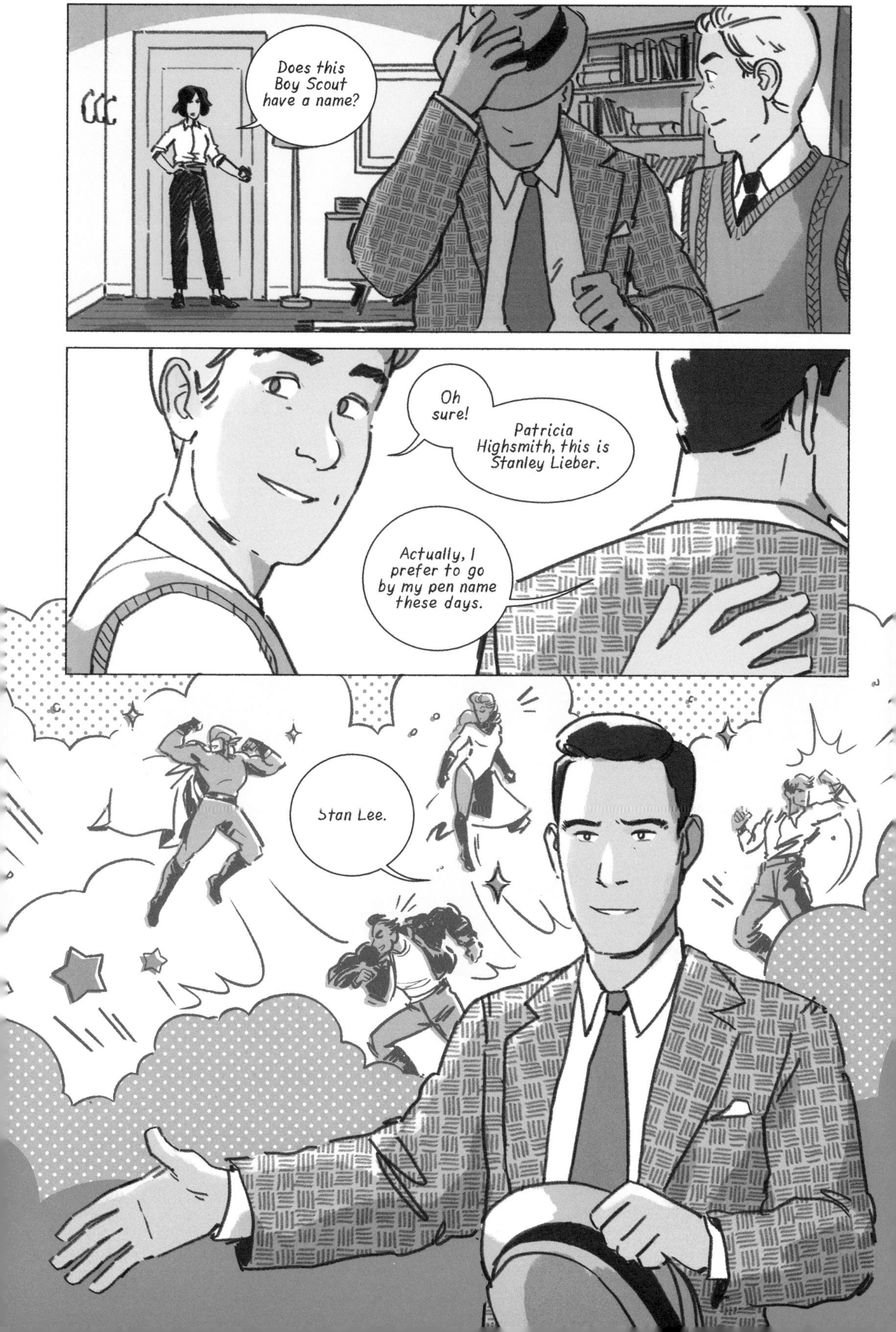
Does this Boy Scout have a name?
Oh sure!
Patricia Highsmith, this is Stanley Lieber.
Actually, I prefer to go by my pen name these days.
Stan Lee.

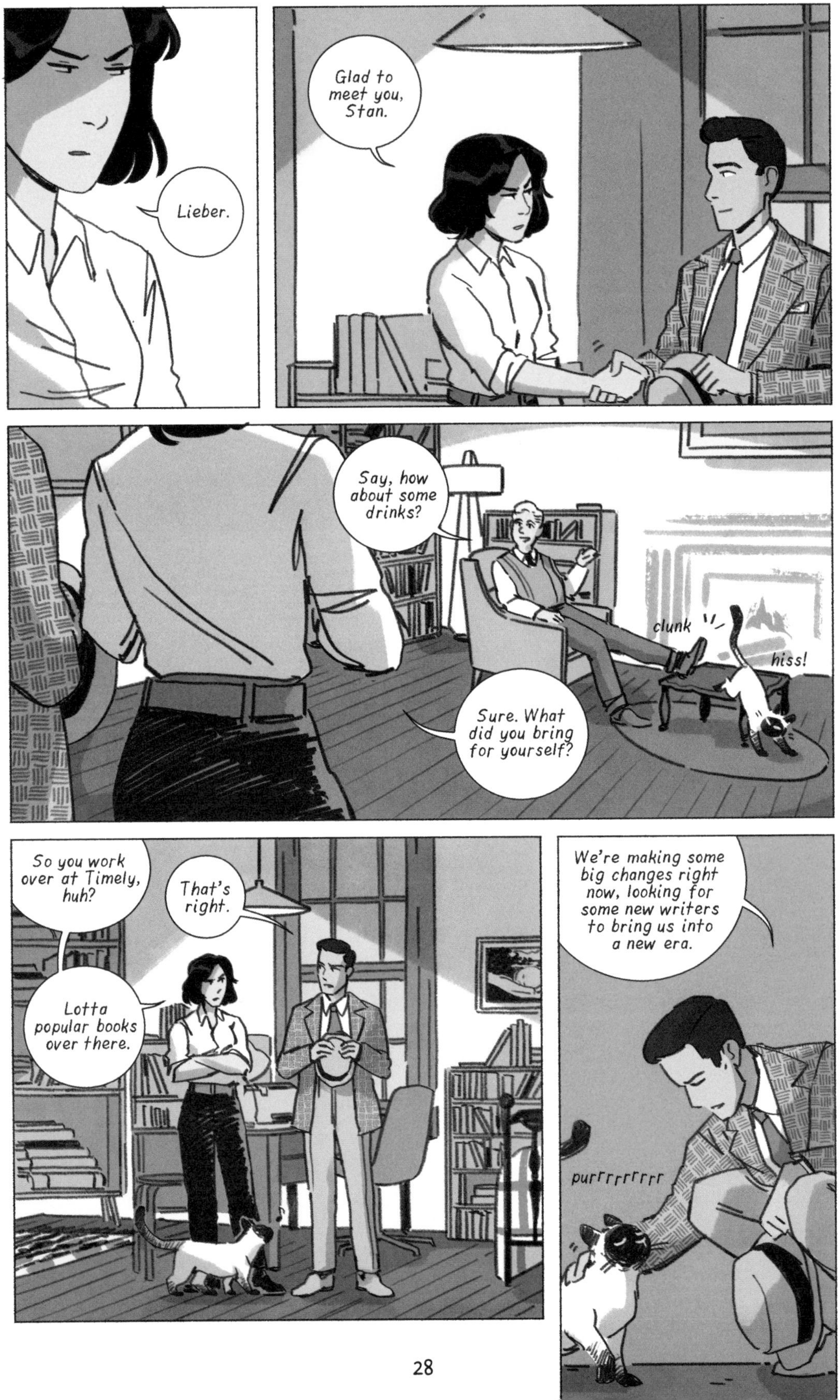
Lieber.
Glad to meet you, Stan.
Say, how about some drinks?
clunk
hiss!
Sure. What did you bring for yourself?
So you work over at Timely, huh?
That's right.
Lotta popular books over there.
We're making some big changes right now, looking for some new writers to bring us into a new era.
purrrrrrrrr

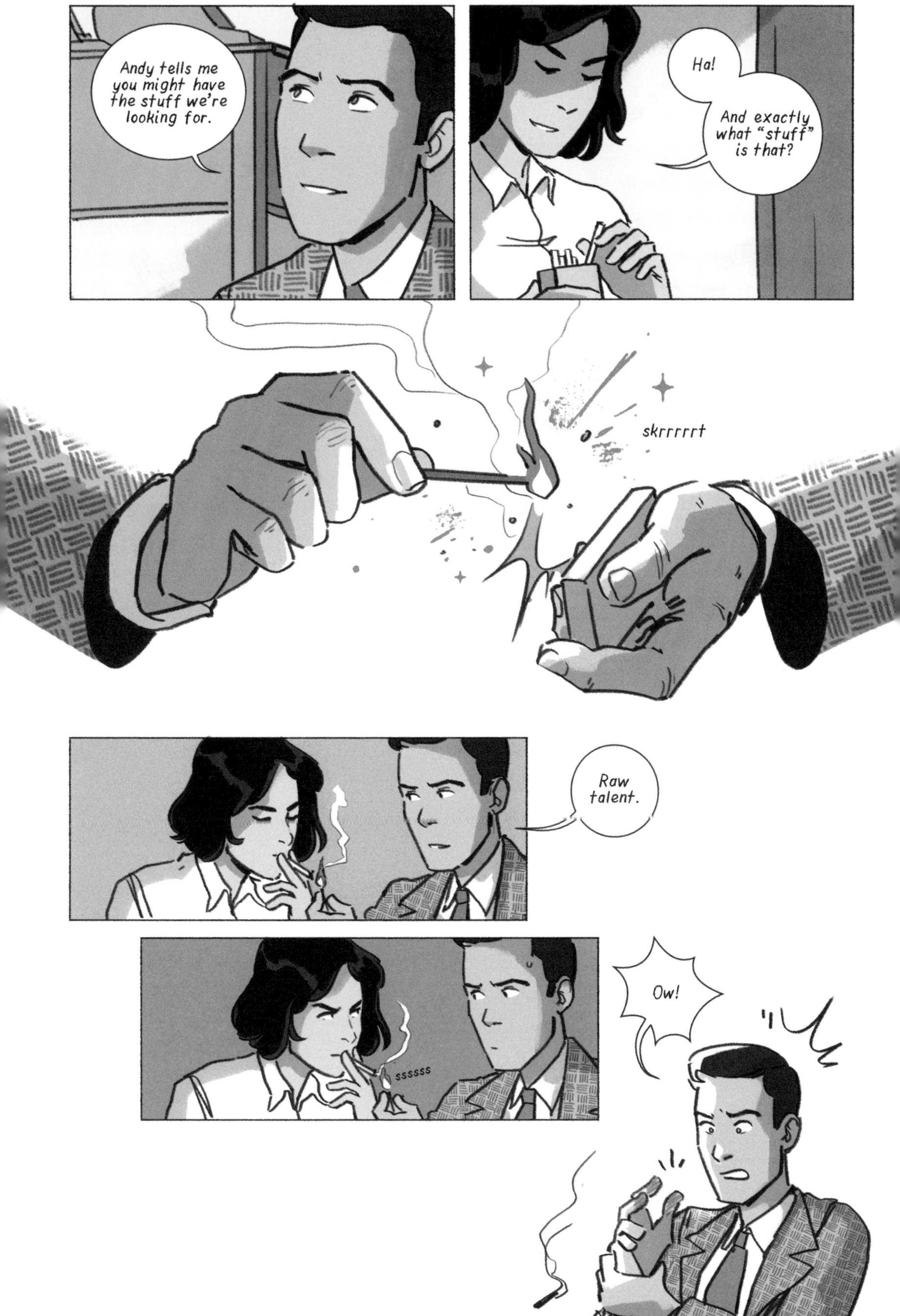
Andy tells me you might have the stuff we're looking for.
Ha!
And exactly what "stuff" is that?
skrrrrrt
Raw talent.
ssssss
Ow!

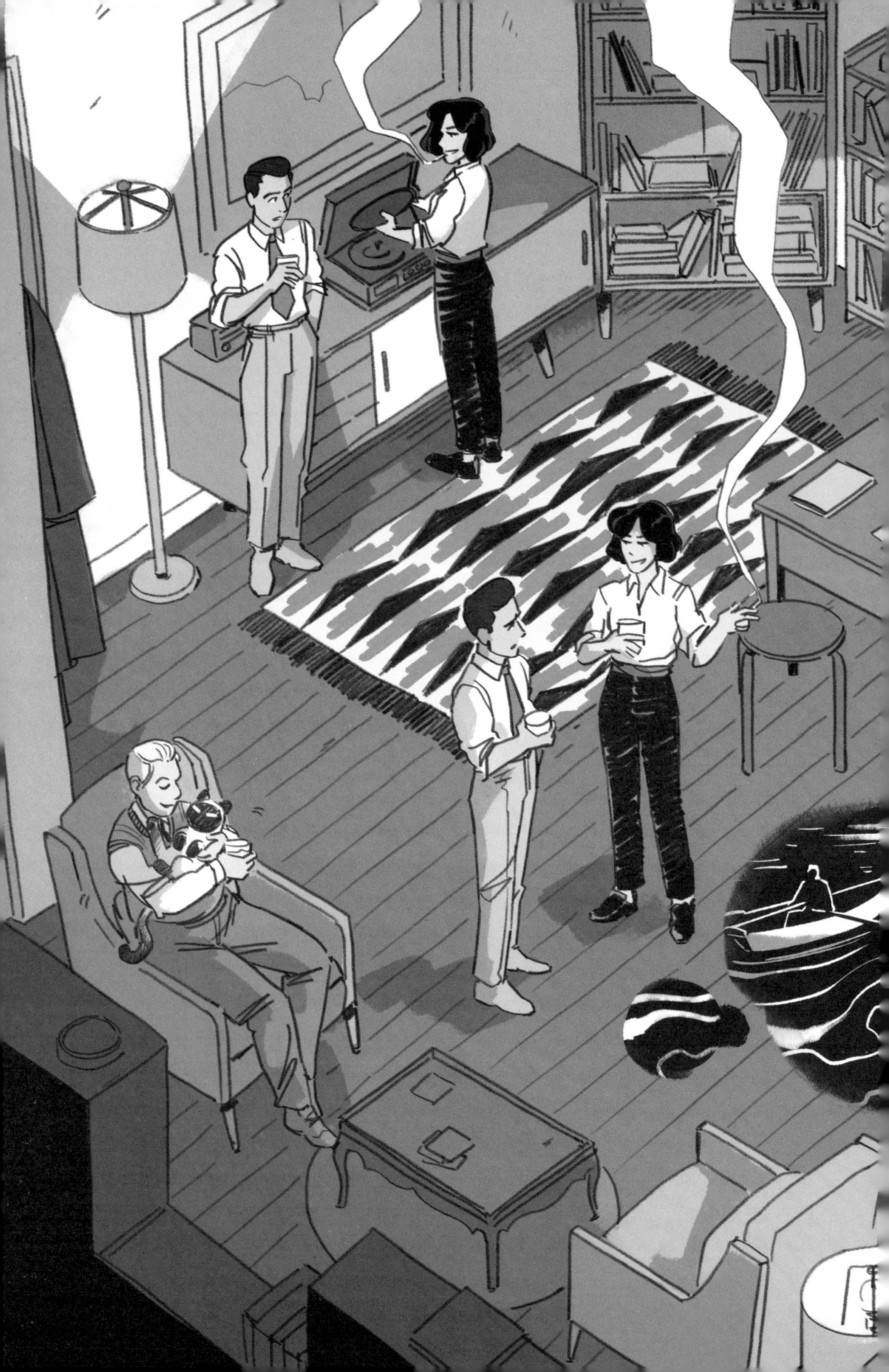

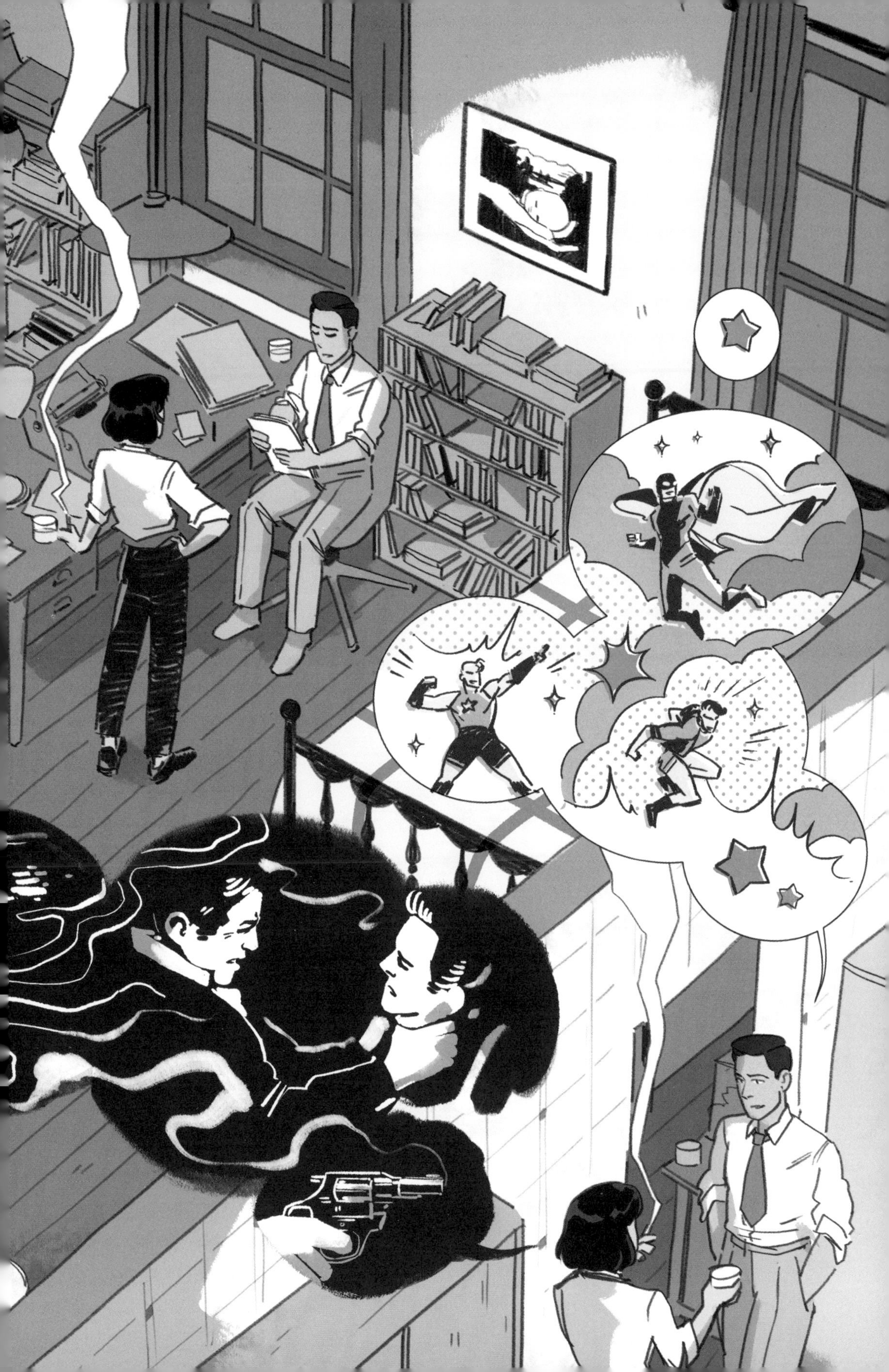

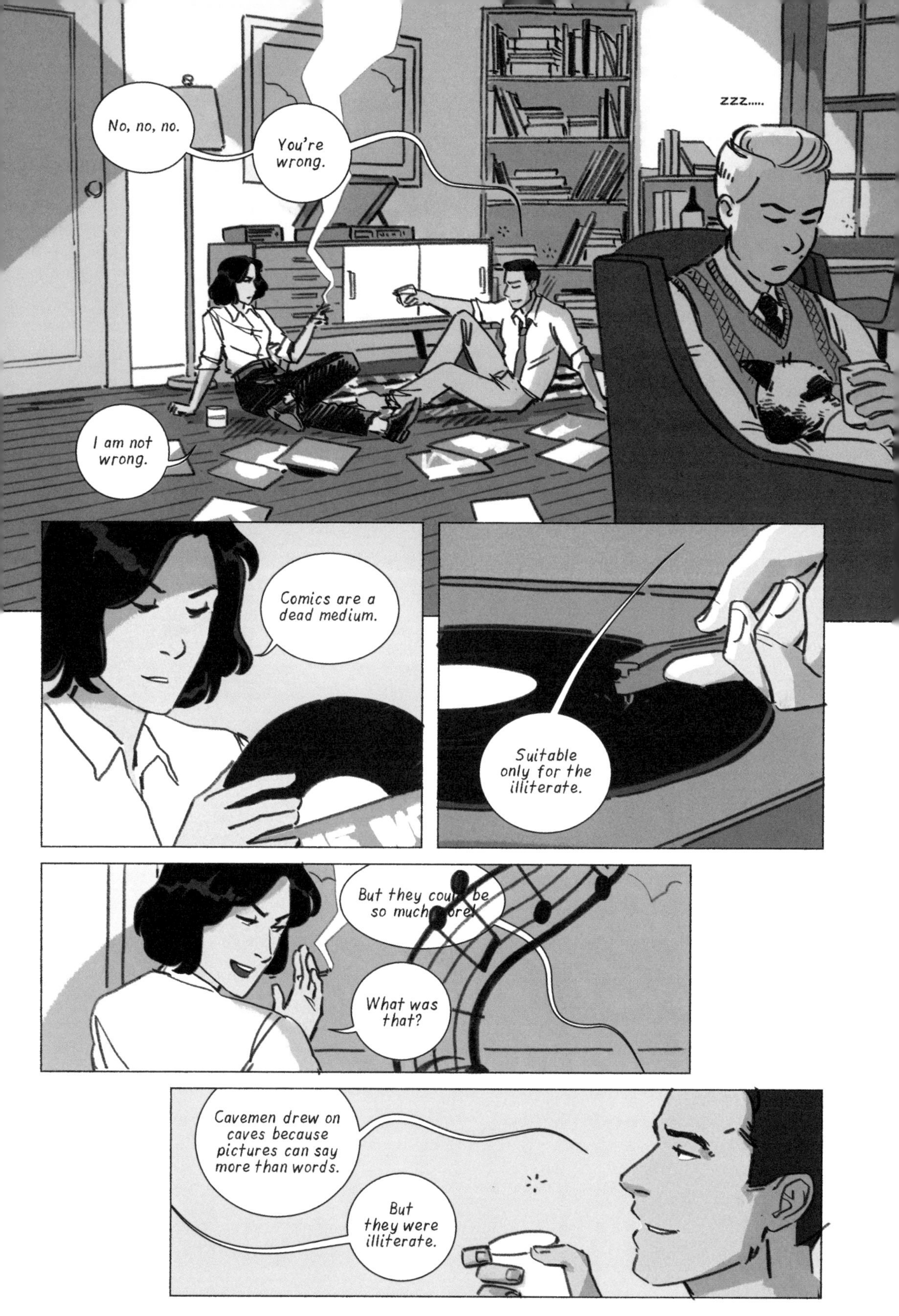
ZZZ.....
No, no, no.
You're wrong.
I am not wrong.
Comics are a dead medium.
Suitable only for the illiterate.
But they cou be so much ore!
What was that?
Cavemen drew on caves because pictures can say more than words.
But they were illiterate.

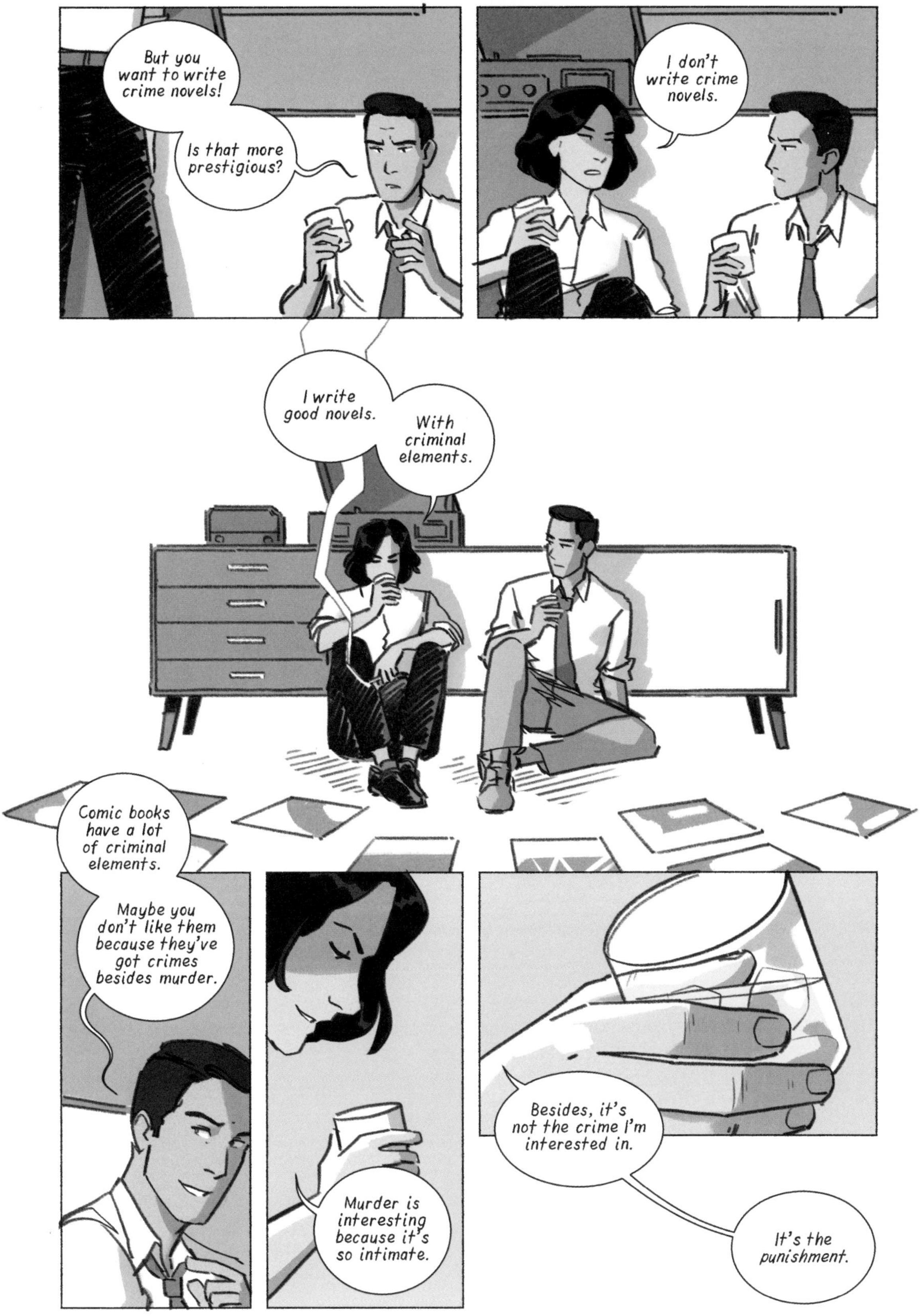

But you want to write crime novels!
Is that more prestigious?
I don't write crime novels.
I write good novels.
With criminal elements.
Comic books have a lot of criminal elements.
Maybe you don't like them because they've got crimes besides murder.
Murder is interesting because it's so intimate.
Besides, it's not the crime I'm interested in.
It's the punishment.

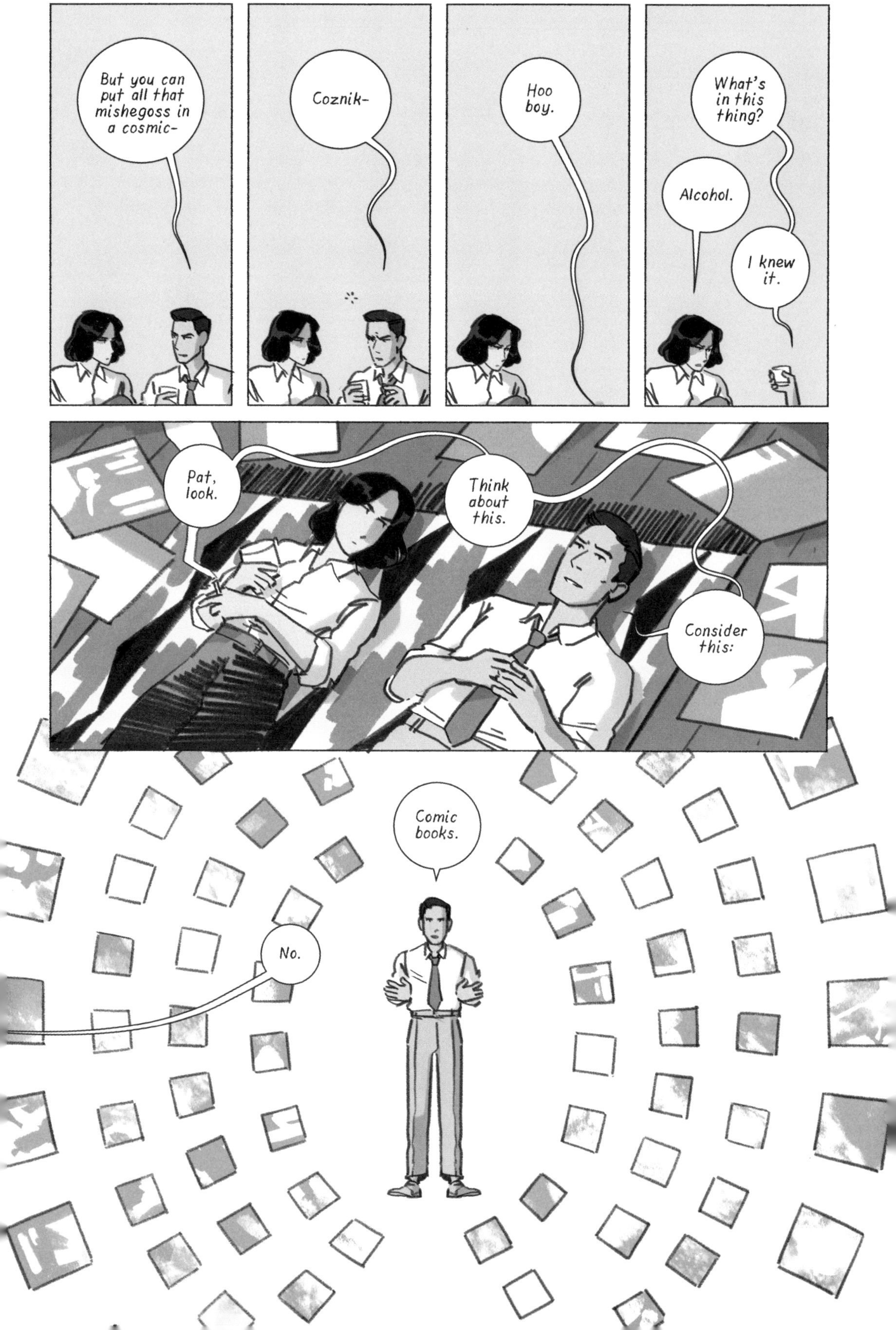
But you can put all that mishegoss in a cosmic-
Coznik-
Hoo boy.
What's in this thing?
Alcohol.
I knew it.
Pat, look.
Think about this.
Consider this:
Comic books.
No.

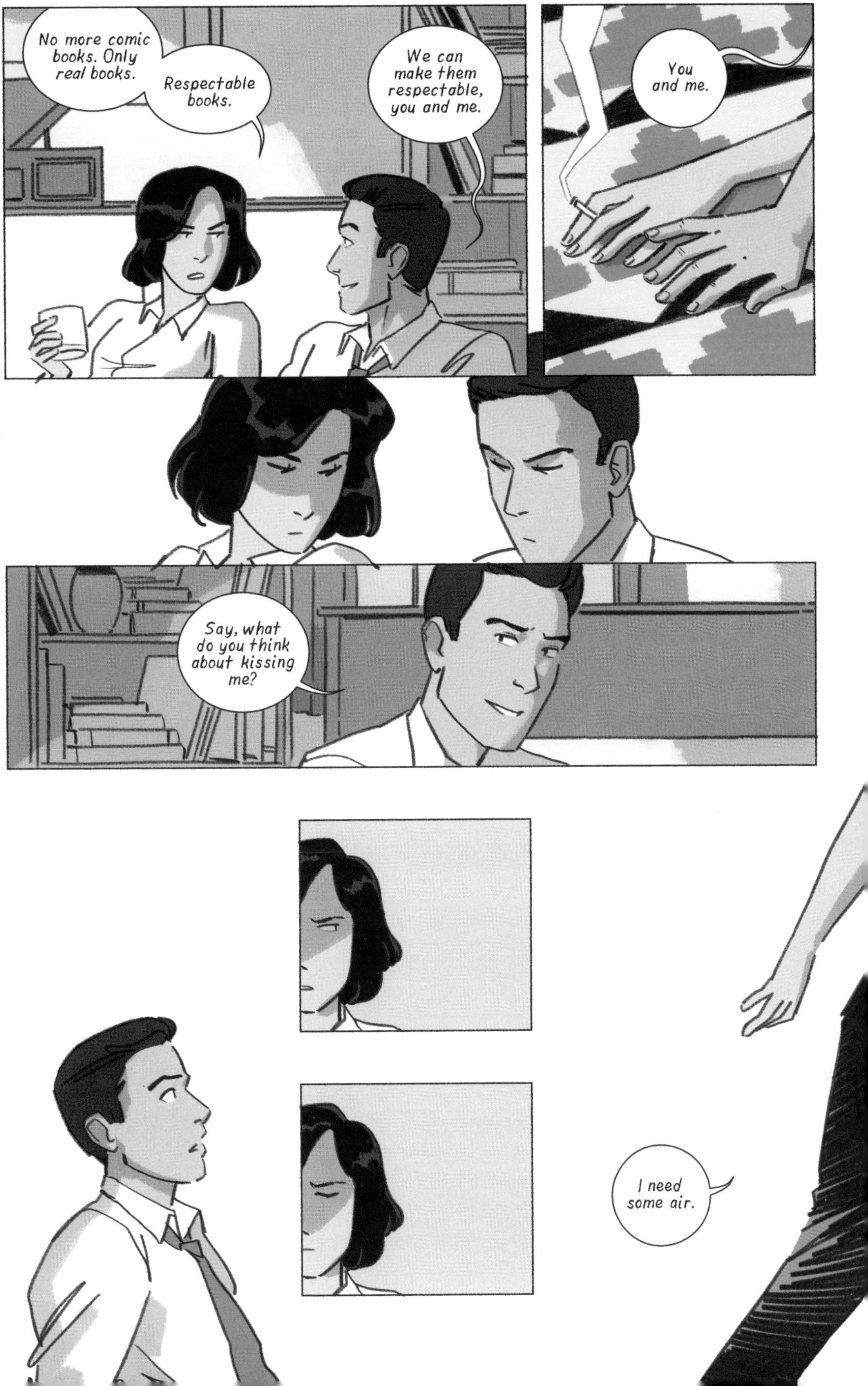
No more comic books. Only real books.
Respectable books.
We can make them respectable, you and me.
You and me.
Say, what do you think about kissing me?
I need some air.

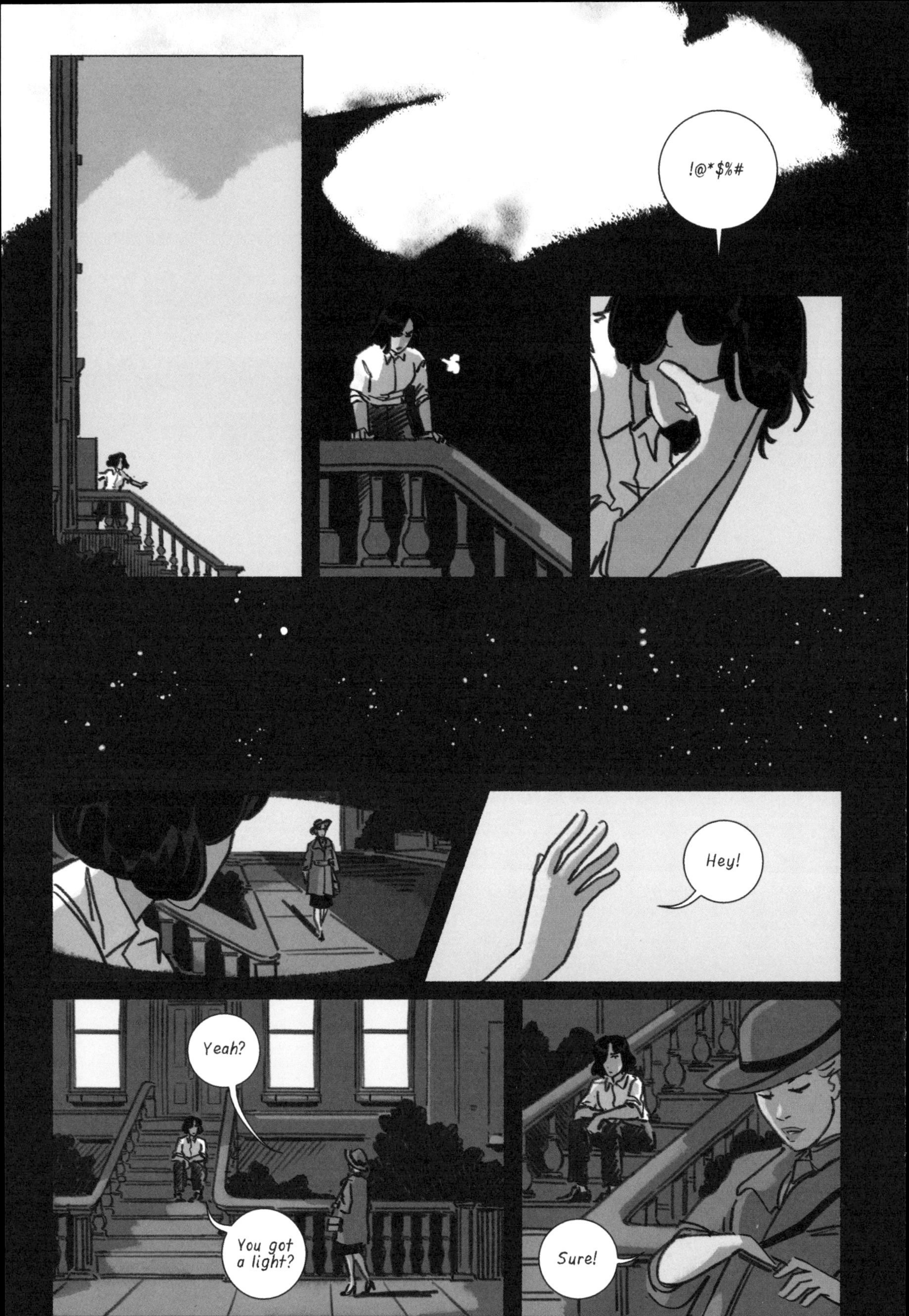
!@*$%#
Hey!
Yeah?
You got a light?
Sure!

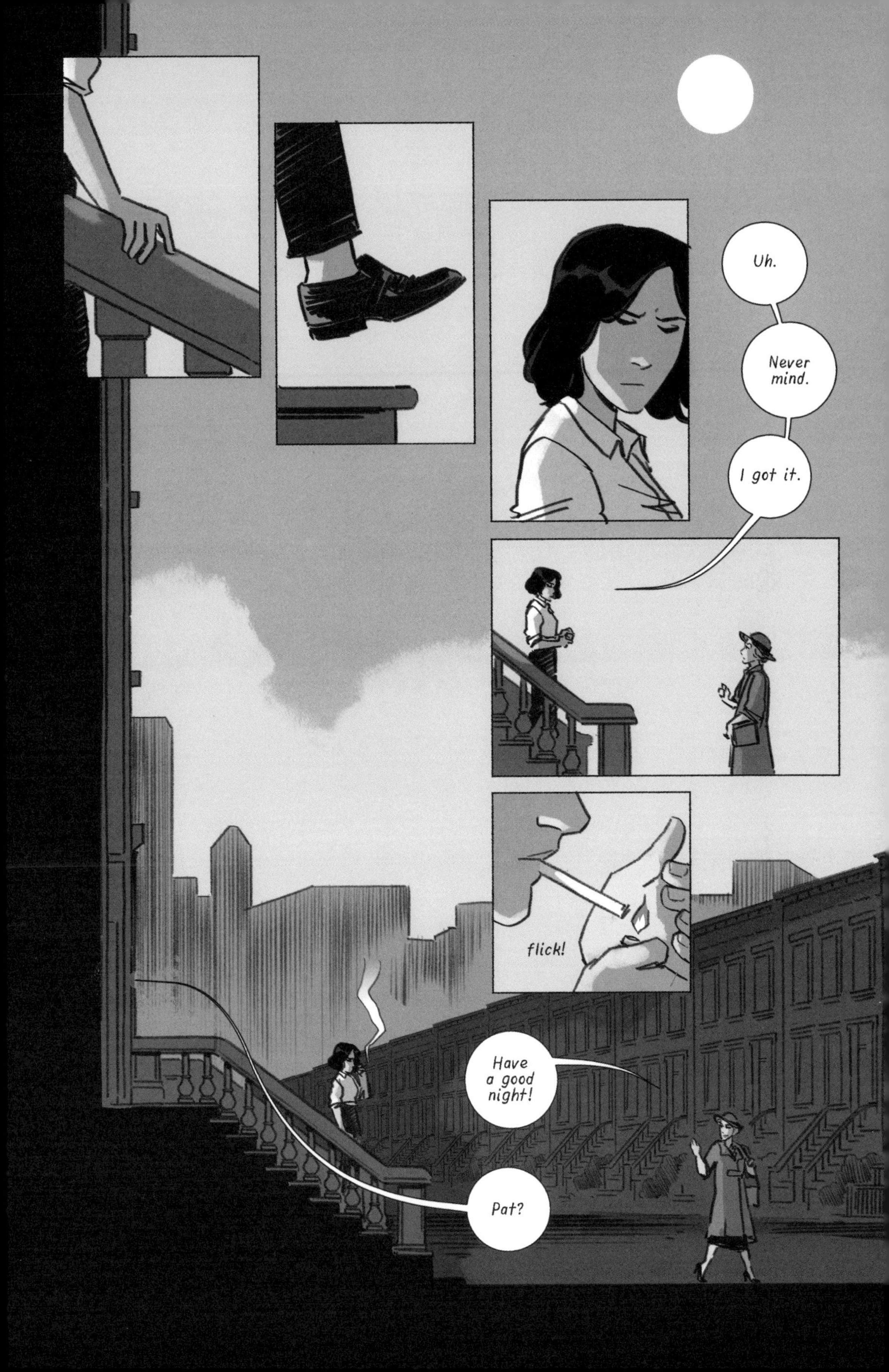
Uh.
Never mind.
I got it.
flick!
Have a good night!
Pat?

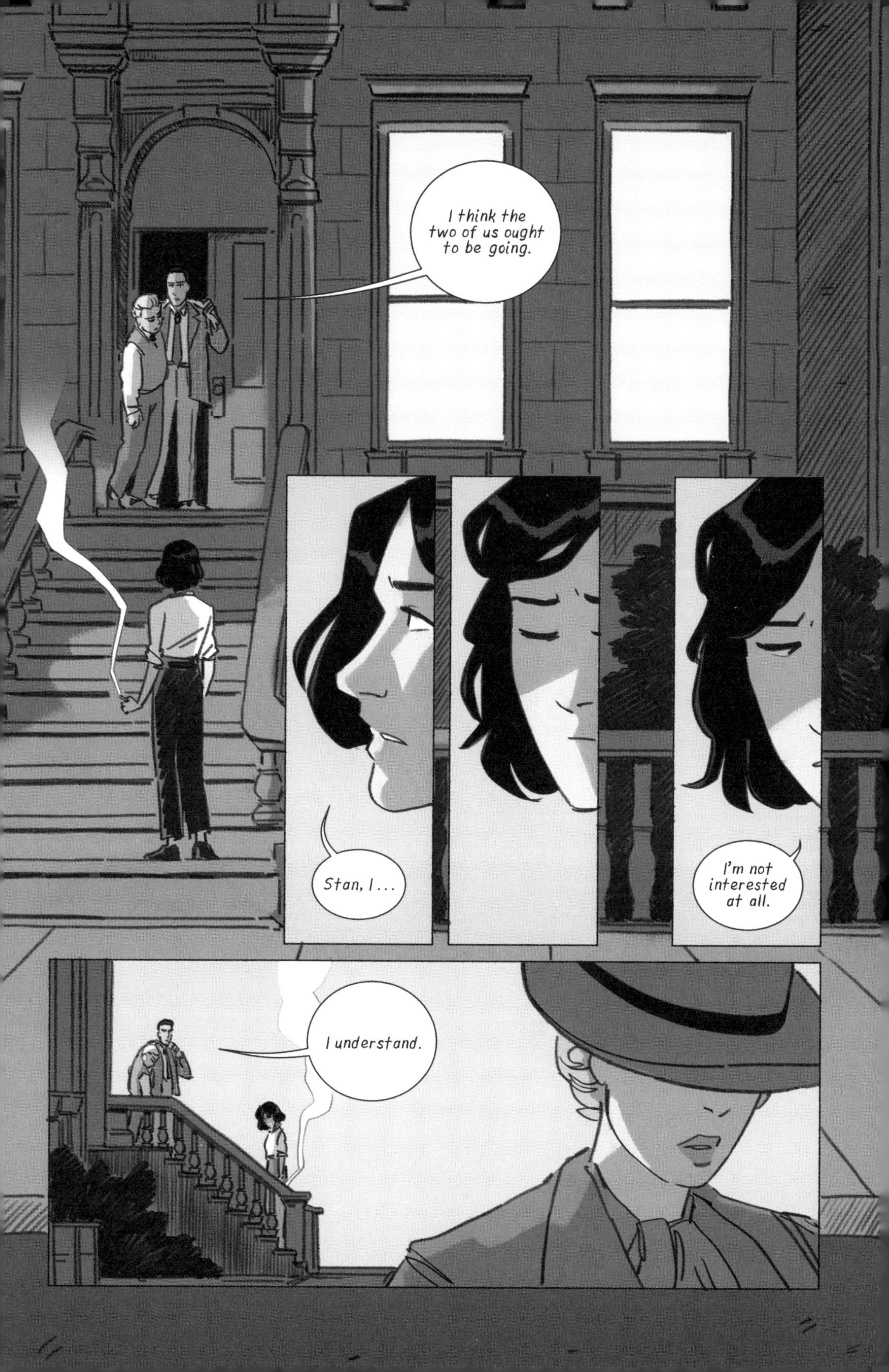
I think the two of us ought to be going.
Stan, I...
I'm not interested at all.
I understand.

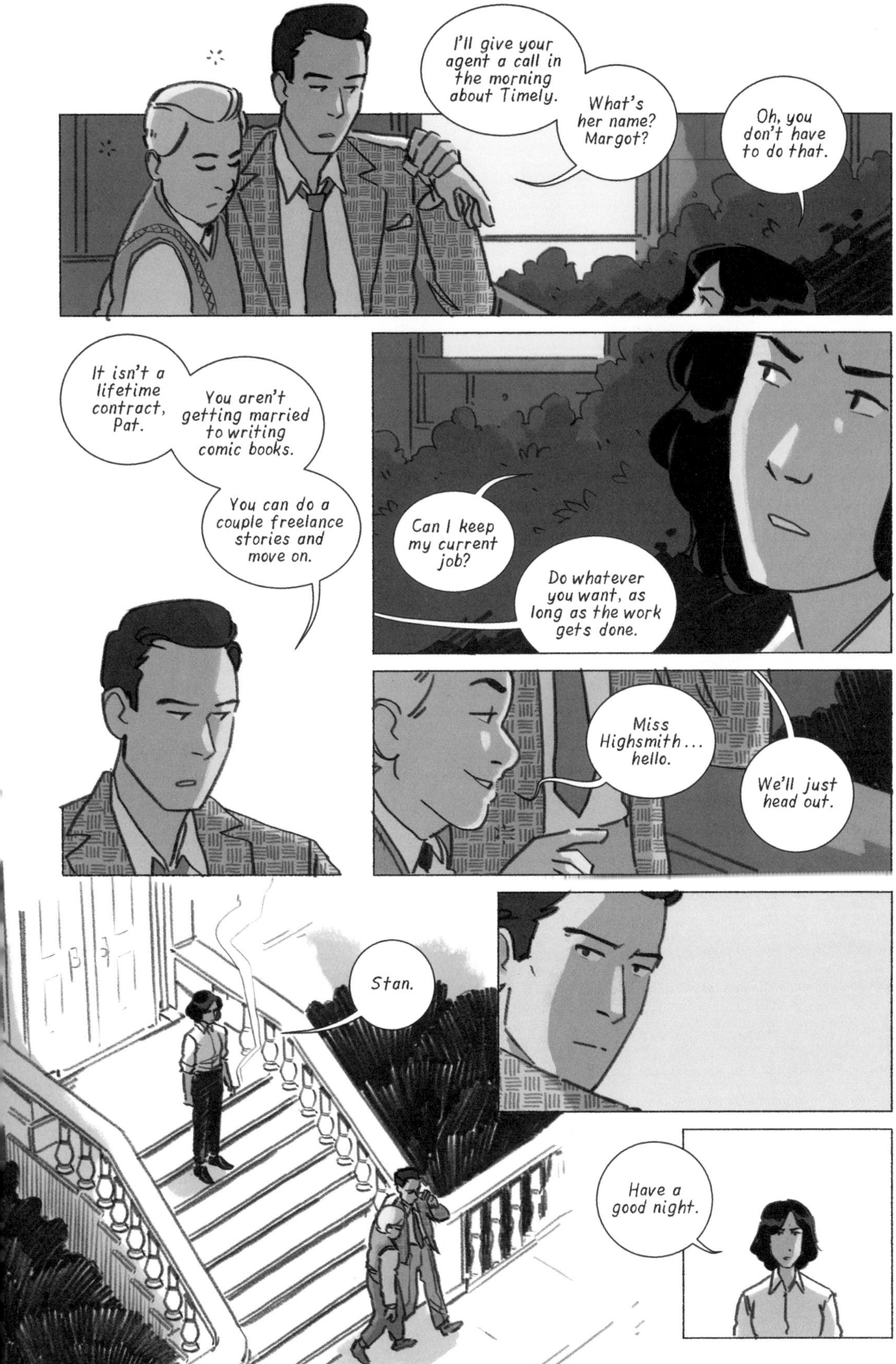
I'll give your agent a call in the morning about Timely.
What's her name? Margot?
Oh, you don't have to do that.
It isn't a lifetime contract, Pat.
You aren't getting married to writing comic books.
You can do a couple freelance stories and move on.
Can I keep my current job?
Do whatever you want, as long as the work gets done.
Miss Highsmith... hello.
We'll just head out.
Stan.
Have a good night.

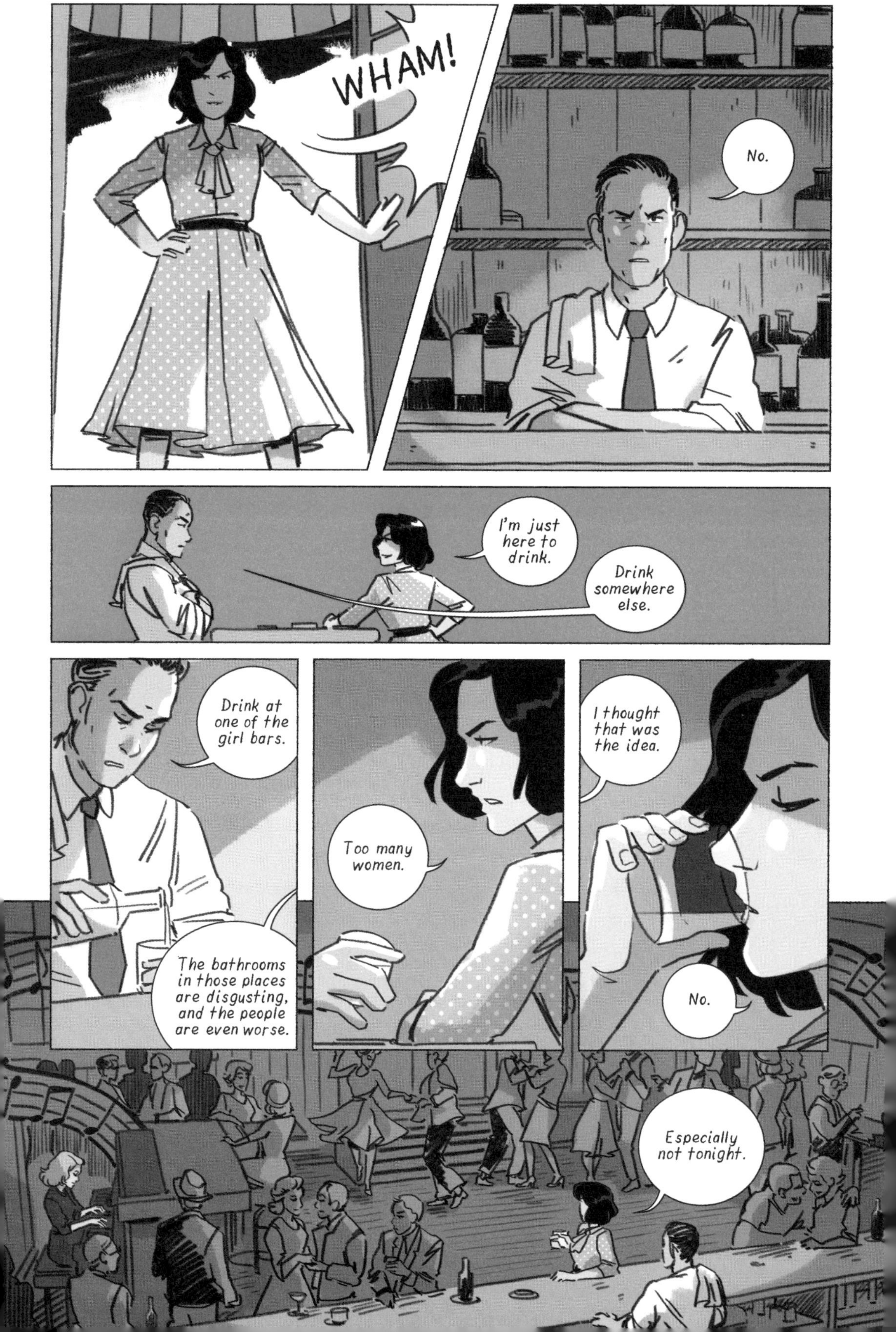

WHAM!
No.
I'm just here to drink.
Drink somewhere else.
Drink at one of the girl bars.
The bathrooms in those places are disgusting, and the people are even worse.
Too many women.
I thought that was the idea.
No.
Especially not tonight.

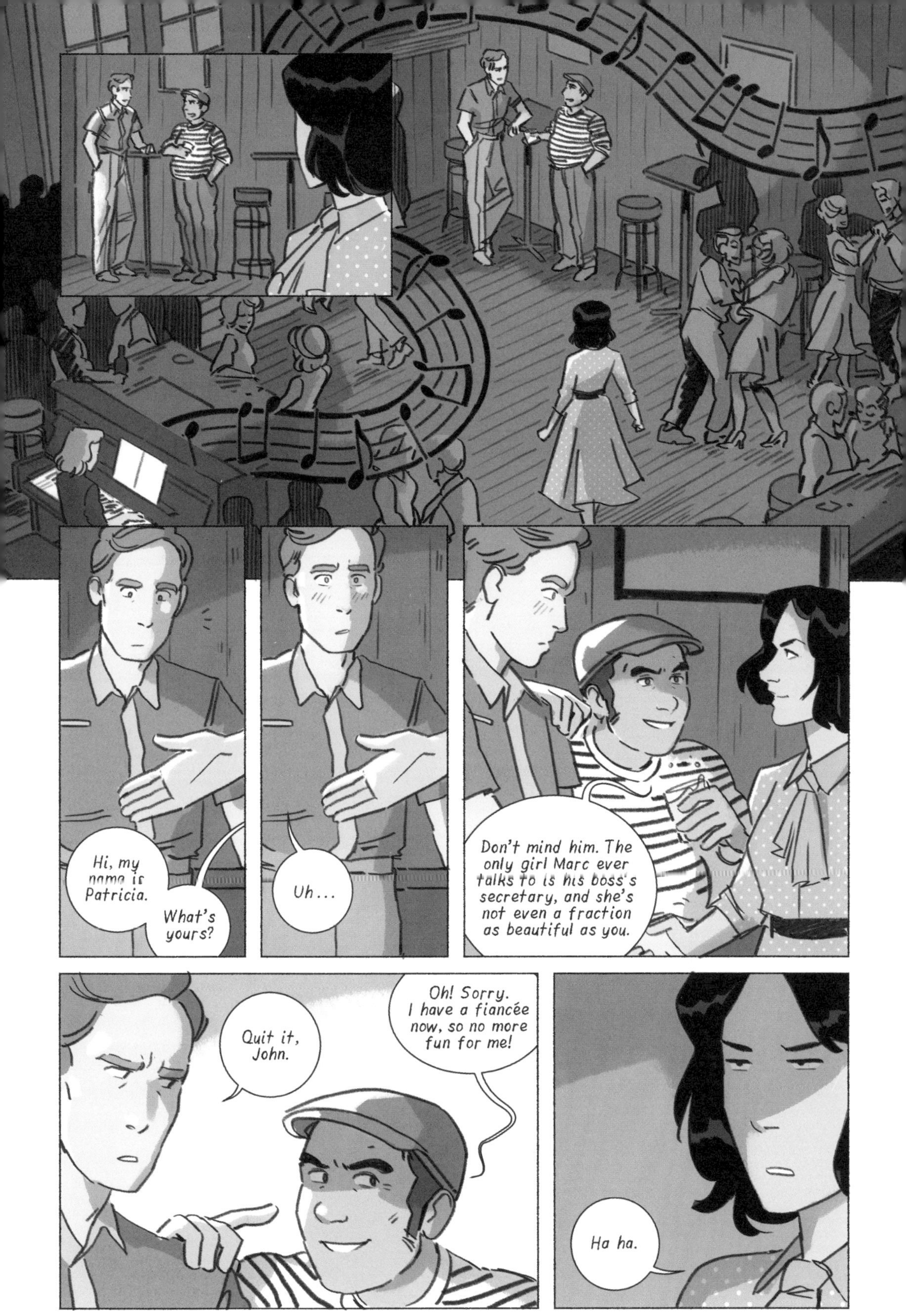
Hi, my name is Patricia.
What's yours?
Uh...
Don't mind him. The only girl Marc ever talks to is his boss's secretary, and she's not even a fraction as beautiful as you.
Quit it, John.
Oh! Sorry. I have a fiancée now, so no more fun for me!
Ha ha.

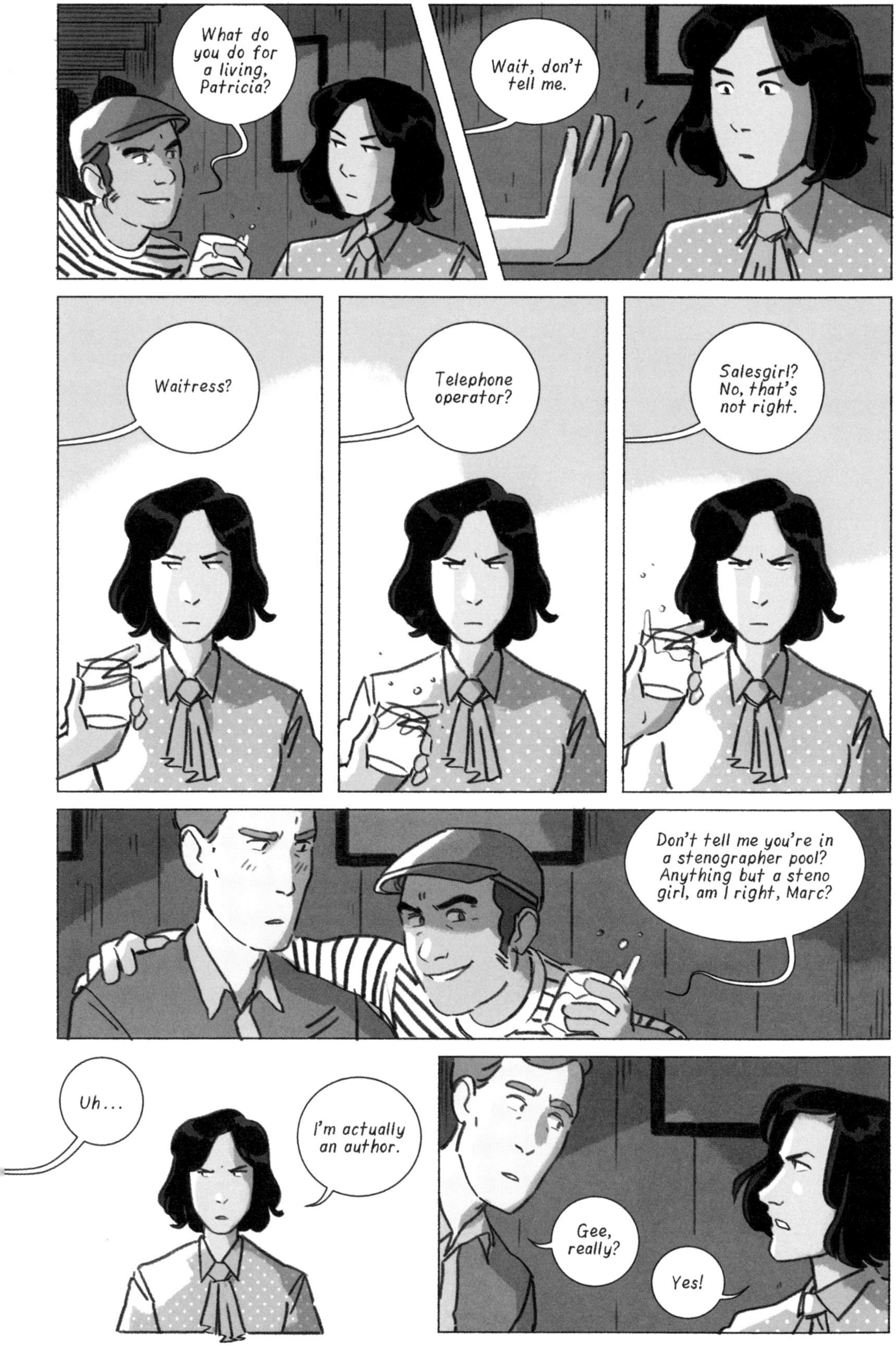
What do you do for a living, Patricia?
Wait, don't tell me.
Waitress?
Telephone operator?
Salesgirl? No, that's not right.
Don't tell me you're in a stenographer pool? Anything but a steno girl, am I right, Marc?
Uh...
I'm actually an author.
Gee, really?
Yes!

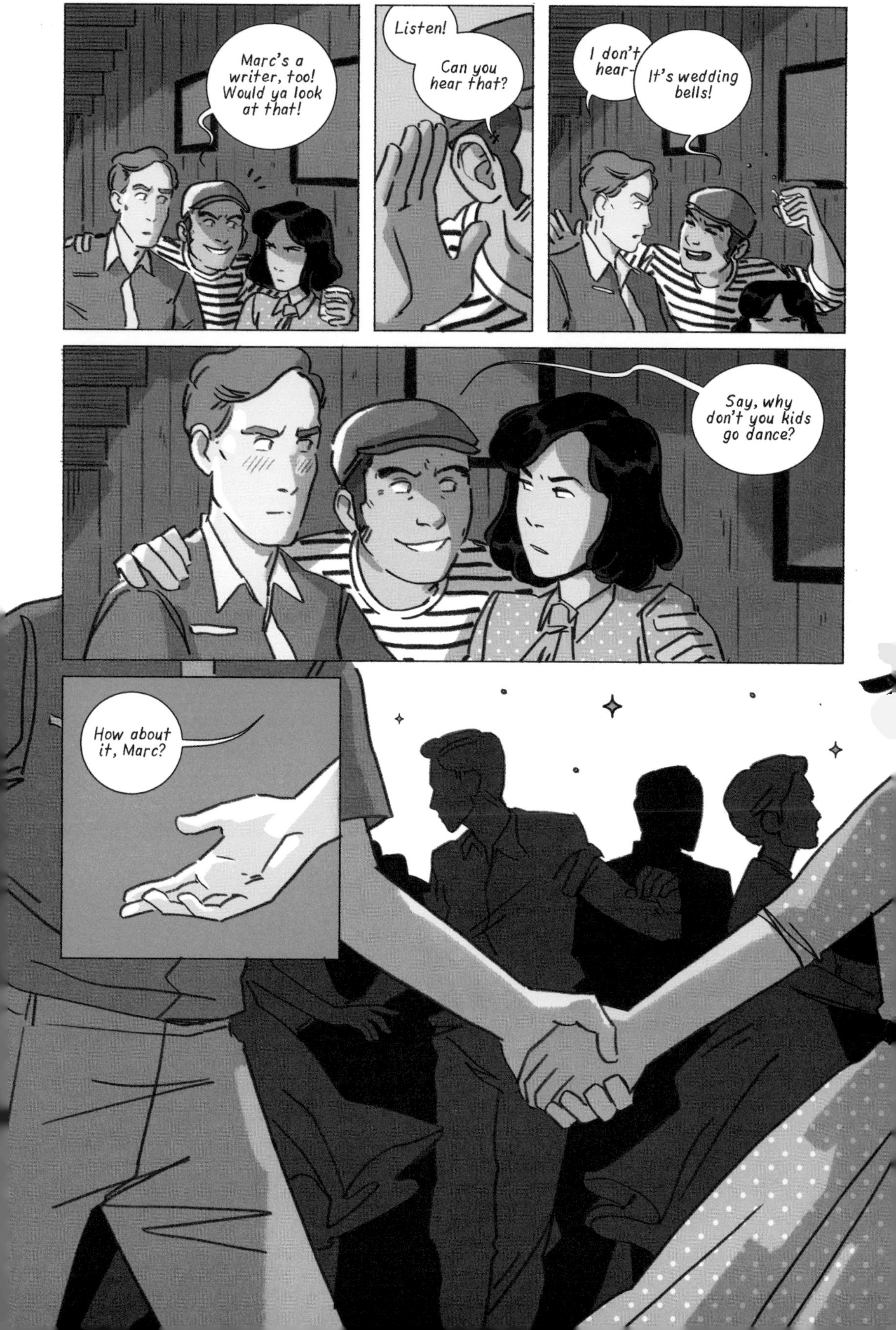
Marc's a writer, too! Would ya look at that!
Listen!
Can you hear that?
I don't hear-
It's wedding bells!
Say, why don't you kids go dance?
How about it, Marc?

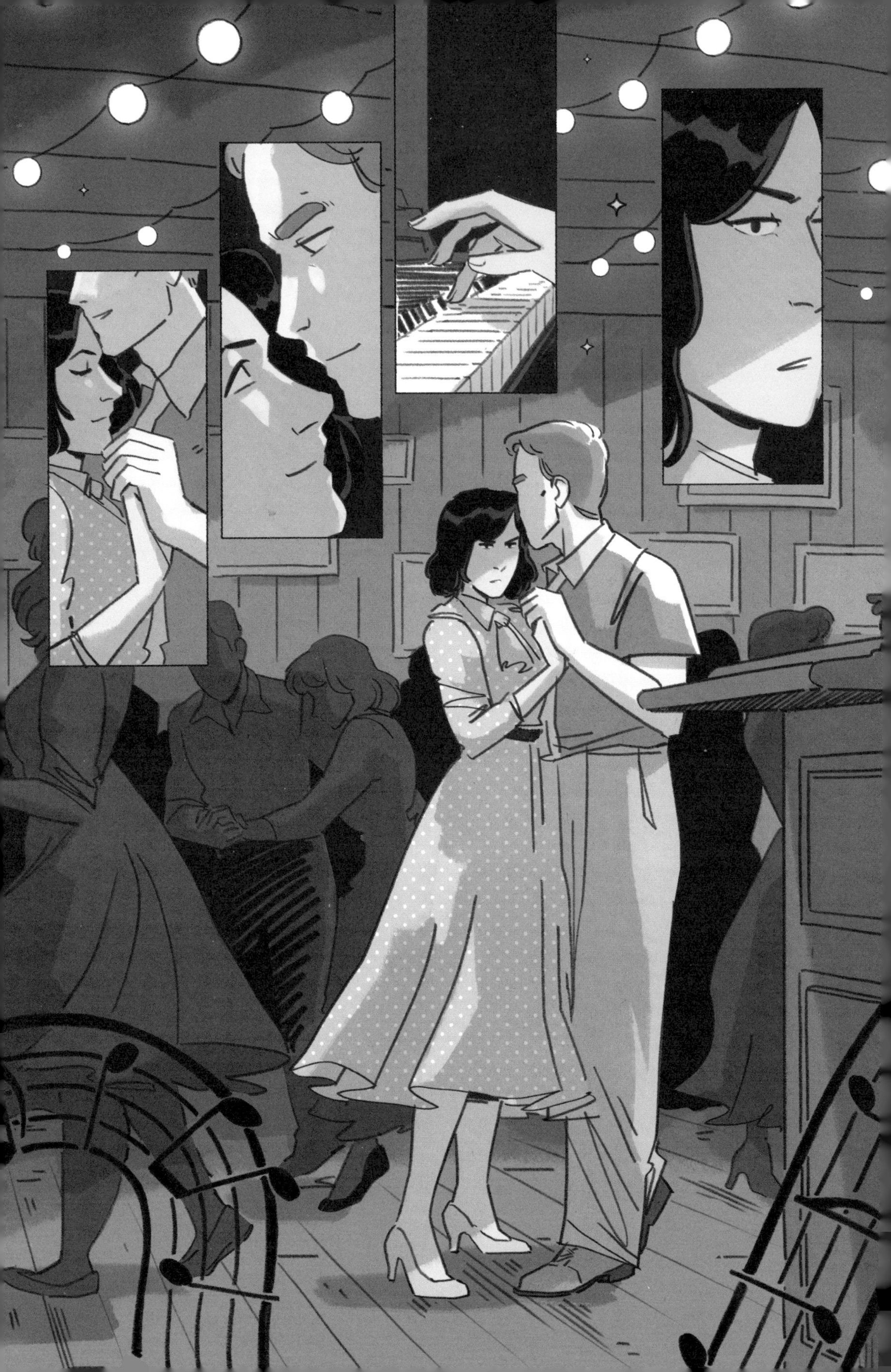

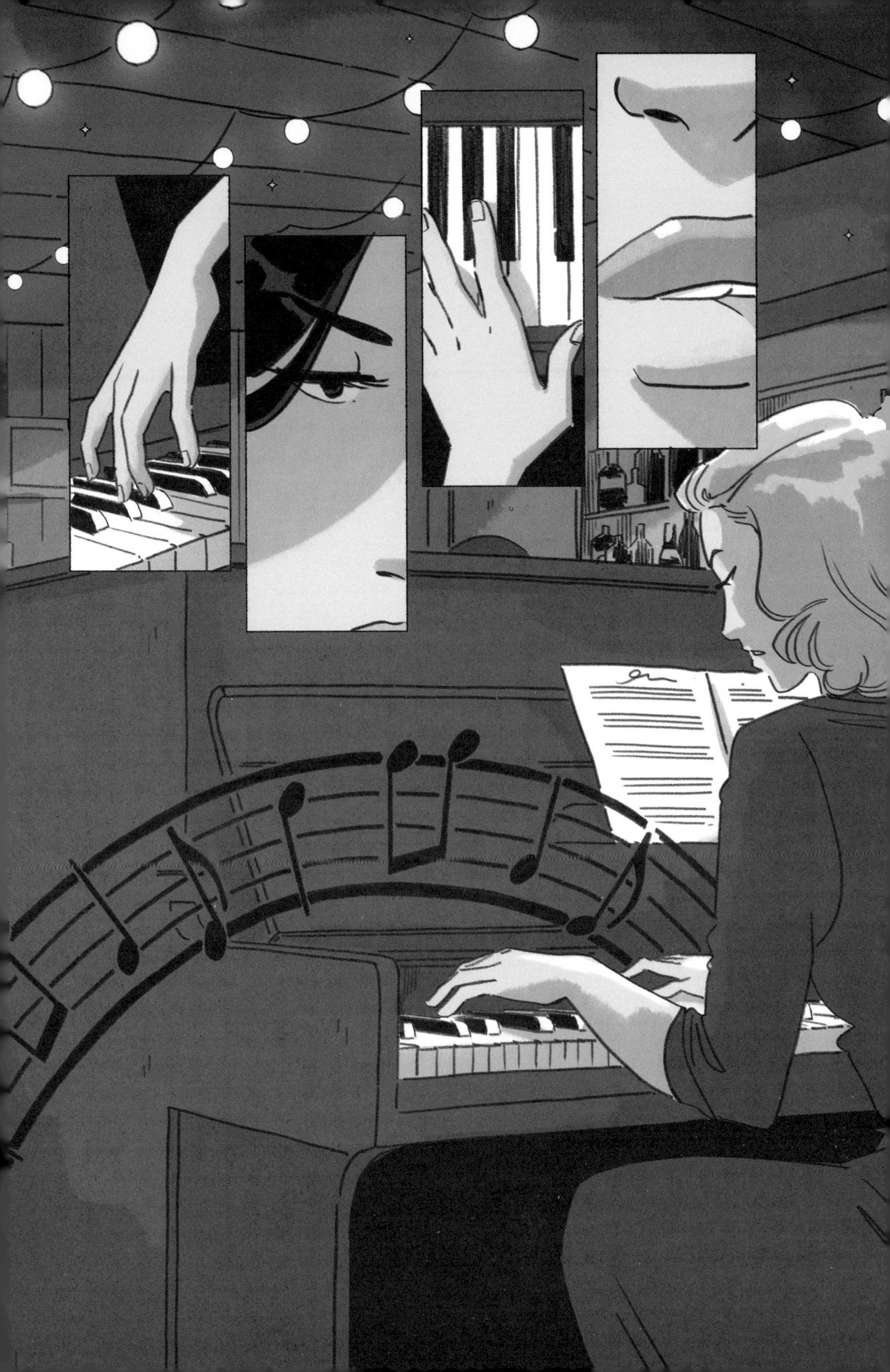

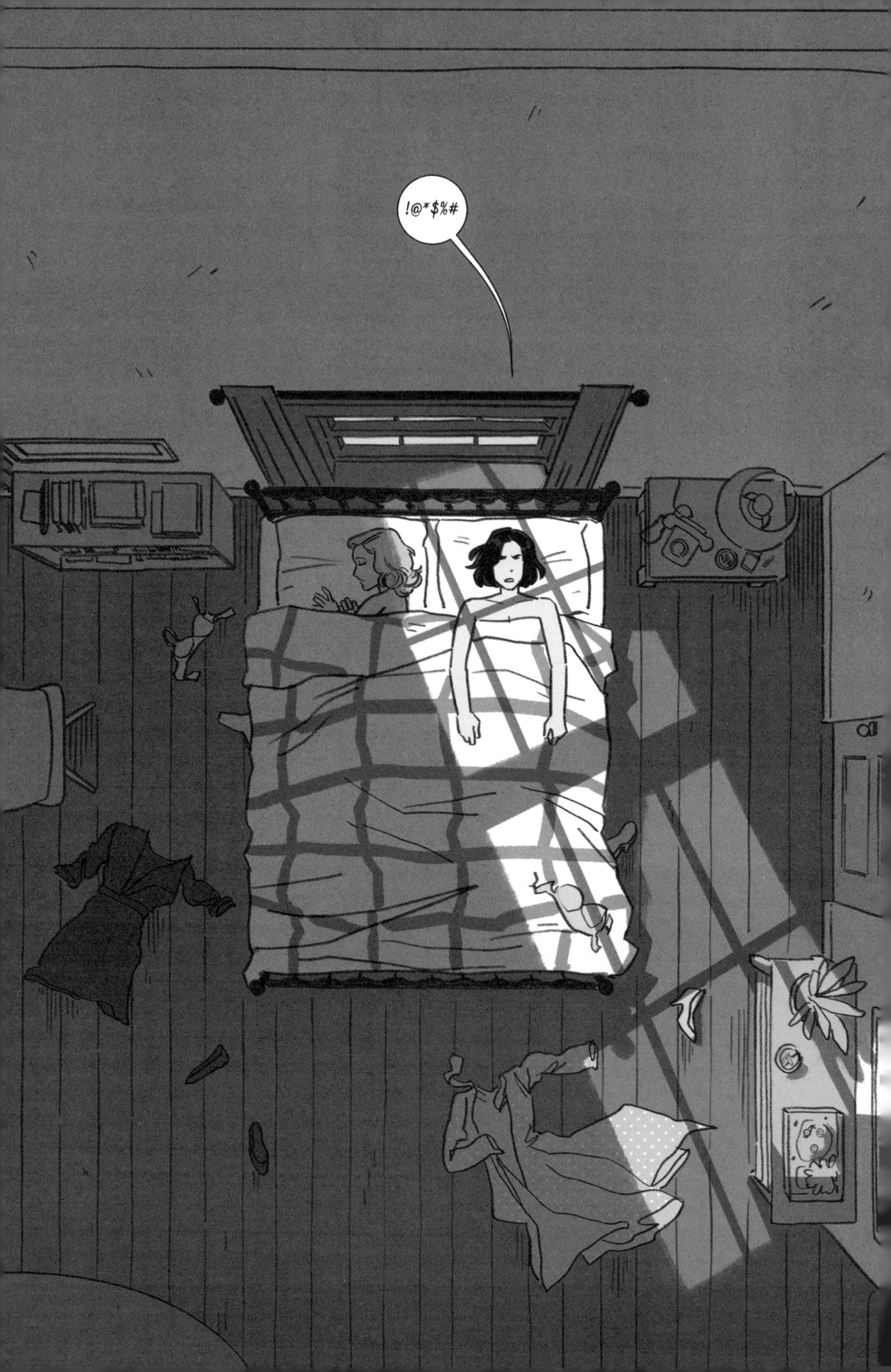
!@*$%#

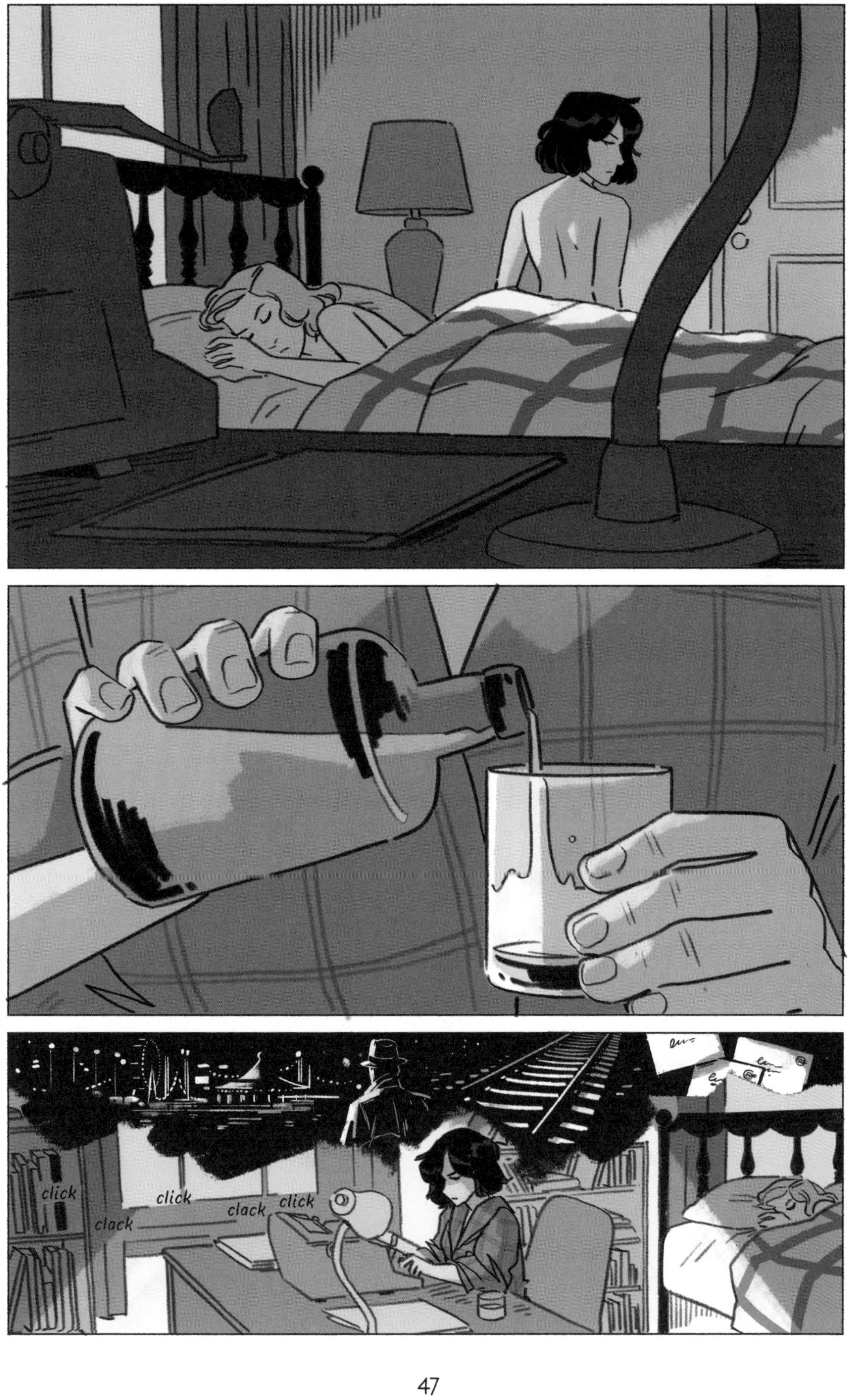
click
clack
click
clack
click

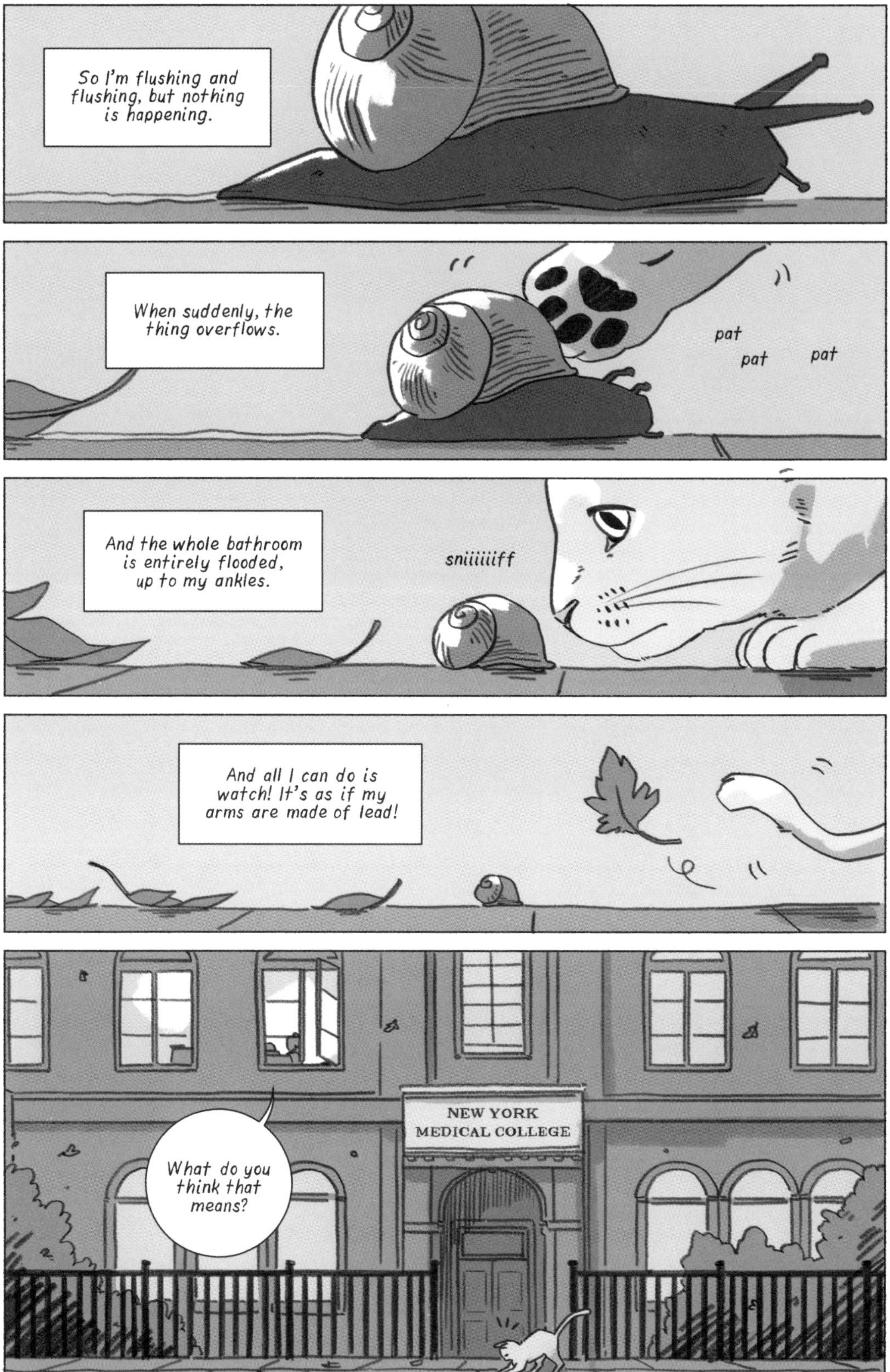
So I'm flushing and flushing, but nothing is happening.
When suddenly, the thing overflows.
pat
pat
pat
And the whole bathroom is entirely flooded, up to my ankles.
sniiiiiiff
And all I can do is watch! It's as if my arms are made of lead!
NEW YORK MEDICAL COLLEGE
What do you think that means?

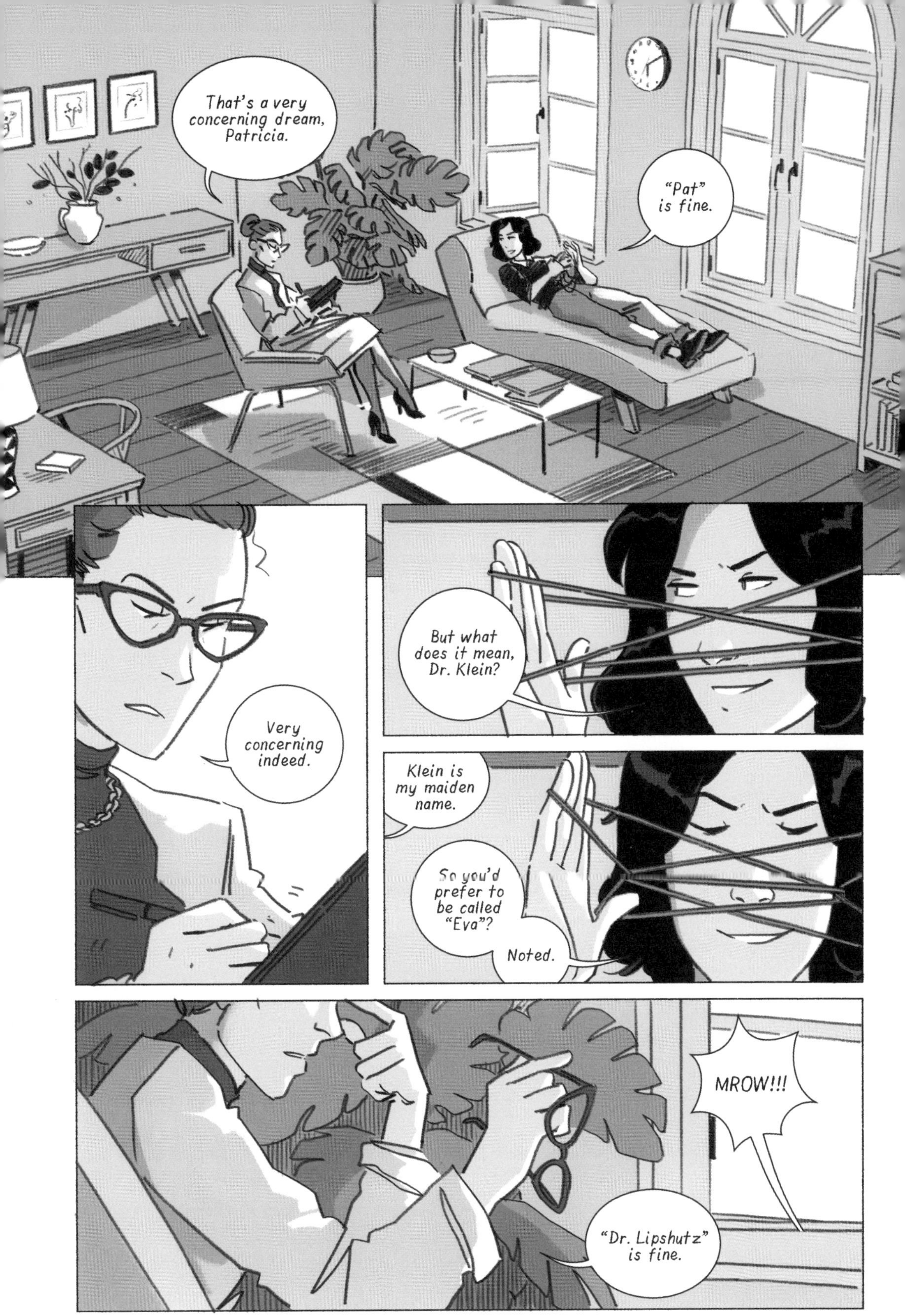
That's a very concerning dream, Patricia.
"Pat" is fine.
Very concerning indeed.
But what does it mean, Dr. Klein?
Klein is my maiden name.
So you'd prefer to be called "Eva"?
Noted.
MROW!!!
"Dr. Lipshutz" is fine.

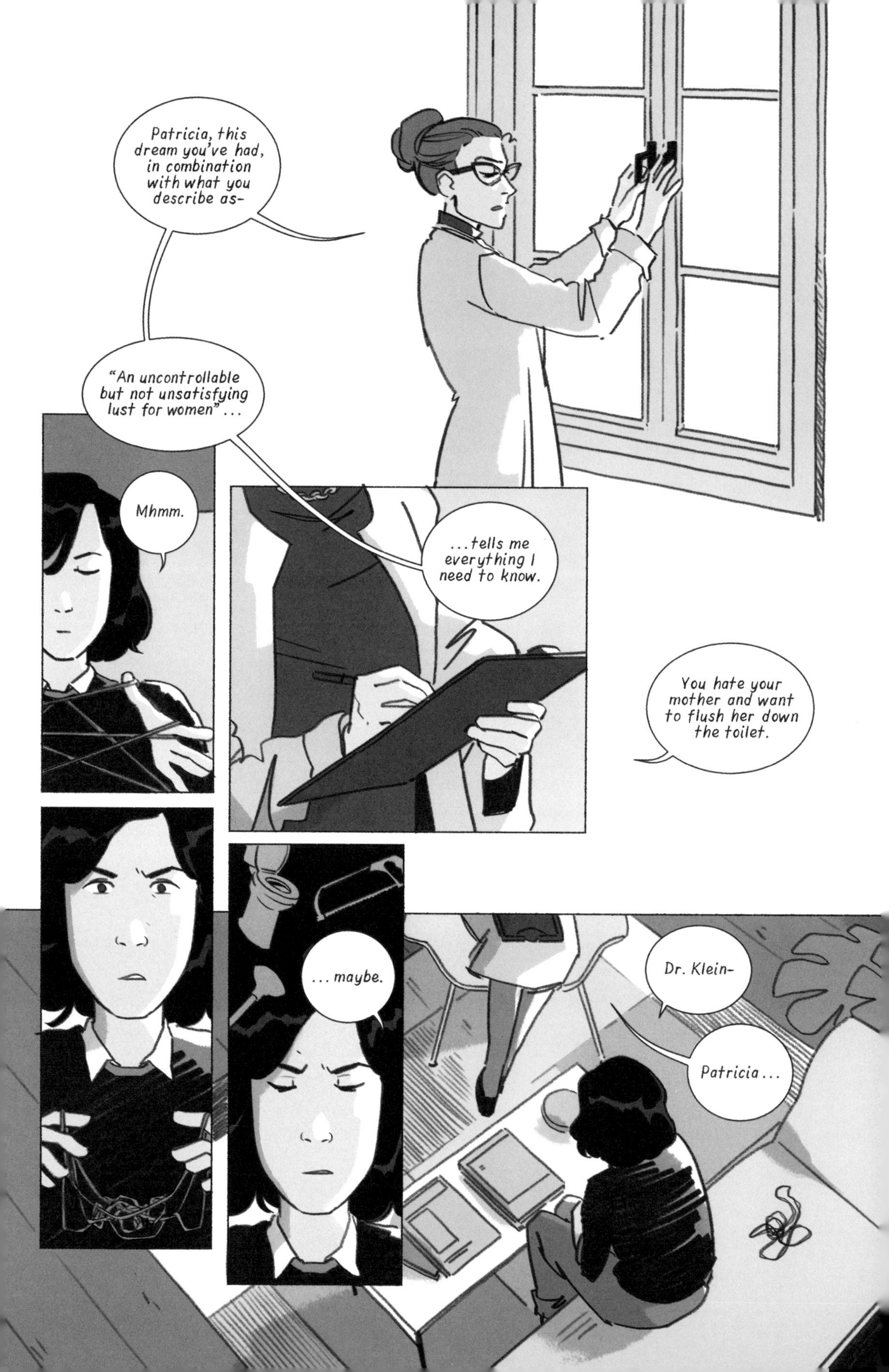
Patricia, this dream you've had, in combination with what you describe as-
"An uncontrollable but not unsatisfying lust for women"...
Mhmm.
...tells me everything I need to know.
You hate your mother and want to flush her down the toilet.
...maybe.
Dr. Klein-
Patricia...

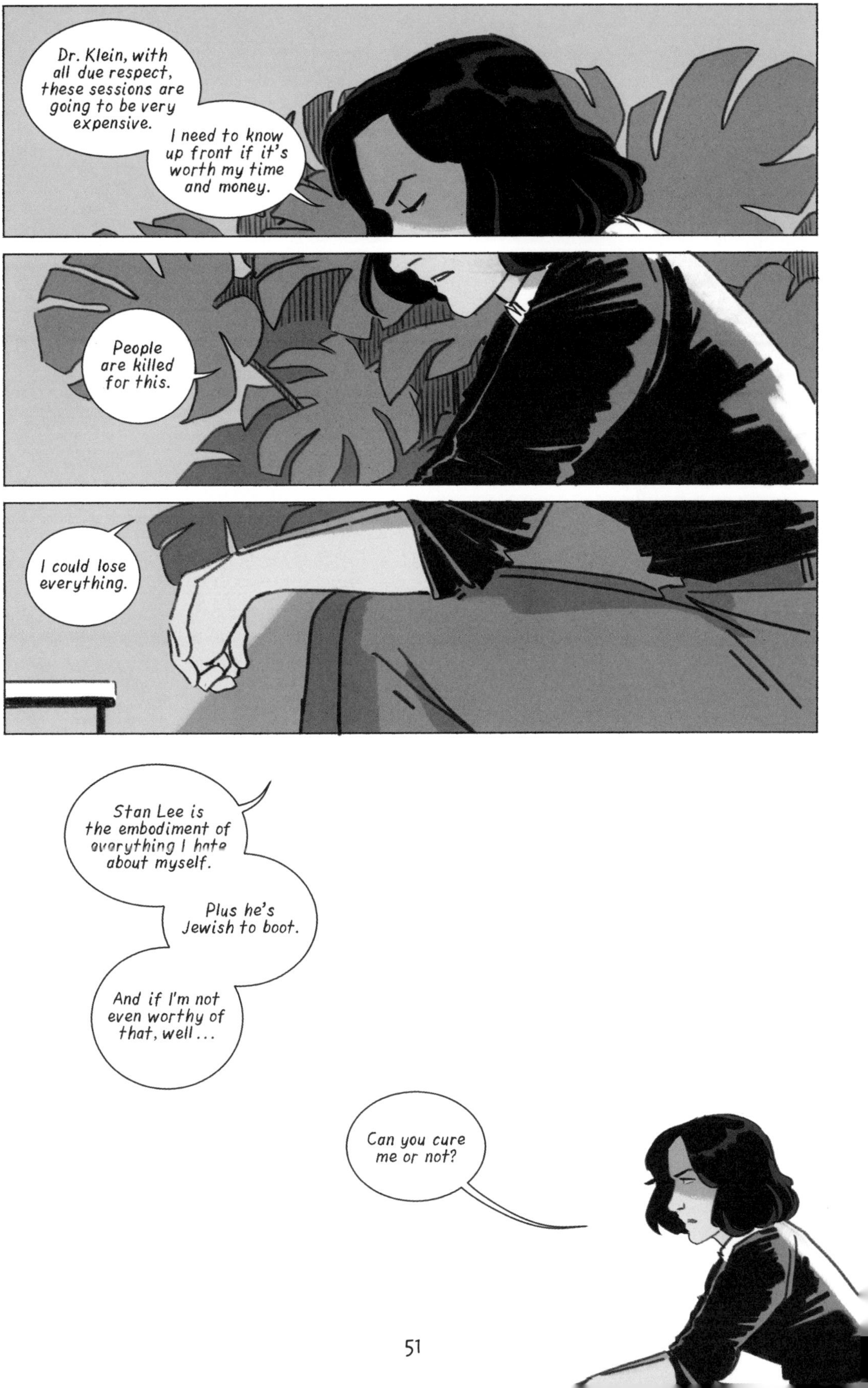

Dr. Klein, with all due respect, these sessions are going to be very expensive.
I need to know up front if it's worth my time and money.
People are killed for this.
I could lose everything.
Stan Lee is the embodiment of everything I hate about myself.
Plus he's Jewish to boot.
And if I'm not even worthy of that, well...
Can you cure me or not?

Sigh.

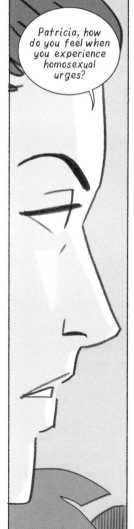

Patricia, how do you feel when you experience homosexual urges?

Happy.

Excited.

Abnormal.

Conflicted.

Guilty.

Interesting.

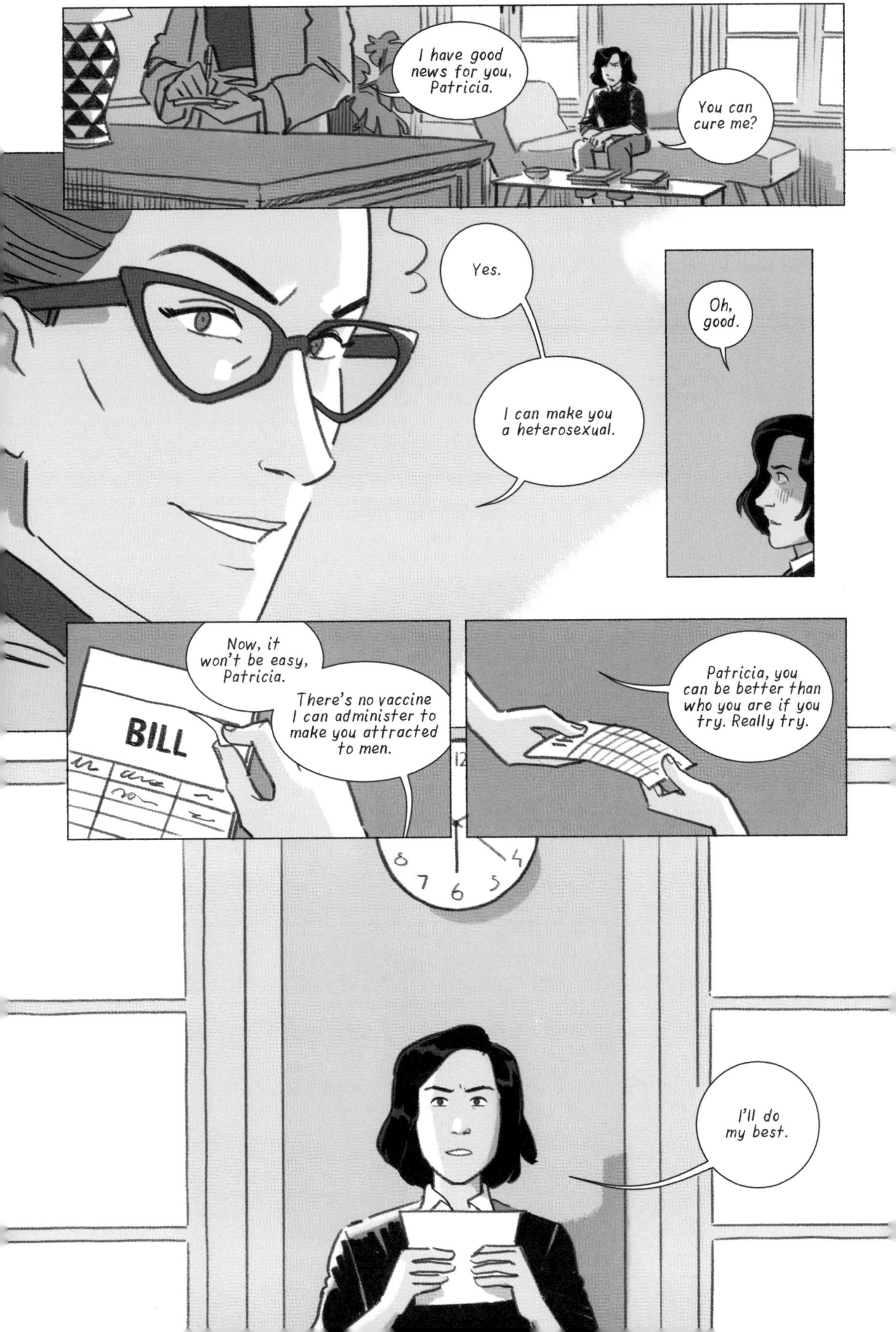
I have good news for you, Patricia.
You can cure me?
Yes.
I can make you a heterosexual.
Oh, good.
Now, it won't be easy, Patricia.
There's no vaccine I can administer to make you attracted to men.
BILL
Patricia, you can be better than who you are if you try. Really try.
I'll do my best.

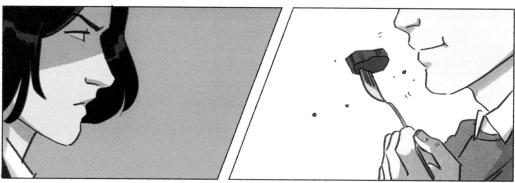

crunch

munch

munch

monch

I'm glad you came by, Marc.

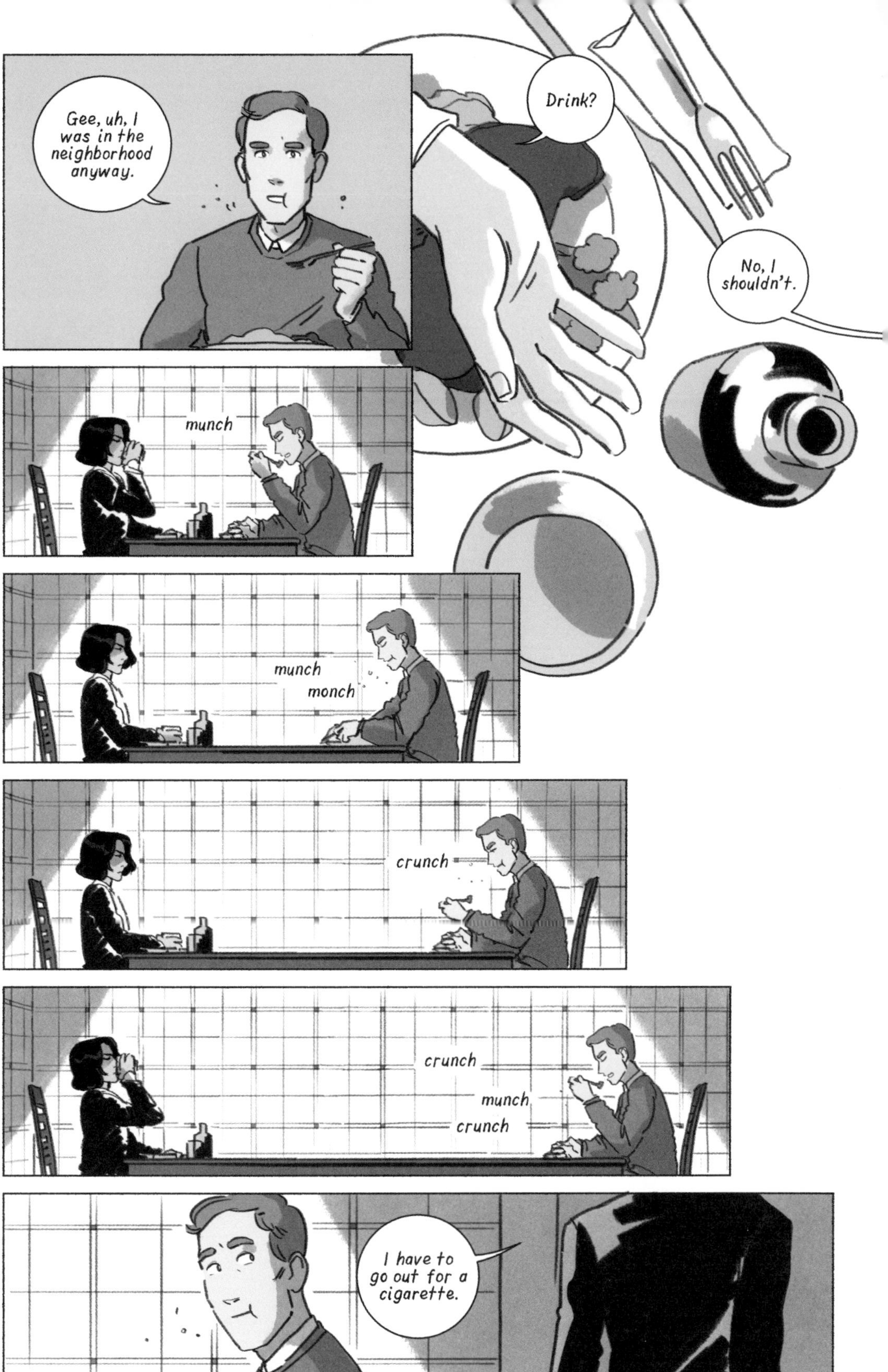
Gee, uh, I was in the neighborhood anyway.
Drink?
No, I shouldn't.
munch
munch
monch
crunch
crunch
munch
crunch
I have to go out for a cigarette.

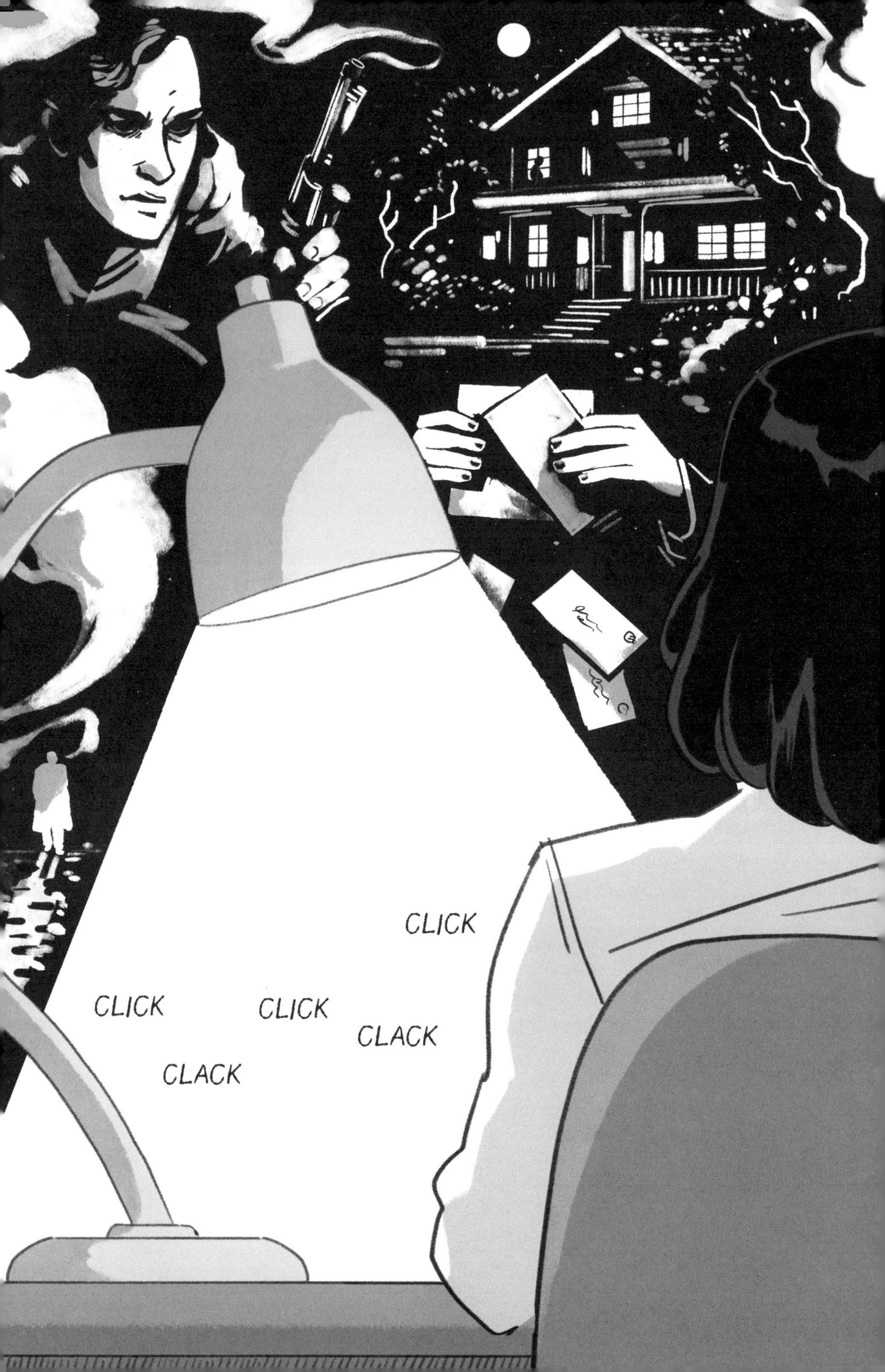
CLICK
CLICK
CLICK
CLACK
CLACK

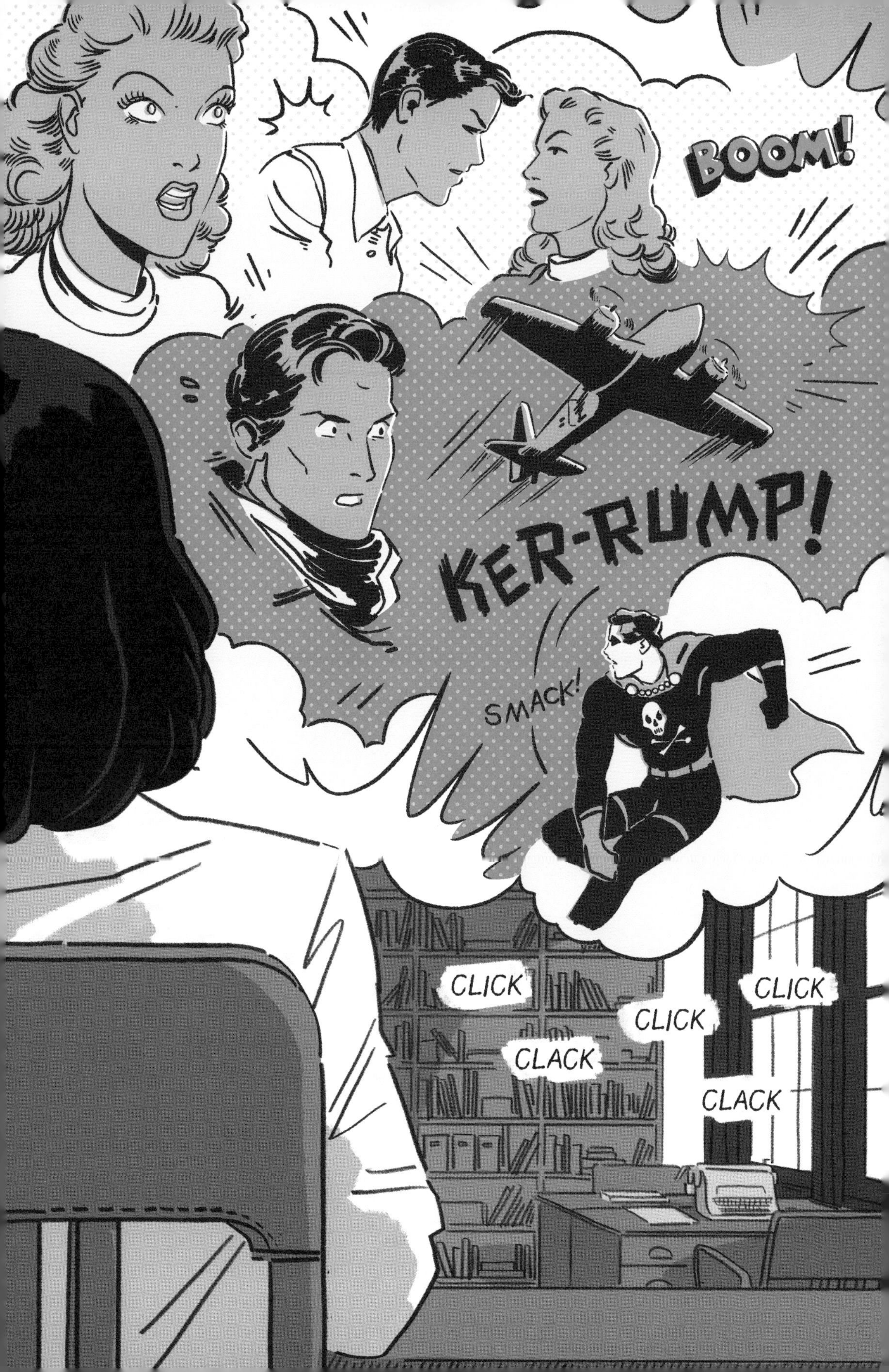
BOOM!
KER-RUMP!
SMACK!
CLICK
CLICK
CLICK
CLACK
CLACK

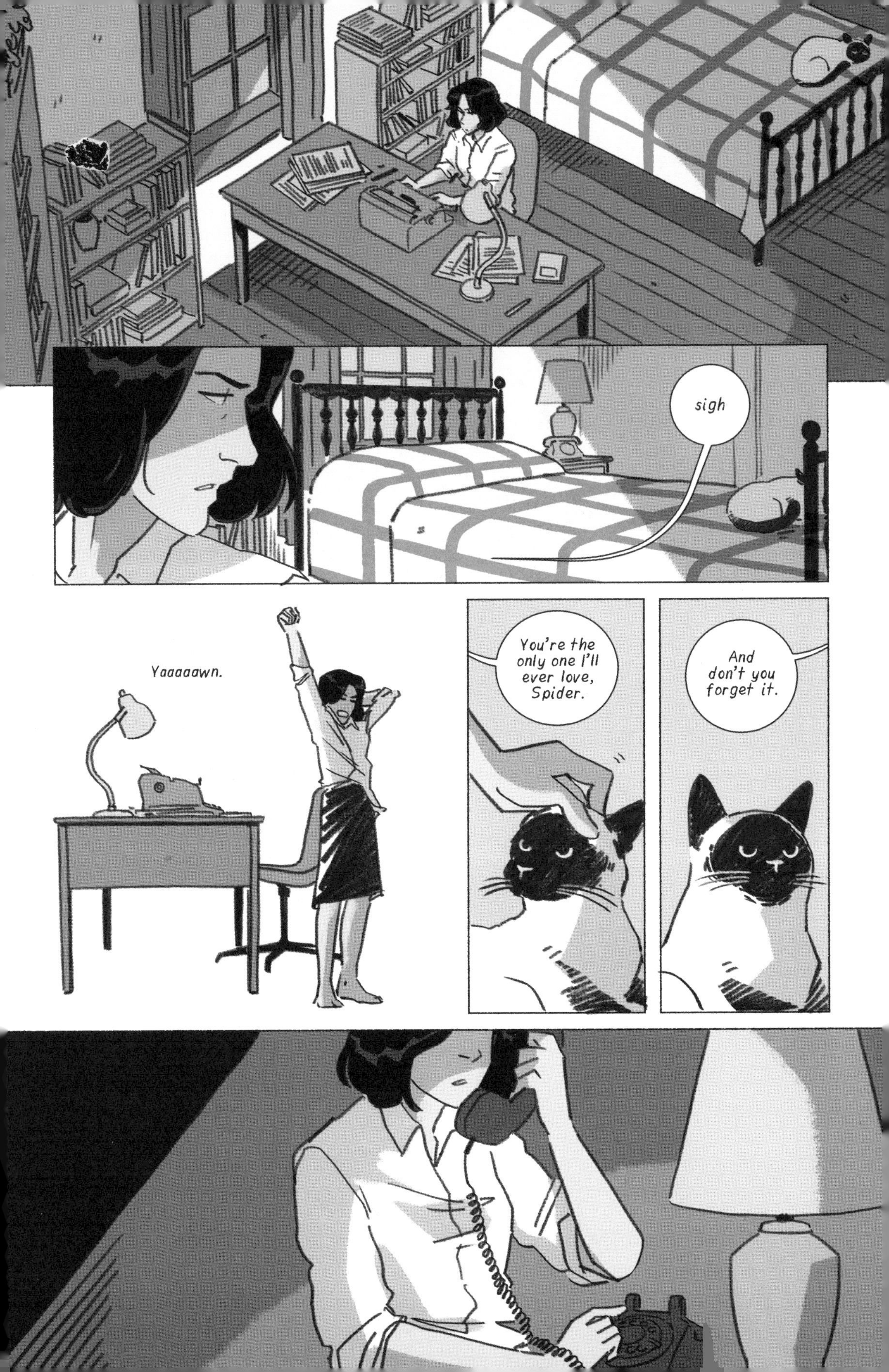
sigh
Yaaaaawn.
You're the only one I'll ever love, Spider.
And don't you forget it.

Hello, Margot?

It's Pat.

What does it matter, you're my agent at all hours.

Listen: It's finished. Fully written.

My book.

Strangers on a Train.

I wanted you to know so you could expect it in the morning.

So you can start taking it to publishers right away.

Is Kay there with you? Are you two still an item? Send her my best.

Hello? Hello?

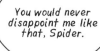

You would never disappoint me like that, Spider.

A butterfly.

A mask.

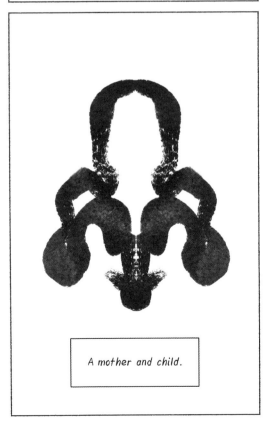

A mother and child.

HA!

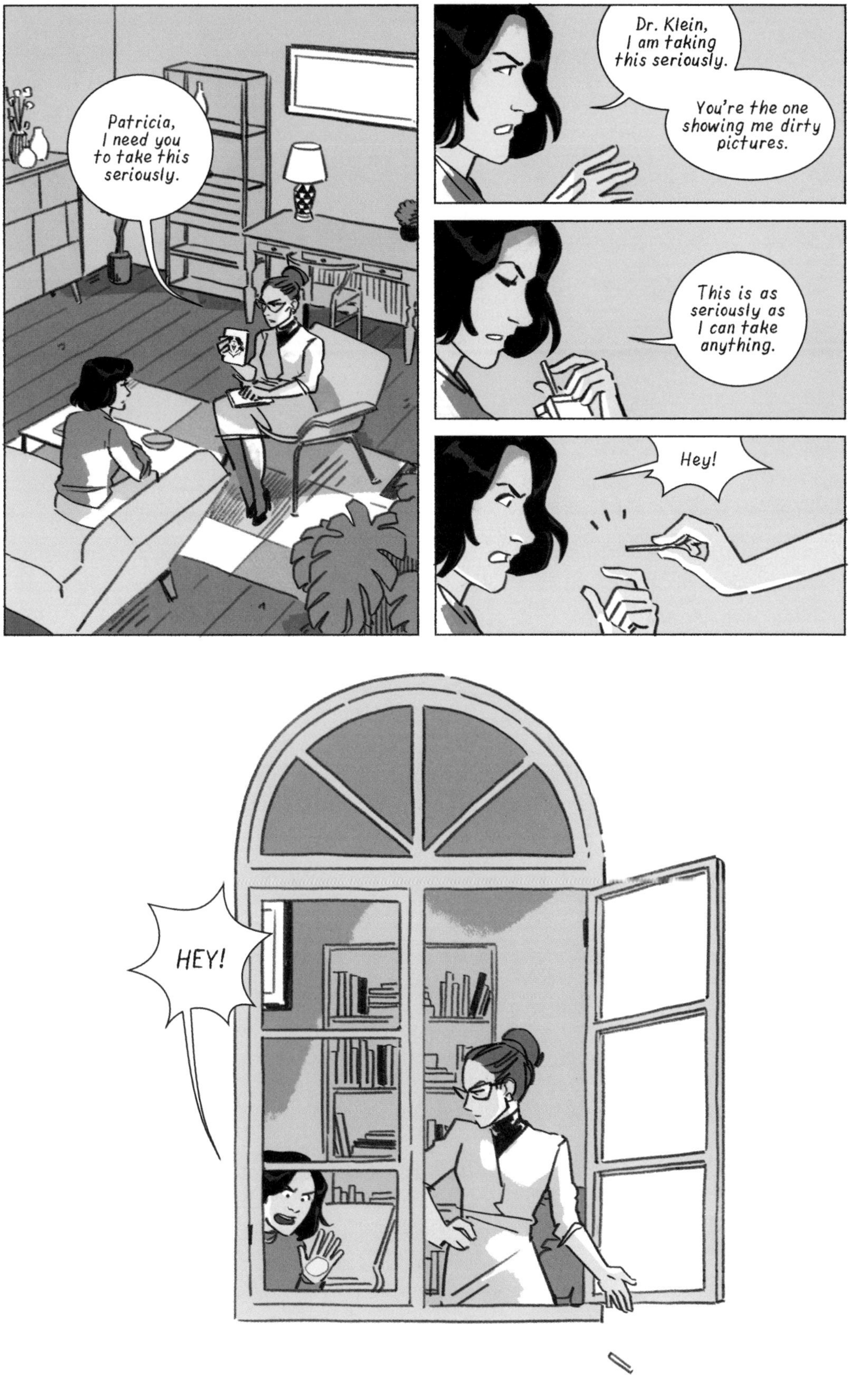

Patricia, I need you to take this seriously.
Dr. Klein, I am taking this seriously.
You're the one showing me dirty pictures.
This is as seriously as I can take anything.
Hey!
HEY!

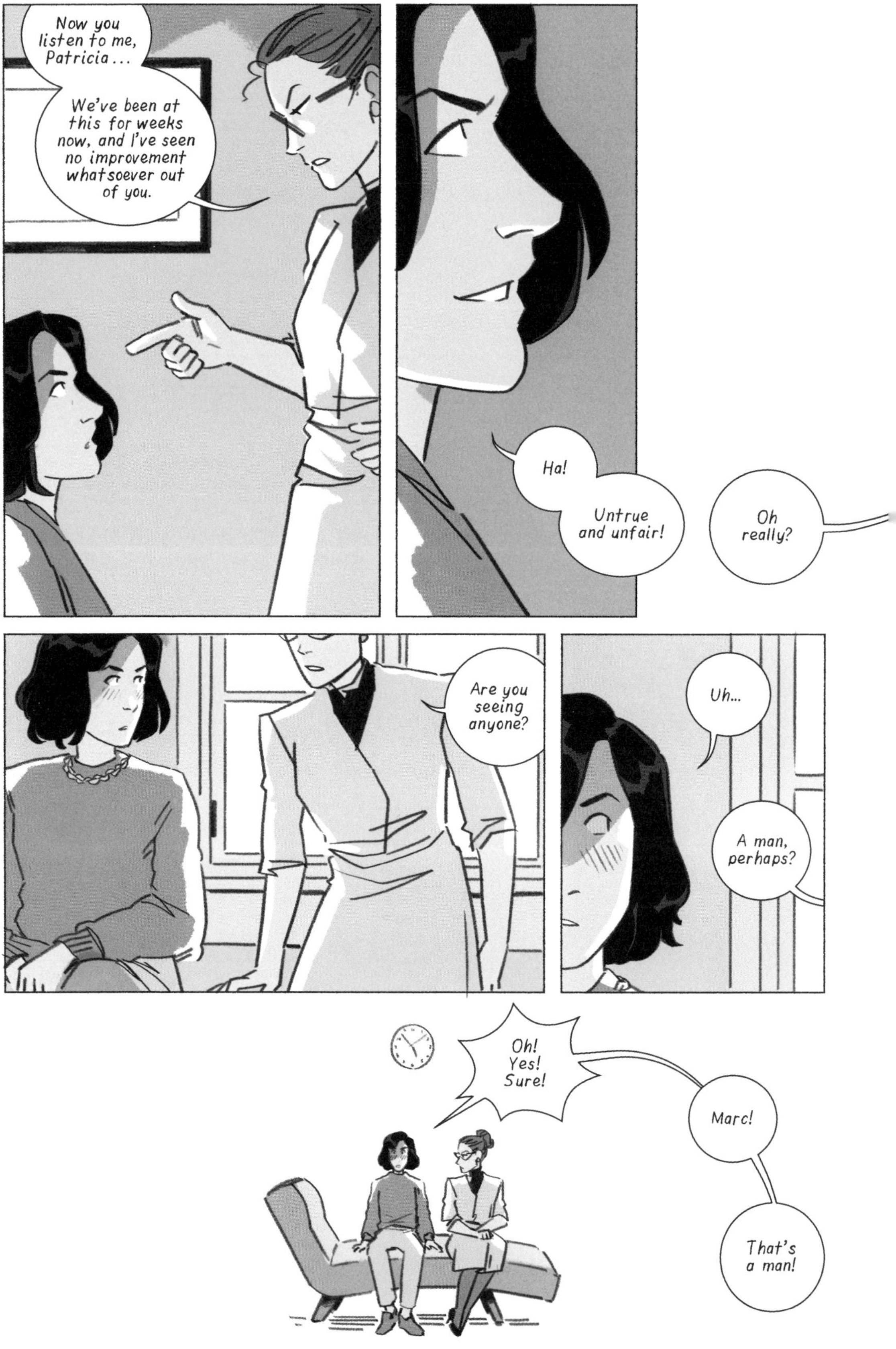

Now you listen to me, Patricia...
We've been at this for weeks now, and I've seen no improvement whatsoever out of you.
Ha!
Untrue and unfair!
Oh really?
Are you seeing anyone?
Uh...
A man, perhaps?
Oh! Yes! Sure!
Marc!
That's a man!

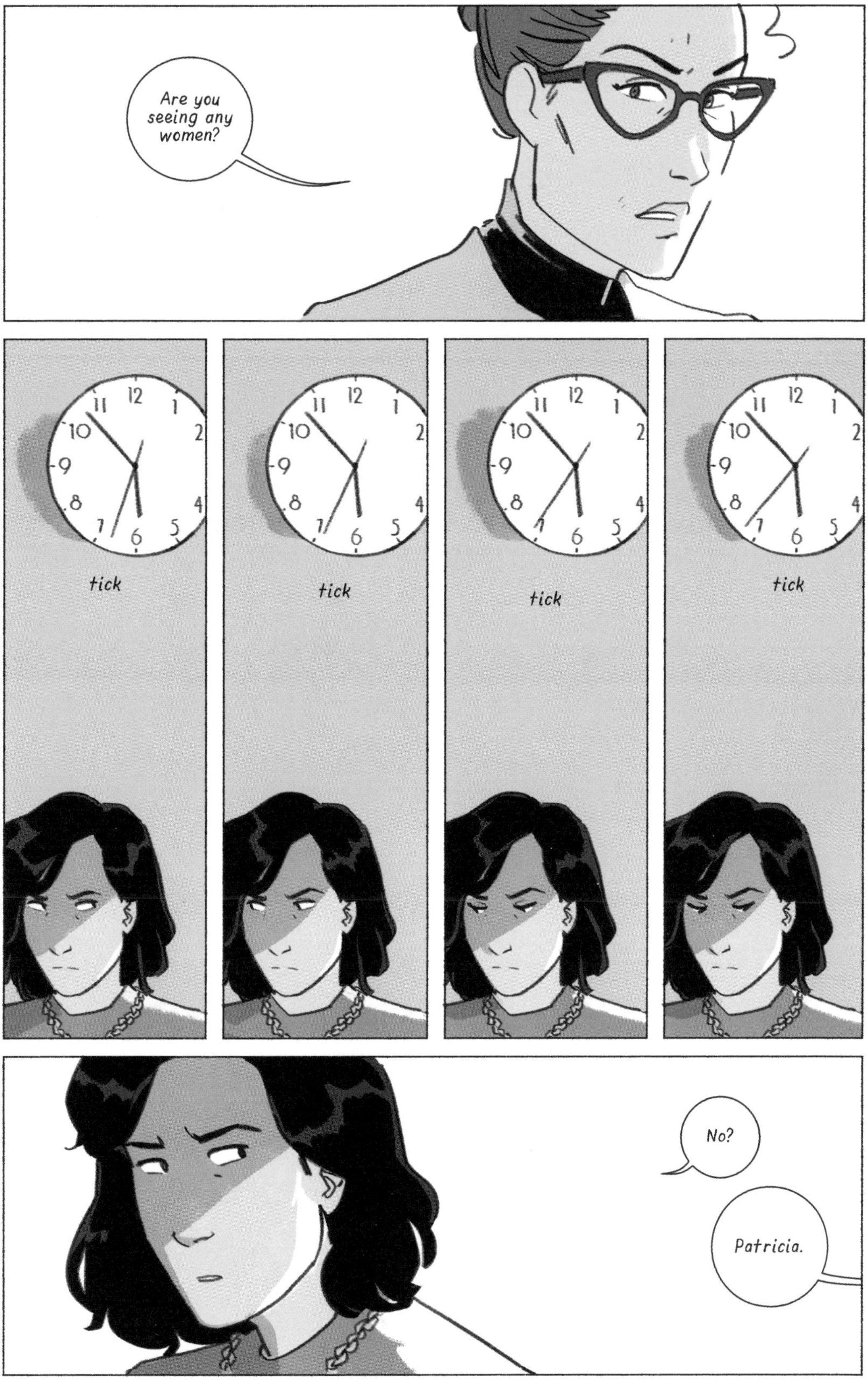

Are you seeing any women?
tick
tick
tick
tick
No?
Patricia.

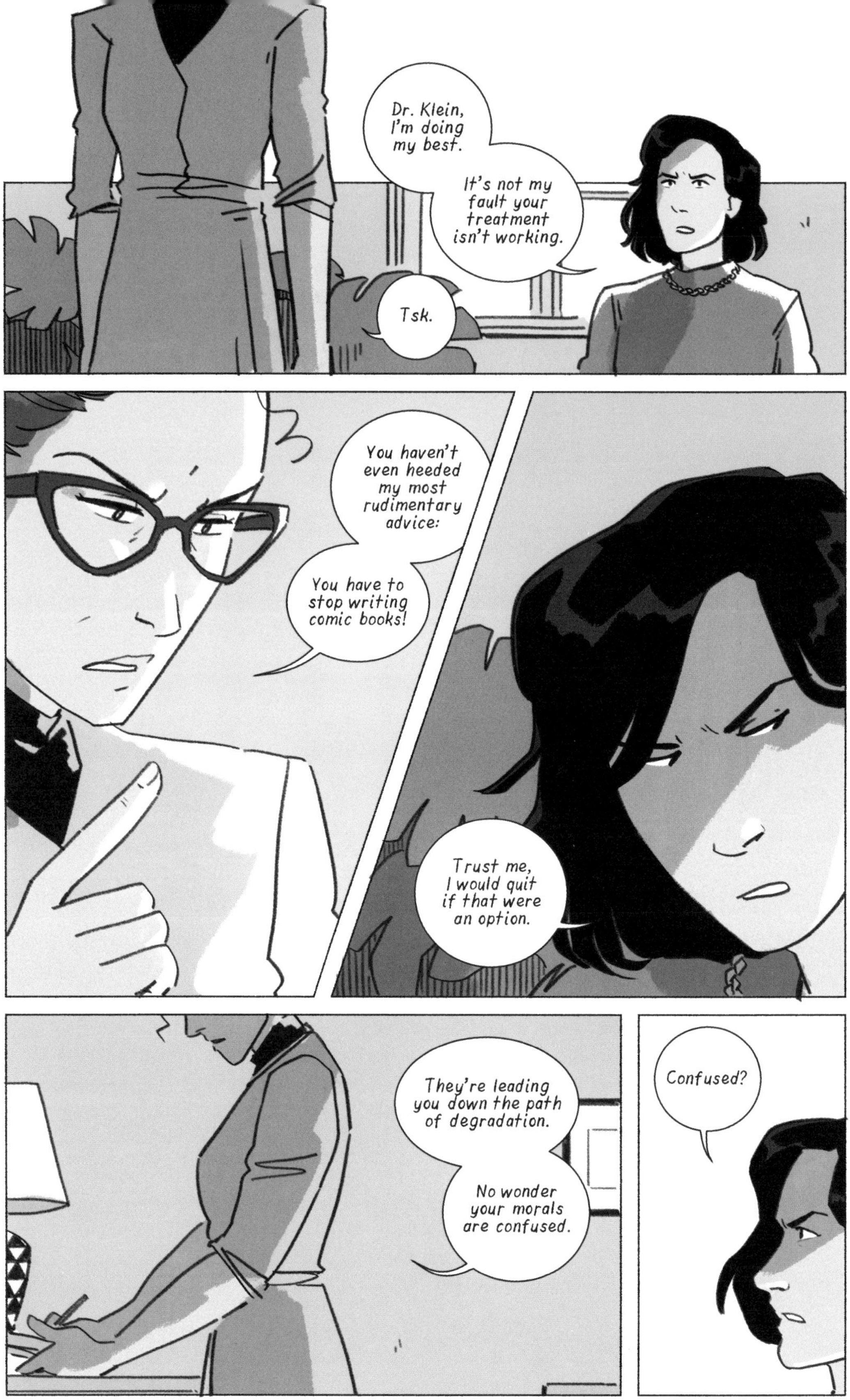
Dr. Klein, I'm doing my best.
It's not my fault your treatment isn't working.
Tsk.
You haven't even heeded my most rudimentary advice:
You have to stop writing comic books!
Trust me, I would quit if that were an option.
They're leading you down the path of degradation.
No wonder your morals are confused.
Confused?

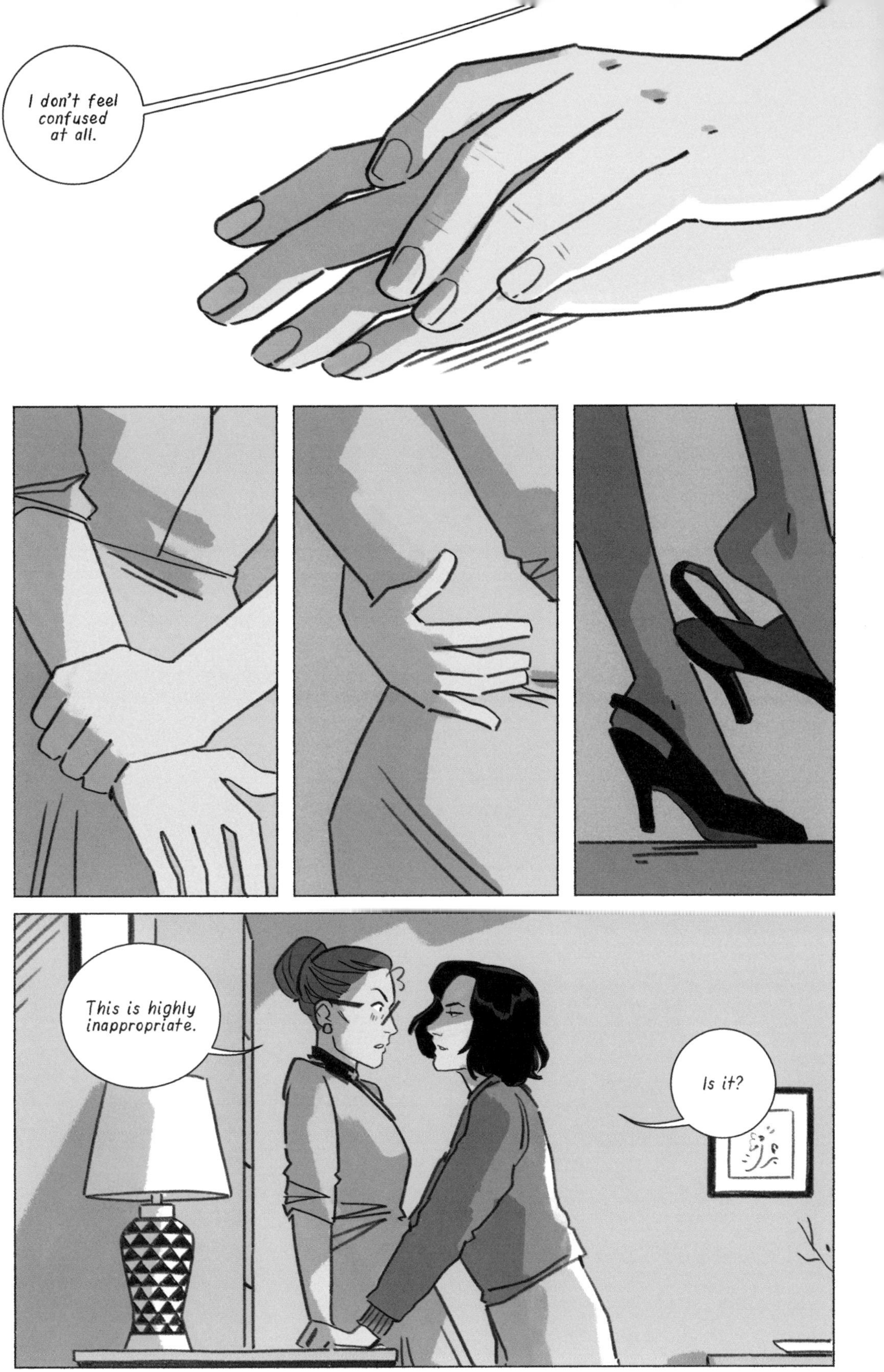

I don't feel confused at all.
This is highly inappropriate.
Is it?

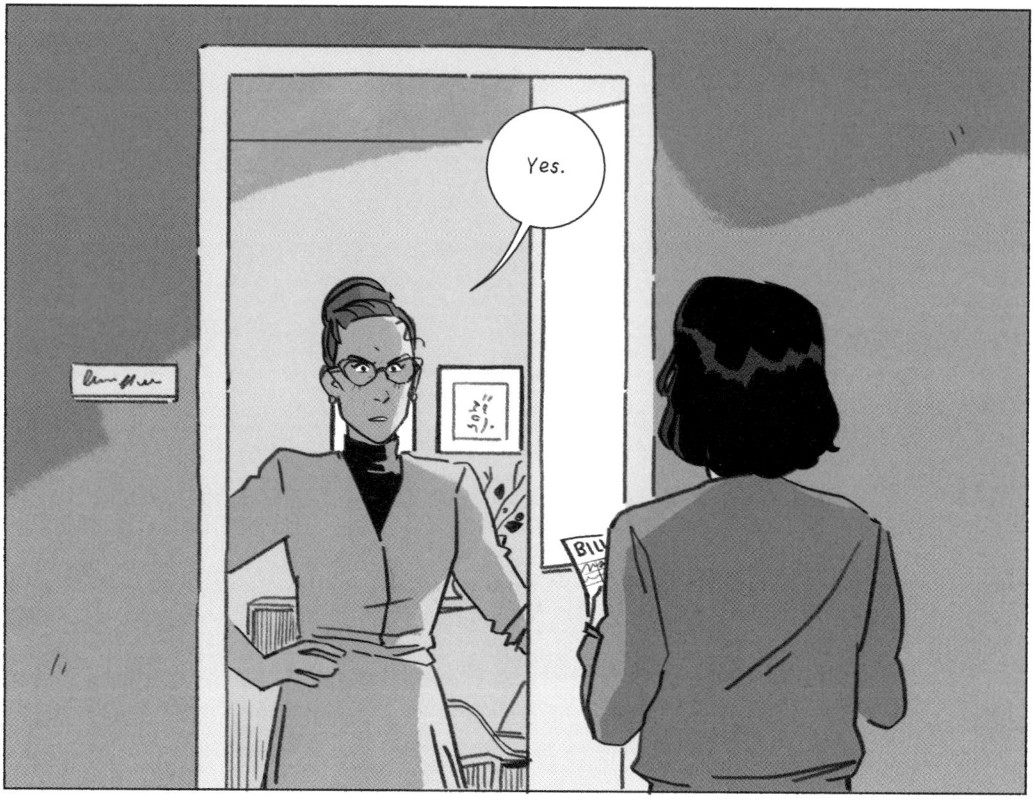
Yes.

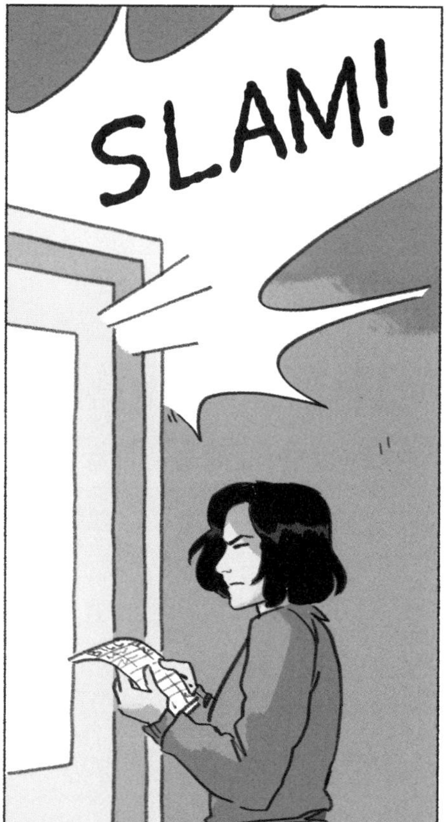
SLAM!

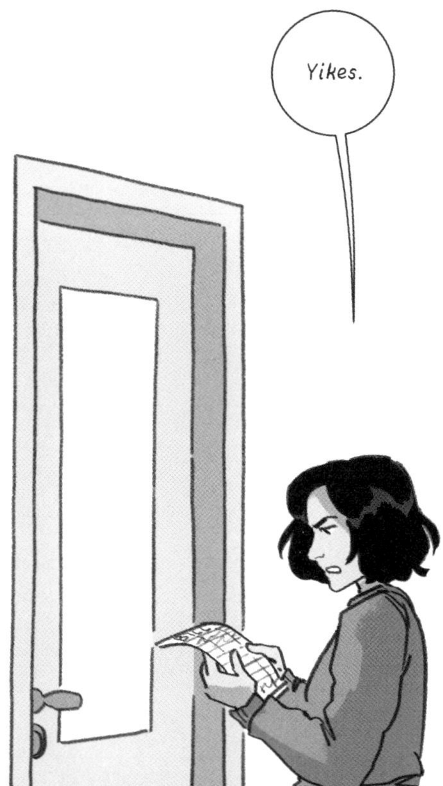
Yikes.

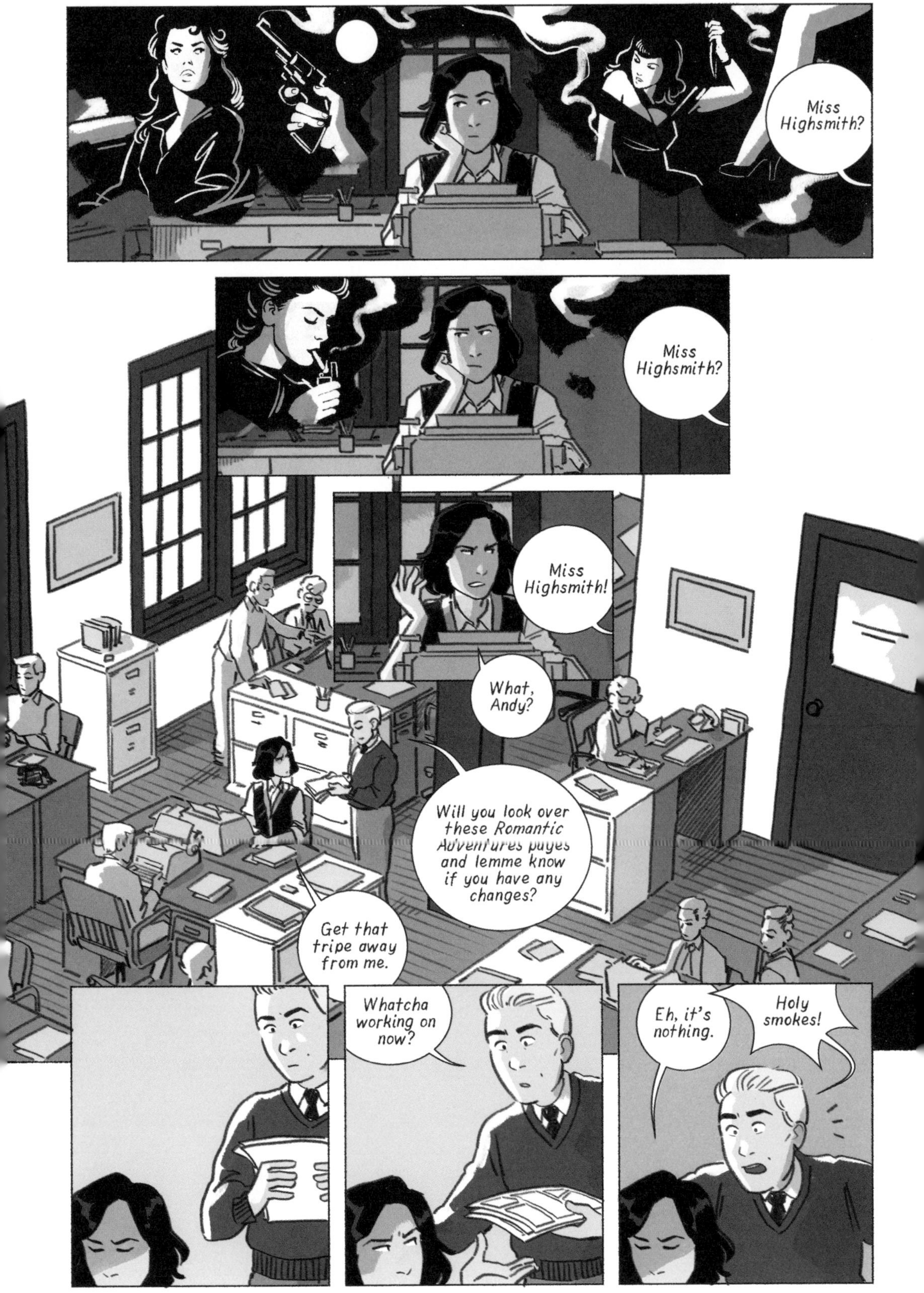

Miss Highsmith?
Miss Highsmith?
Miss Highsmith!
What, Andy?
Will you look over these *Romantic Adventures* pages and lemme know if you have any changes?
Get that tripe away from me.
Whatcha working on now?
Eh, it's nothing.
Holy smokes!

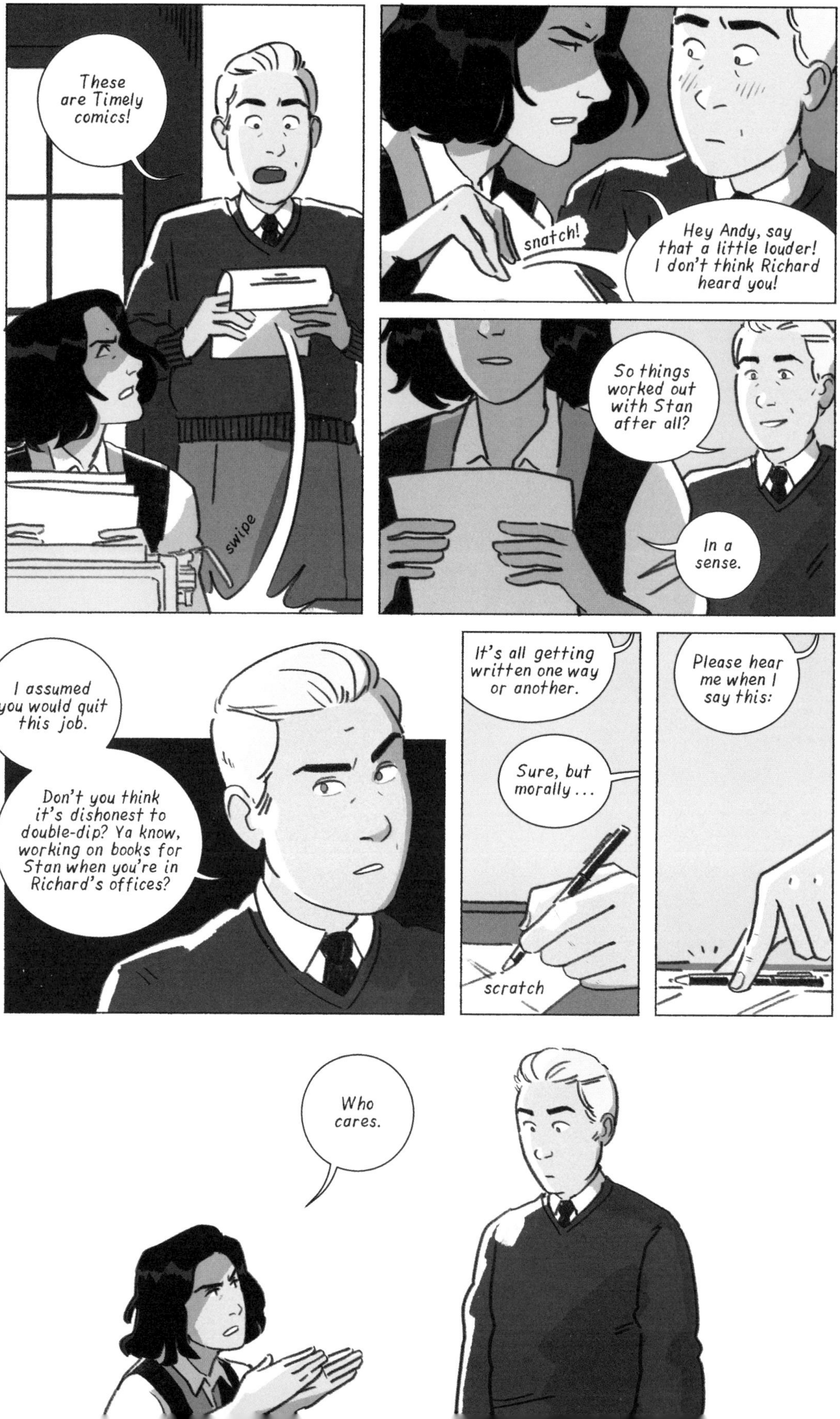
These are Timely comics!
swipe
snatch!
Hey Andy, say that a little louder! I don't think Richard heard you!
So things worked out with Stan after all?
In a sense.
I assumed you would quit this job.
Don't you think it's dishonest to double-dip? Ya know, working on books for Stan when you're in Richard's offices?
It's all getting written one way or another.
Sure, but morally . . .
scratch
Please hear me when I say this:
Who cares.

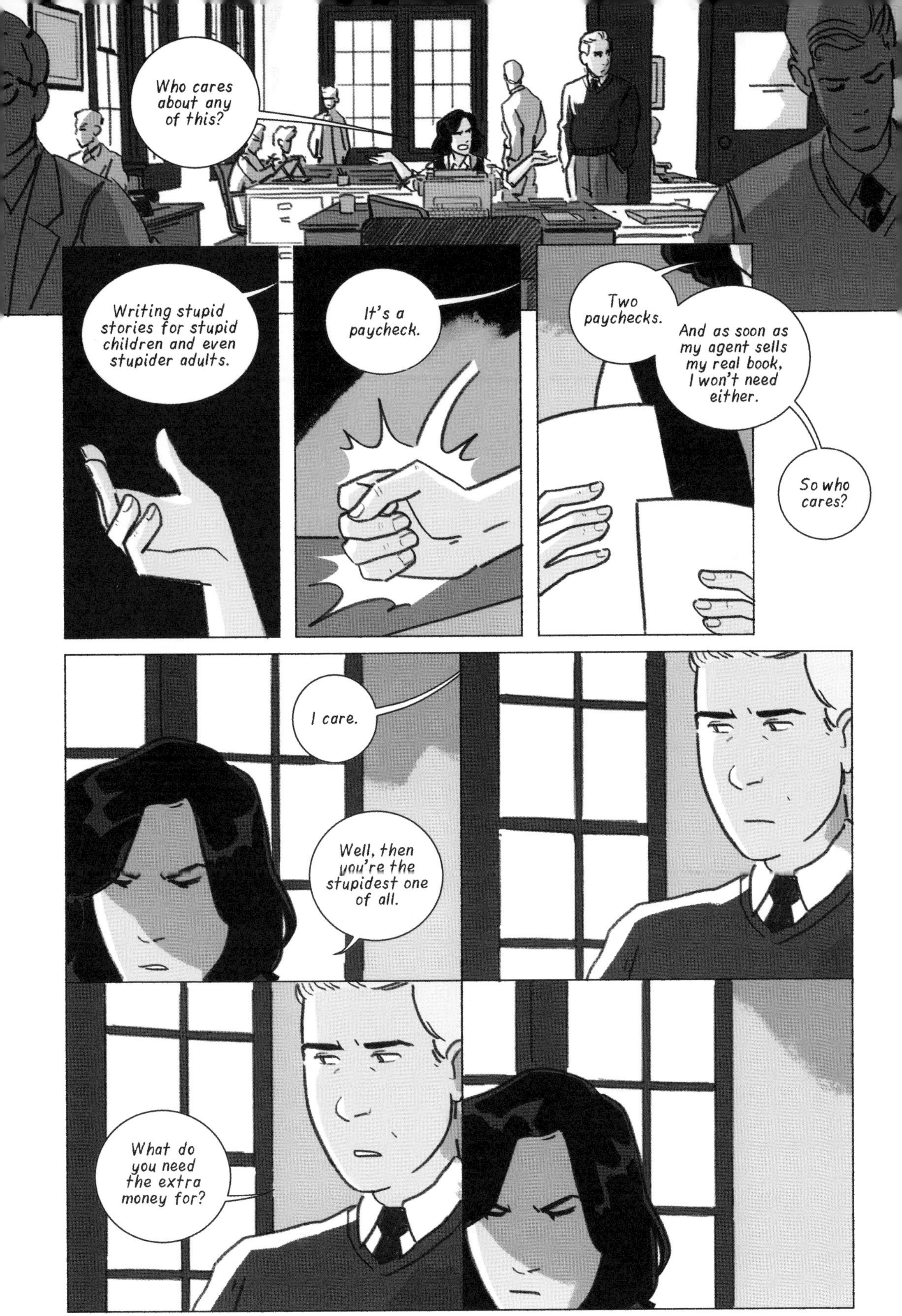
Who cares about any of this?
Writing stupid stories for stupid children and even stupider adults.
It's a paycheck.
Two paychecks.
And as soon as my agent sells my real book, I won't need either.
So who cares?
I care.
Well, then you're the stupidest one of all.
What do you need the extra money for?

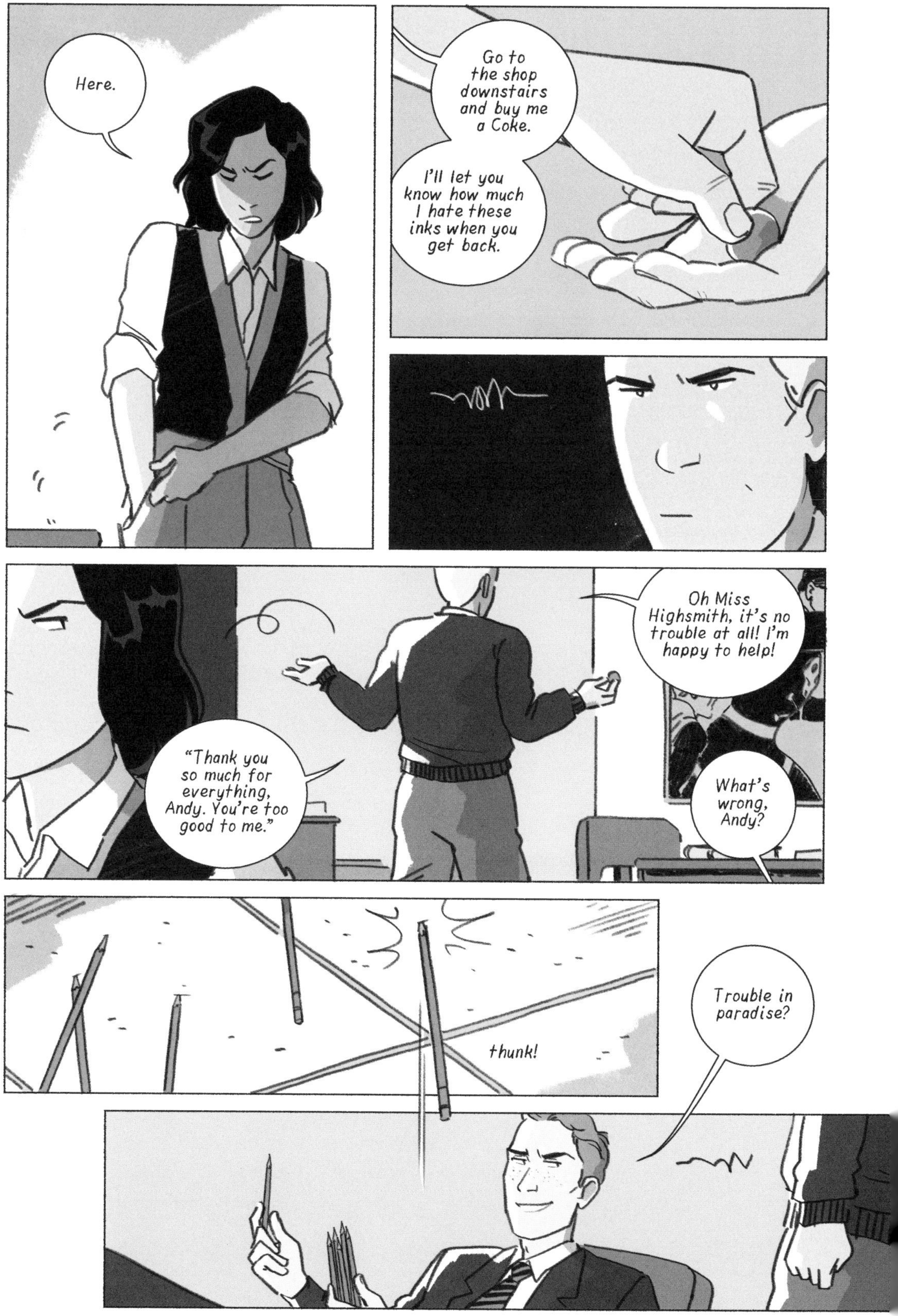
Here.
Go to the shop downstairs and buy me a Coke.
I'll let you know how much I hate these inks when you get back.
Oh Miss Highsmith, it's no trouble at all! I'm happy to help!
"Thank you so much for everything, Andy. You're too good to me."
What's wrong, Andy?
thunk!
Trouble in paradise?

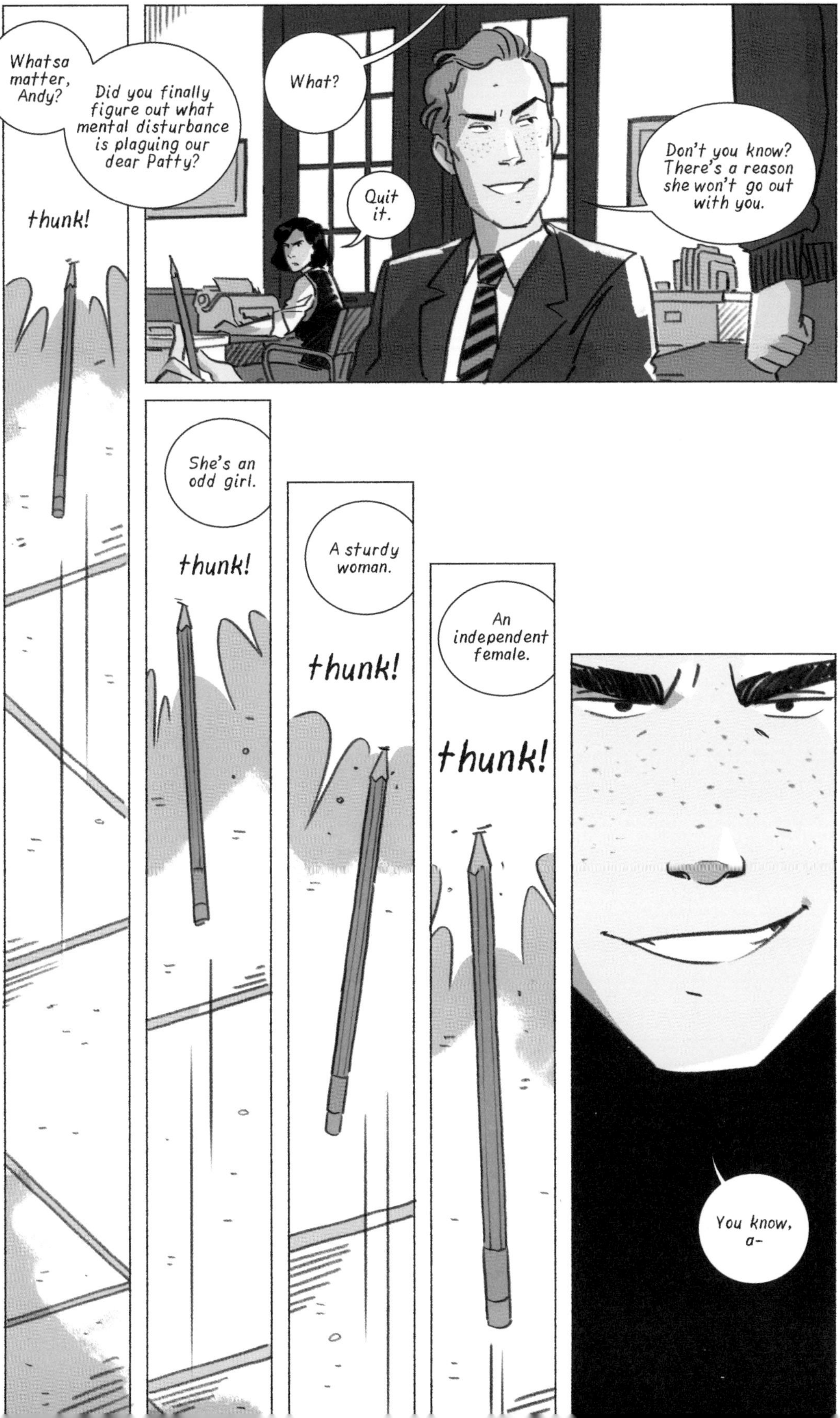
Whatsa matter, Andy?
Did you finally figure out what mental disturbance is plaguing our dear Patty?
thunk!
What?
Quit it.
Don't you know? There's a reason she won't go out with you.
She's an odd girl.
thunk!
A sturdy woman.
thunk!
An independent female.
thunk!
You know, a-

DY

KE

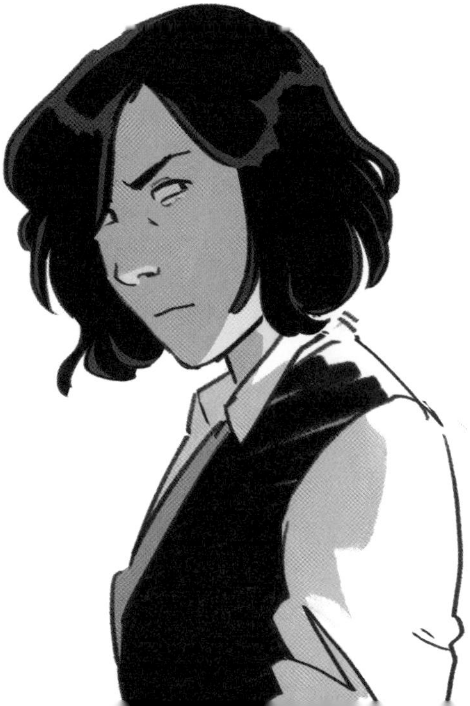

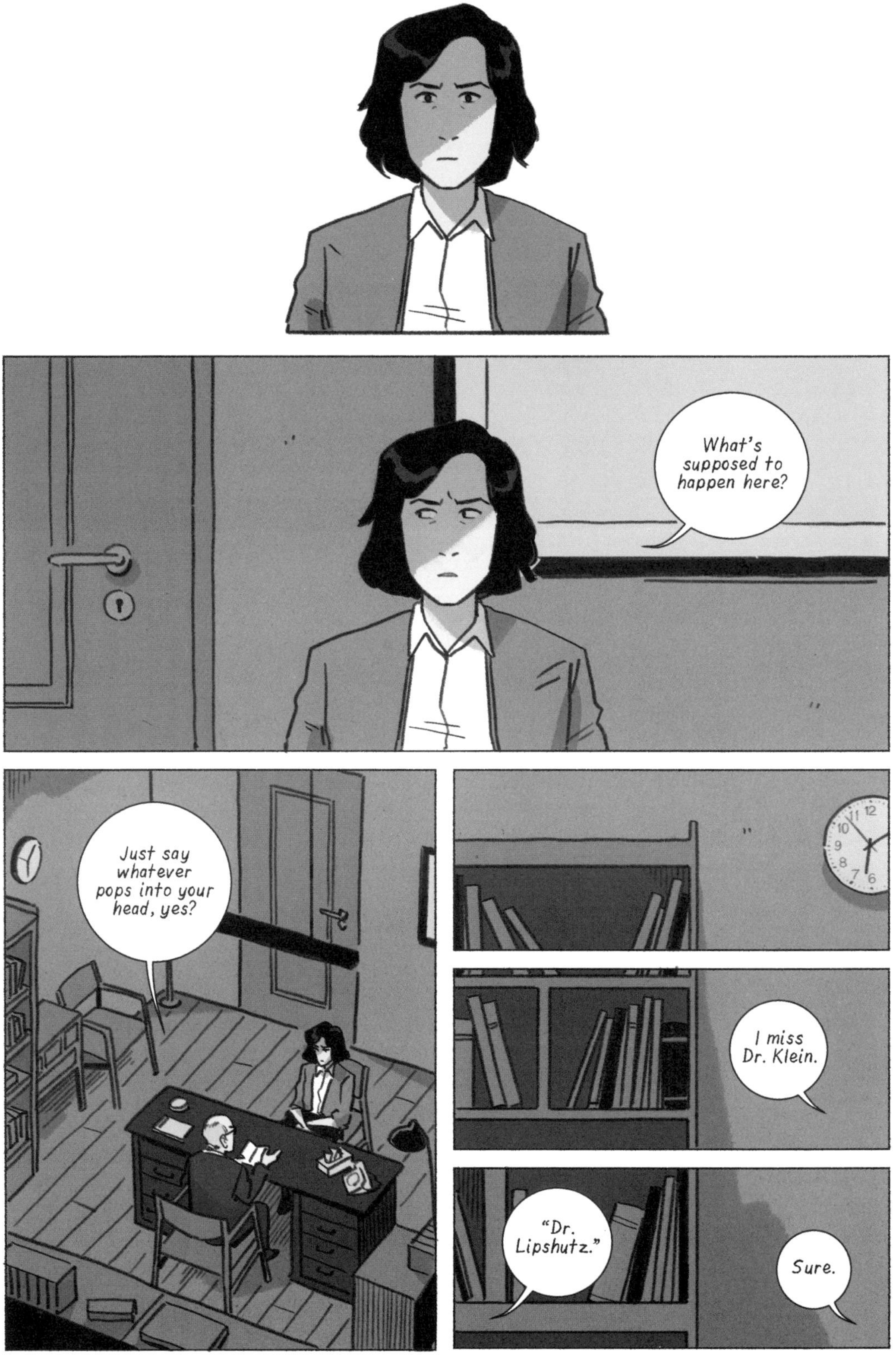
What's supposed to happen here?
Just say whatever pops into your head, yes?
I miss Dr. Klein.
"Dr. Lipshutz."
Sure.

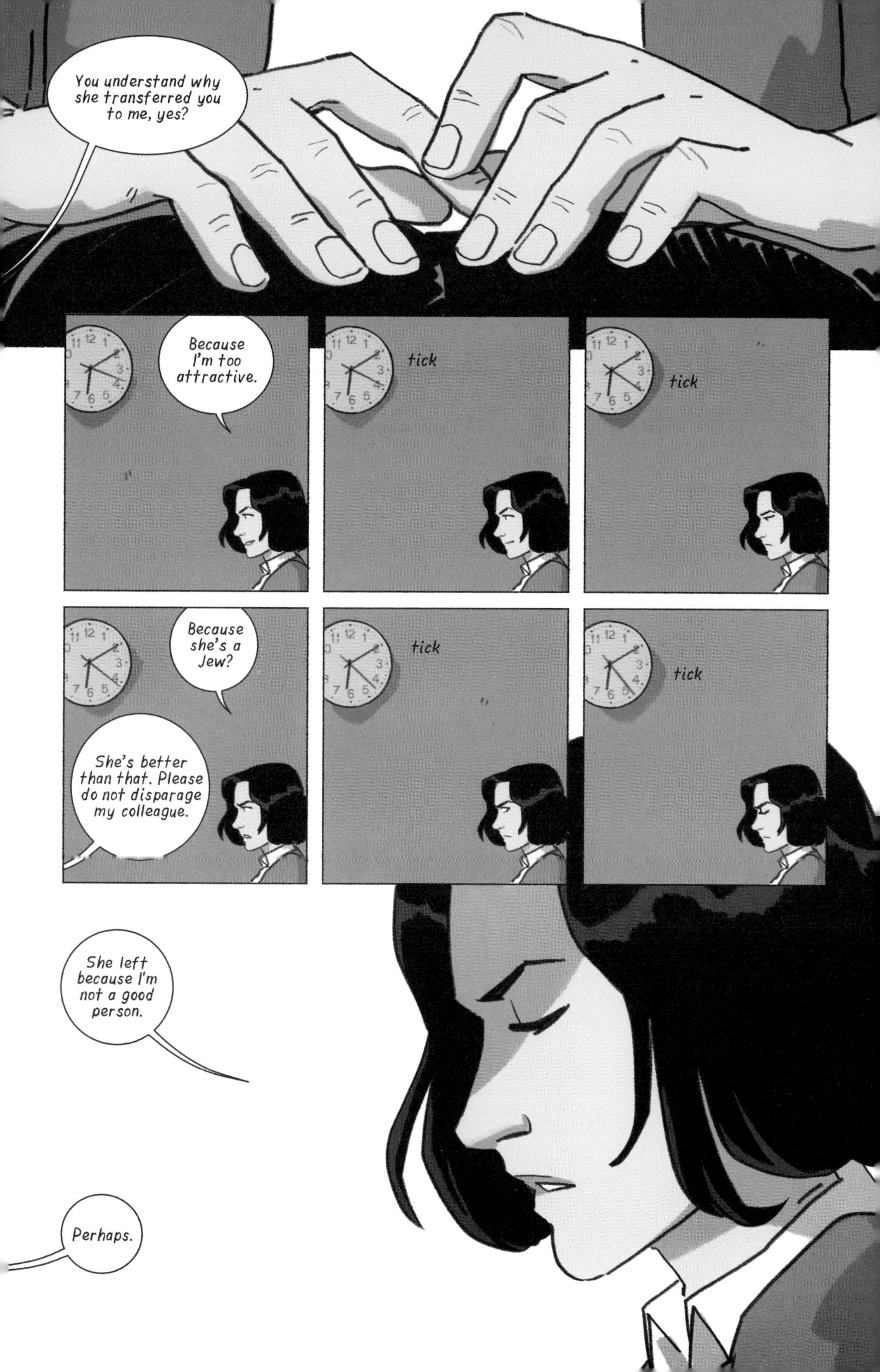

You understand why she transferred you to me, yes?
Because I'm too attractive.
tick
tick
Because she's a Jew?
She's better than that. Please do not disparage my colleague.
tick
tick
She left because I'm not a good person.
Perhaps.

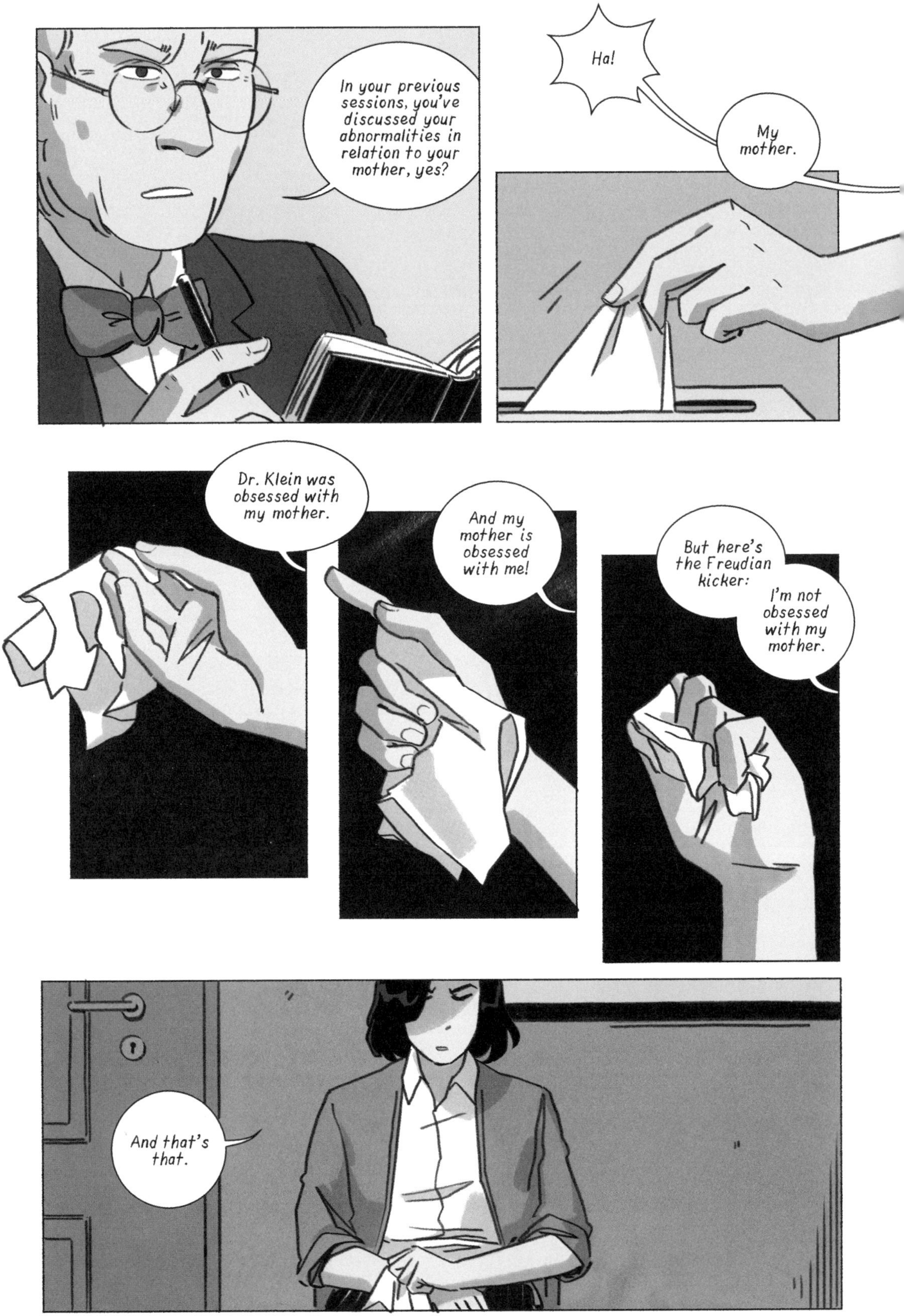
In your previous sessions, you've discussed your abnormalities in relation to your mother, yes?
Ha!
My mother.
Dr. Klein was obsessed with my mother.
And my mother is obsessed with me!
But here's the Freudian kicker:
I'm not obsessed with my mother.
And that's that.

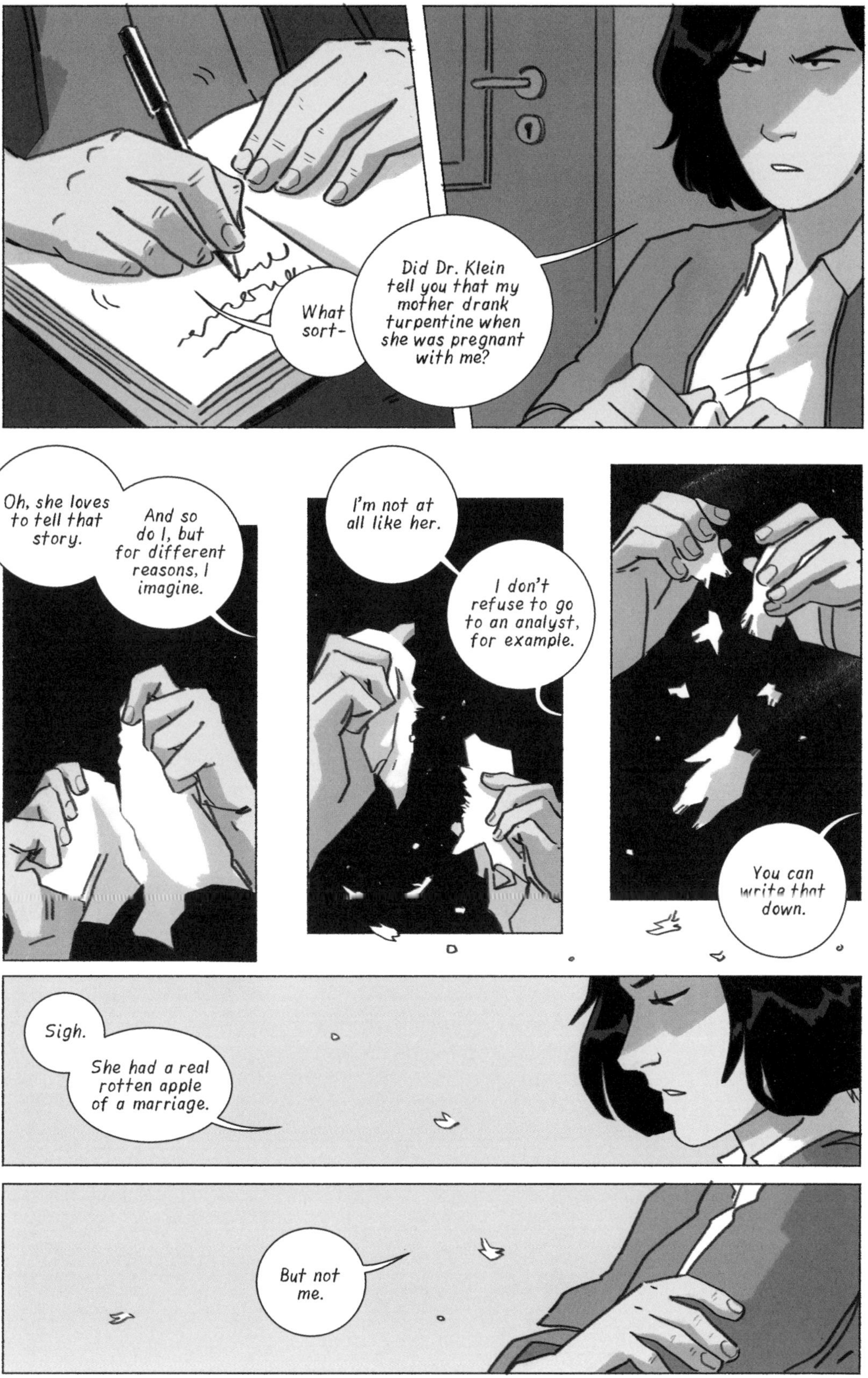
What sort-
Did Dr. Klein tell you that my mother drank turpentine when she was pregnant with me?
Oh, she loves to tell that story.
And so do I, but for different reasons, I imagine.
I'm not at all like her.
I don't refuse to go to an analyst, for example.
You can write that down.
Sigh.
She had a real rotten apple of a marriage.
But not me.

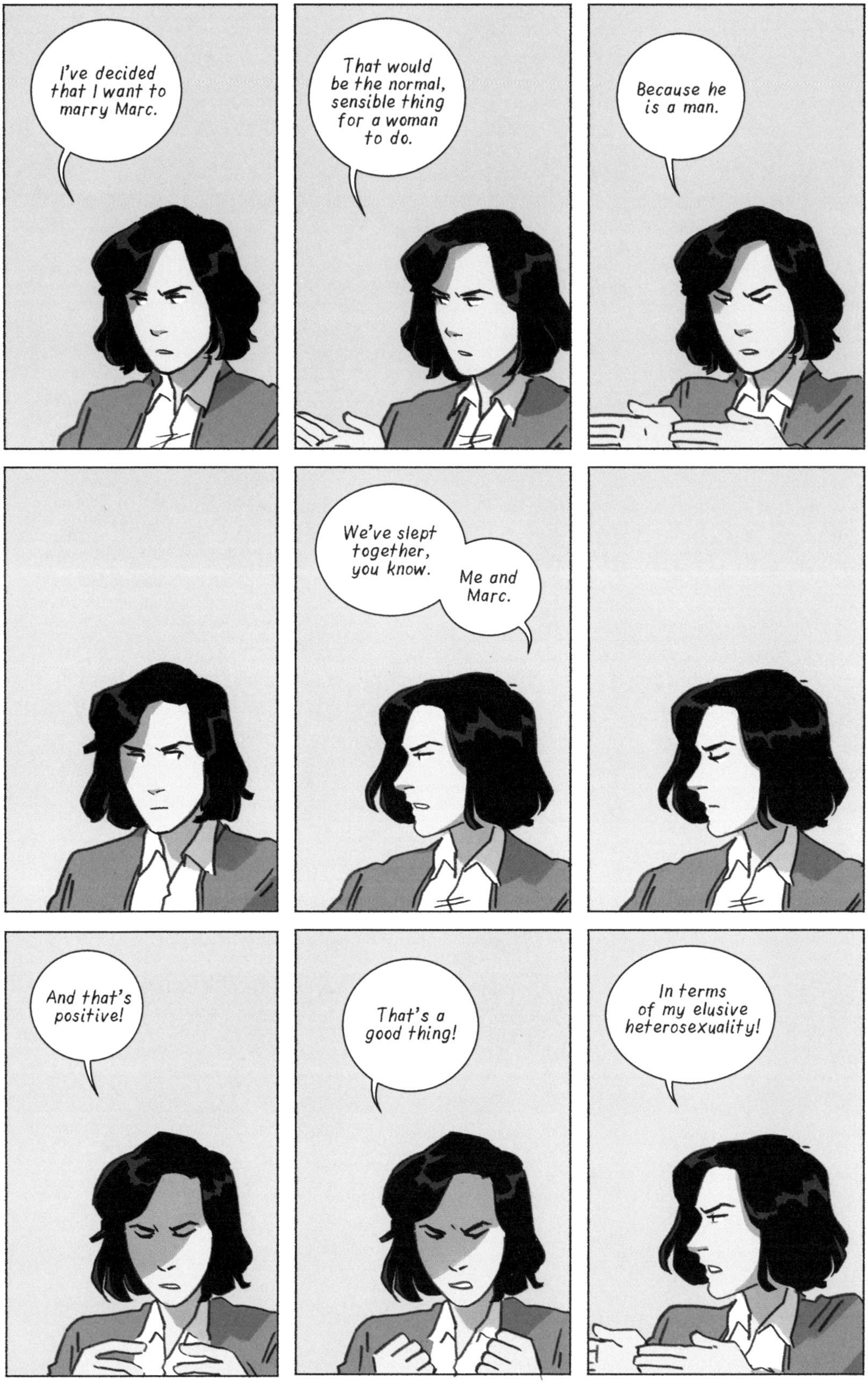
I've decided that I want to marry Marc.
That would be the normal, sensible thing for a woman to do.
Because he is a man.
We've slept together, you know.
Me and Marc.
And that's positive!
That's a good thing!
In terms of my elusive heterosexuality!

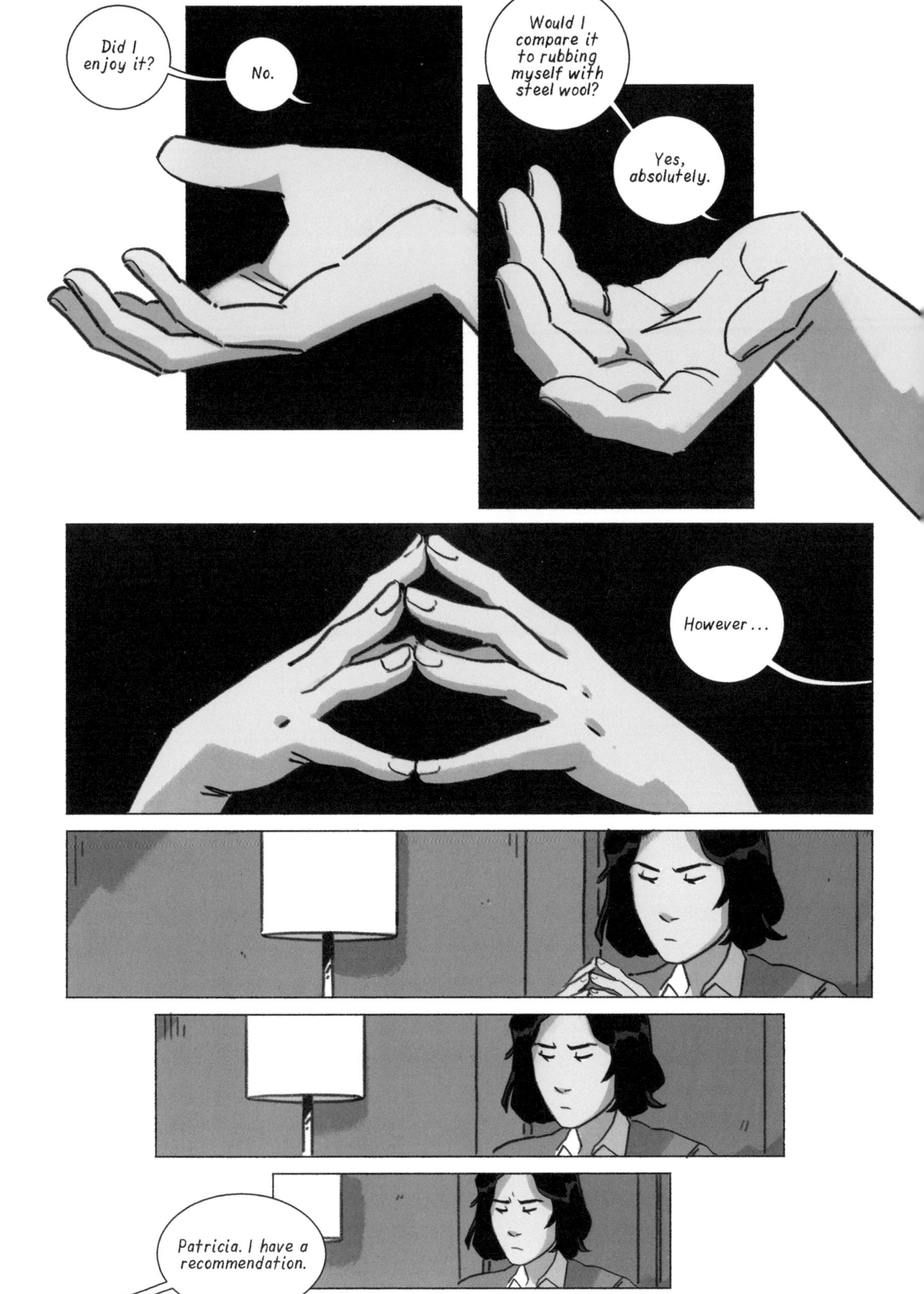
Did I enjoy it?
No.
Would I compare it to rubbing myself with steel wool?
Yes, absolutely.
However...
Patricia. I have a recommendation.

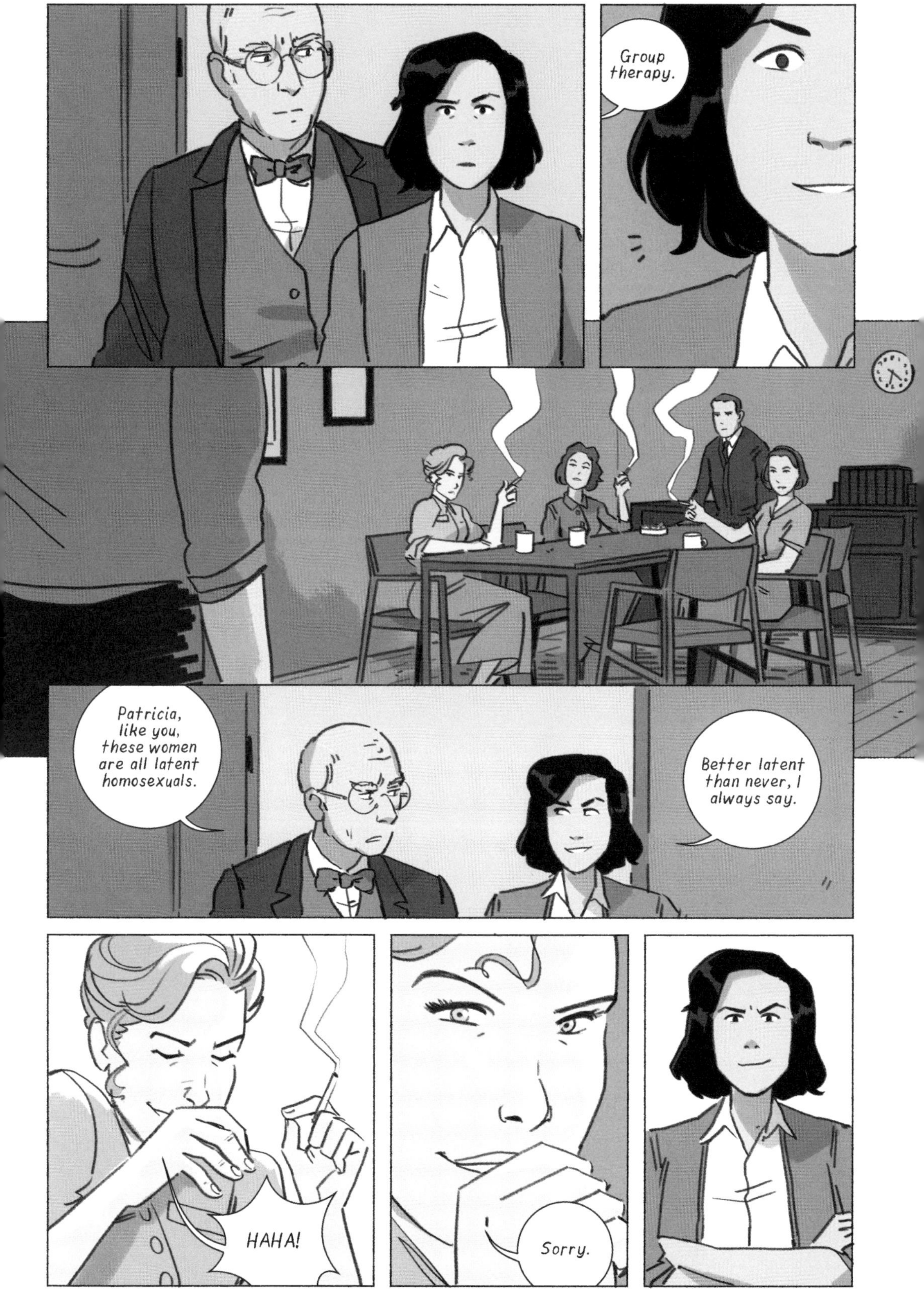
Group therapy.
Patricia, like you, these women are all latent homosexuals.
Better latent than never, I always say.
HAHA!
Sorry.

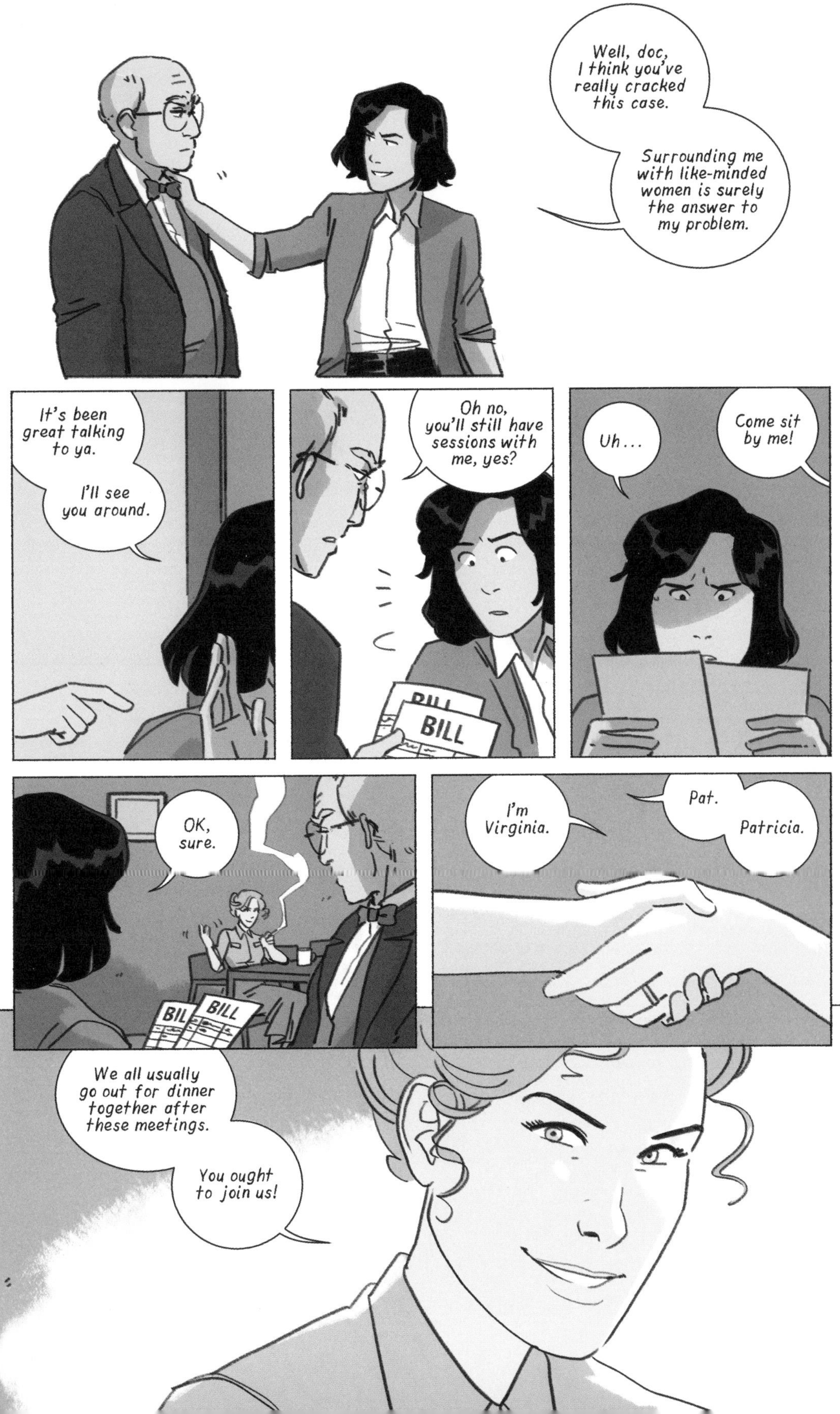
Well, doc, I think you've really cracked this case.
Surrounding me with like-minded women is surely the answer to my problem.
It's been great talking to ya.
I'll see you around.
Oh no, you'll still have sessions with me, yes?
BILL
BILL
Uh...
Come sit by me!
OK, sure.
BILL
BILL
I'm Virginia.
Pat.
Patricia.
We all usually go out for dinner together after these meetings.
You ought to join us!

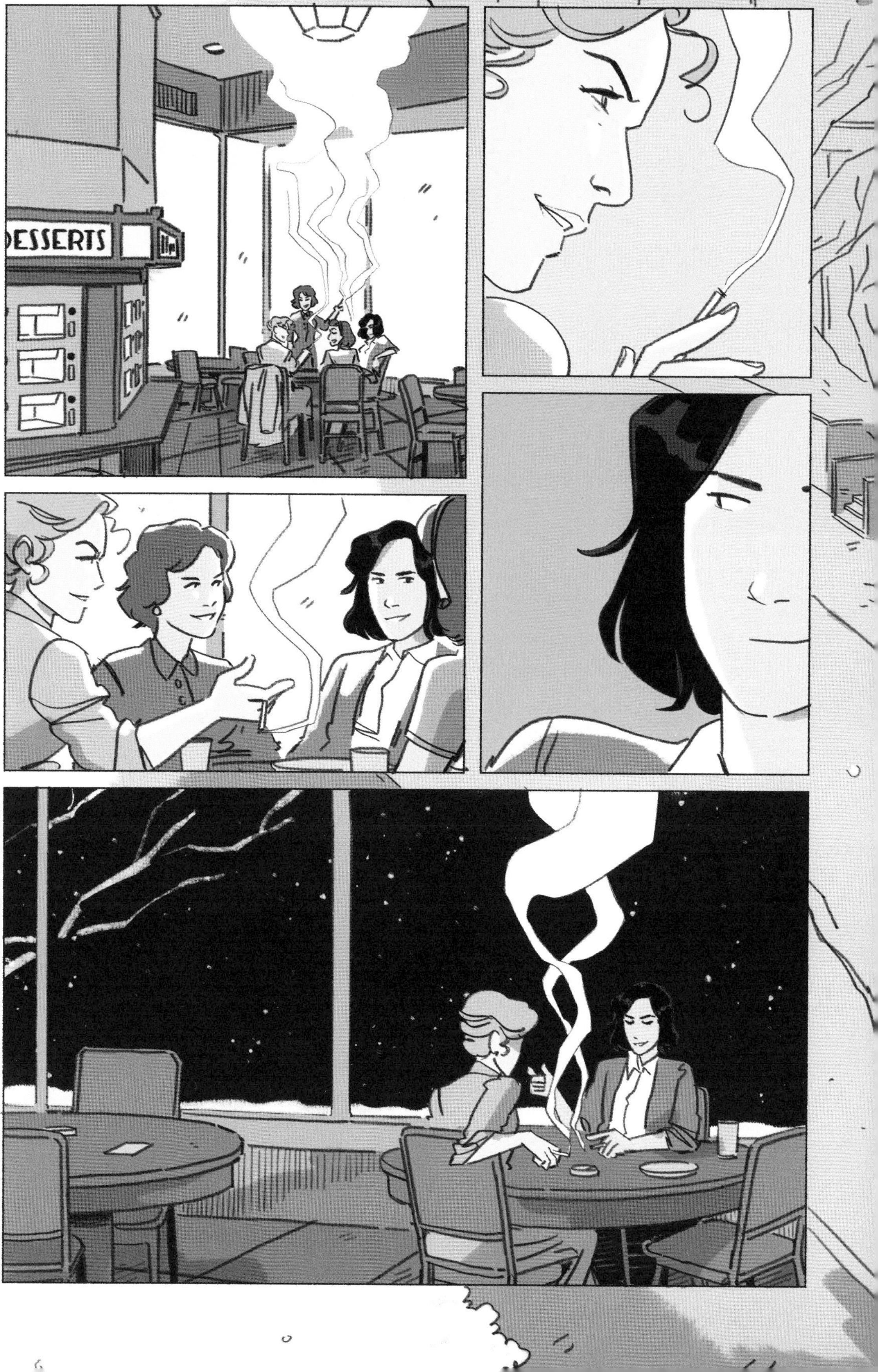
DESSERTS

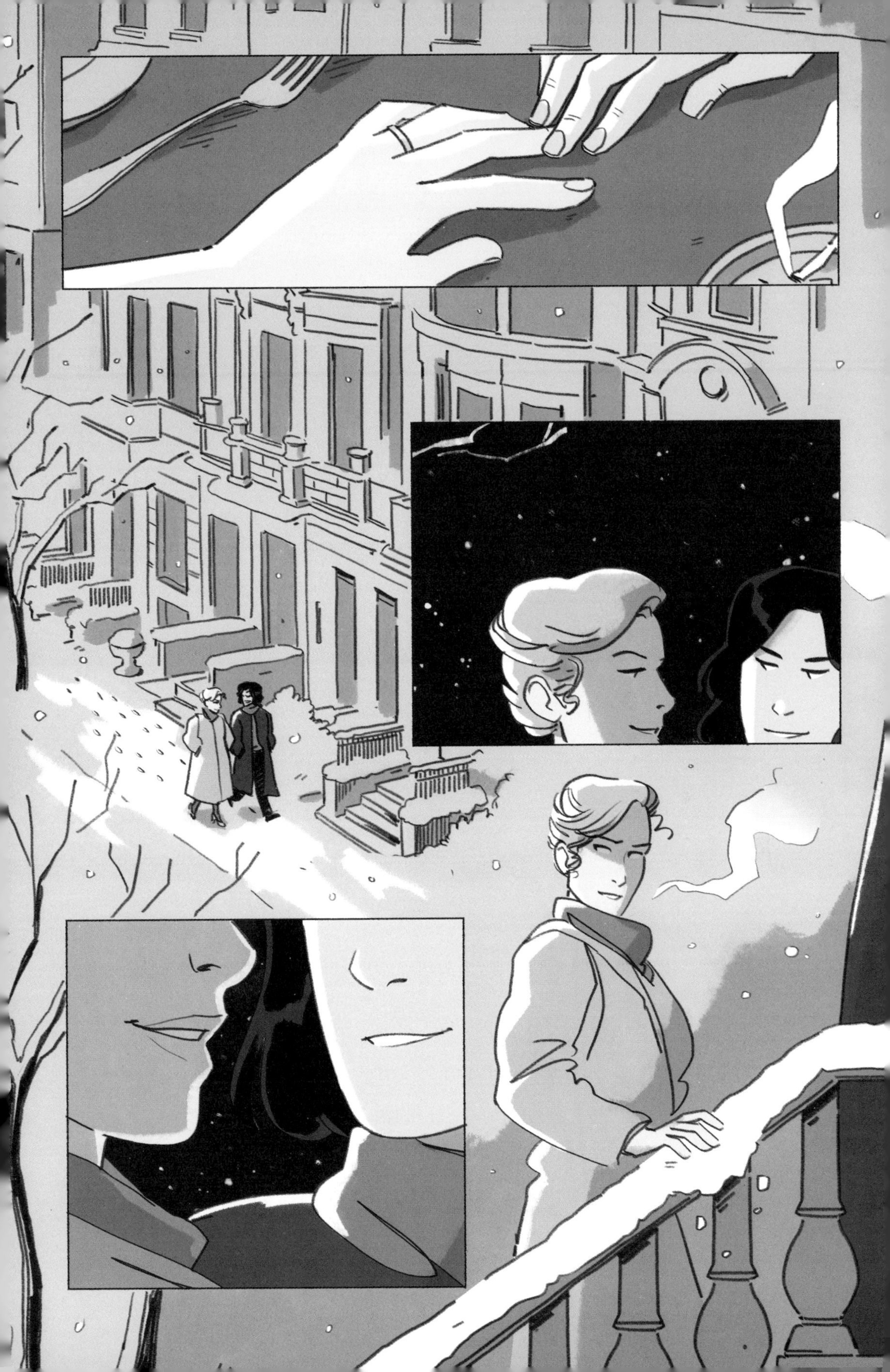

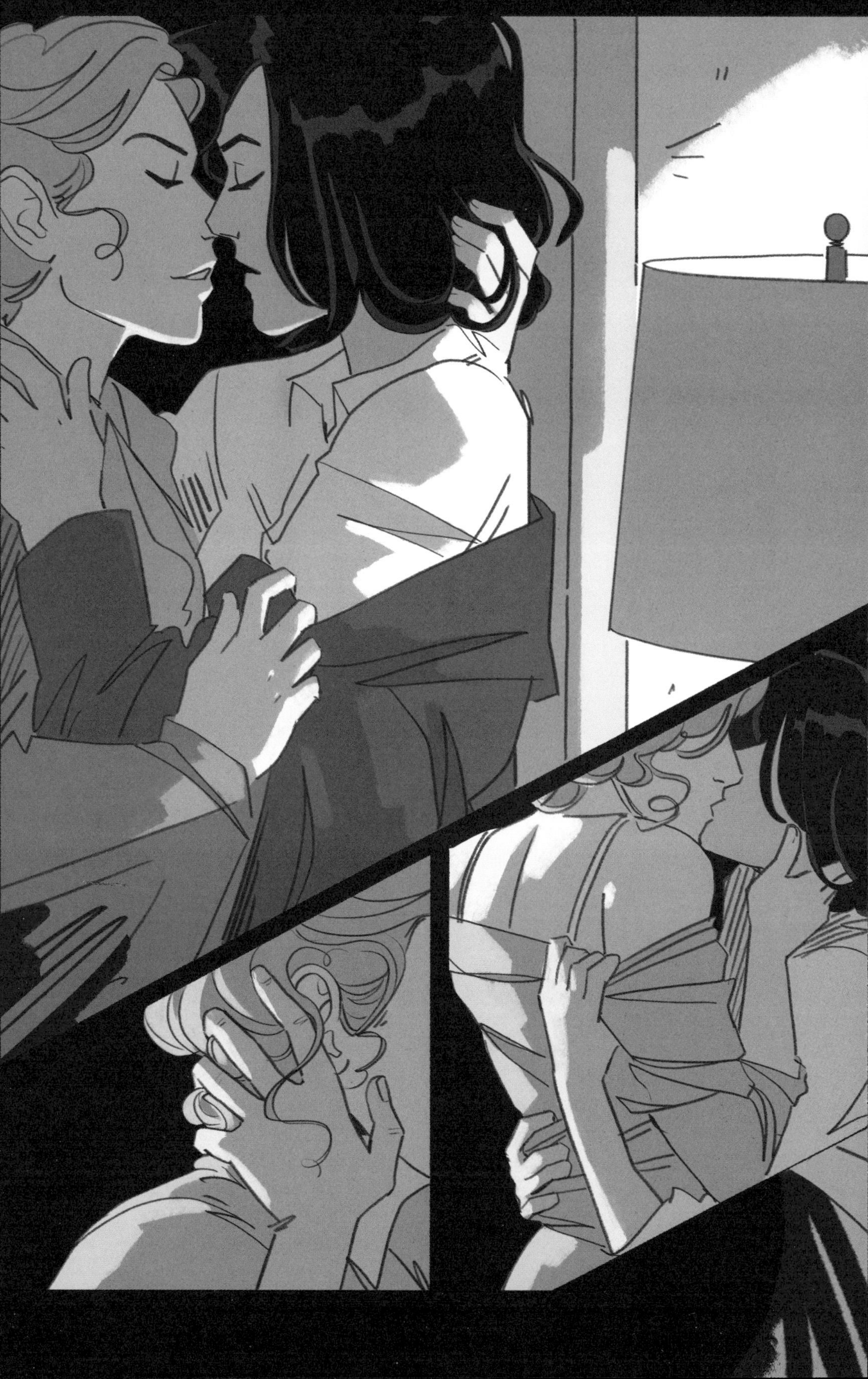

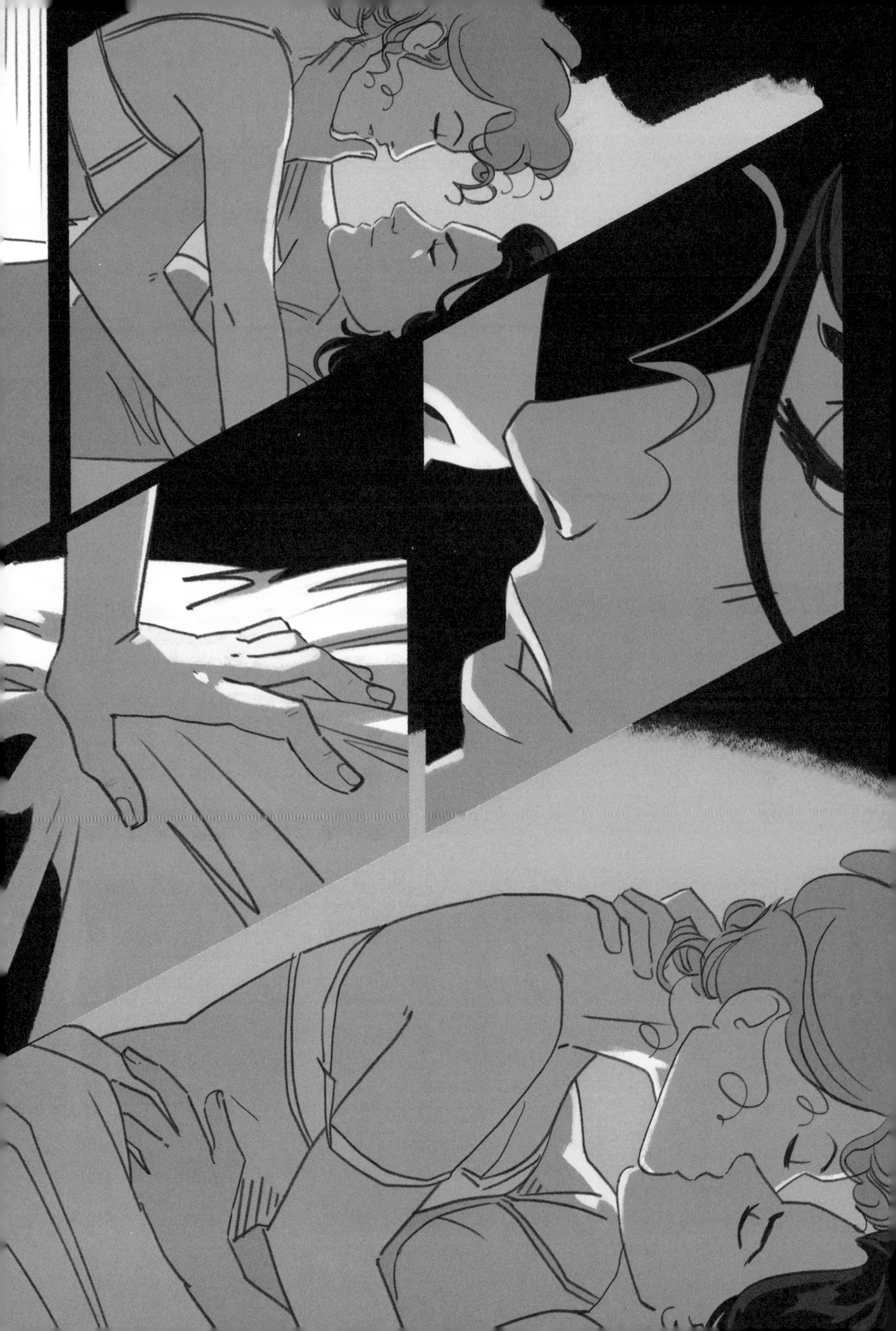

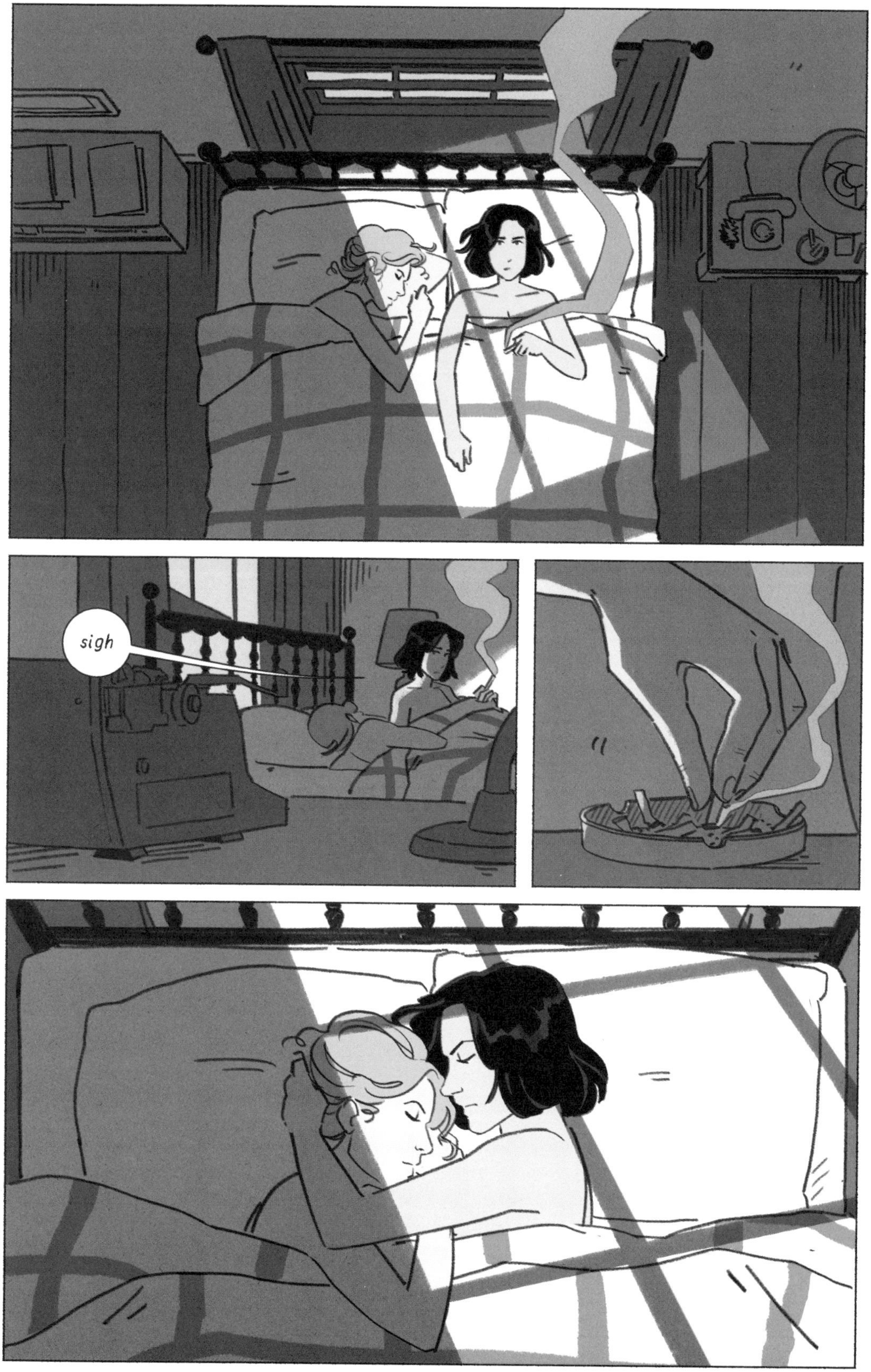
sigh

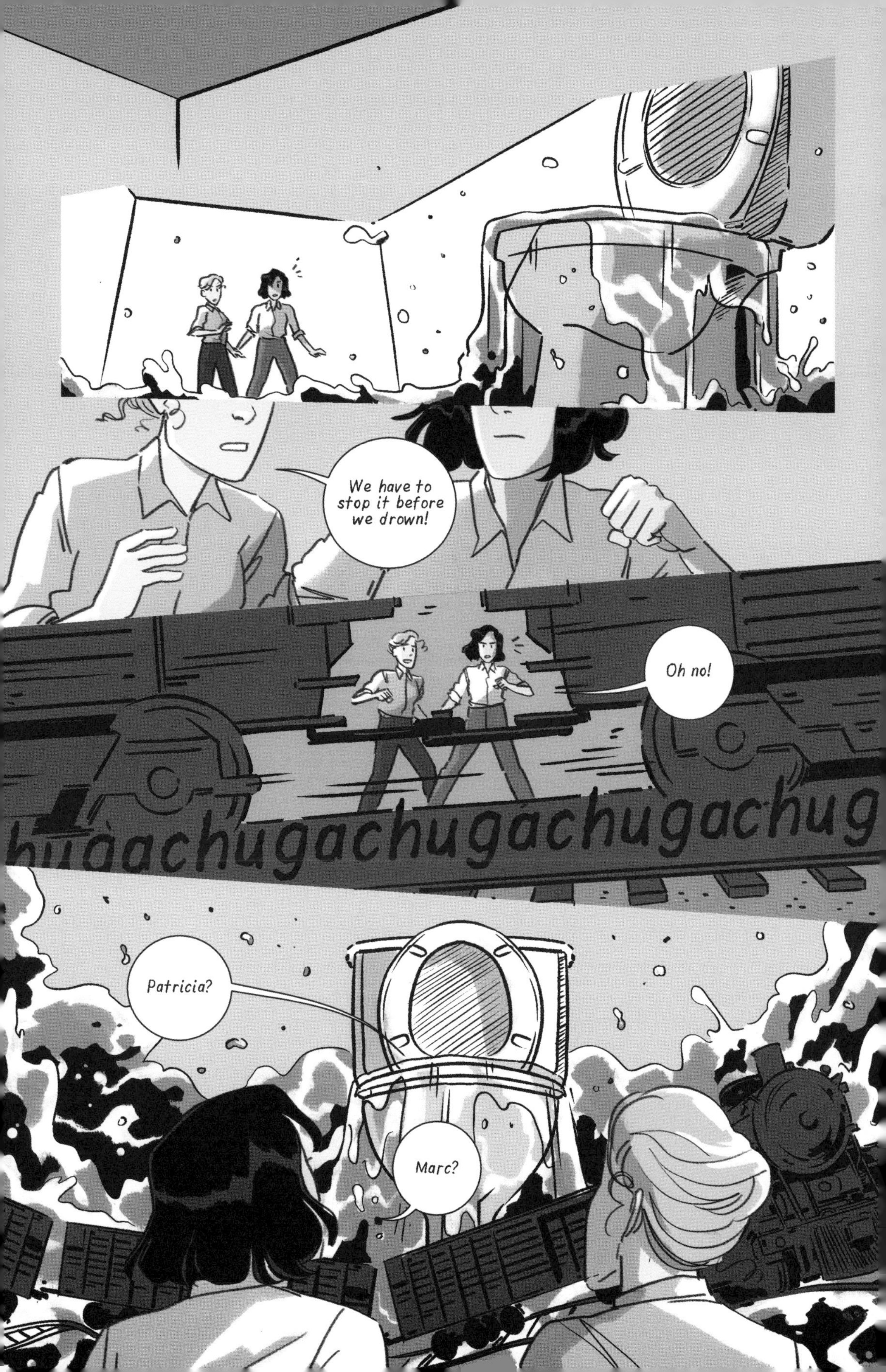
We have to stop it before we drown!
Oh no!
chugachugachugachug
Patricia?
Marc?

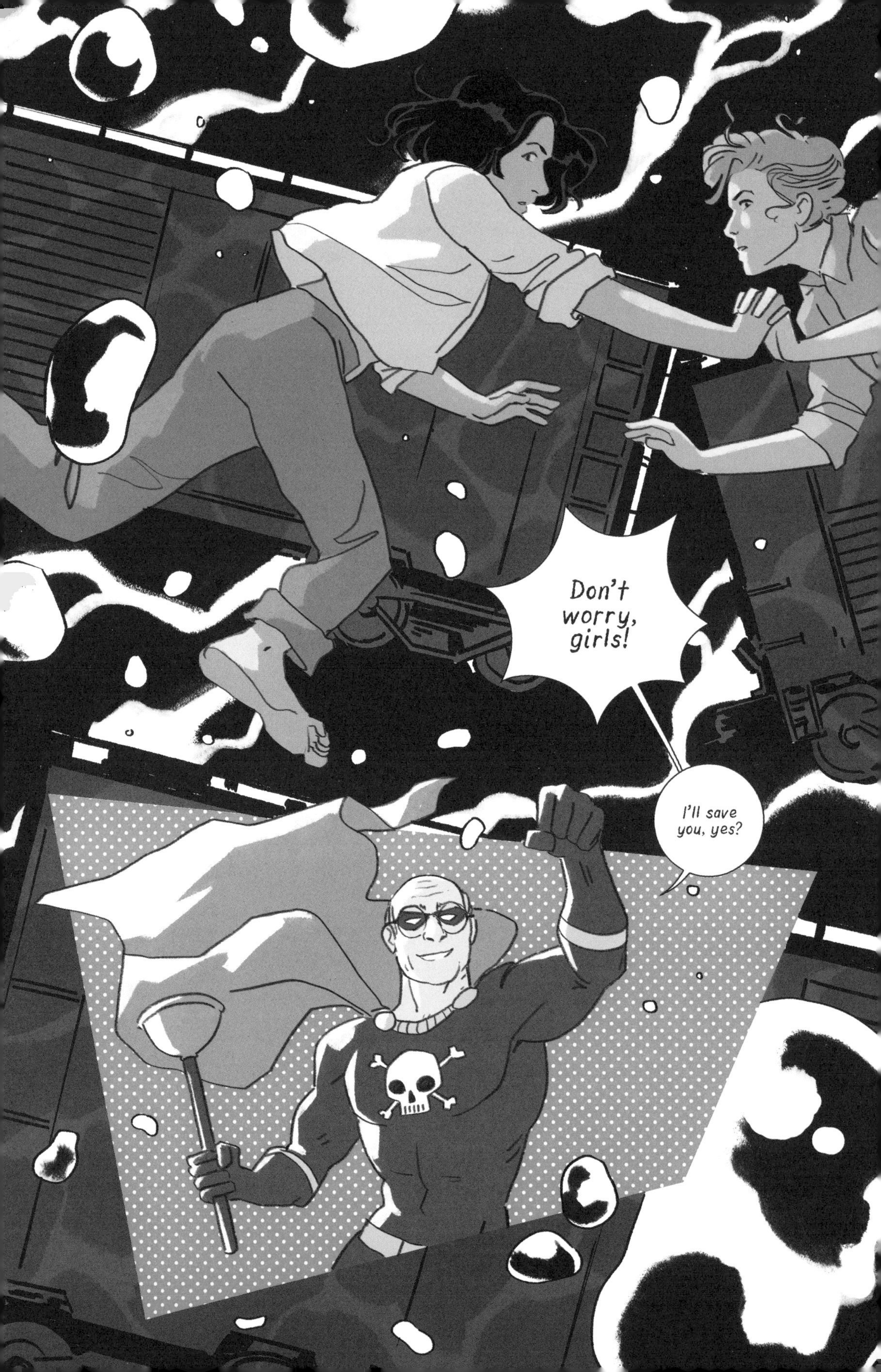
Don't worry, girls!
I'll save you, yes?

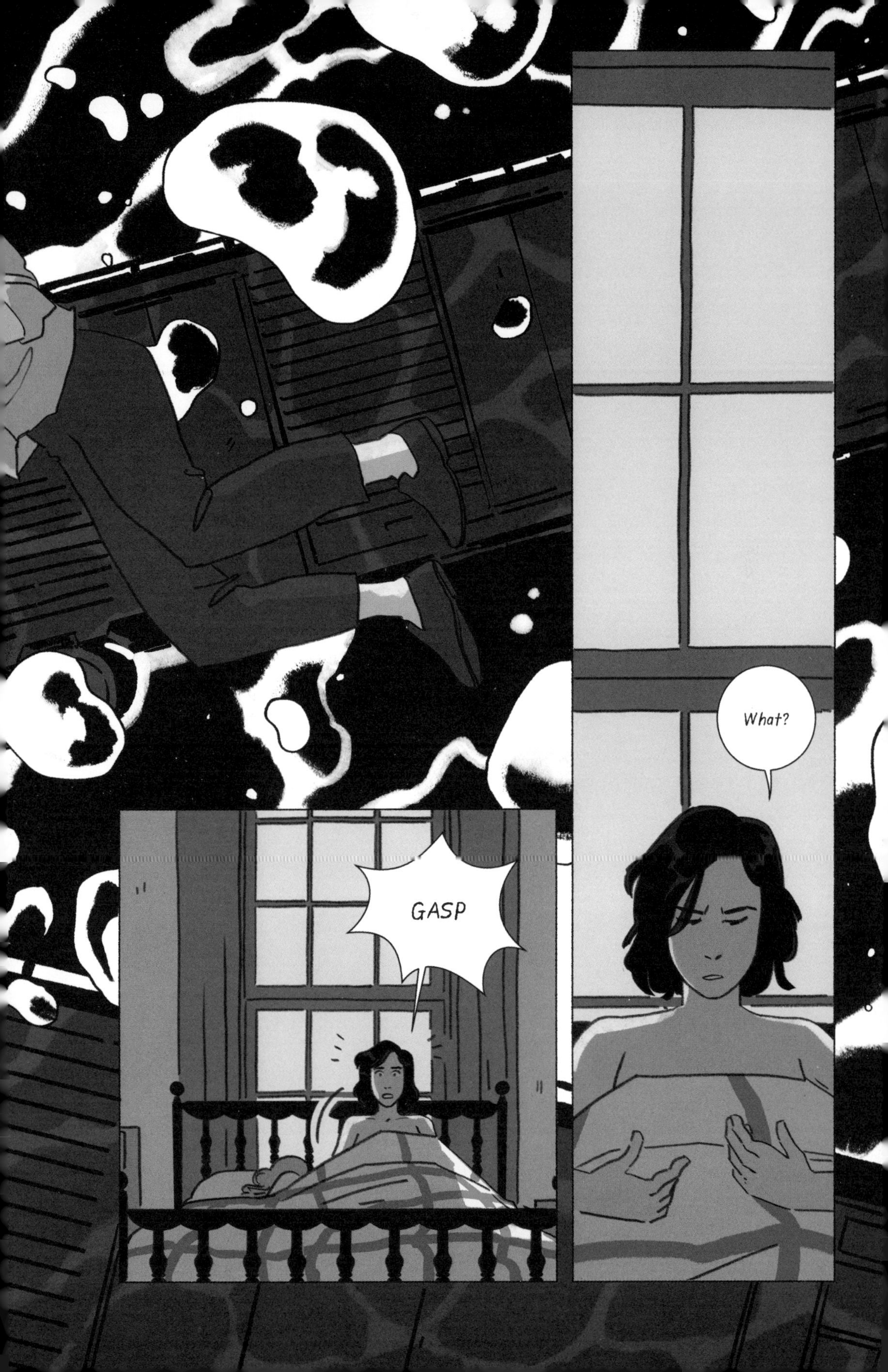
GASP
What?

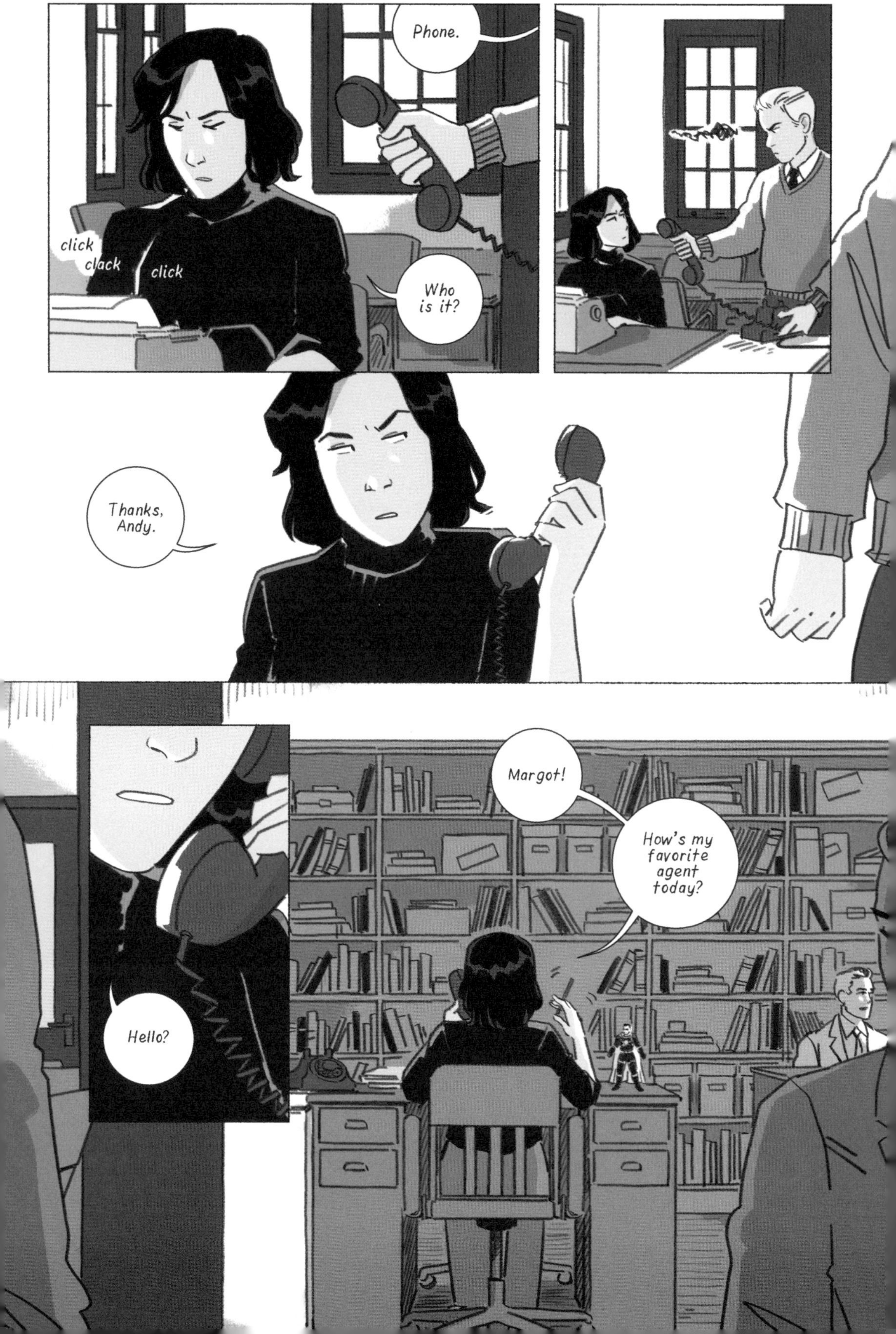
click
clack
click
Phone.
Who is it?
Thanks, Andy.
Hello?
Margot!
How's my favorite agent today?

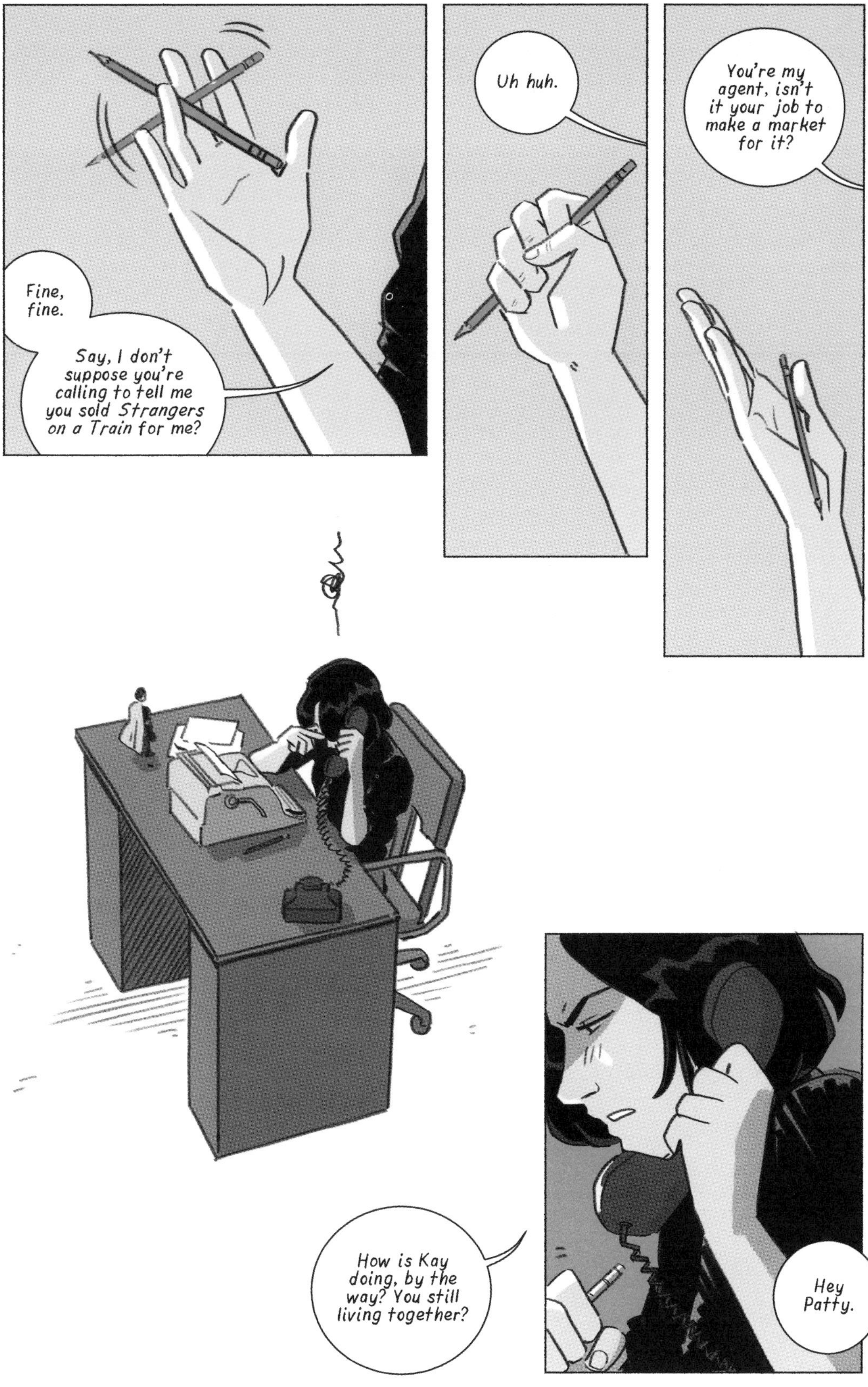

Fine, fine.
Say, I don't suppose you're calling to tell me you sold Strangers on a Train for me?
Uh huh.
You're my agent, isn't it your job to make a market for it?
Hey Patty.
How is Kay doing, by the way? You still living together?

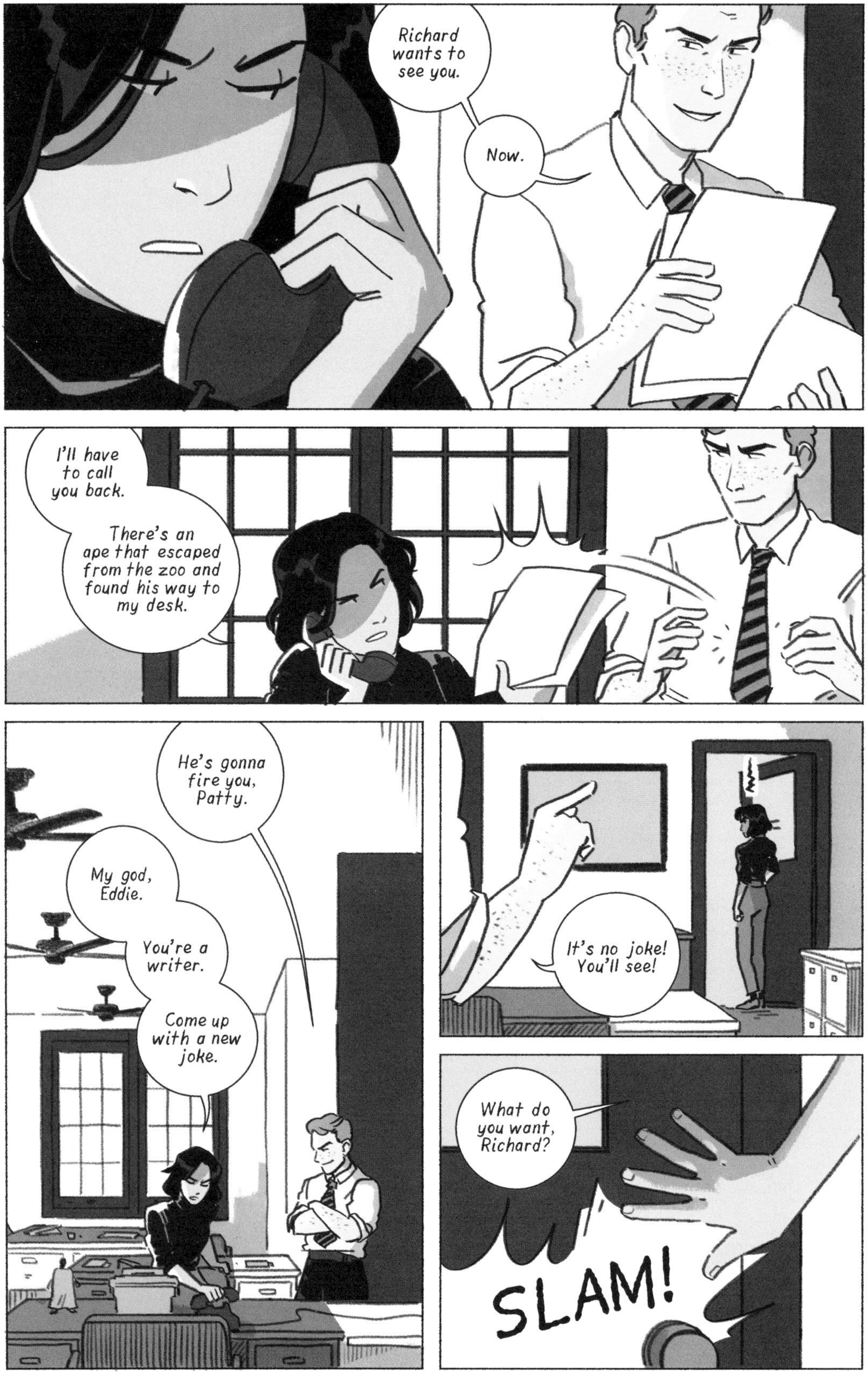
Richard wants to see you.
Now.
I'll have to call you back.
There's an ape that escaped from the zoo and found his way to my desk.
He's gonna fire you, Patty.
My god, Eddie.
You're a writer.
Come up with a new joke.
It's no joke! You'll see!
What do you want, Richard?
SLAM!

Have a
seat, kid.

What
is it,
Richard?

Do you
respect
me?

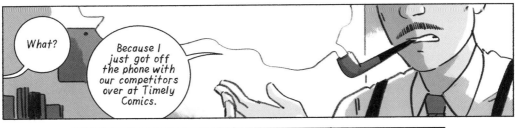

What?

Because I
just got off
the phone with
our competitors
over at Timely
Comics.

Oh.

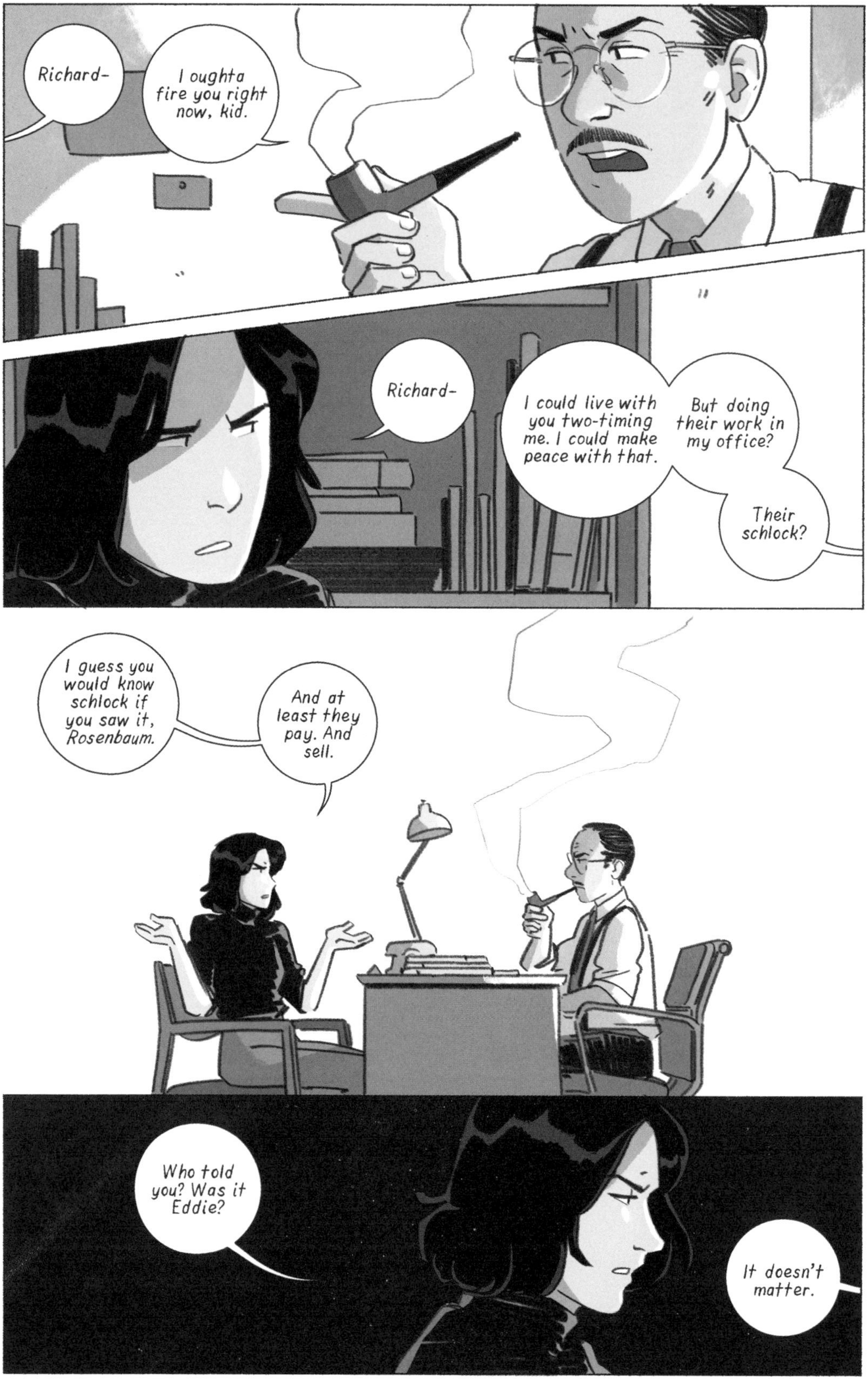

Richard-
I oughta fire you right now, kid.
"
"
Richard-
I could live with you two-timing me. I could make peace with that.
But doing their work in my office?
Their schlock?
I guess you would know schlock if you saw it, Rosenbaum.
And at least they pay. And sell.
Who told you? Was it Eddie?
It doesn't matter.

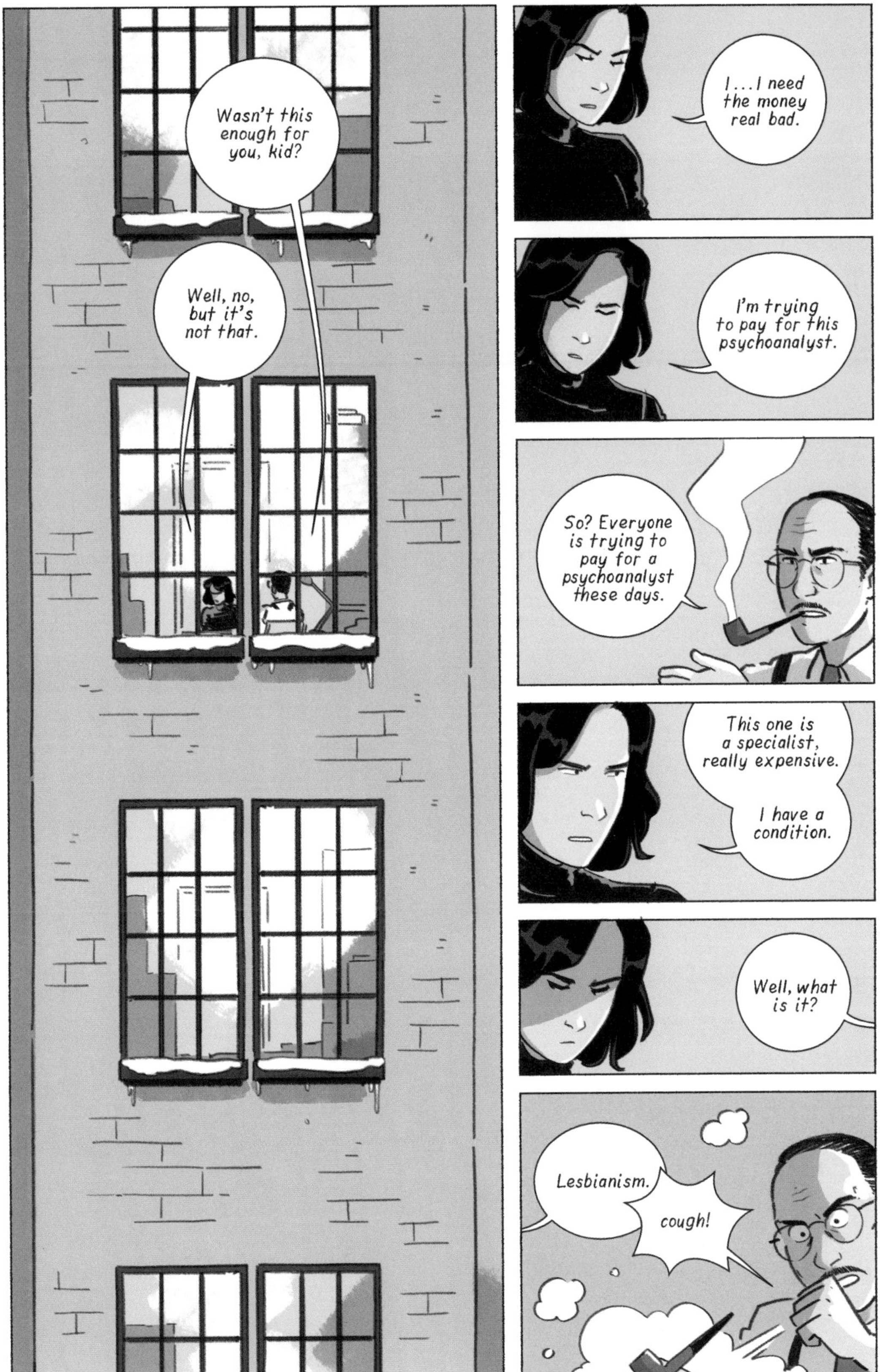

Wasn't this enough for you, kid?
Well, no, but it's not that.
I...I need the money real bad.
I'm trying to pay for this psychoanalyst.
So? Everyone is trying to pay for a psychoanalyst these days.
This one is a specialist, really expensive.
I have a condition.
Well, what is it?
Lesbianism.
cough!

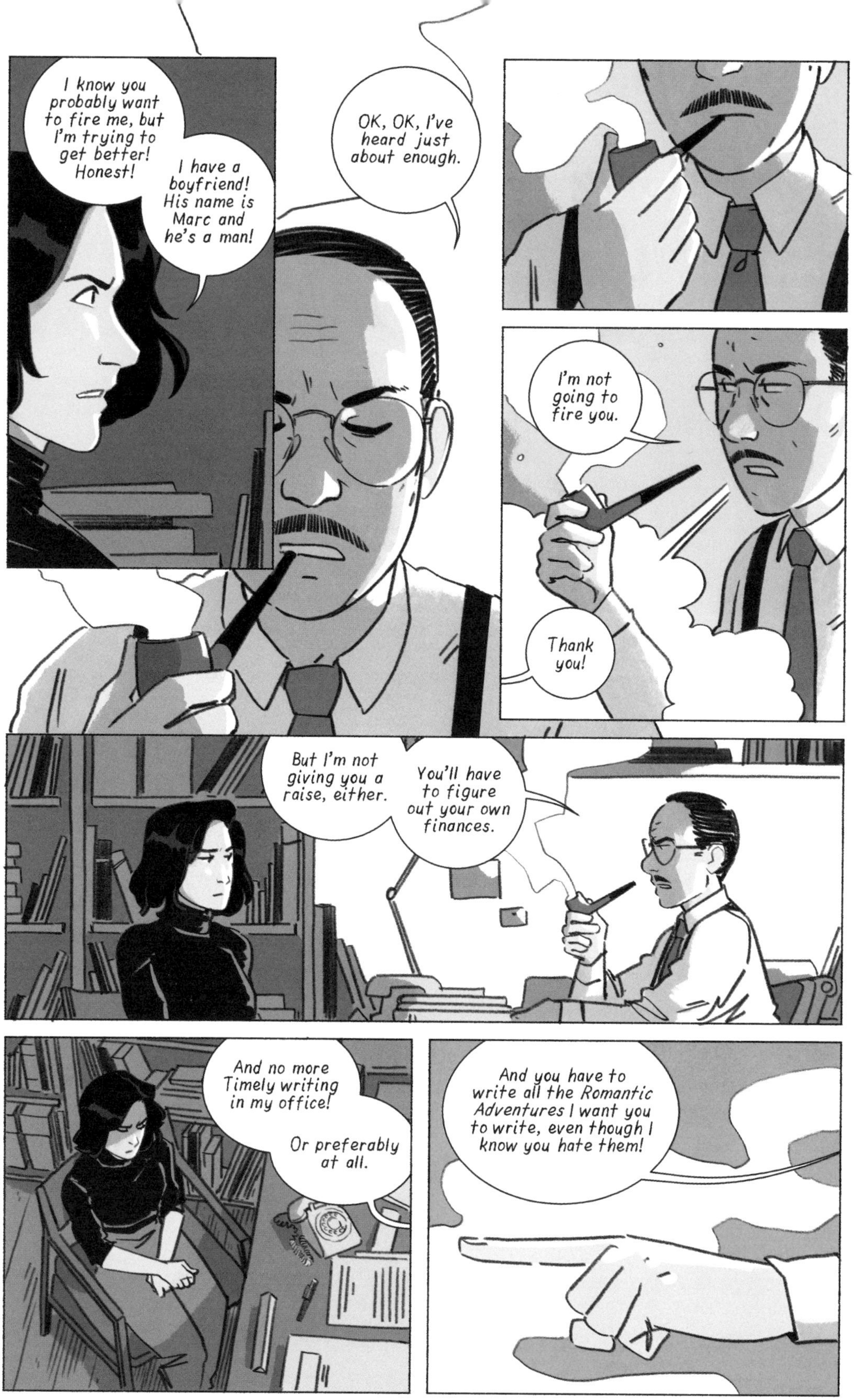
I know you probably want to fire me, but I'm trying to get better! Honest!
I have a boyfriend! His name is Marc and he's a man!
OK, OK, I've heard just about enough.
I'm not going to fire you.
Thank you!
But I'm not giving you a raise, either.
You'll have to figure out your own finances.
And no more Timely writing in my office!
Or preferably at all.
And you have to write all the Romantic Adventures I want you to write, even though I know you hate them!

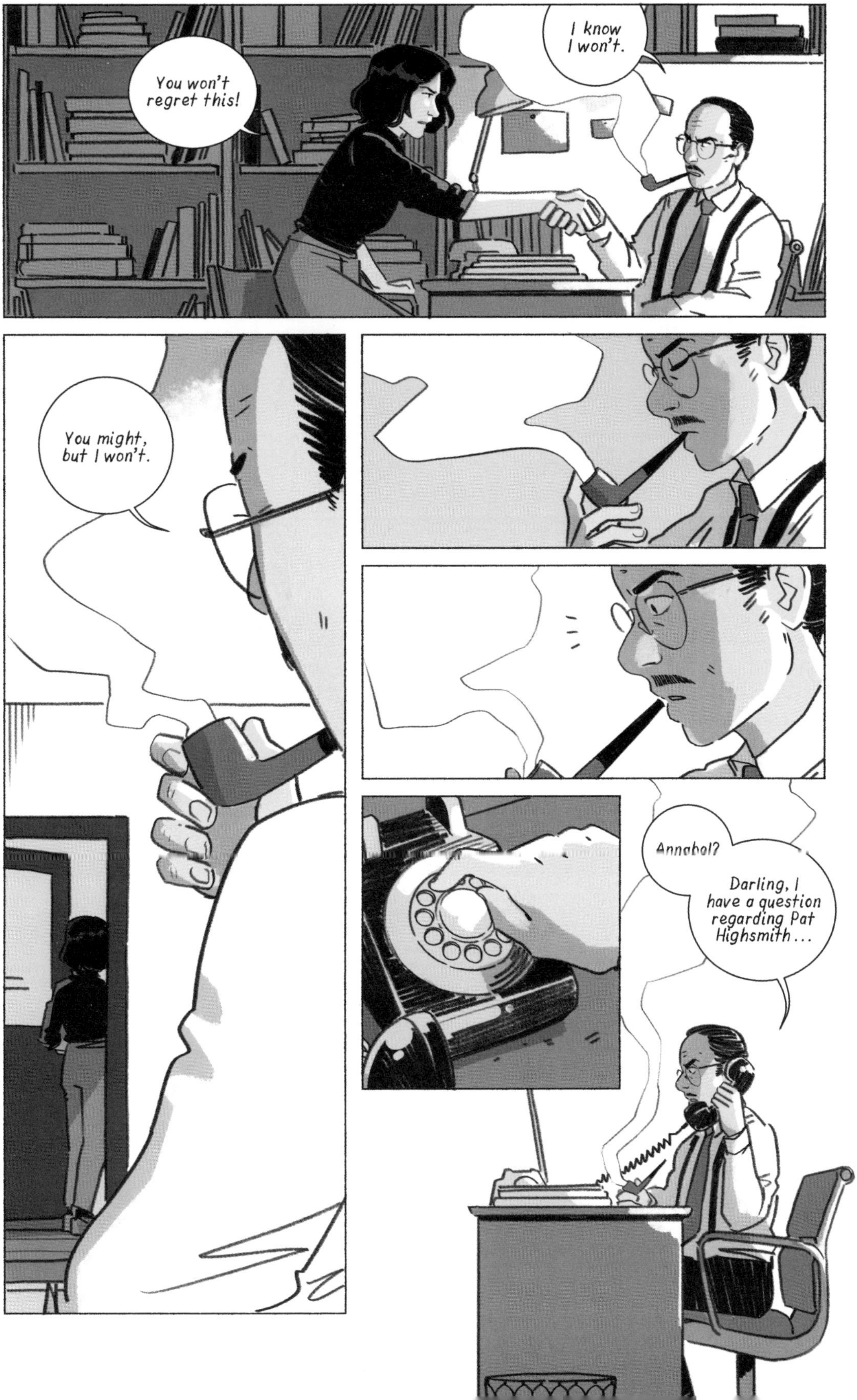
You won't regret this!
I know I won't.
You might, but I won't.
Annabel?
Darling, I have a question regarding Pat Highsmith...

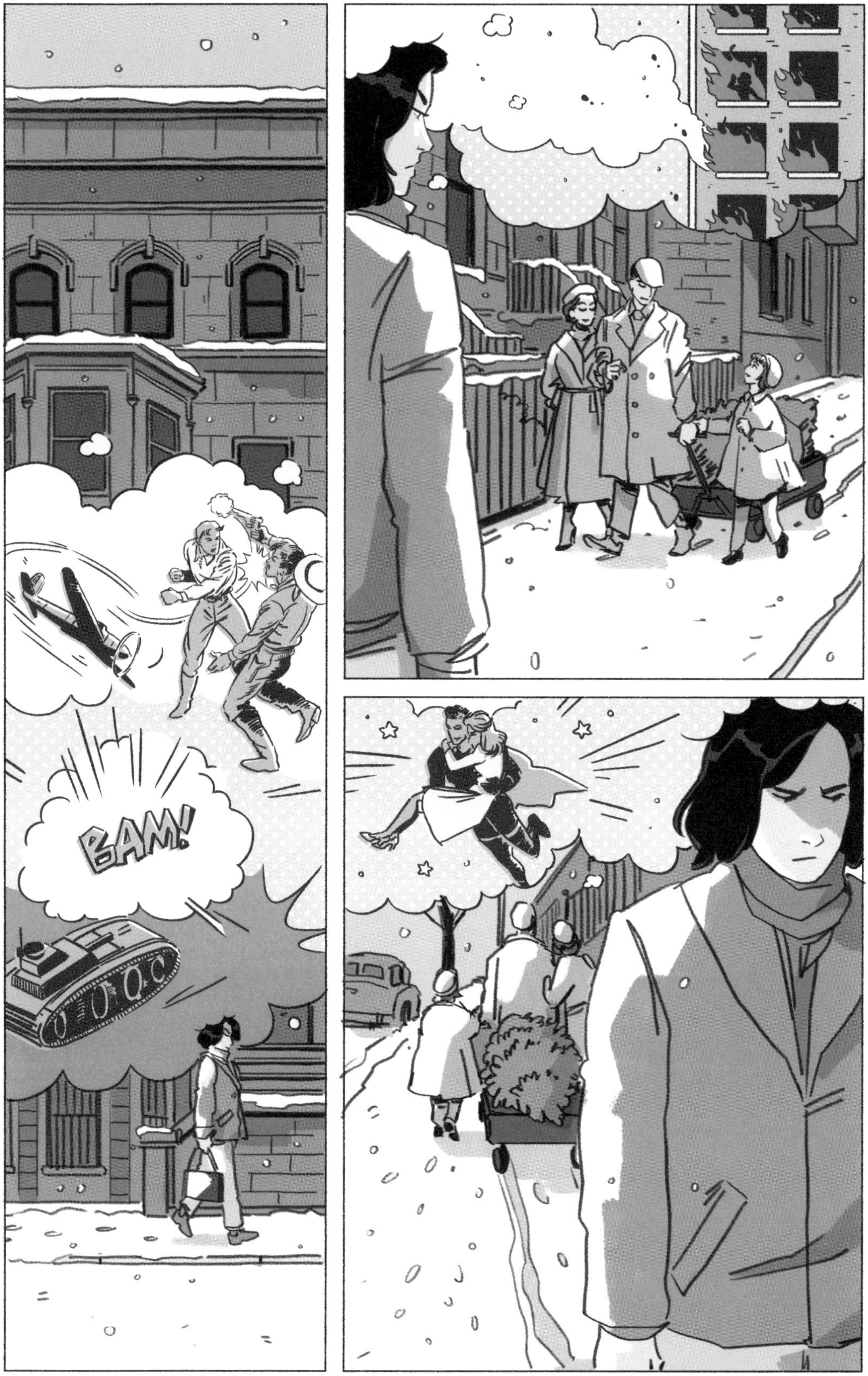

BAM!

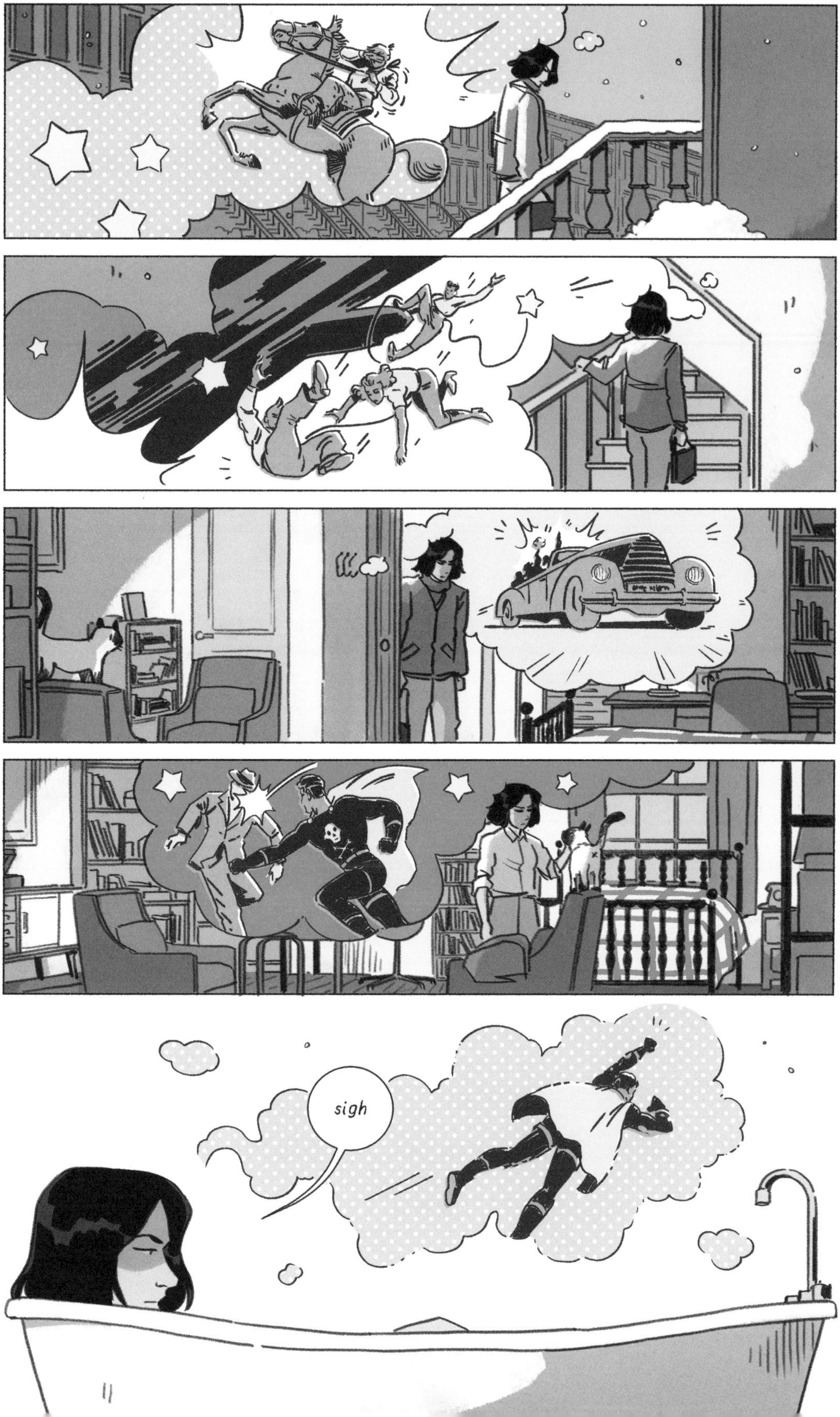
sigh

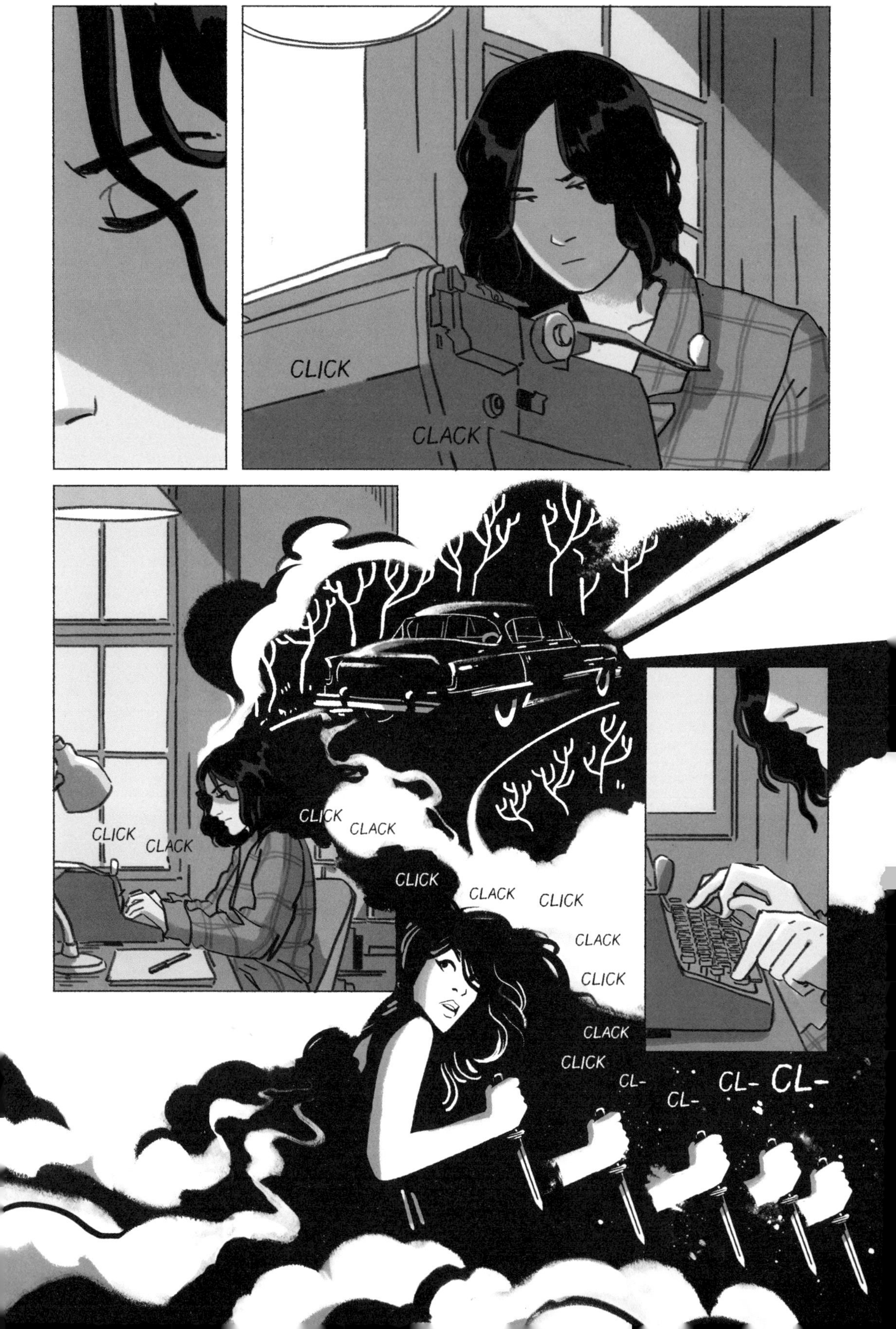

CLICK
CLACK
CLICK
CLACK
CLICK
CLACK
CLICK
CLACK
CLICK
CLACK
CLICK
CLACK
CLICK
CL-
CL-
CL-
CL-

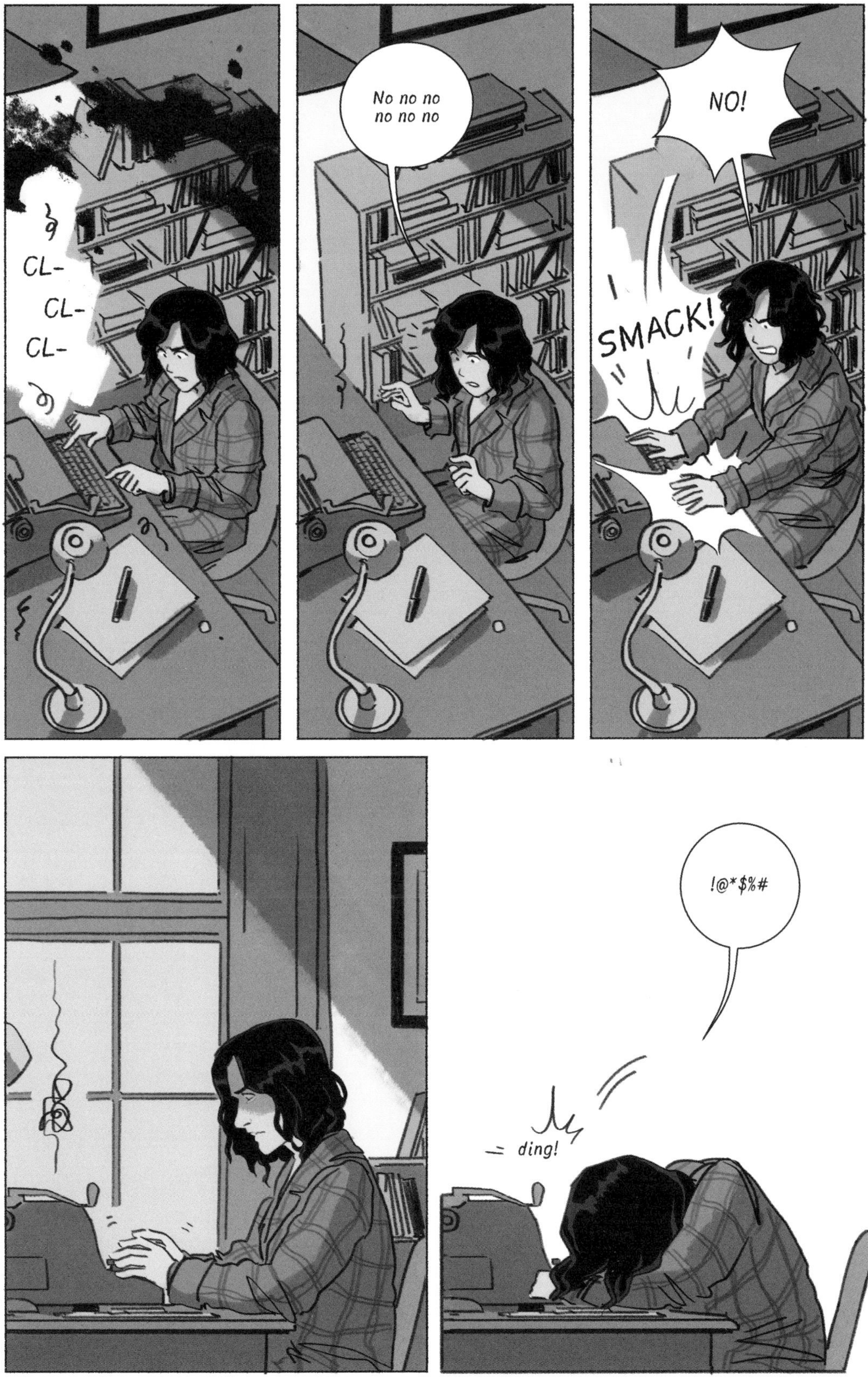
CL-
CL-
CL-
No no no
no no no
NO!
SMACK!
ding!
!@*$%#

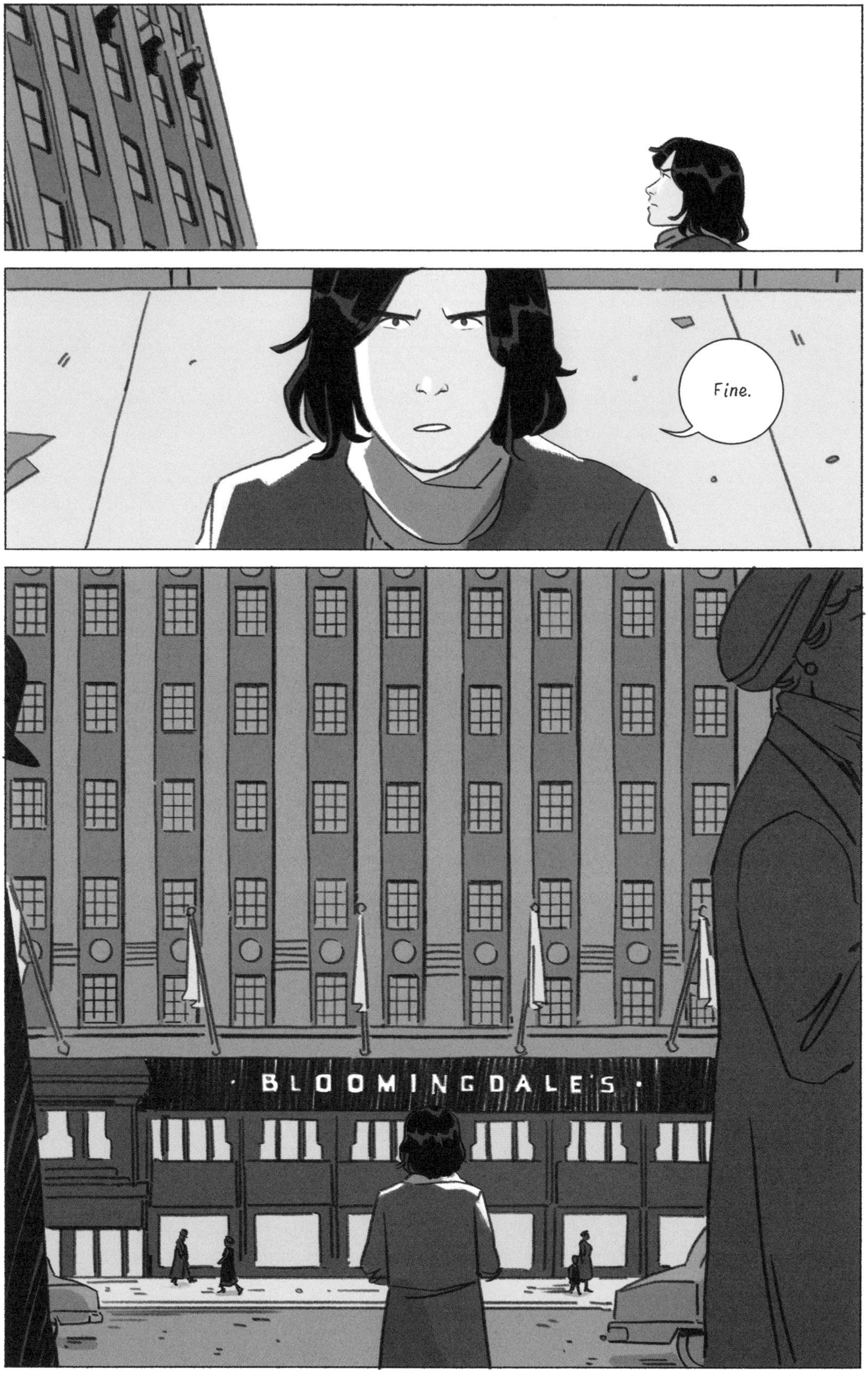
Fine.
· BLOOMINGDALE'S ·

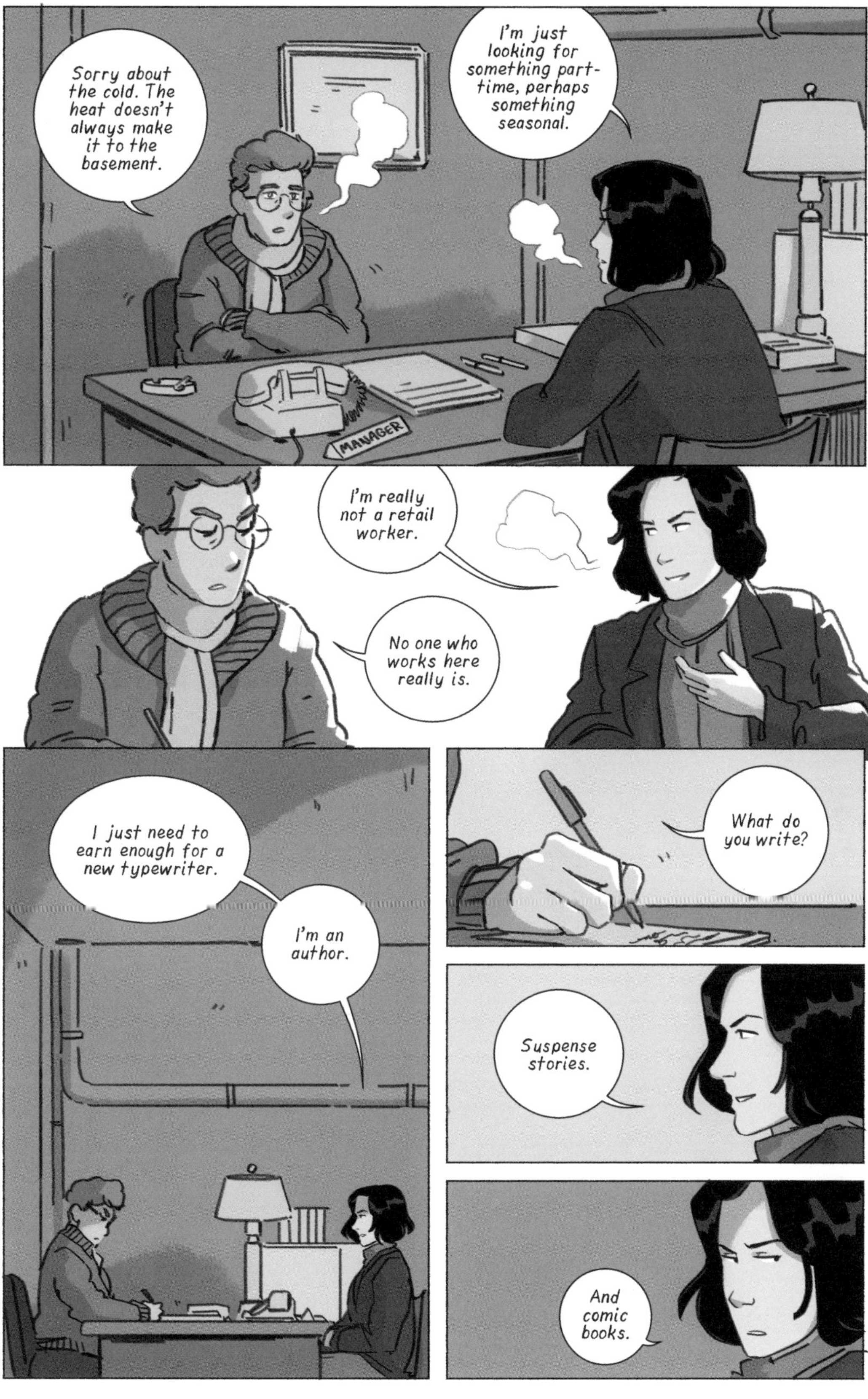
Sorry about the cold. The heat doesn't always make it to the basement.
I'm just looking for something part-time, perhaps something seasonal.
MANAGER
I'm really not a retail worker.
No one who works here really is.
I just need to earn enough for a new typewriter.
I'm an author.
What do you write?
Suspense stories.
And comic books.

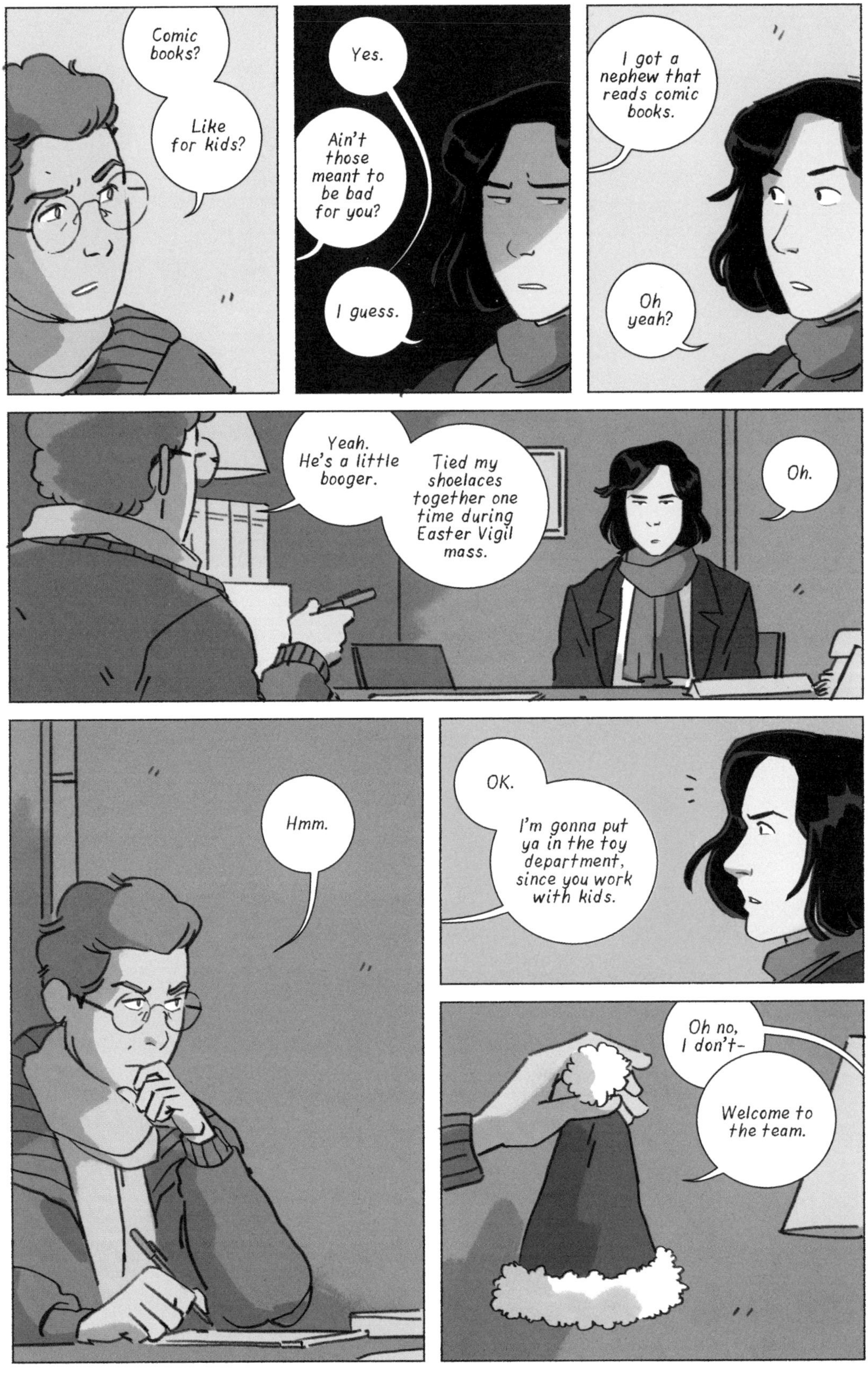

Comic books?
Like for kids?
Yes.
Ain't those meant to be bad for you?
I guess.
I got a nephew that reads comic books.
Oh yeah?
Yeah. He's a little booger.
Tied my shoelaces together one time during Easter Vigil mass.
Oh.
Hmm.
OK.
I'm gonna put ya in the toy department, since you work with kids.
Oh no, I don't-
Welcome to the team.

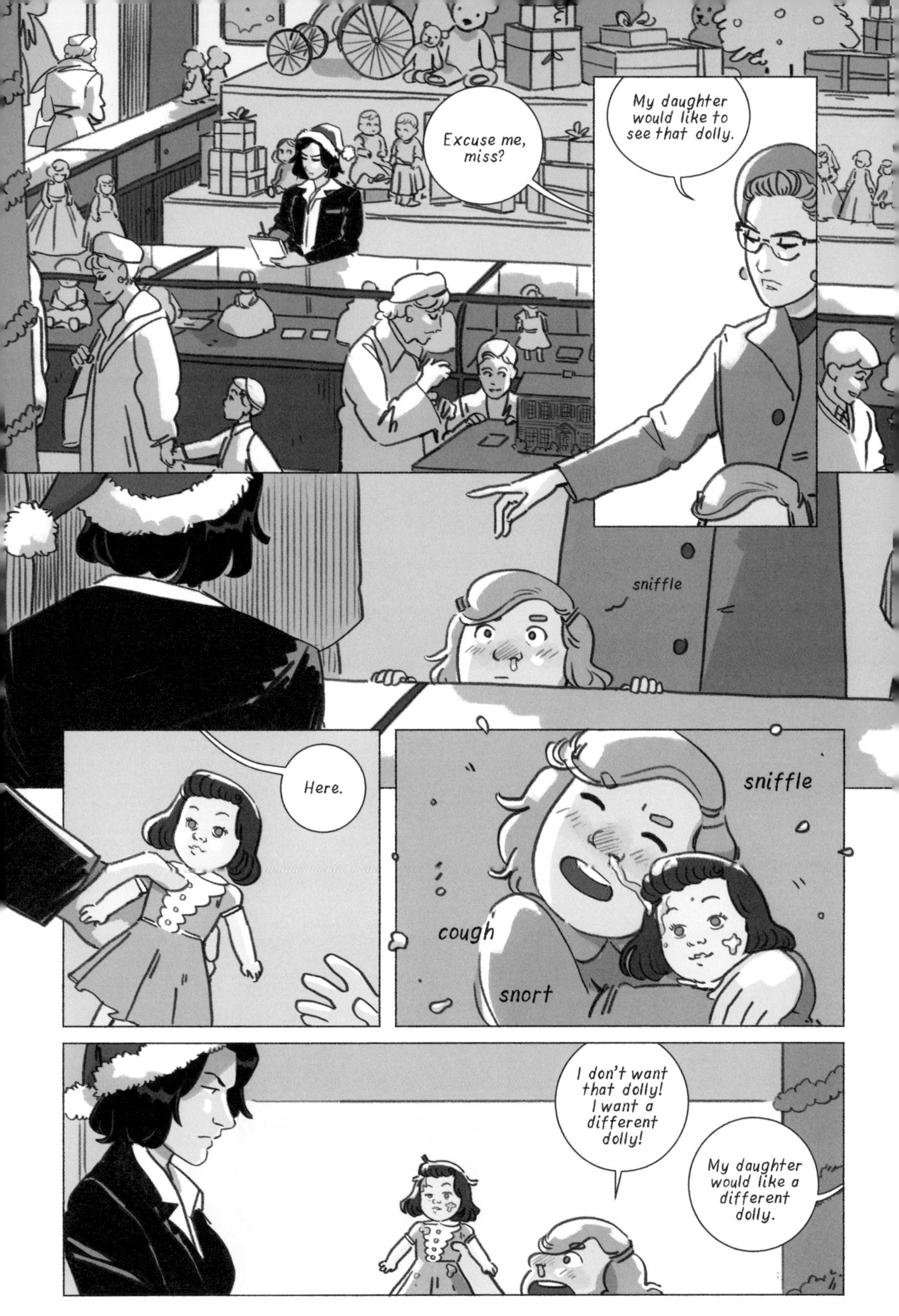
Excuse me, miss?
My daughter would like to see that dolly.
sniffle
Here.
sniffle
cough
snort
I don't want that dolly! I want a different dolly!
My daughter would like a different dolly.

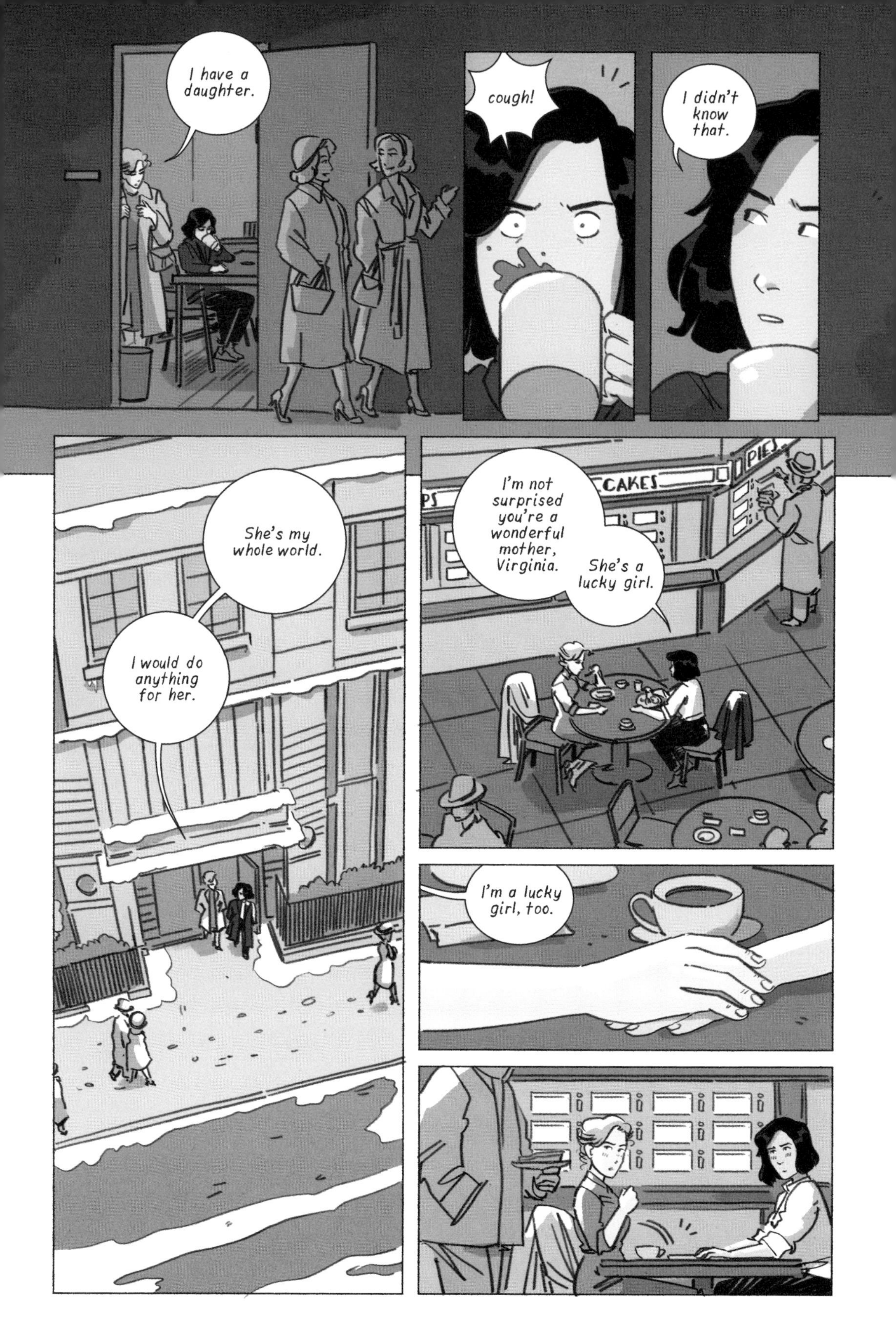

I have a daughter.
cough!
I didn't know that.
She's my whole world.
I would do anything for her.
CAKES
PIES
I'm not surprised you're a wonderful mother, Virginia.
She's a lucky girl.
I'm a lucky girl, too.

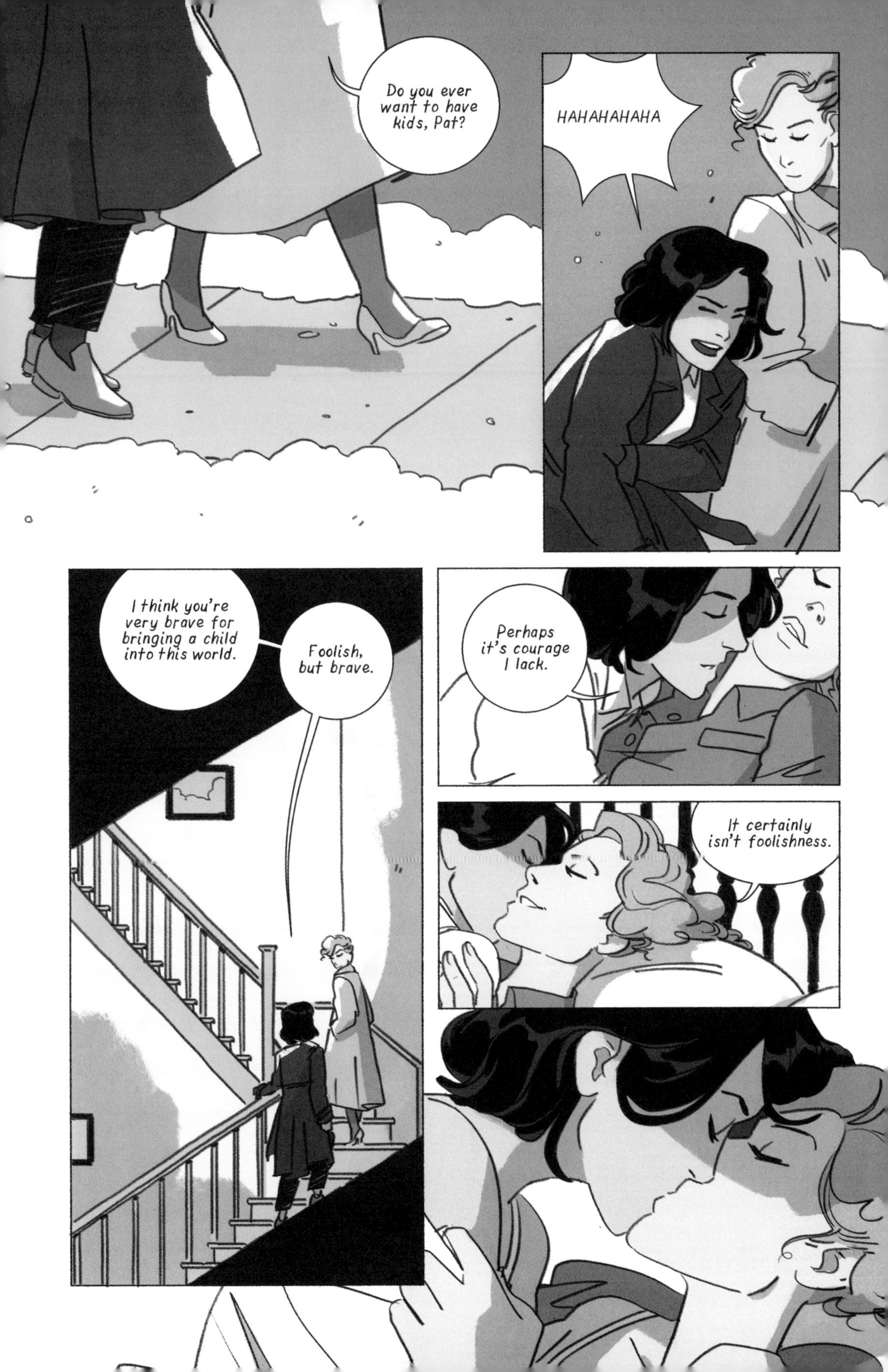
Do you ever want to have kids, Pat?
HAHAHAHAHA
I think you're very brave for bringing a child into this world.
Foolish, but brave.
Perhaps it's courage I lack.
It certainly isn't foolishness.

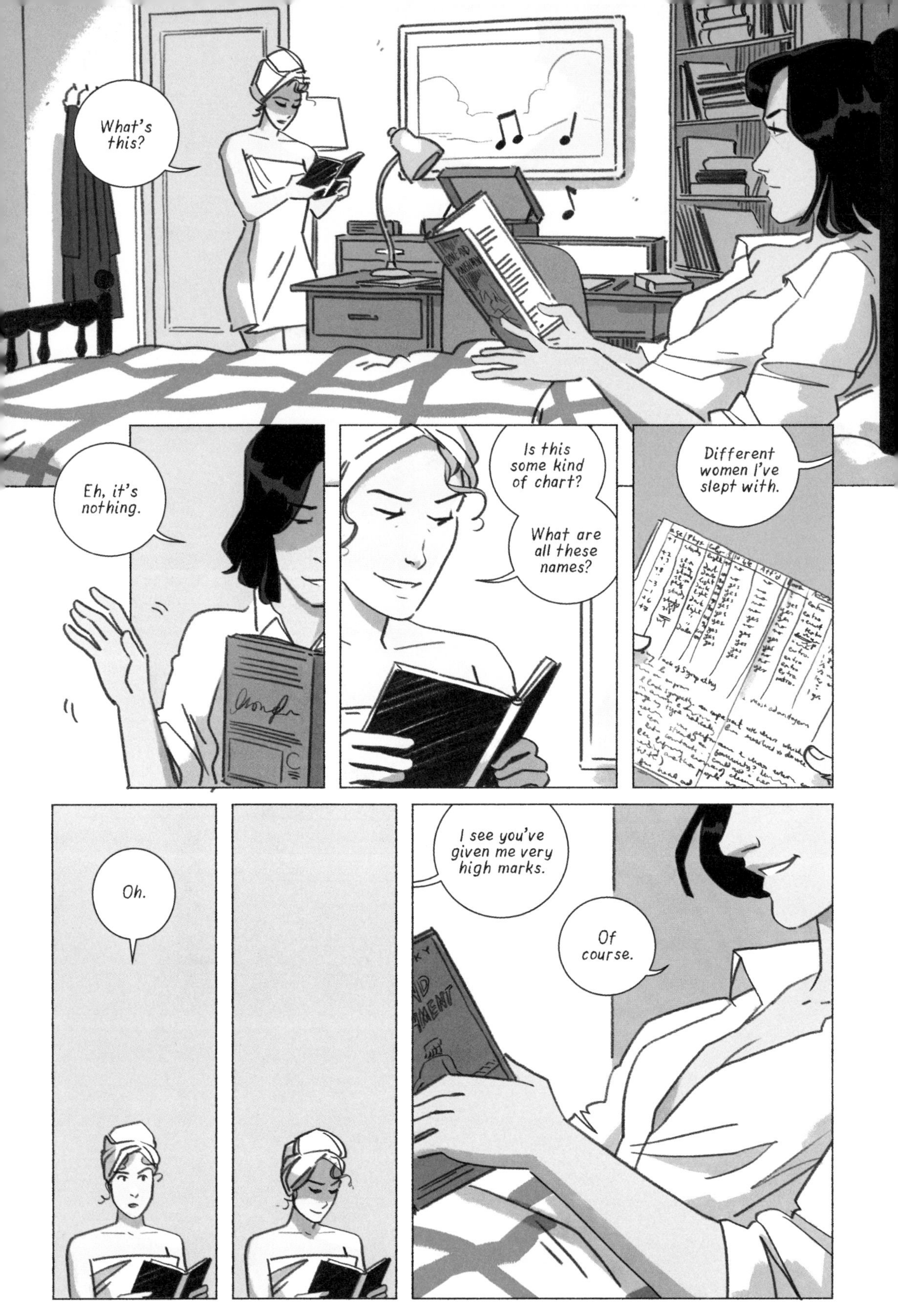
What's this?
Eh, it's nothing.
Is this some kind of chart?
What are all these names?
Different women I've slept with.
Oh.
I see you've given me very high marks.
Of course.

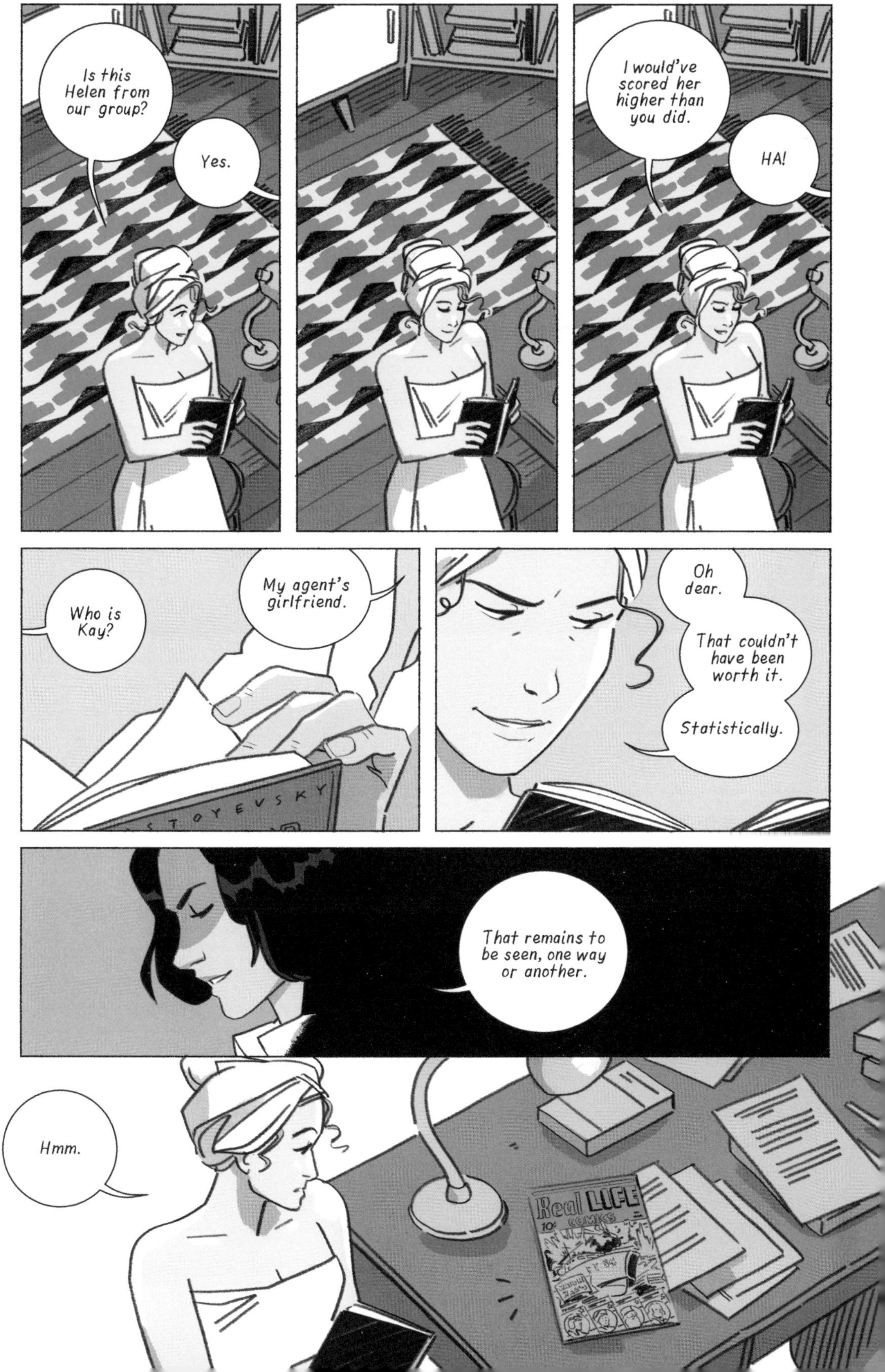

Is this Helen from our group?
Yes.
I would've scored her higher than you did.
HA!
Who is Kay?
My agent's girlfriend.
DOSTOYEVSKY
Oh dear.
That couldn't have been worth it.
Statistically.
That remains to be seen, one way or another.
Hmm.
Real LIFE COMICS
10¢

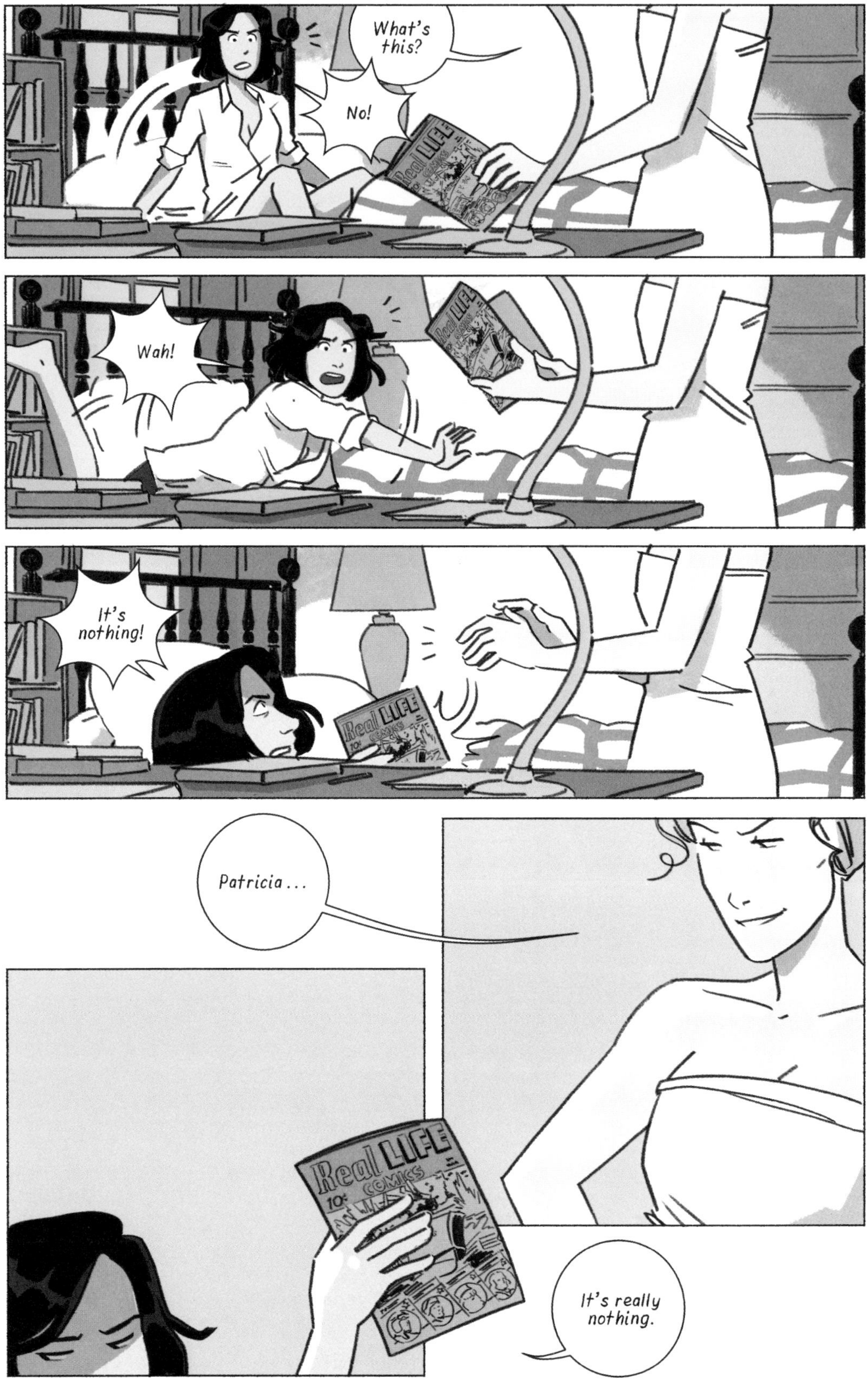

What's this?
No!
Wah!
It's nothing!
Patricia...
It's really nothing.

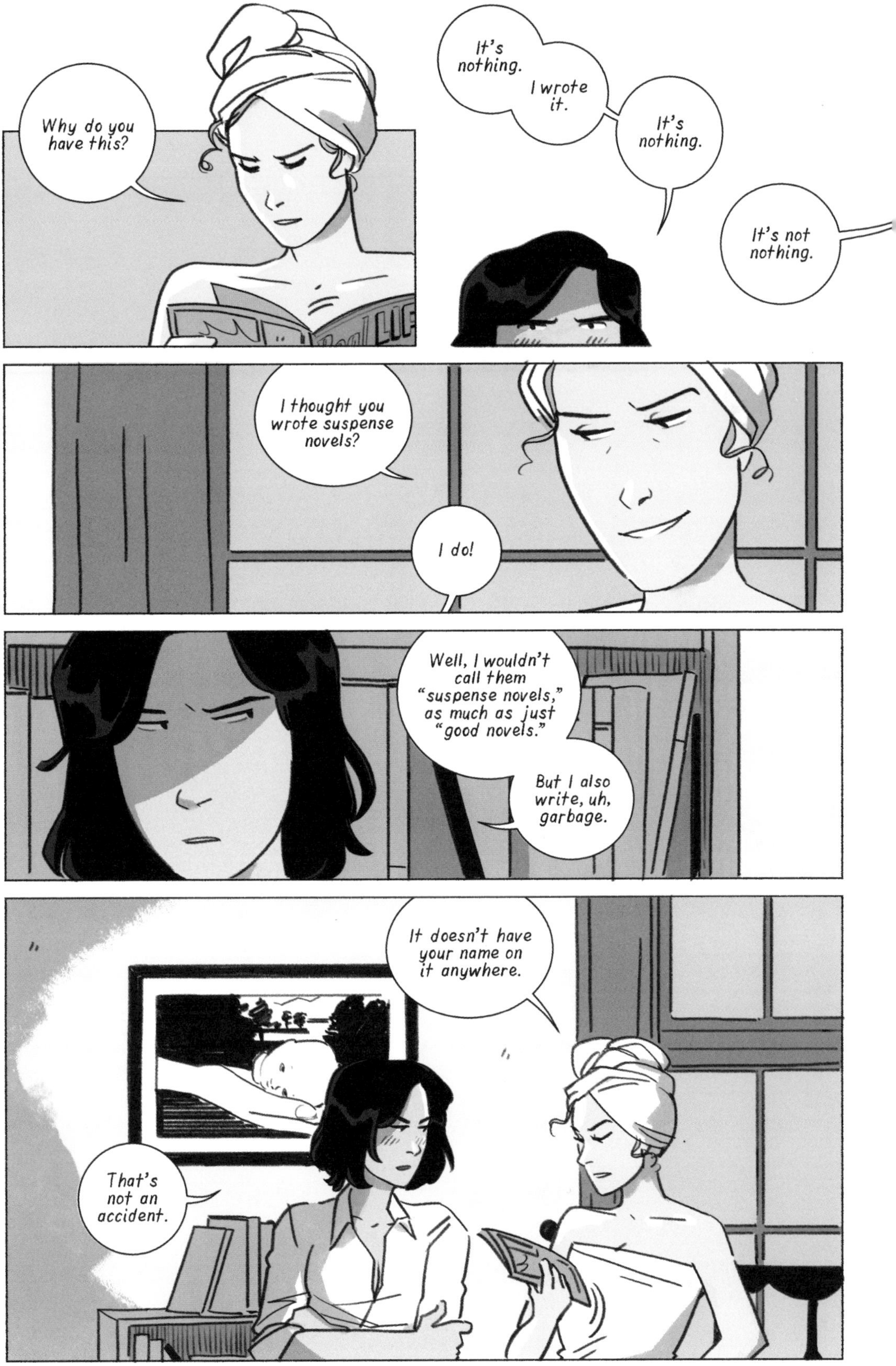
Why do you have this?
It's nothing.
I wrote it.
It's nothing.
It's not nothing.
I thought you wrote suspense novels?
I do!
Well, I wouldn't call them "suspense novels," as much as just "good novels."
But I also write, uh, garbage.
It doesn't have your name on it anywhere.
That's not an accident.

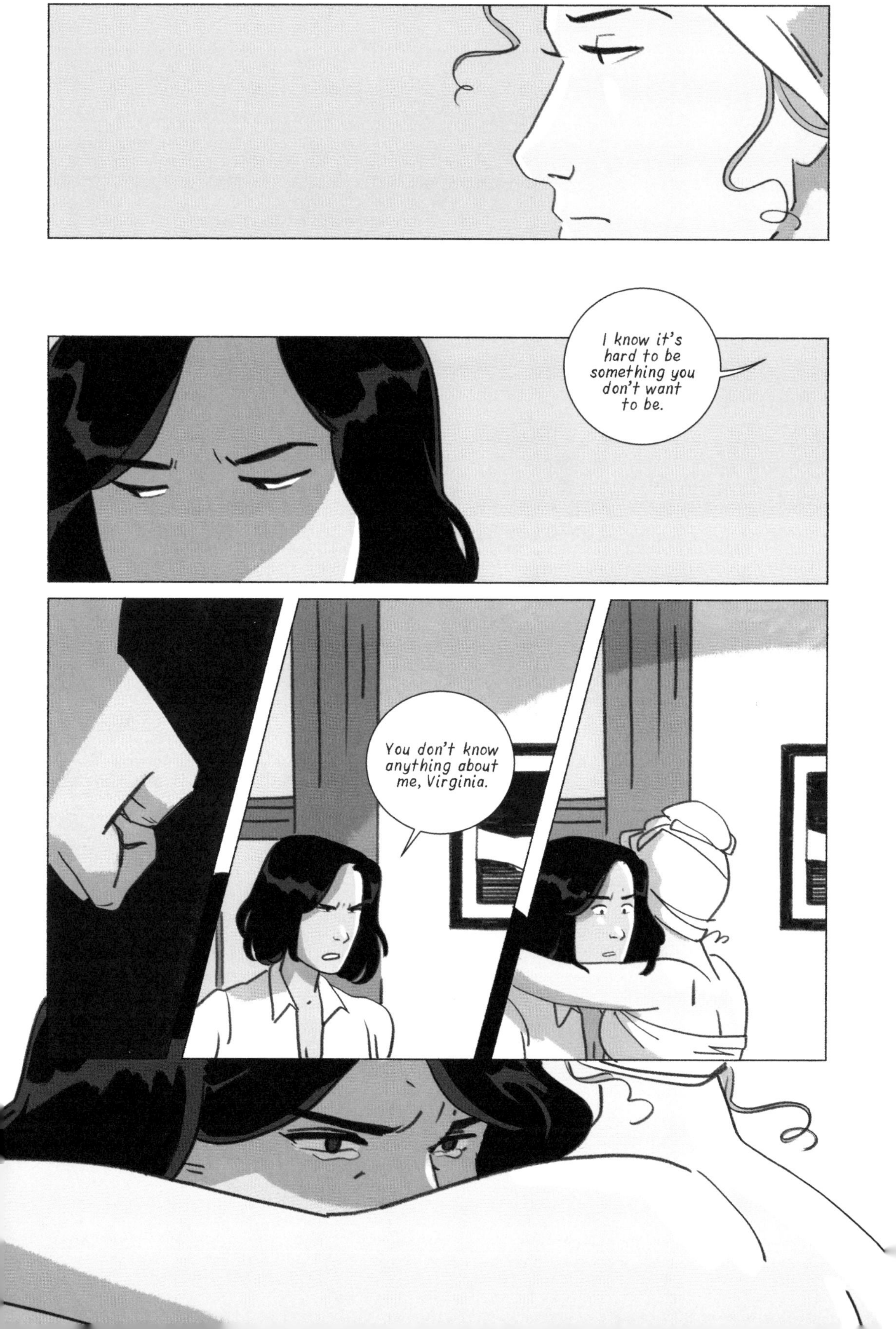
I know it's hard to be something you don't want to be.
You don't know anything about me, Virginia.

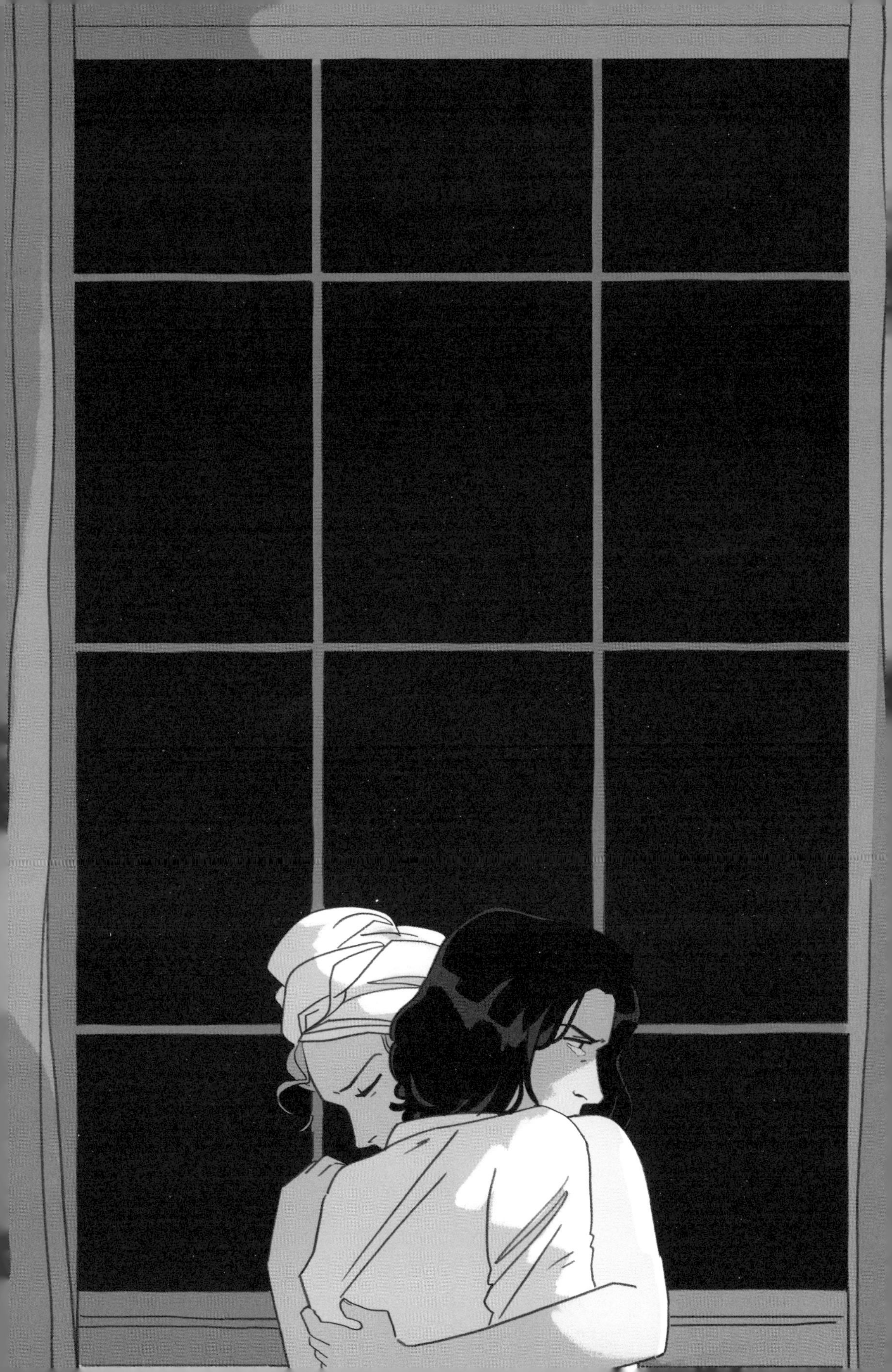

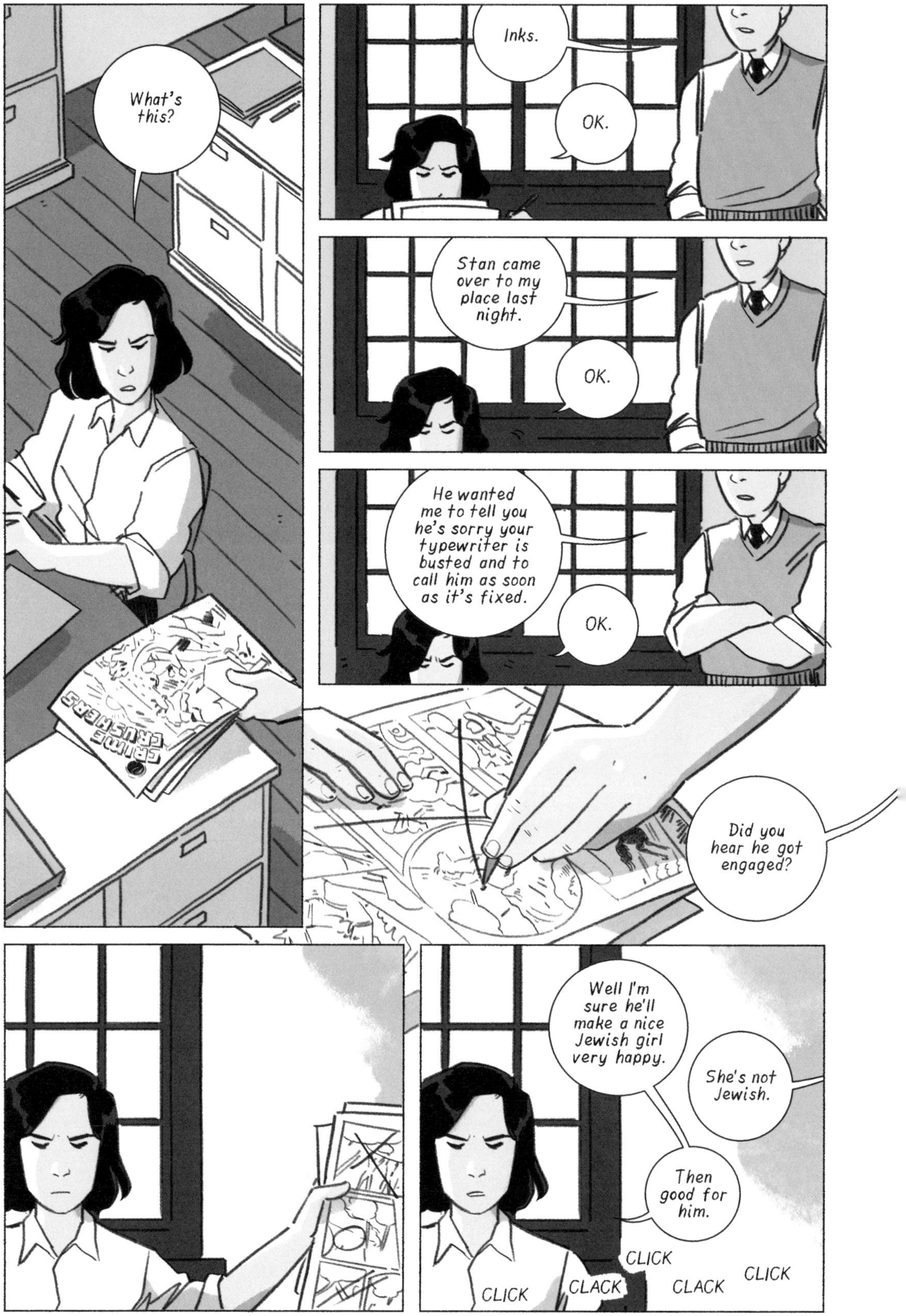
What's this?
Inks.
OK.
Stan came over to my place last night.
OK.
He wanted me to tell you he's sorry your typewriter is busted and to call him as soon as it's fixed.
OK.
CRIME CRUSHERS
Did you hear he got engaged?
Well I'm sure he'll make a nice Jewish girl very happy.
She's not Jewish.
Then good for him.
CLICK
CLACK
CLICK
CLACK
CLICK

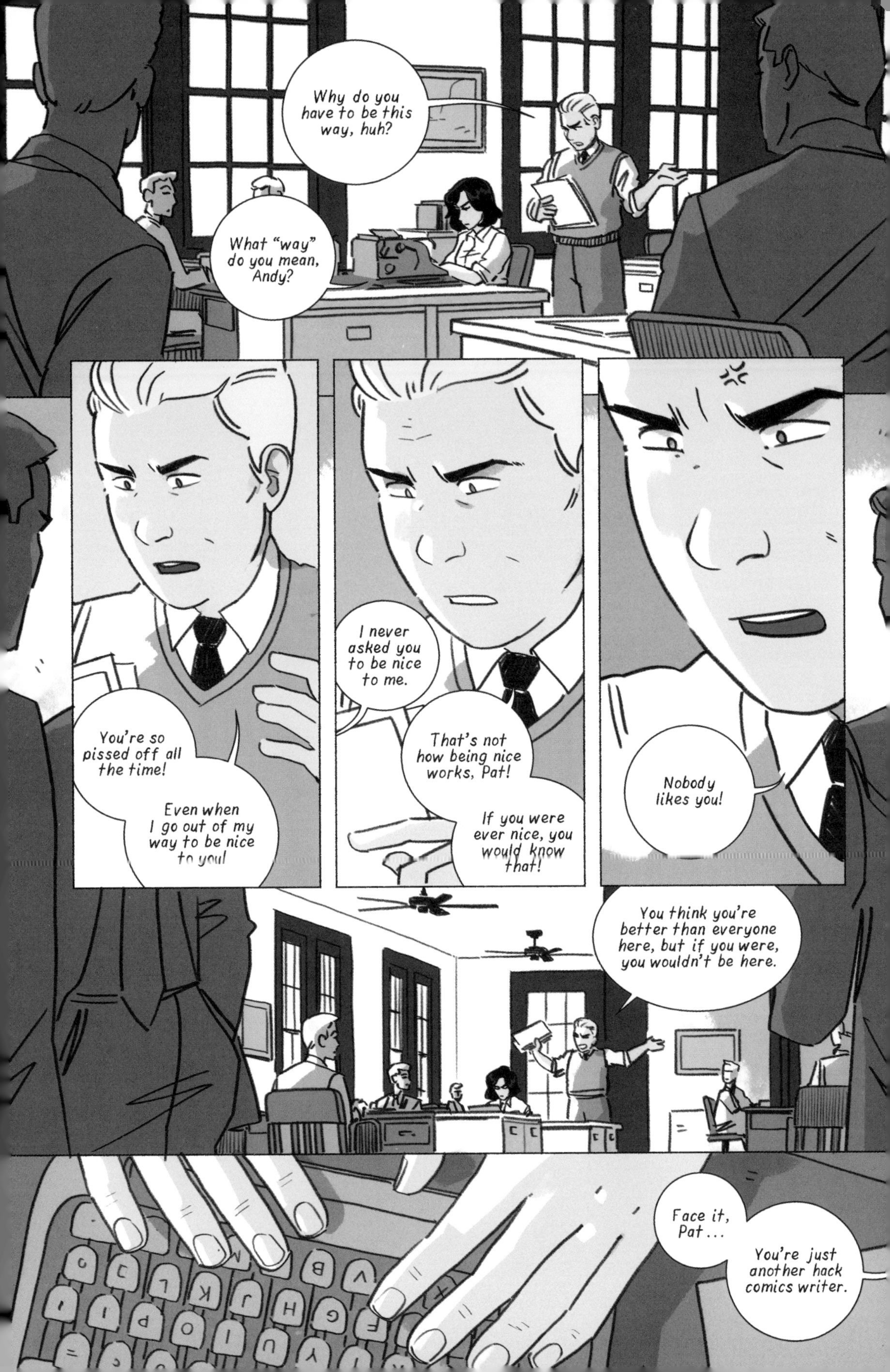
Why do you have to be this way, huh?
What "way" do you mean, Andy?
You're so pissed off all the time!
Even when I go out of my way to be nice to you!
I never asked you to be nice to me.
That's not how being nice works, Pat!
If you were ever nice, you would know that!
Nobody likes you!
You think you're better than everyone here, but if you were, you wouldn't be here.
Face it, Pat...
You're just another hack comics writer.

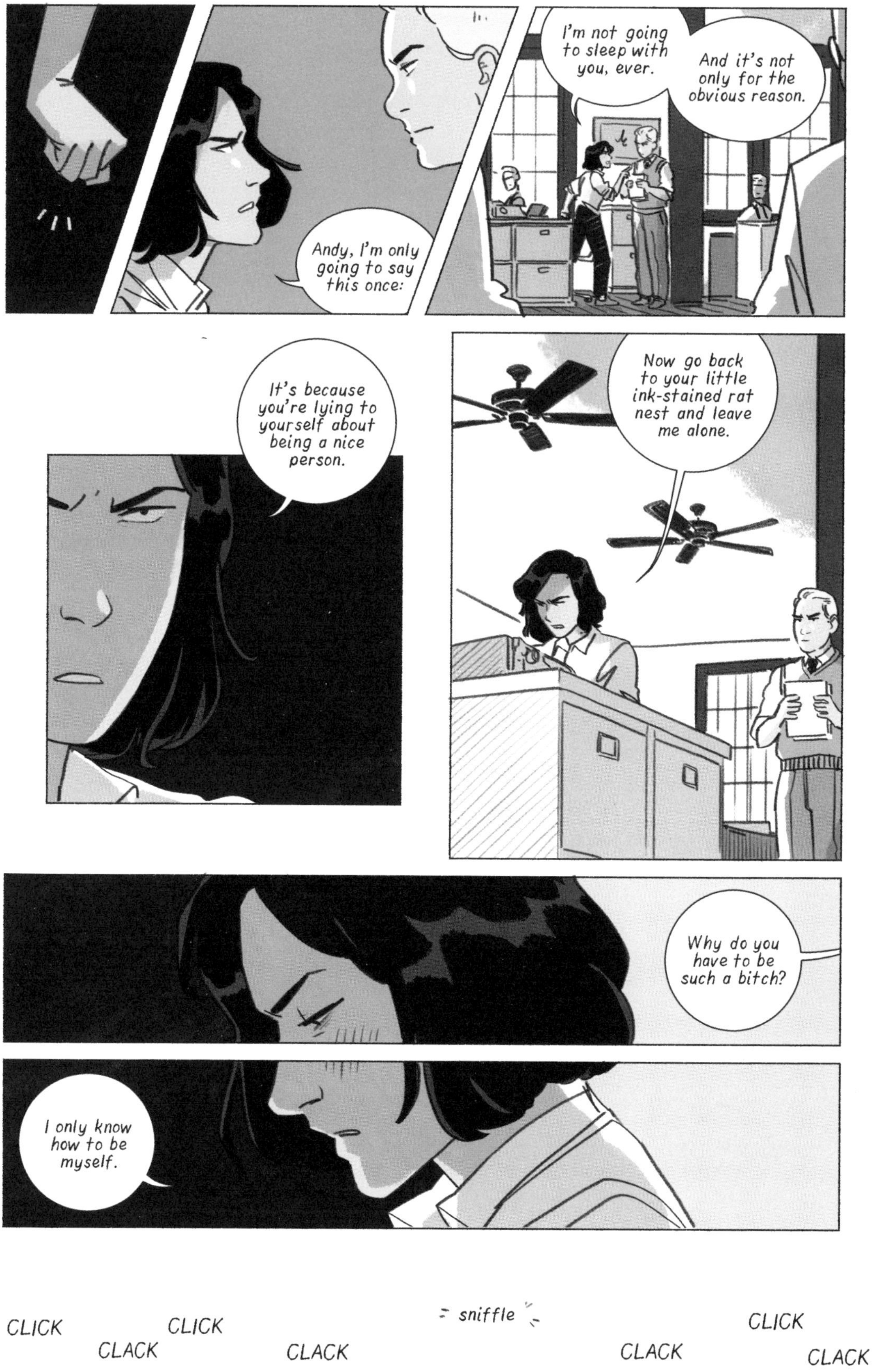
Andy, I'm only going to say this once:
I'm not going to sleep with you, ever.
And it's not only for the obvious reason.
It's because you're lying to yourself about being a nice person.
Now go back to your little ink-stained rat nest and leave me alone.
Why do you have to be such a bitch?
I only know how to be myself.
CLICK
CLACK
CLICK
CLACK
sniffle
CLACK
CLICK
CLACK

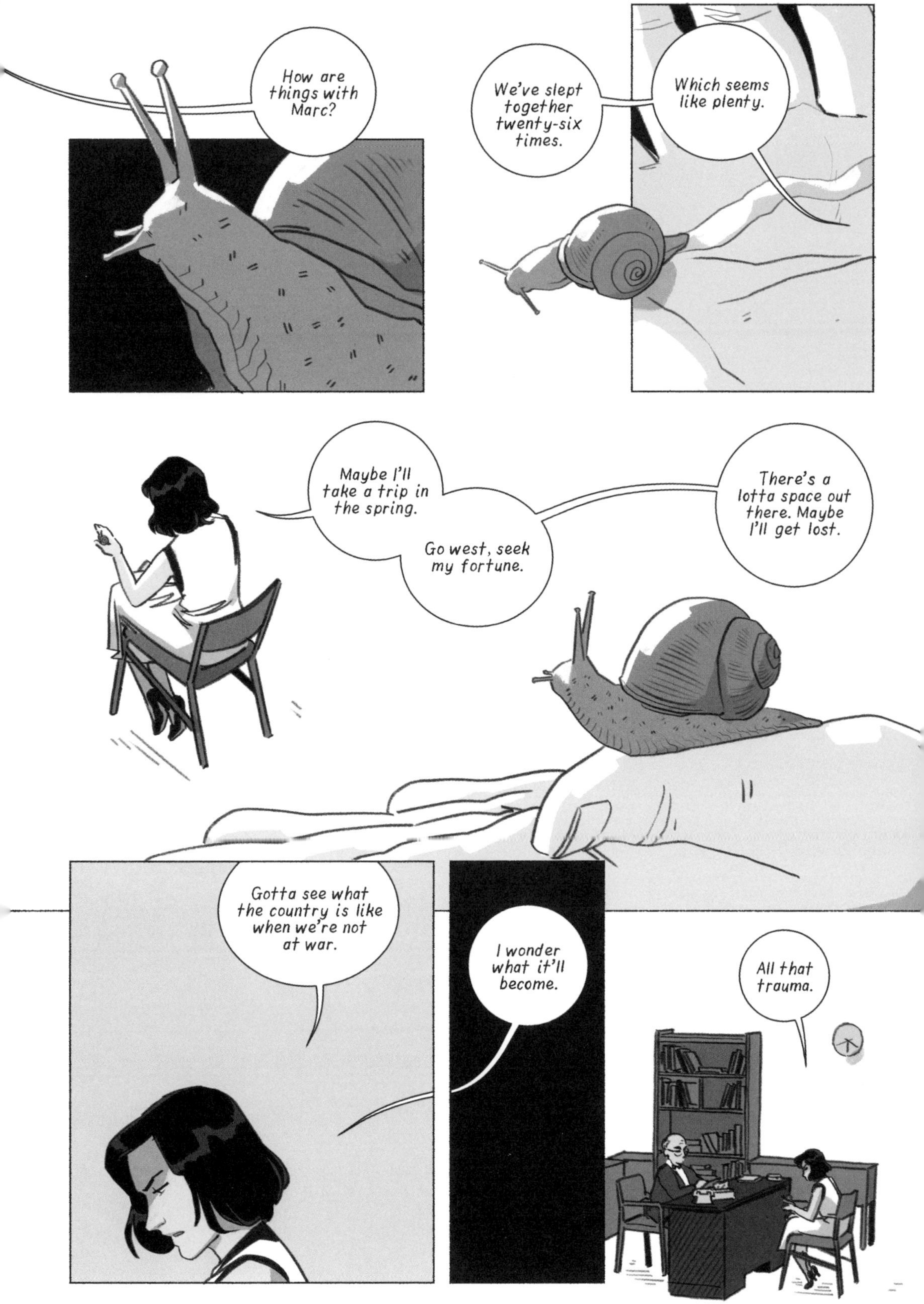
How are things with Marc?
We've slept together twenty-six times.
Which seems like plenty.
Maybe I'll take a trip in the spring.
Go west, seek my fortune.
There's a lotta space out there. Maybe I'll get lost.
Gotta see what the country is like when we're not at war.
I wonder what it'll become.
All that trauma.

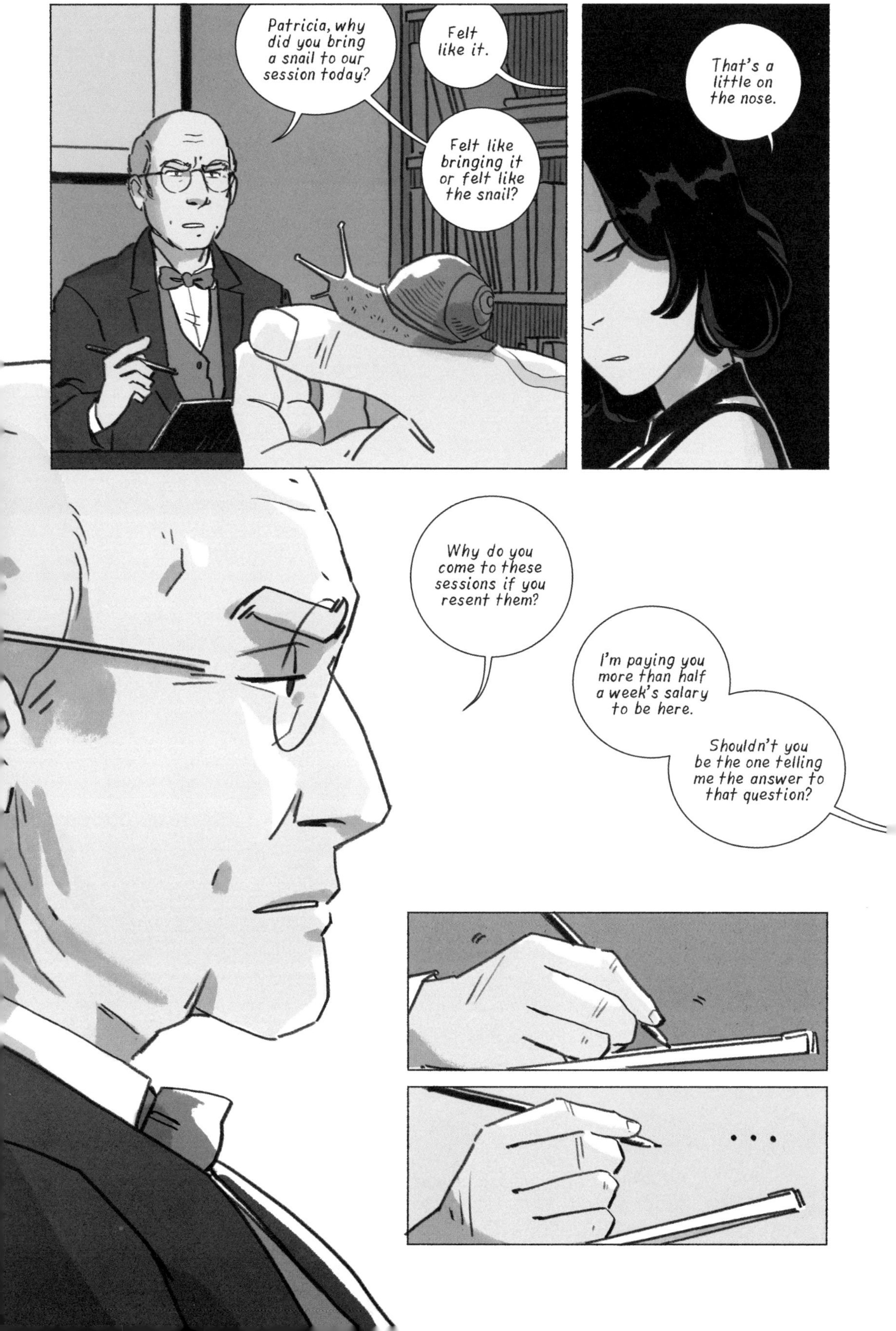
Patricia, why did you bring a snail to our session today?
Felt like it.
Felt like bringing it or felt like the snail?
That's a little on the nose.
Why do you come to these sessions if you resent them?
I'm paying you more than half a week's salary to be here.
Shouldn't you be the one telling me the answer to that question?
. . .

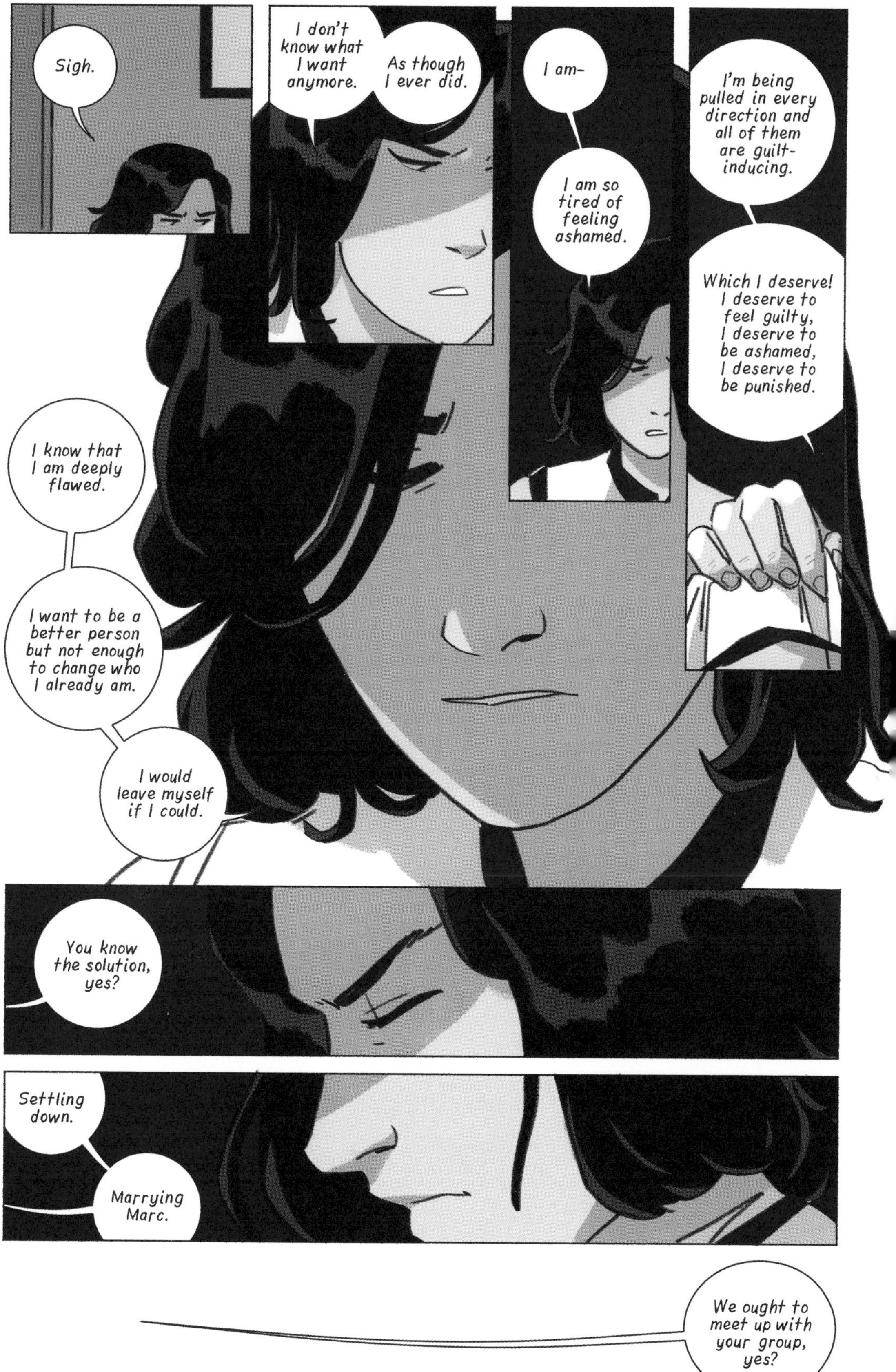
Sigh.
I don't know what I want anymore.
As though I ever did.
I am-
I am so tired of feeling ashamed.
I'm being pulled in every direction and all of them are guilt-inducing.
Which I deserve! I deserve to feel guilty, I deserve to be ashamed, I deserve to be punished.
I know that I am deeply flawed.
I want to be a better person but not enough to change who I already am.
I would leave myself if I could.
You know the solution, yes?
Settling down.
Marrying Marc.
We ought to meet up with your group, yes?

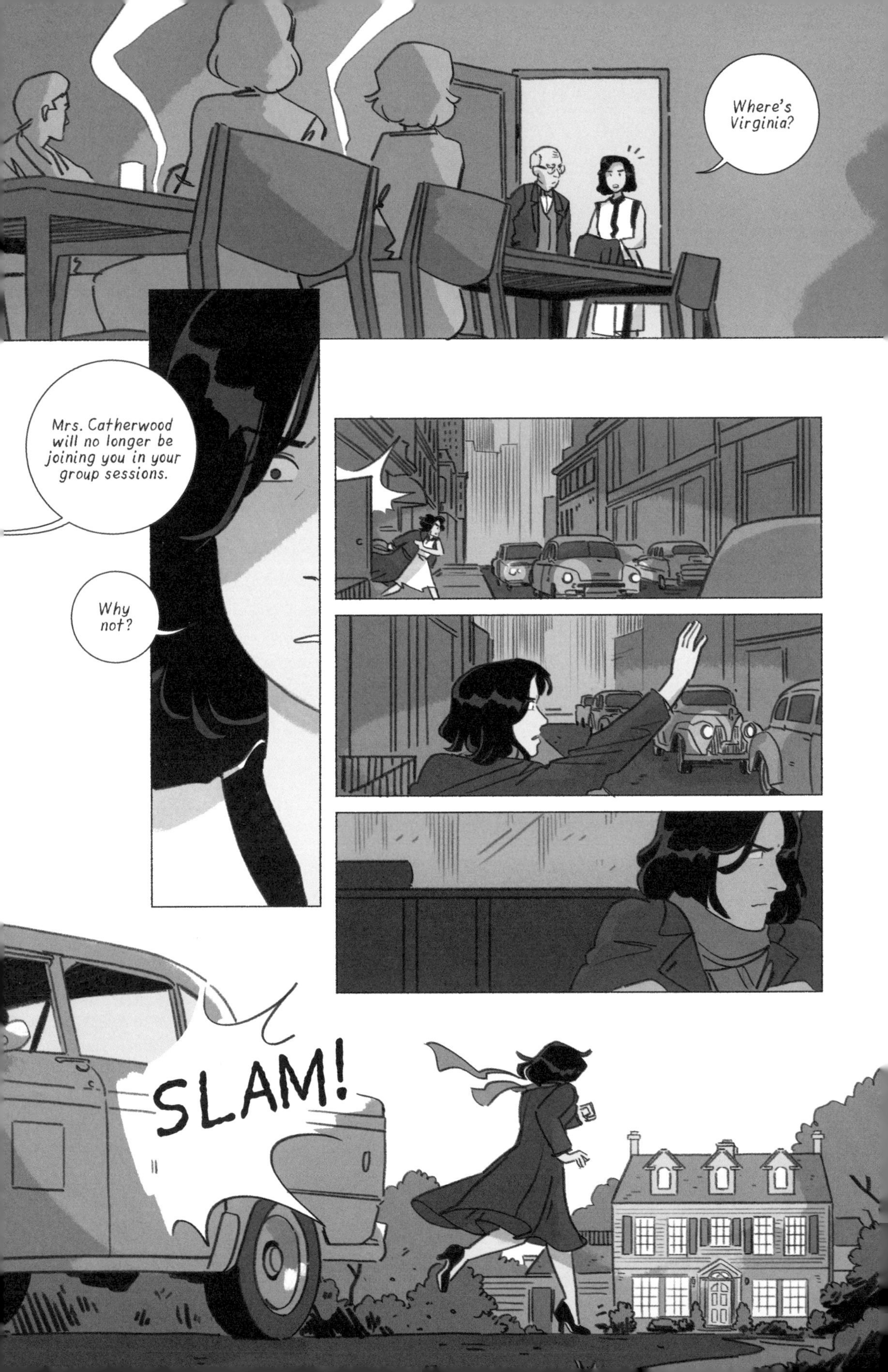
Where's Virginia?
Mrs. Catherwood will no longer be joining you in your group sessions.
Why not?
SLAM!

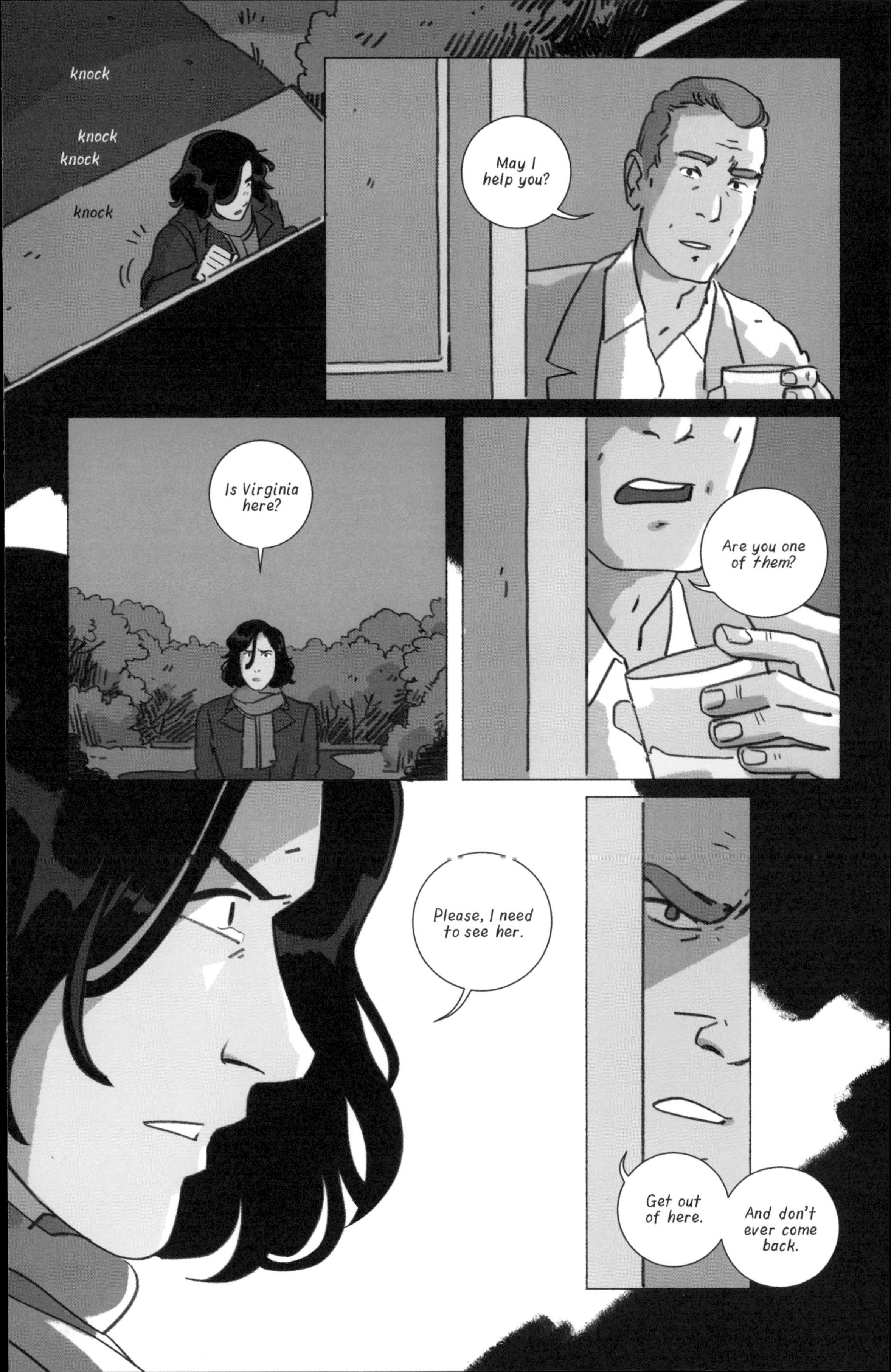
knock
knock
knock
knock
May I help you?
Is Virginia here?
Are you one of *them*?
Please, I need to see her.
Get out of here.
And don't ever come back.

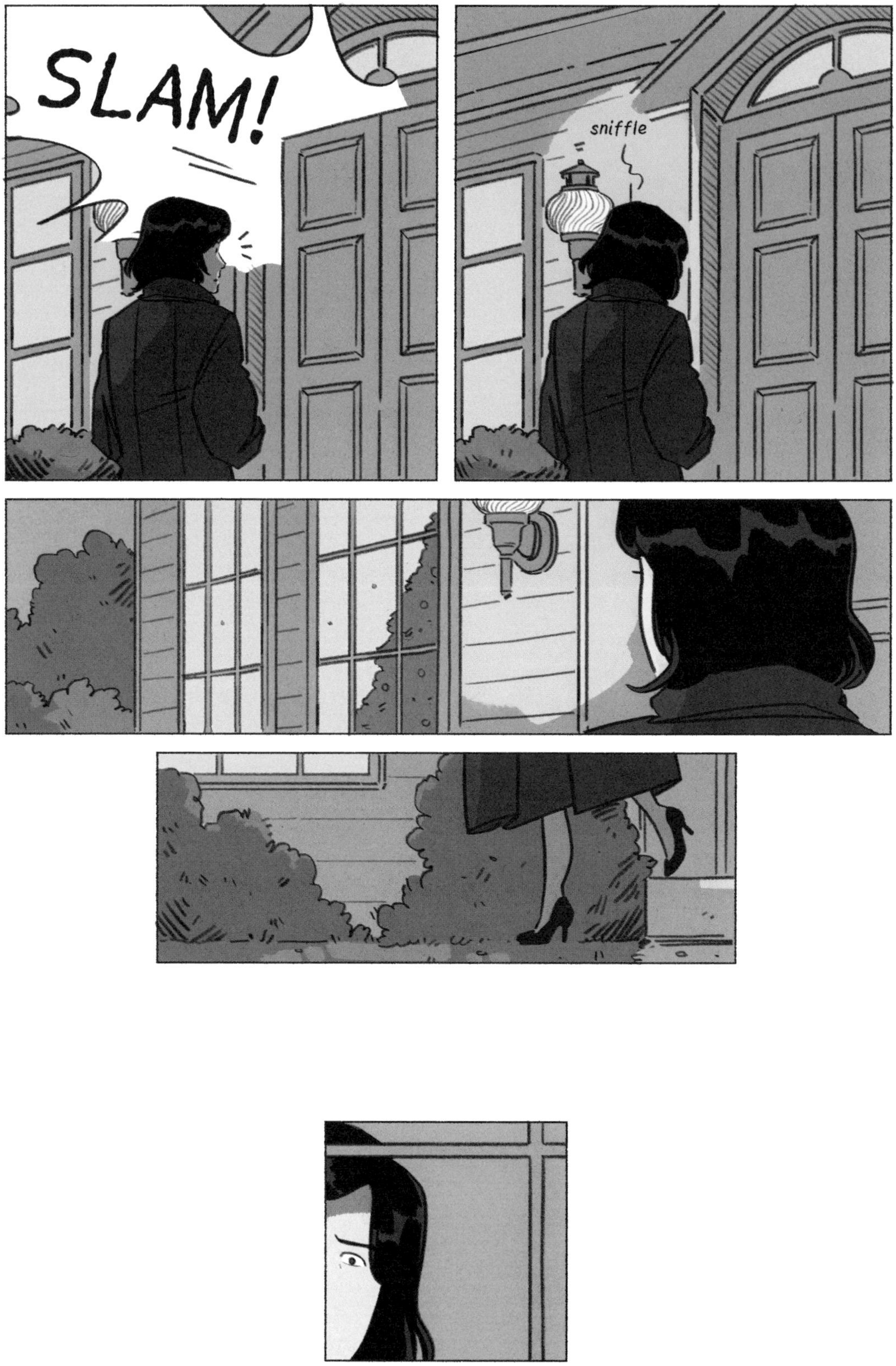
SLAM!
sniffle

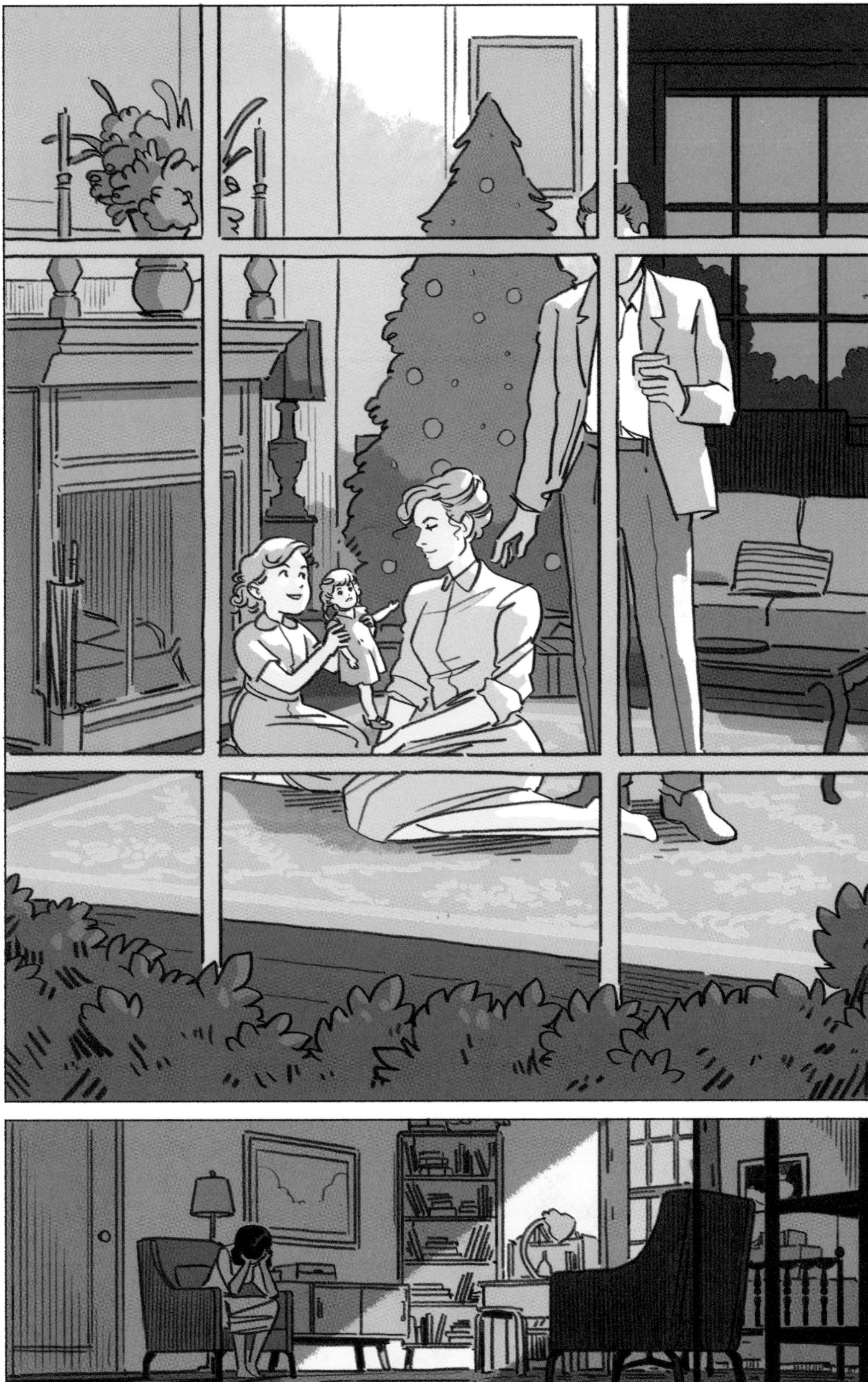

flick!
cough
cough
cough
cough
cough
Ugh.
crackle
crackle
crackle

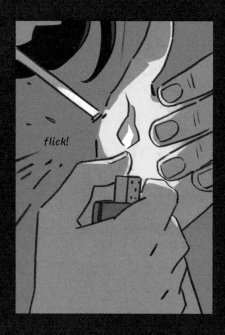

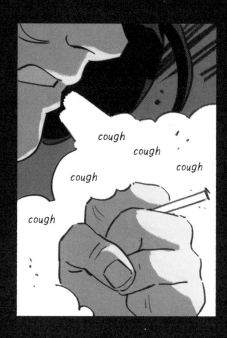

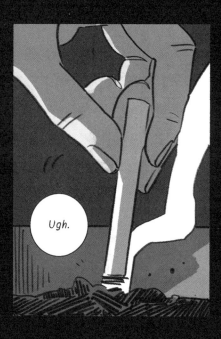

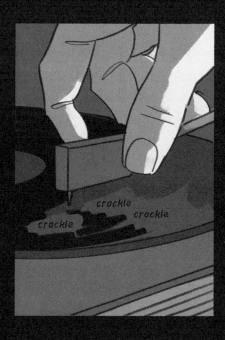

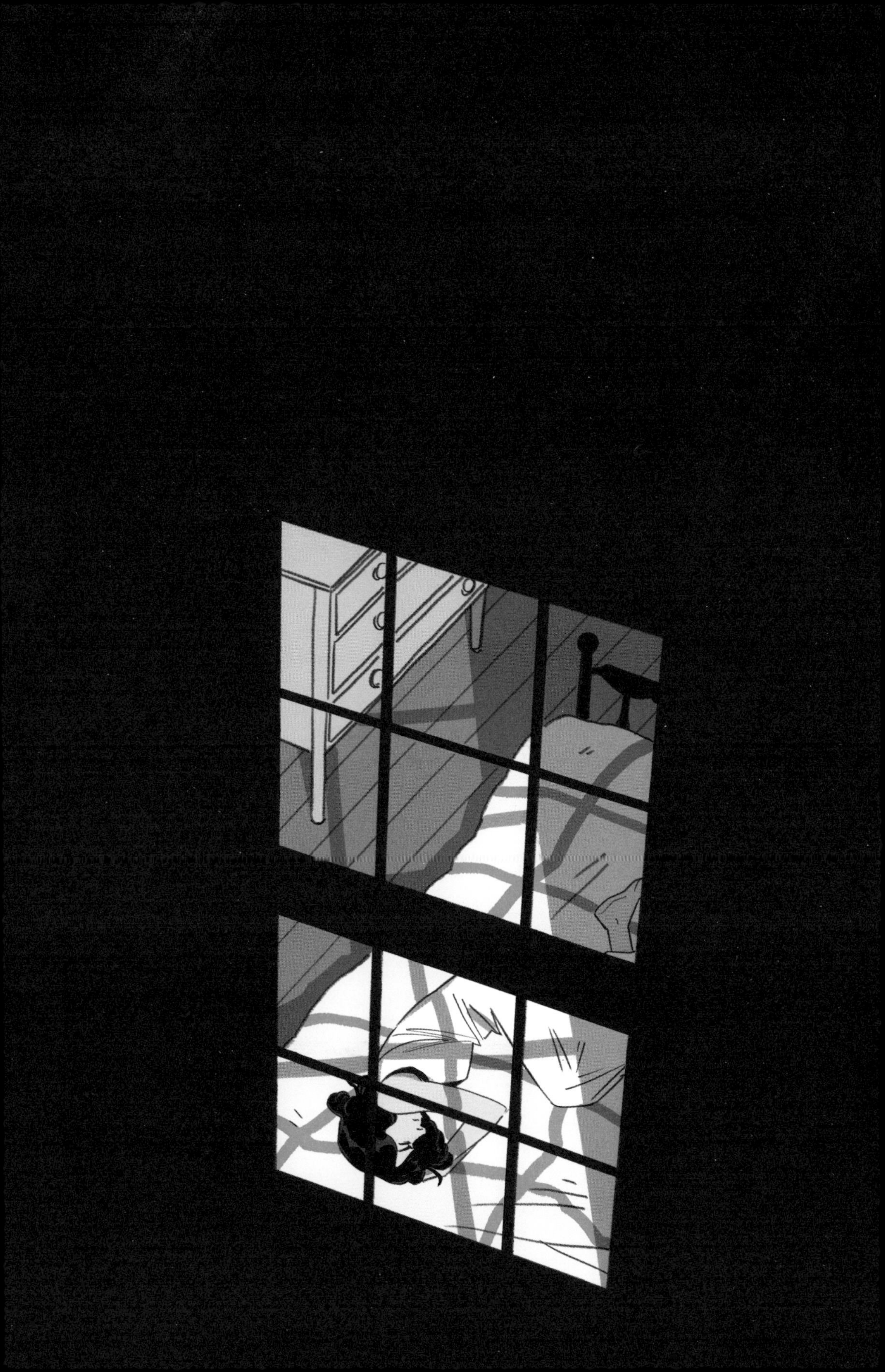

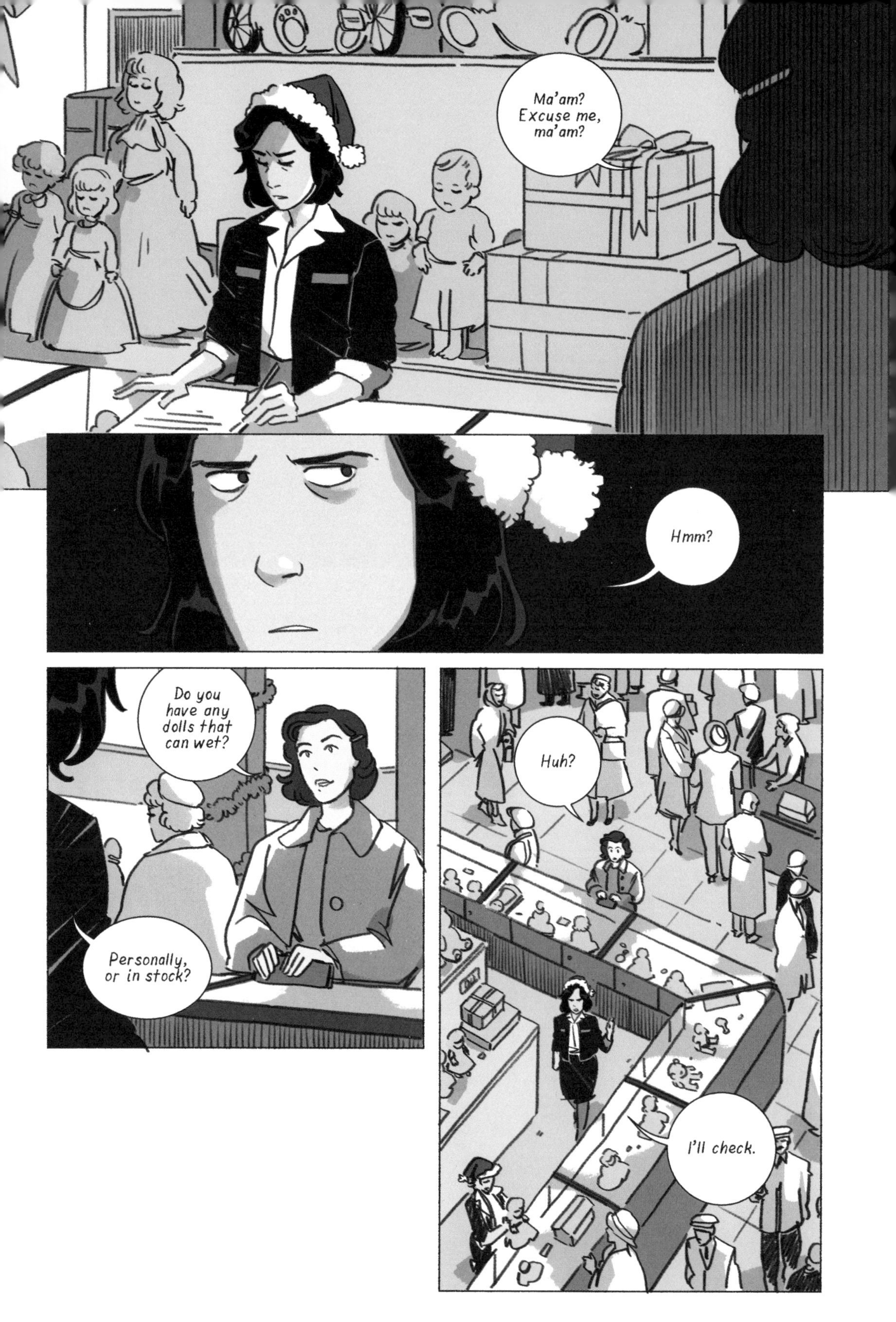
Ma'am? Excuse me, ma'am?
Hmm?
Do you have any dolls that can wet?
Personally, or in stock?
Huh?
I'll check.

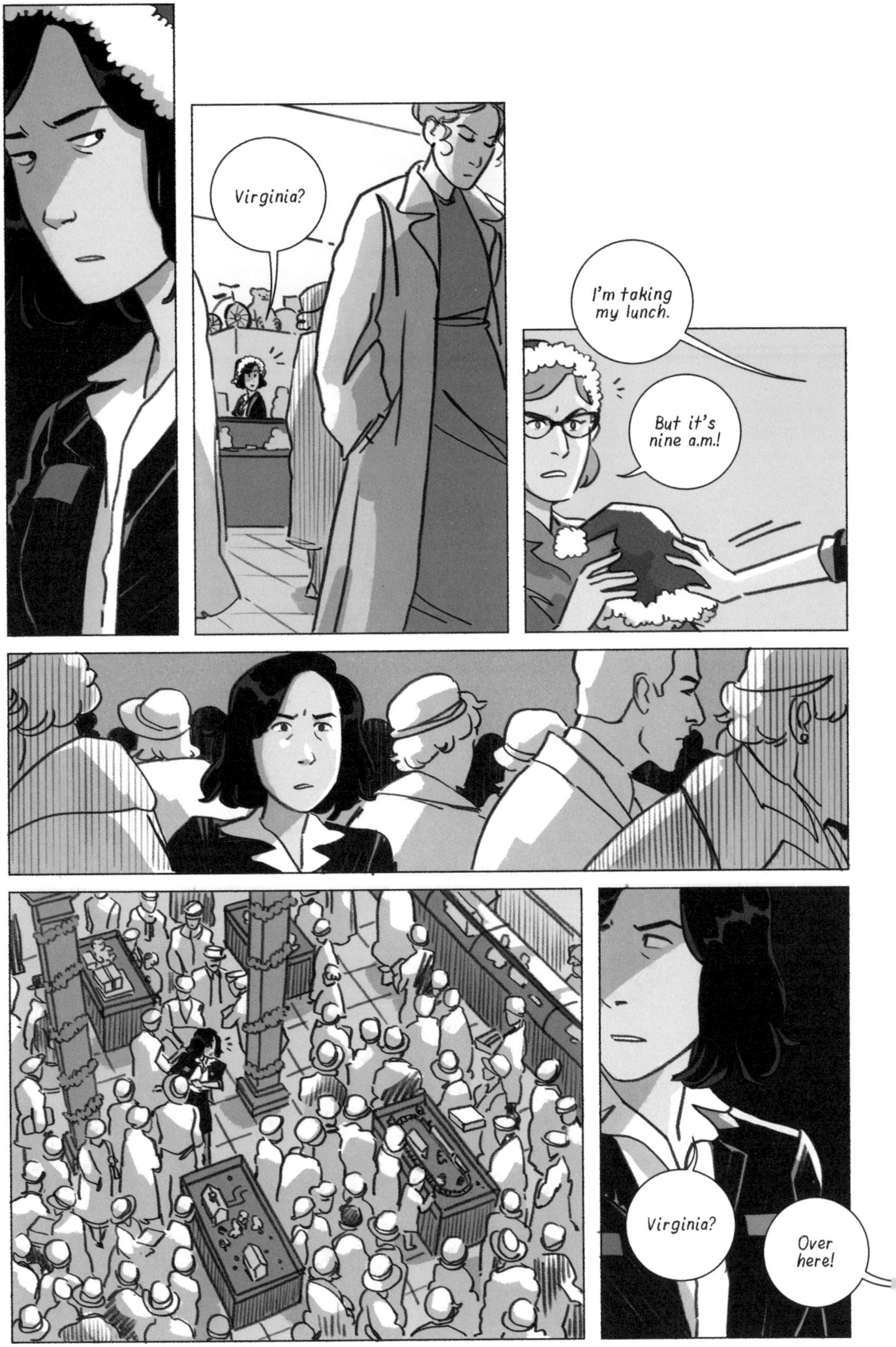
Virginia?
I'm taking my lunch.
But it's nine a.m.!
Virginia?
Over here!

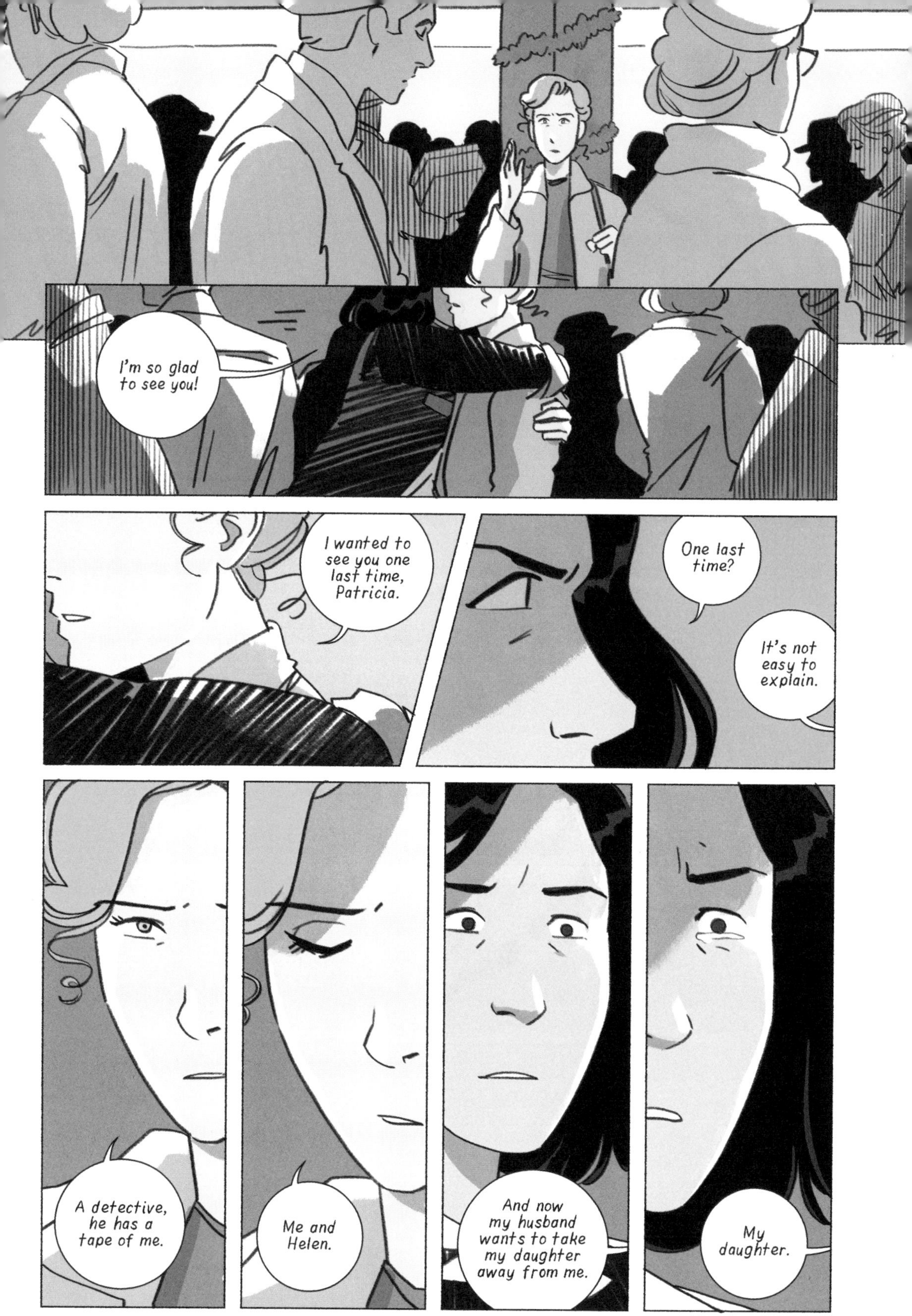
I'm so glad to see you!
I wanted to see you one last time, Patricia.
One last time?
It's not easy to explain.
A detective, he has a tape of me.
Me and Helen.
And now my husband wants to take my daughter away from me.
My daughter.

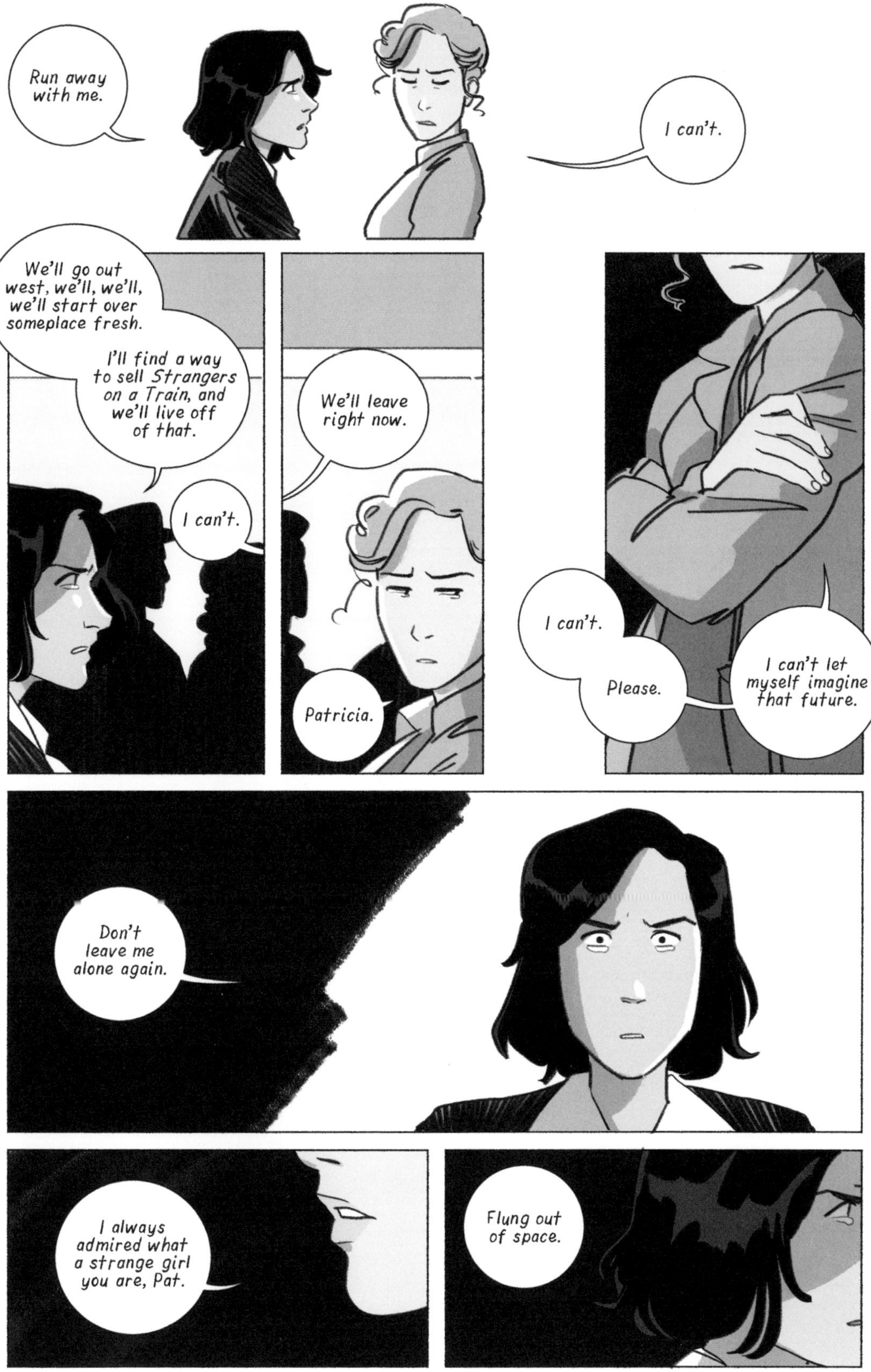
Run away with me.
I can't.
We'll go out west, we'll, we'll, we'll start over someplace fresh.
I'll find a way to sell *Strangers on a Train*, and we'll live off of that.
I can't.
We'll leave right now.
Patricia.
I can't.
Please.
I can't let myself imagine that future.
Don't leave me alone again.
I always admired what a strange girl you are, Pat.
Flung out of space.

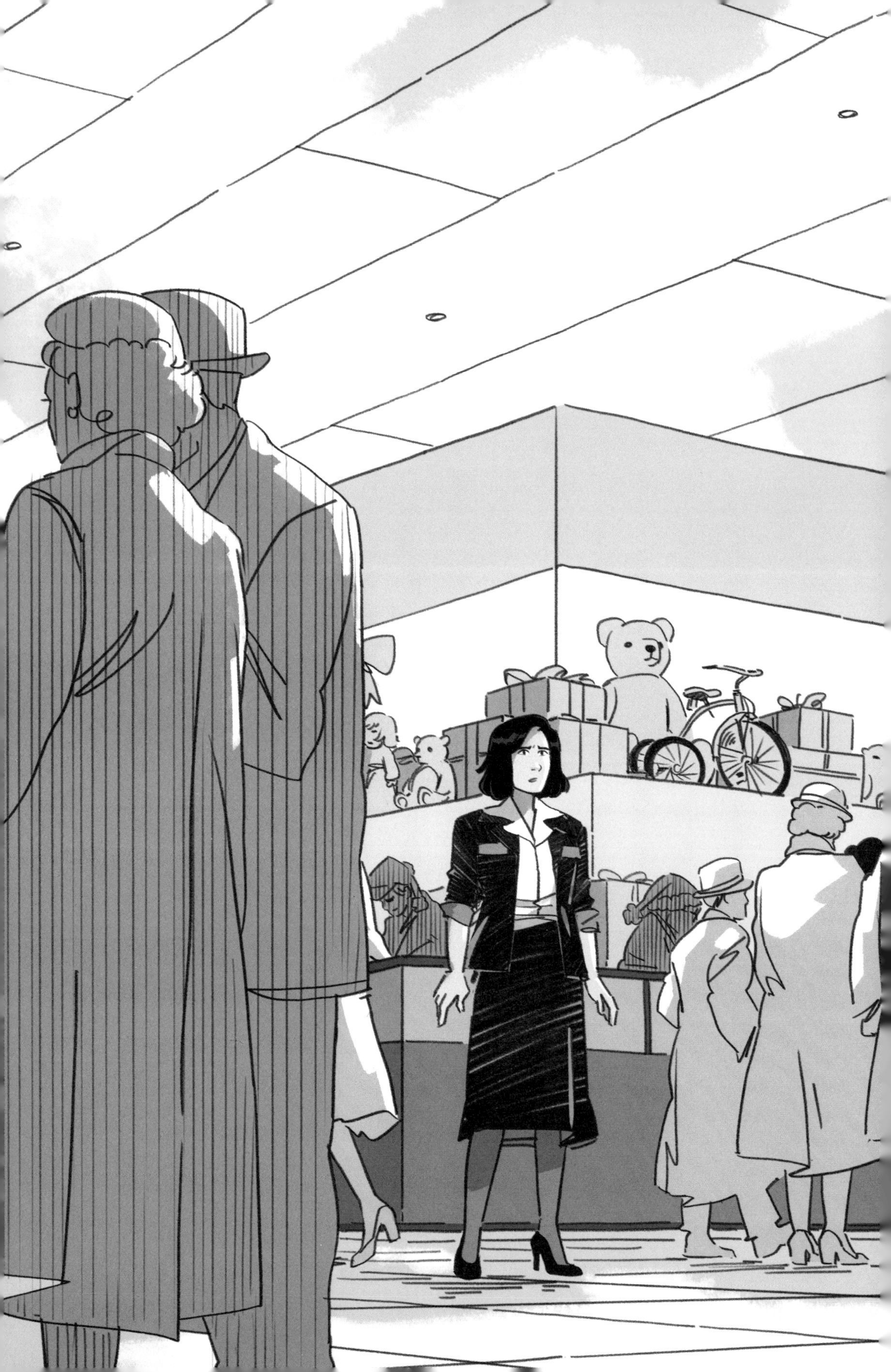

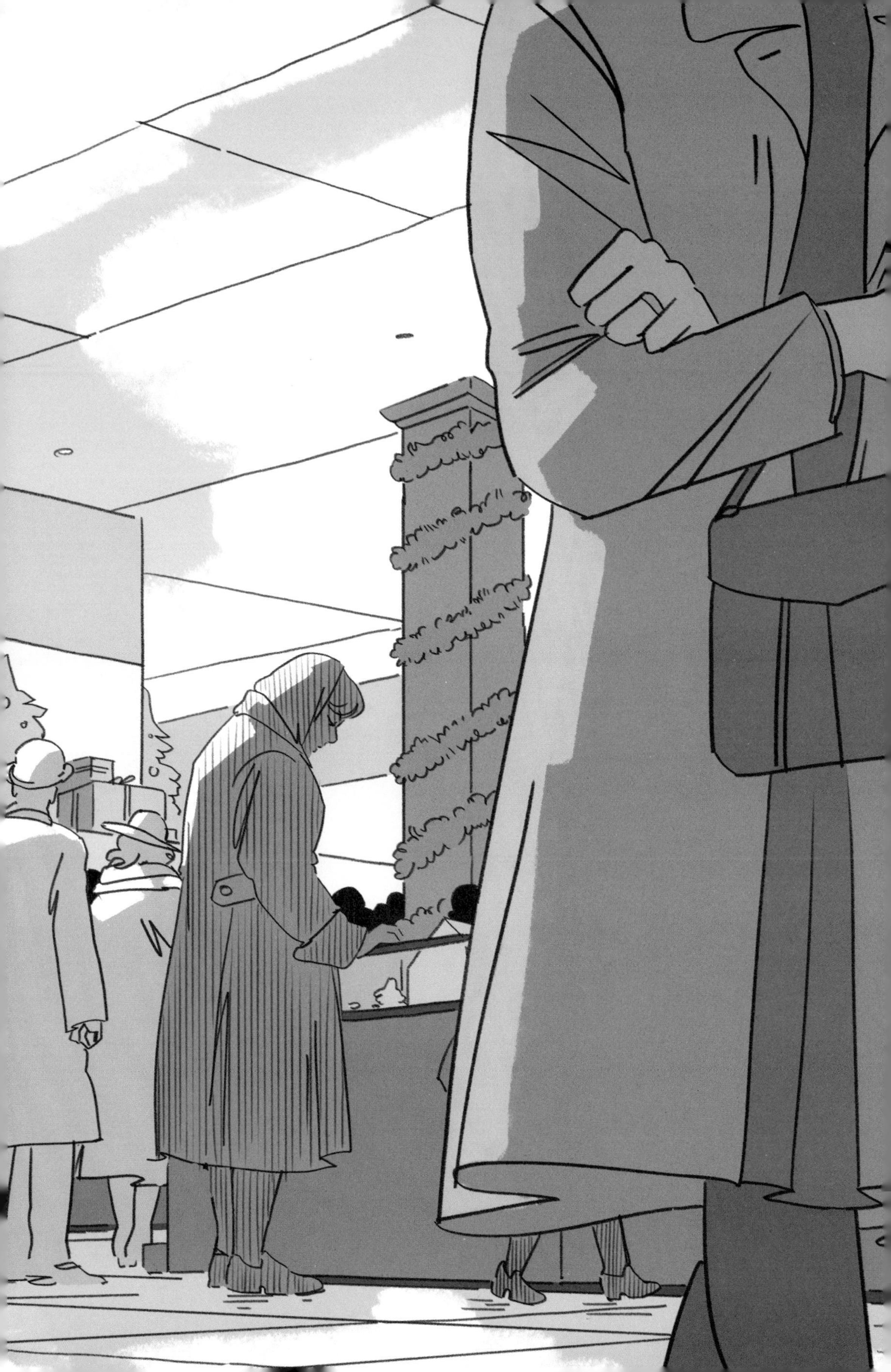

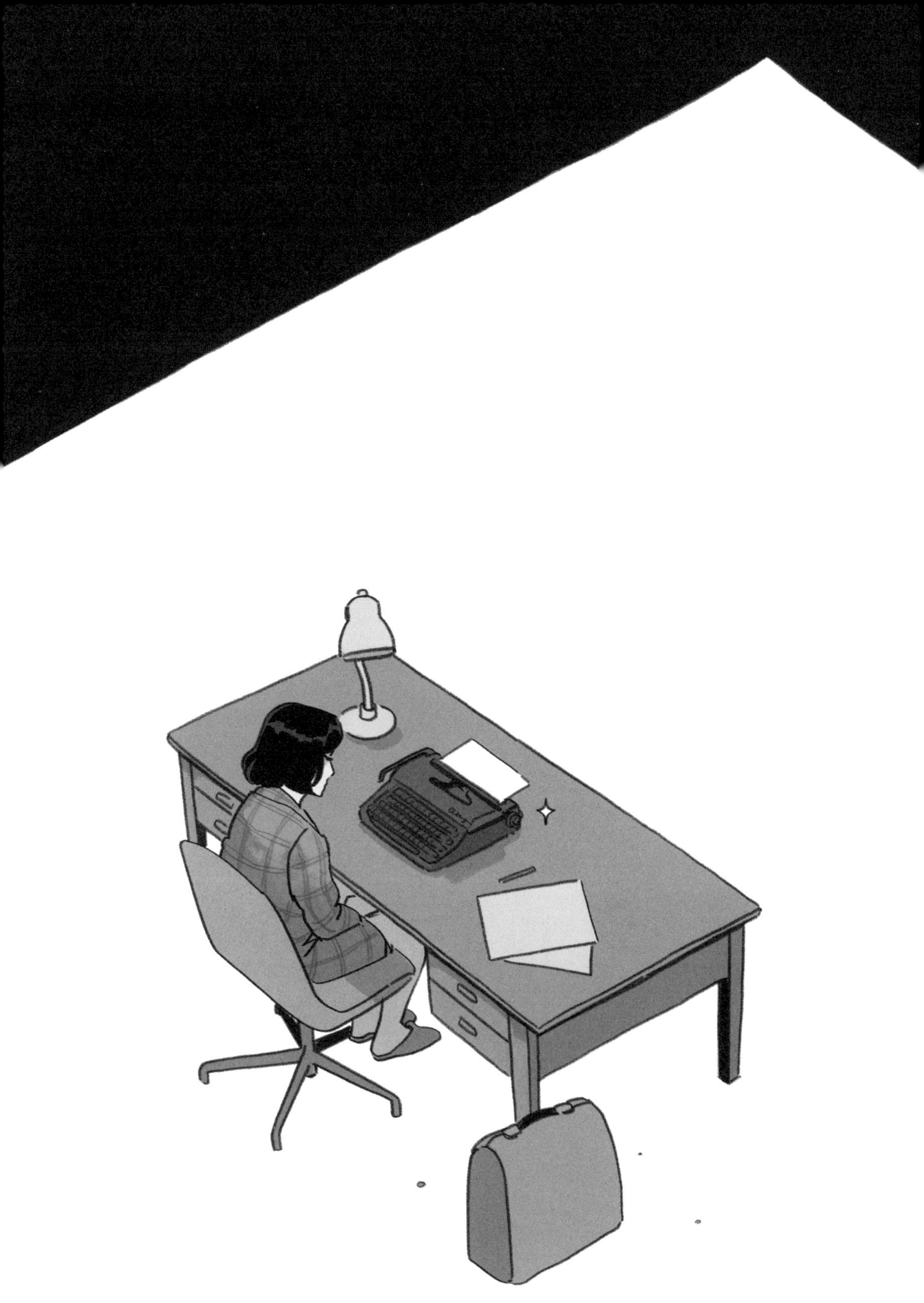

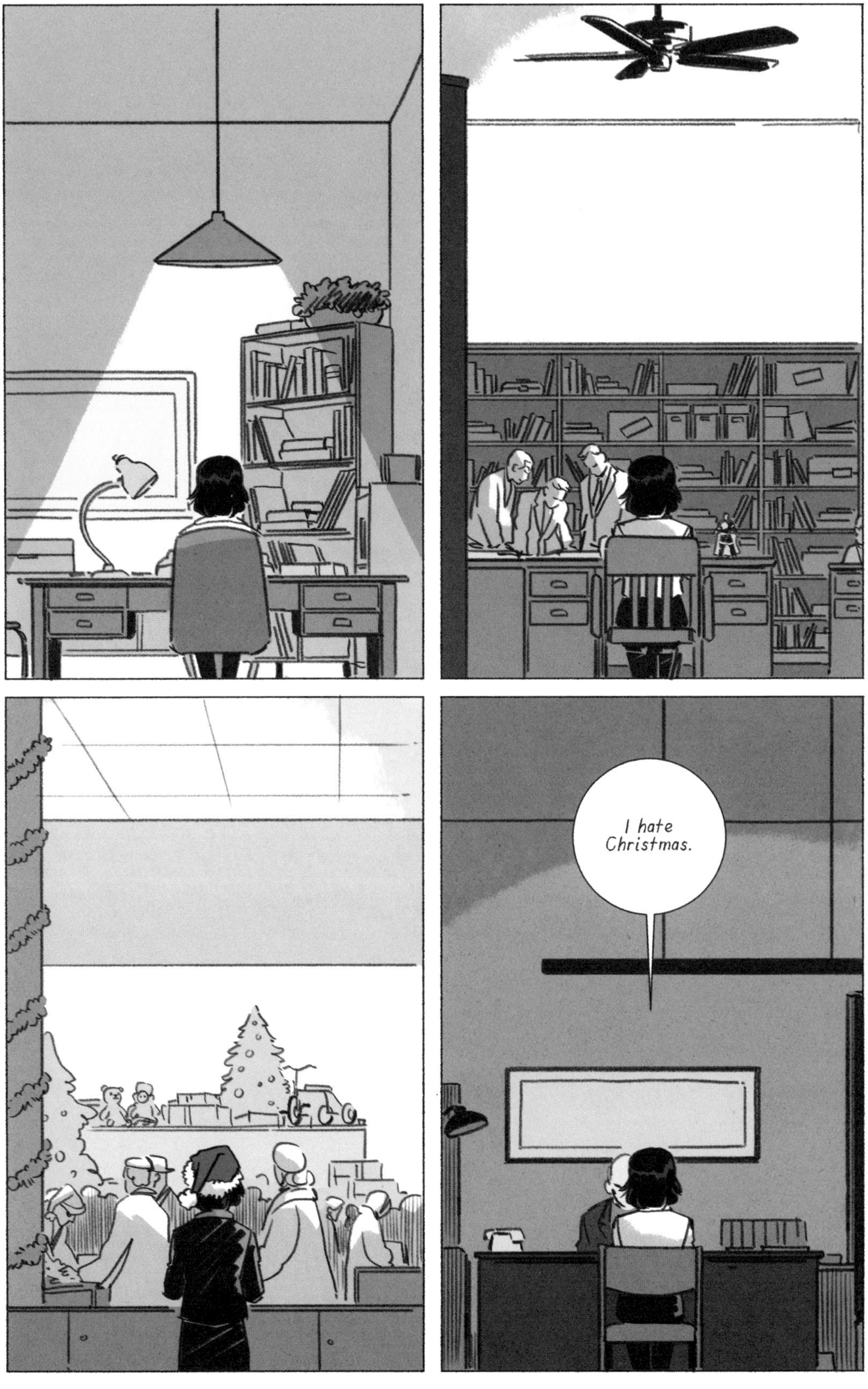
I hate Christmas.

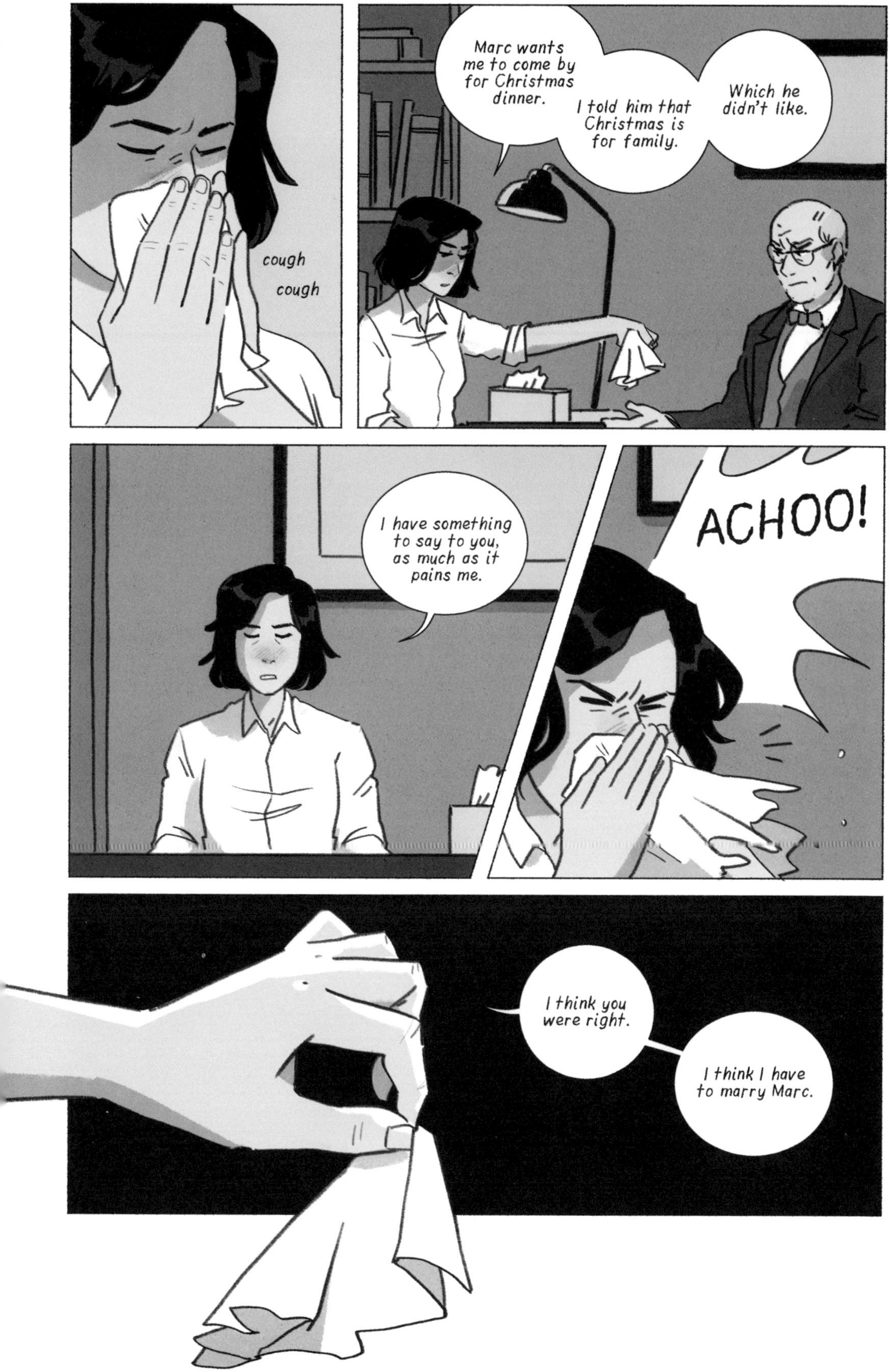
cough
cough
Marc wants me to come by for Christmas dinner.
I told him that Christmas is for family.
Which he didn't like.
I have something to say to you, as much as it pains me.
ACHOO!
I think you were right.
I think I have to marry Marc.

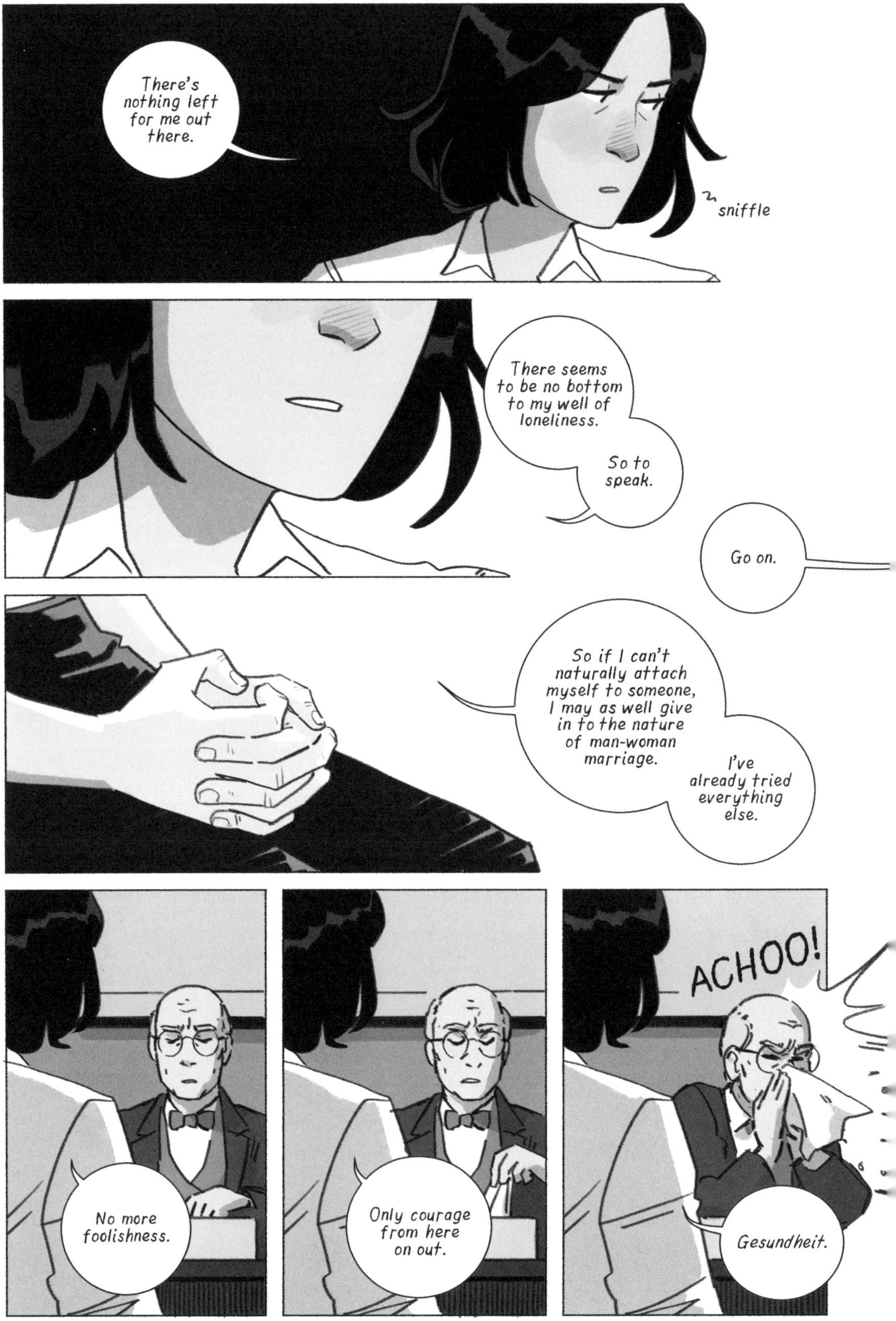
There's nothing left for me out there.
sniffle
There seems to be no bottom to my well of loneliness.
So to speak.
Go on.
So if I can't naturally attach myself to someone, I may as well give in to the nature of man-woman marriage.
I've already tried everything else.
No more foolishness.
Only courage from here on out.
ACHOO!
Gesundheit.

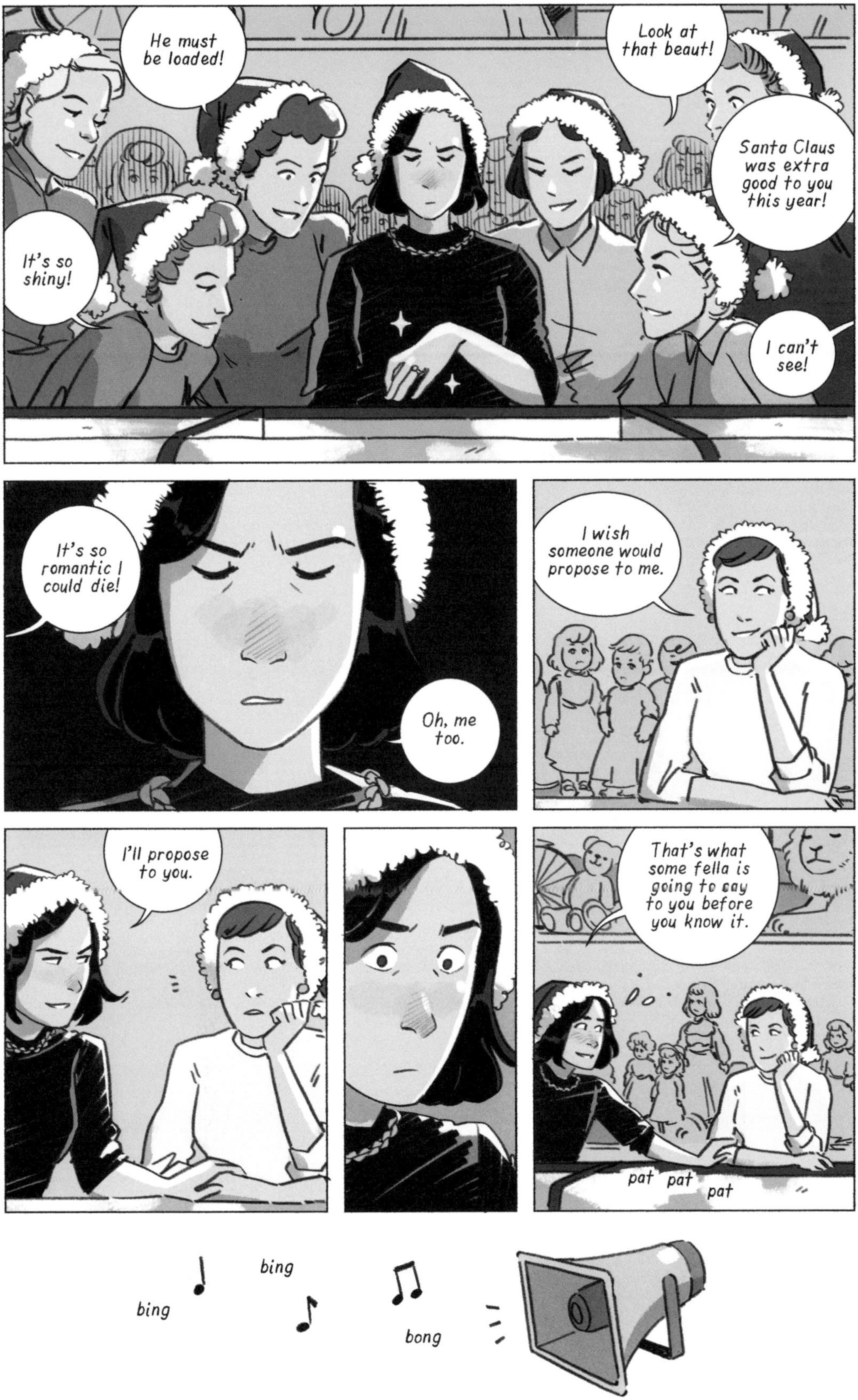
He must be loaded!
Look at that beaut!
Santa Claus was extra good to you this year!
It's so shiny!
I can't see!
It's so romantic I could die!
Oh, me too.
I wish someone would propose to me.
I'll propose to you.
That's what some fella is going to say to you before you know it.
pat pat pat
bing
bing
bong

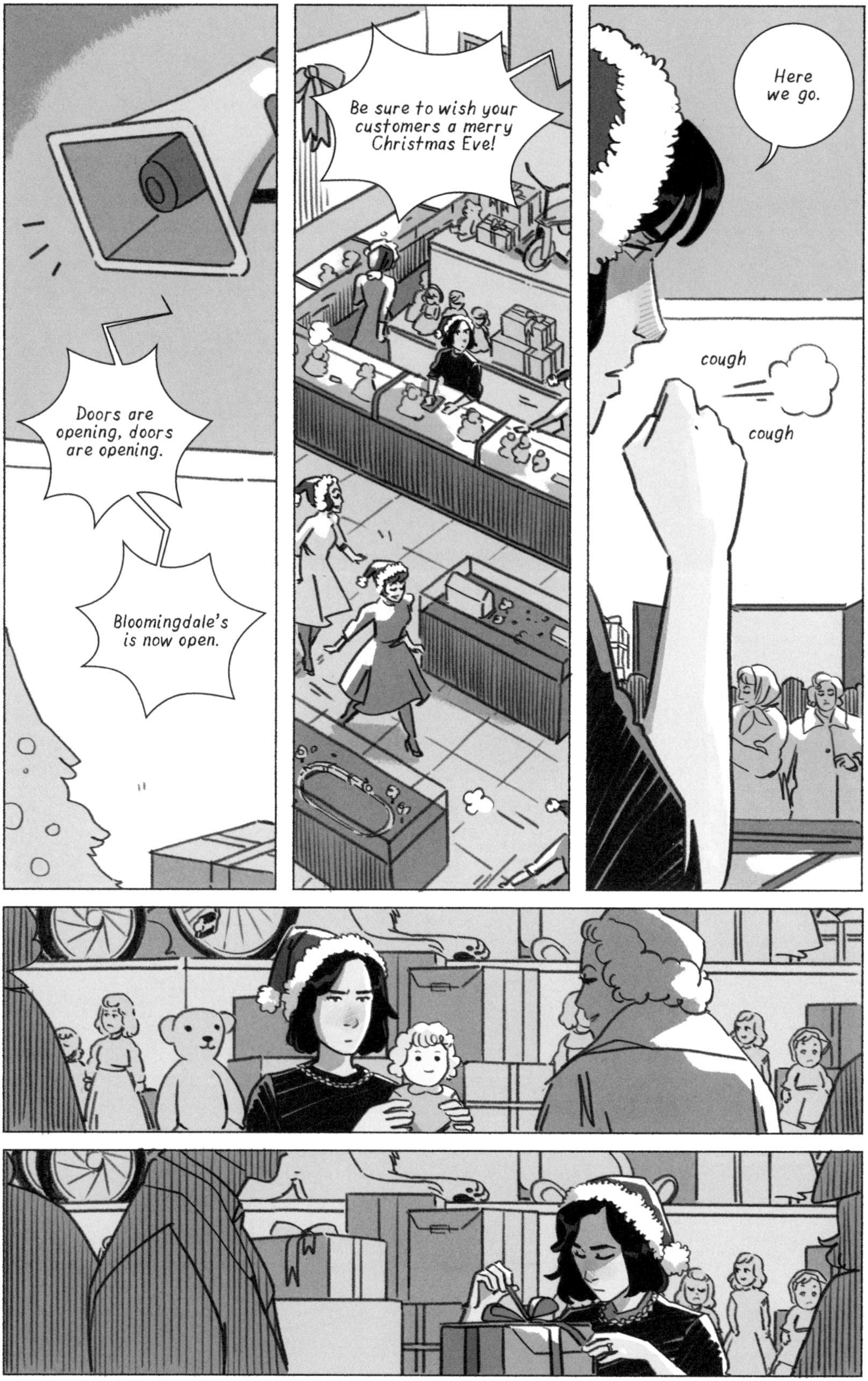
Doors are opening, doors are opening.
Bloomingdale's is now open.
Be sure to wish your customers a merry Christmas Eve!
Here we go.
cough
cough

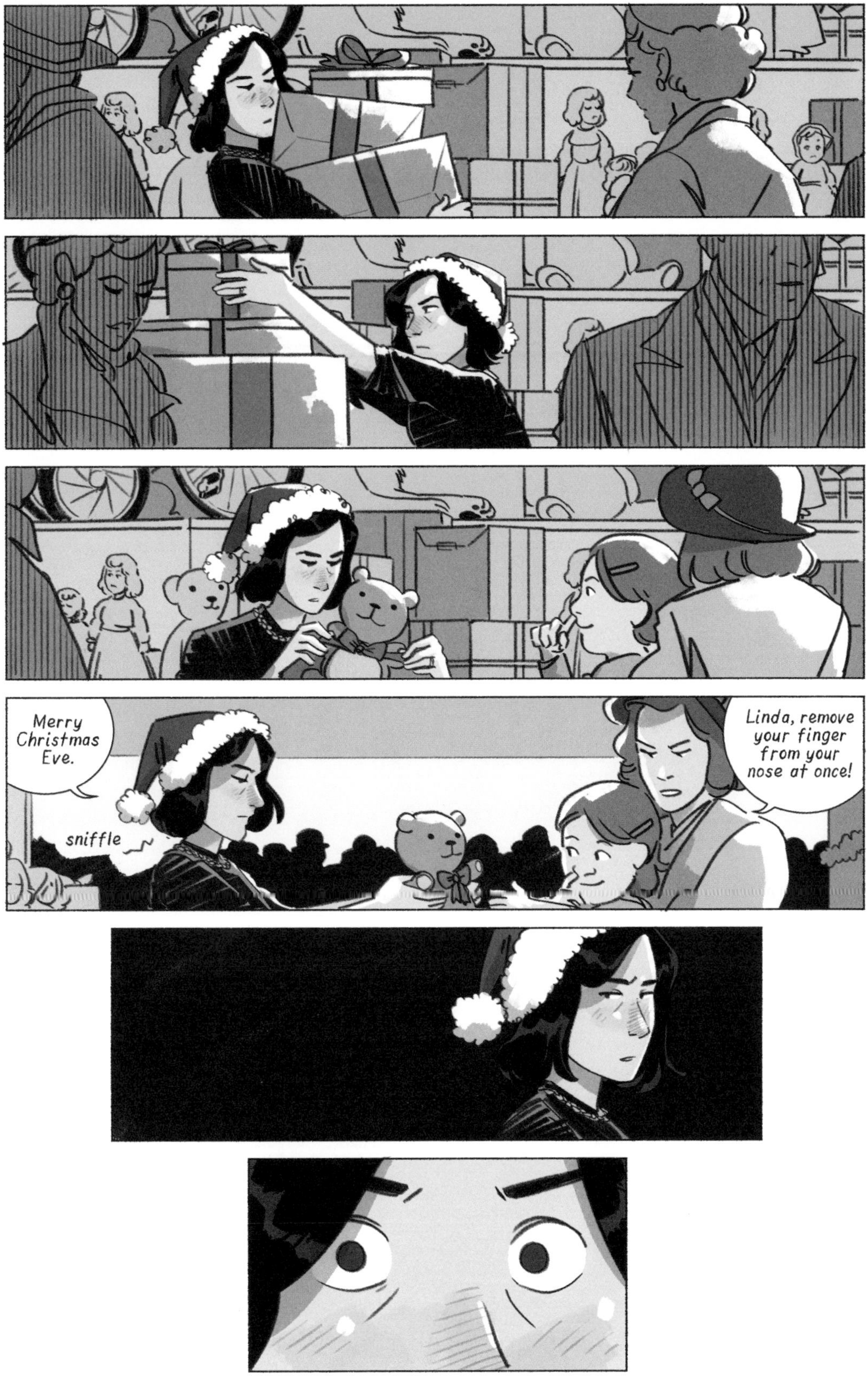
Merry Christmas Eve.
sniffle
Linda, remove your finger from your nose at once!

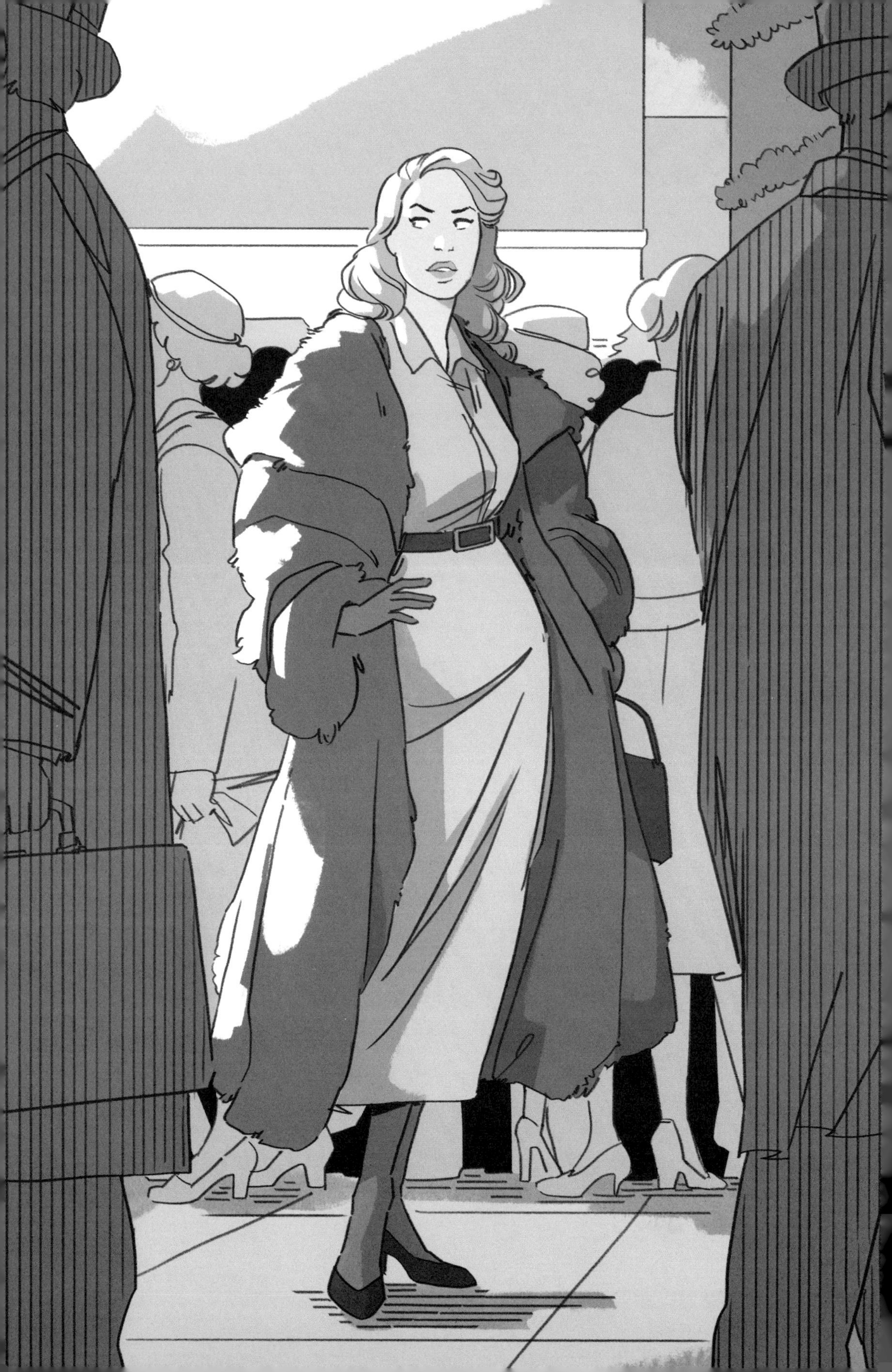

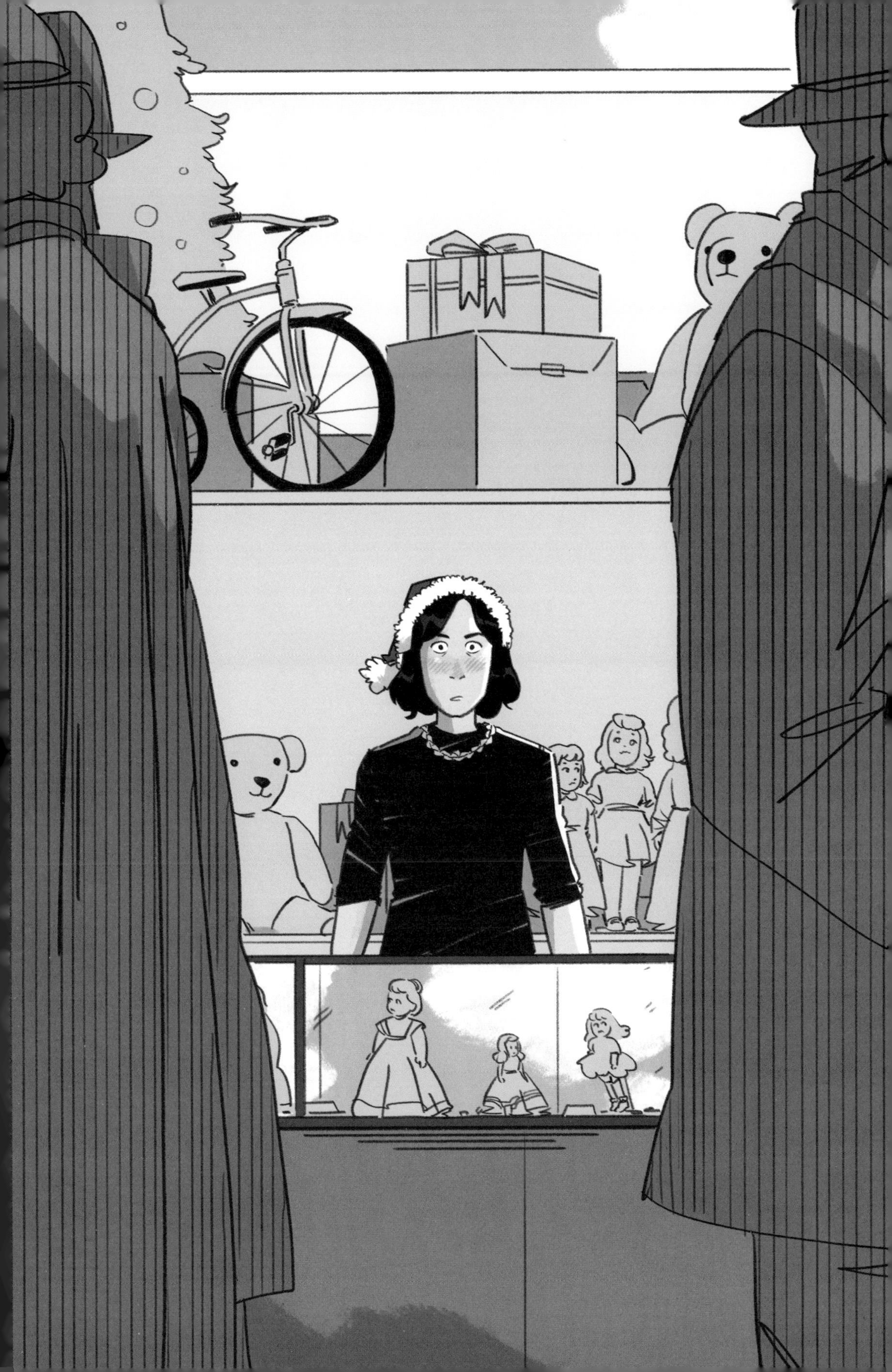

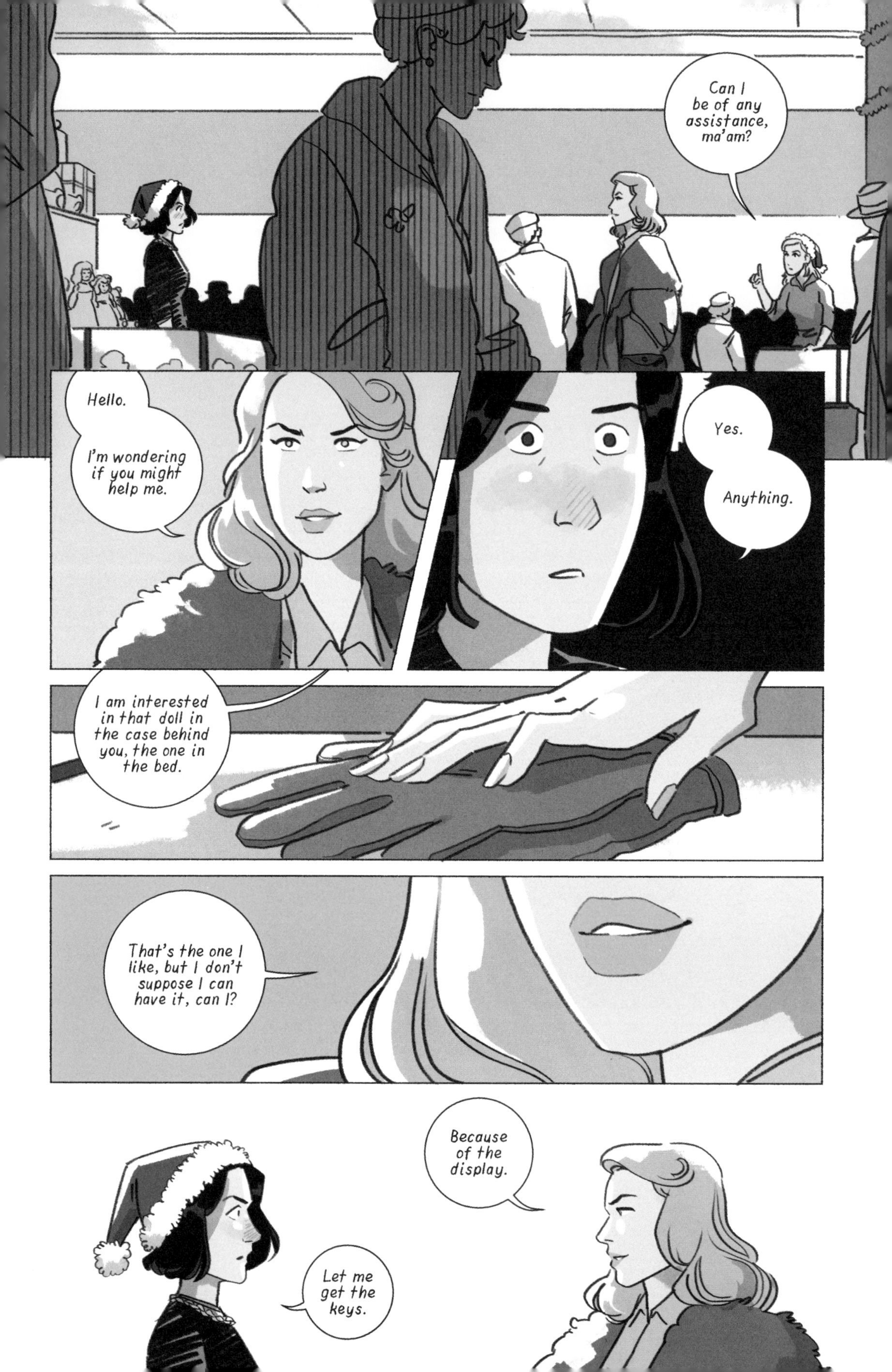

Can I be of any assistance, ma'am?
Hello.
I'm wondering if you might help me.
Yes.
Anything.
I am interested in that doll in the case behind you, the one in the bed.
That's the one I like, but I don't suppose I can have it, can I?
Because of the display.
Let me get the keys.

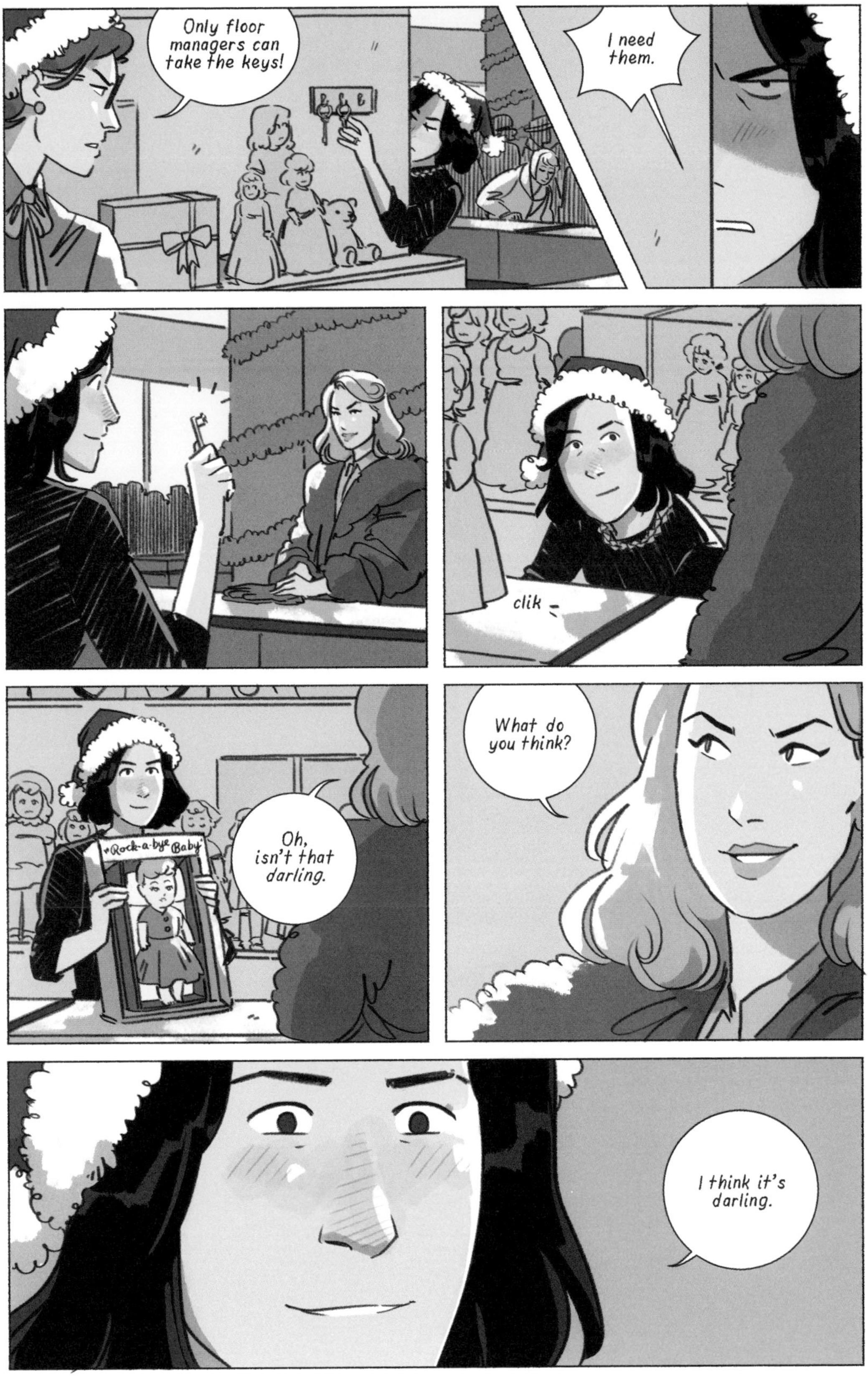
Only floor managers can take the keys!
I need them.
clik
"Rock-a-bye Baby"
Oh, isn't that darling.
What do you think?
I think it's darling.

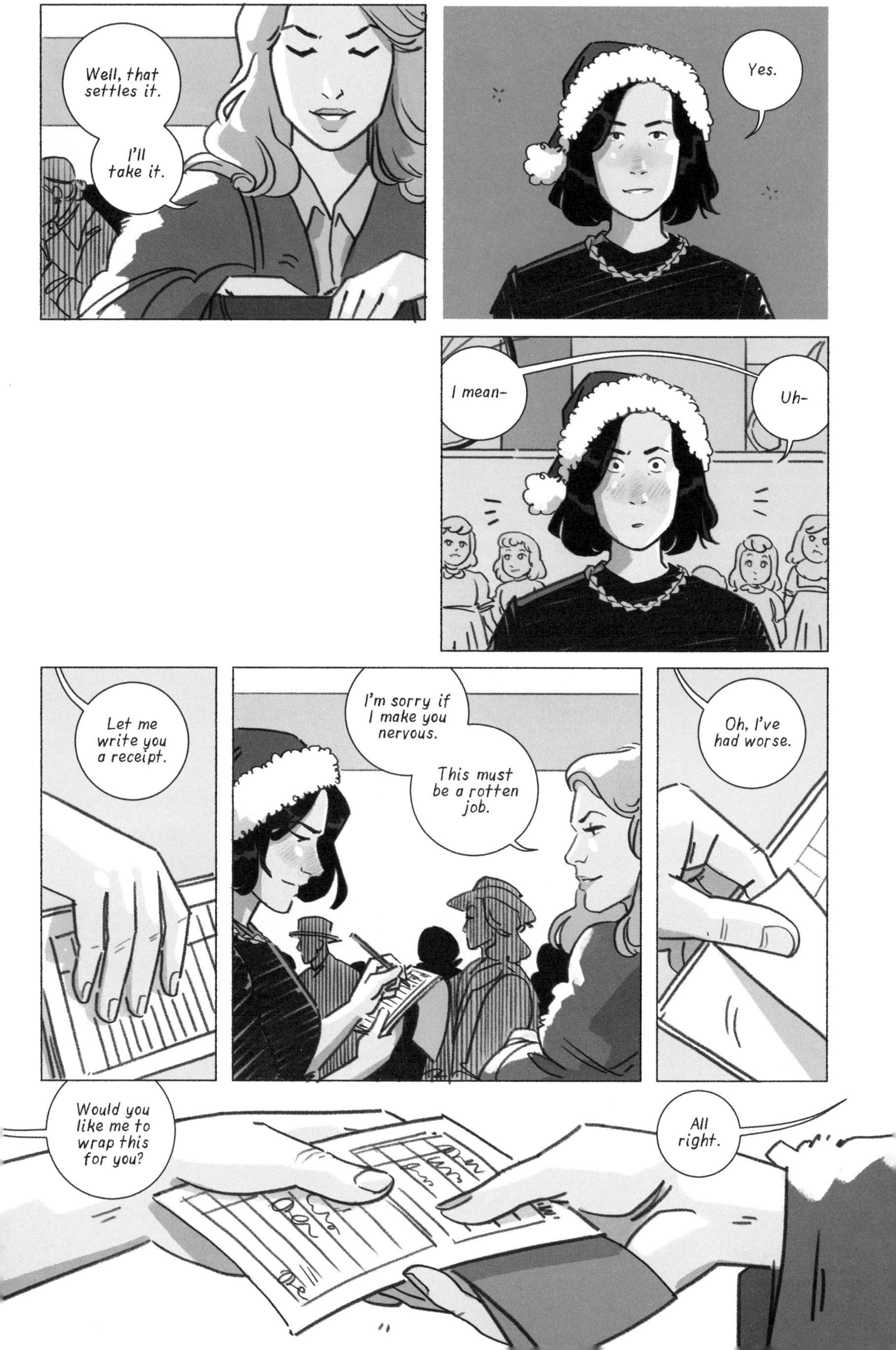
Well, that settles it.
I'll take it.
Yes.
I mean-
Uh-
Let me write you a receipt.
I'm sorry if I make you nervous.
This must be a rotten job.
Oh, I've had worse.
Would you like me to wrap this for you?
All right.

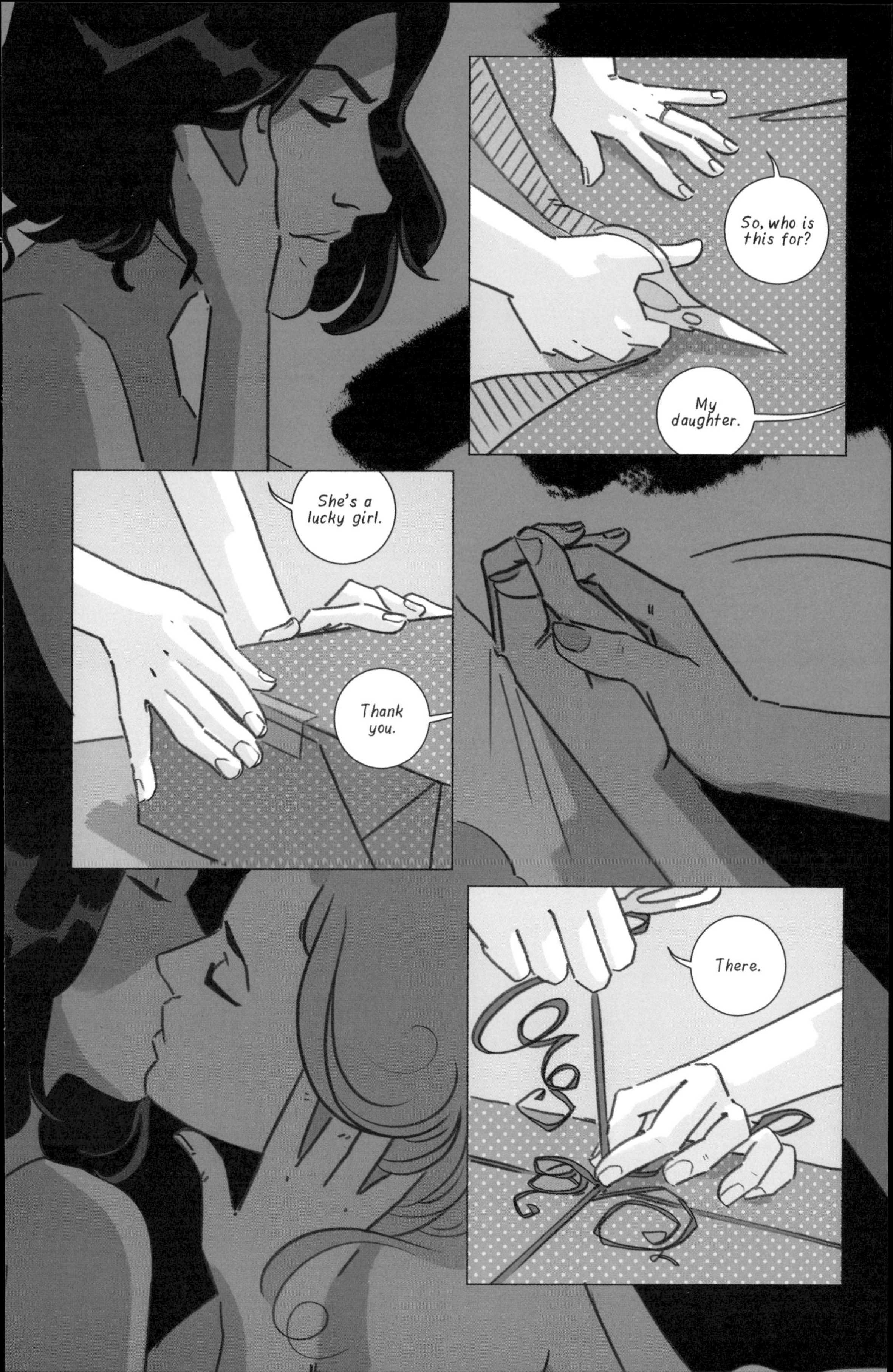
So, who is this for?
My daughter.
She's a lucky girl.
Thank you.
There.

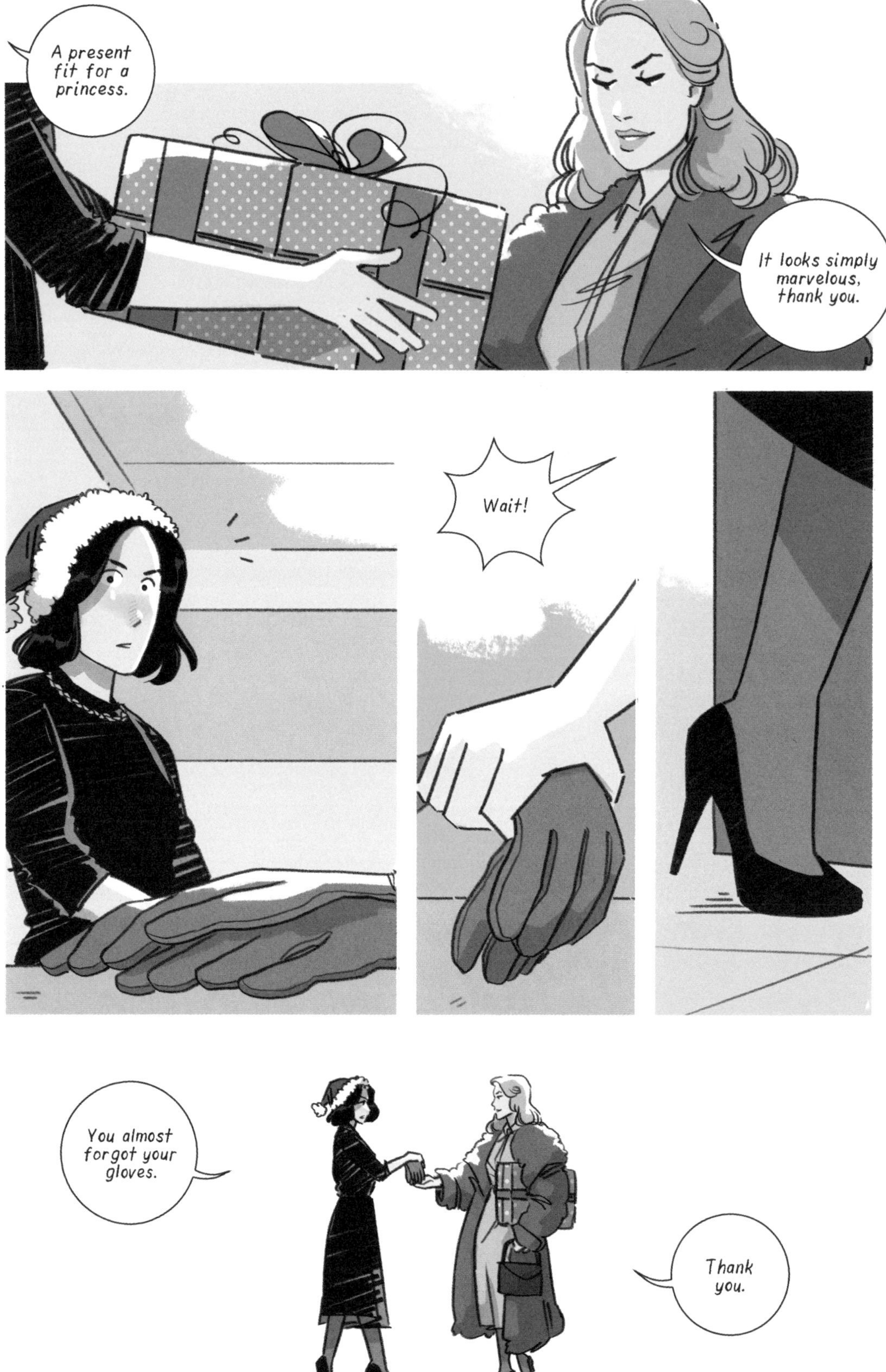
A present fit for a princess.
It looks simply marvelous, thank you.
Wait!
You almost forgot your gloves.
Thank you.

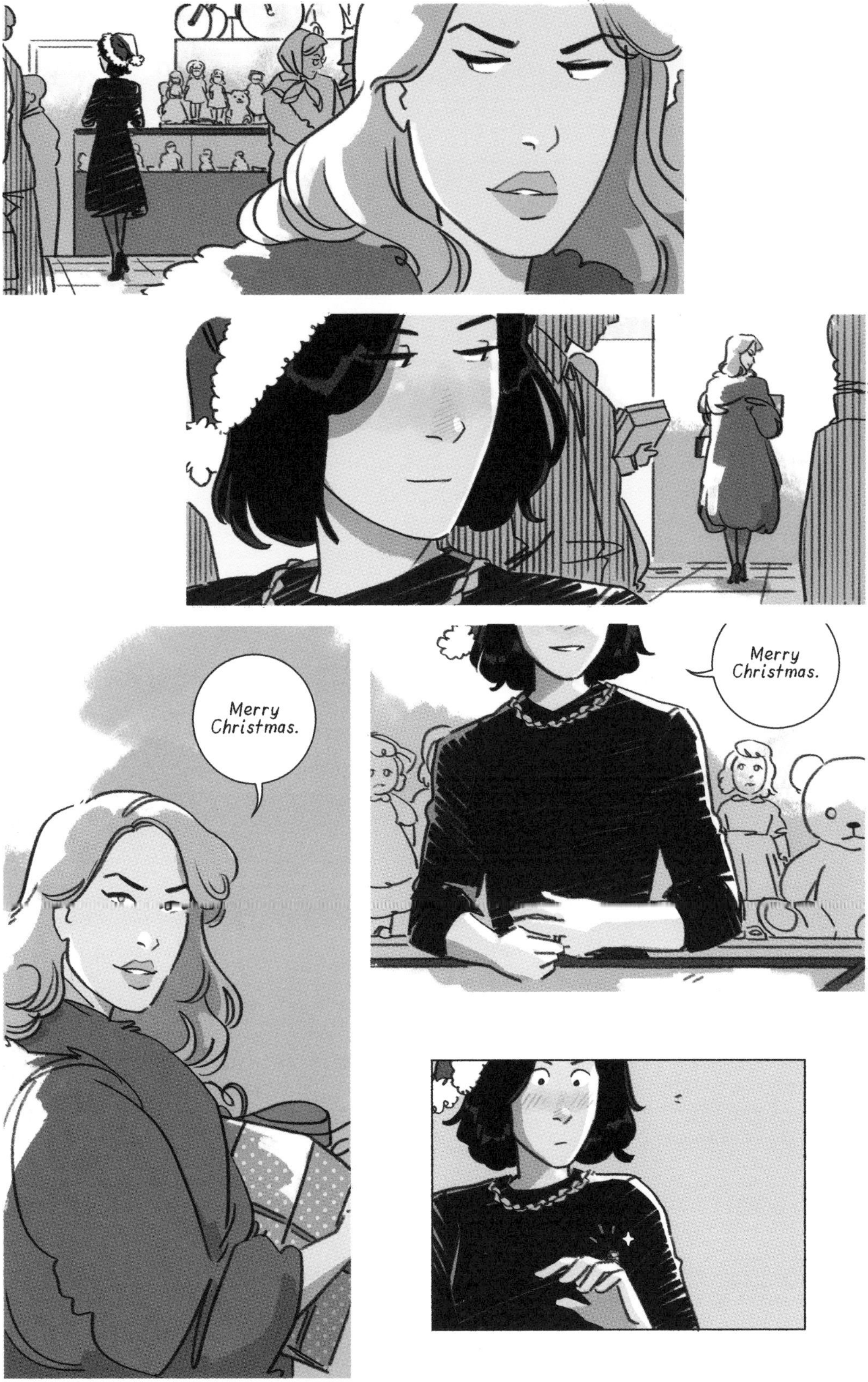
Merry Christmas.
Merry Christmas.

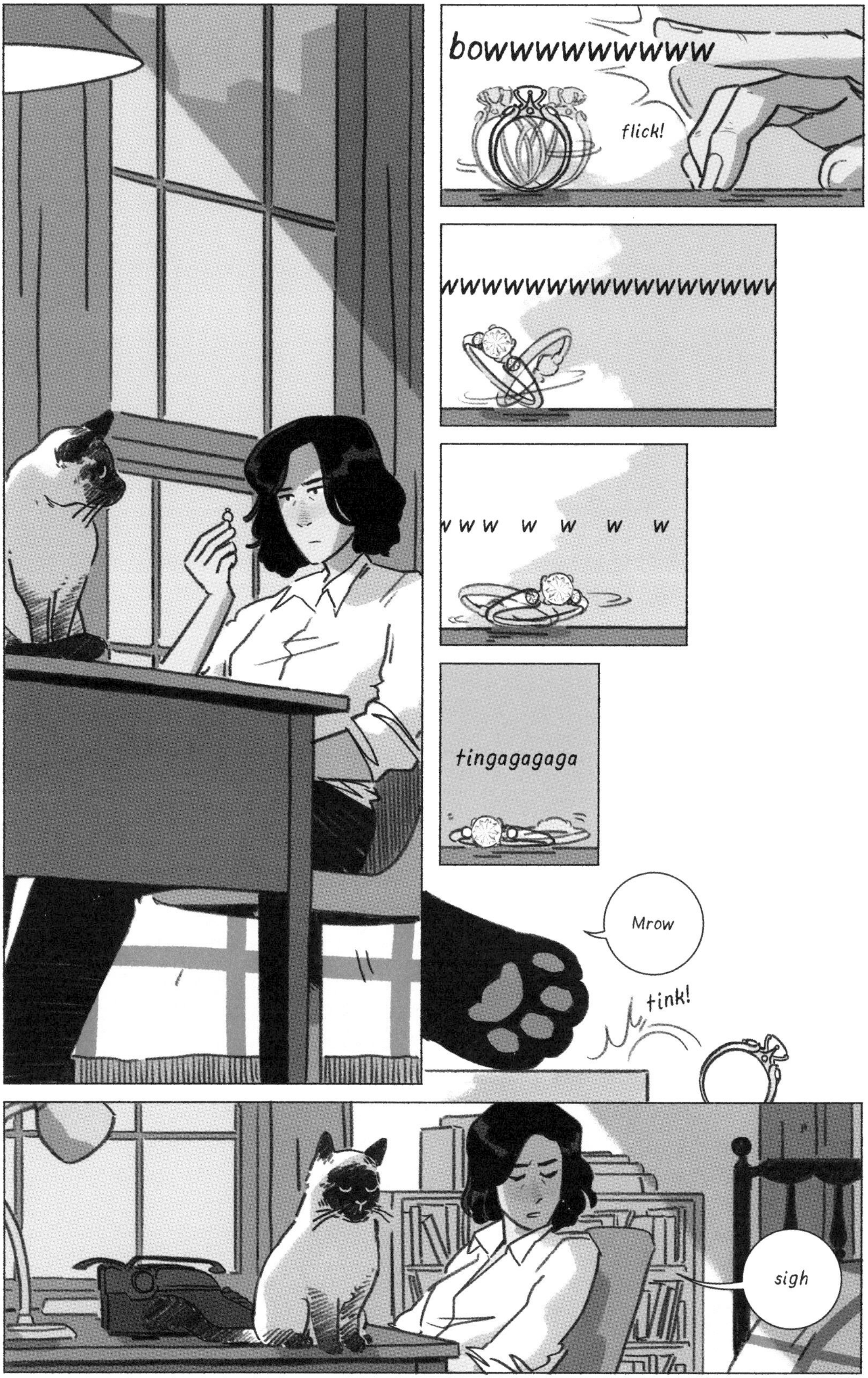
bowwwwwwwwww
flick!
wwwwwwwwwwwwwwwwww
www w w w w
tingagagaga
Mrow
tink!
sigh

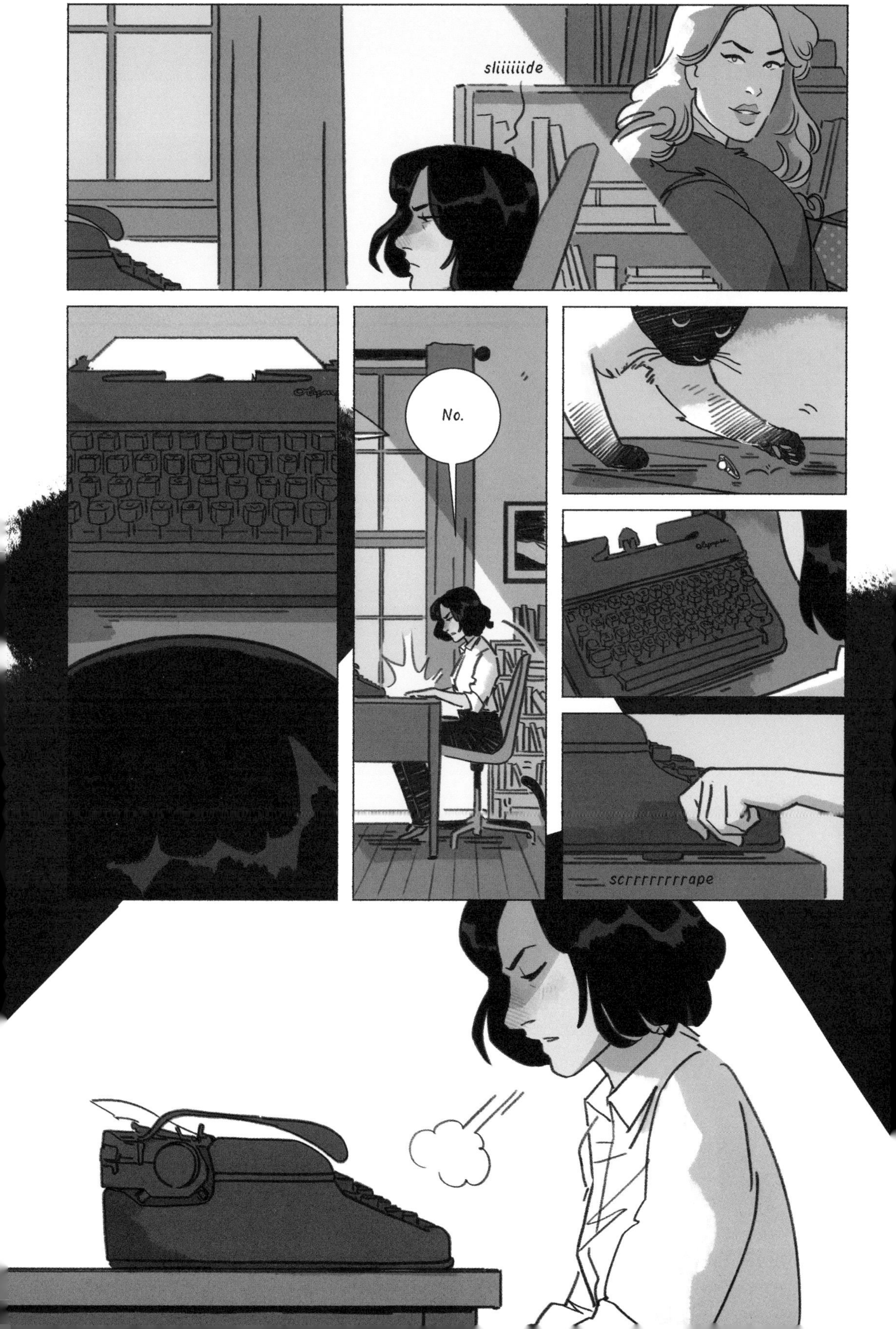
sliiiiiide
No.
scrrrrrrrrape

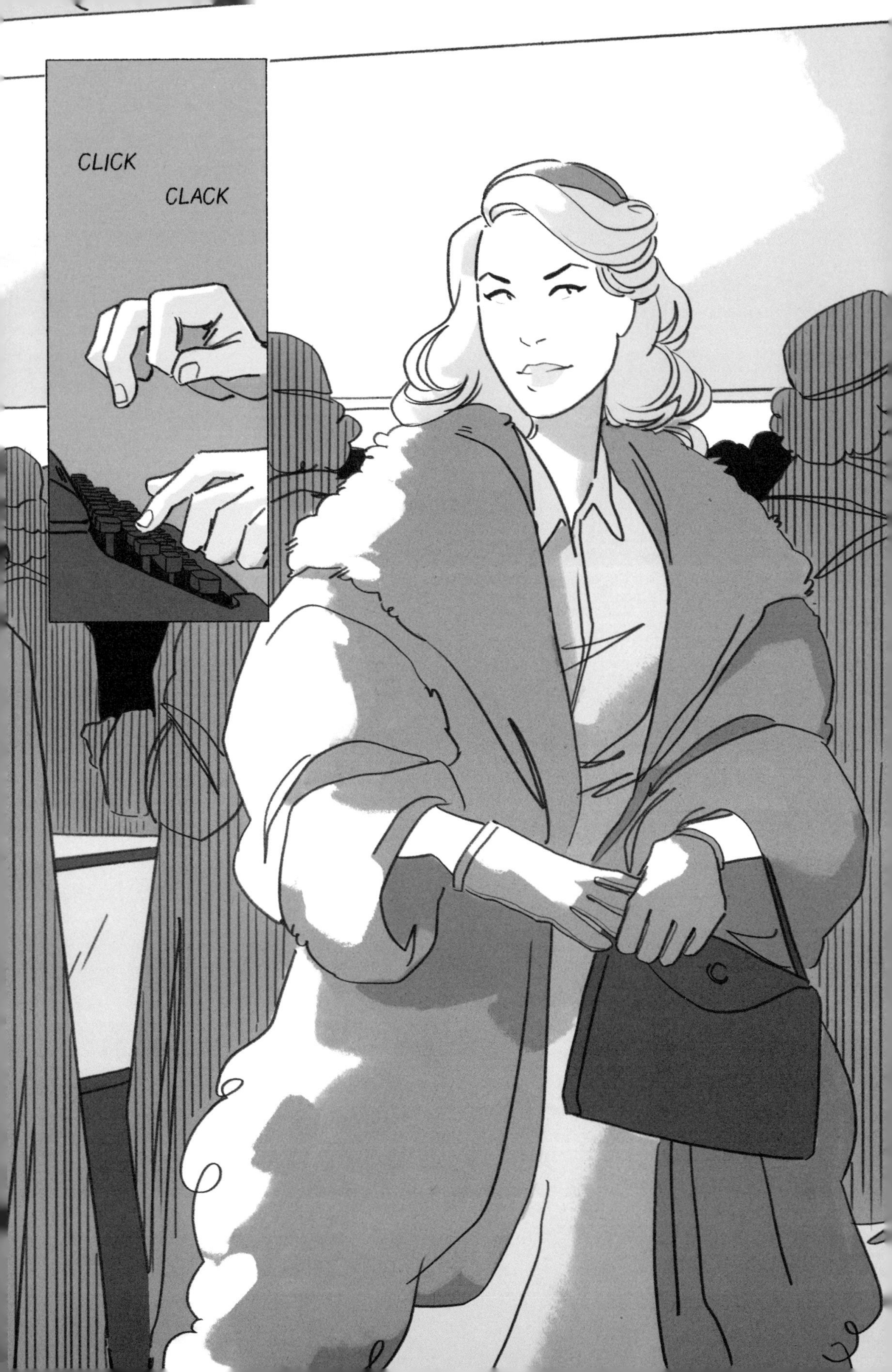
CLICK
CLACK

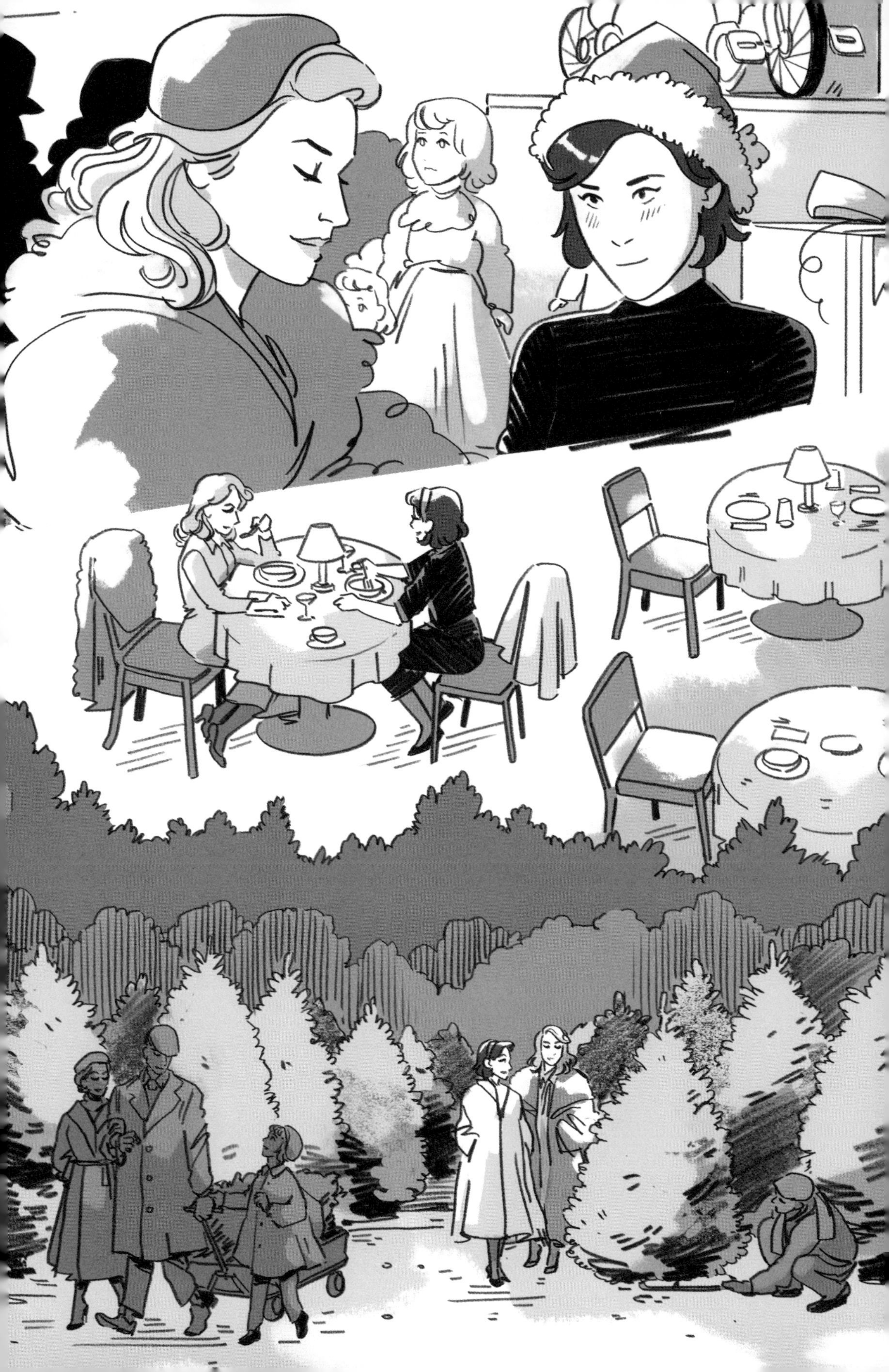

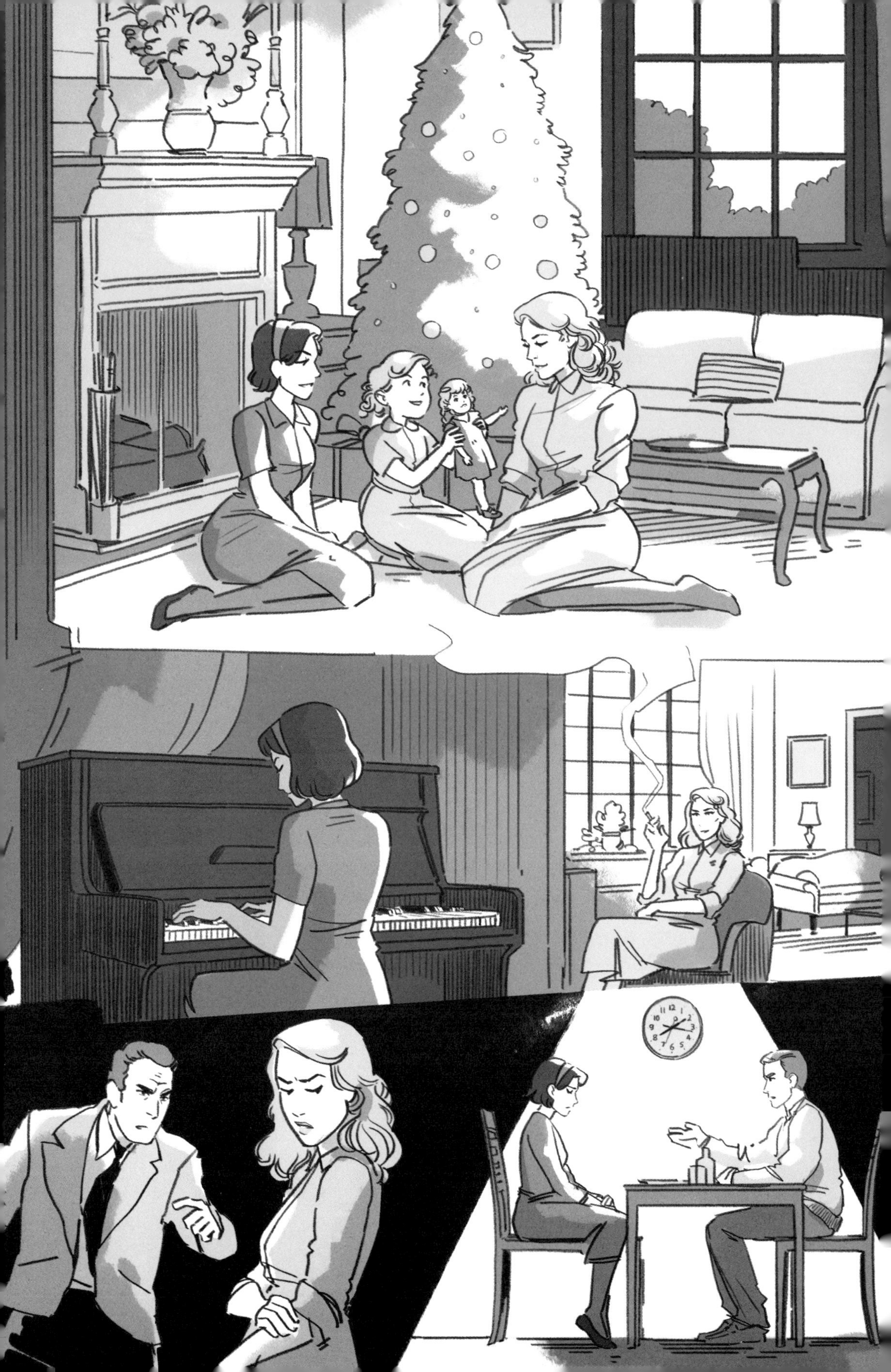

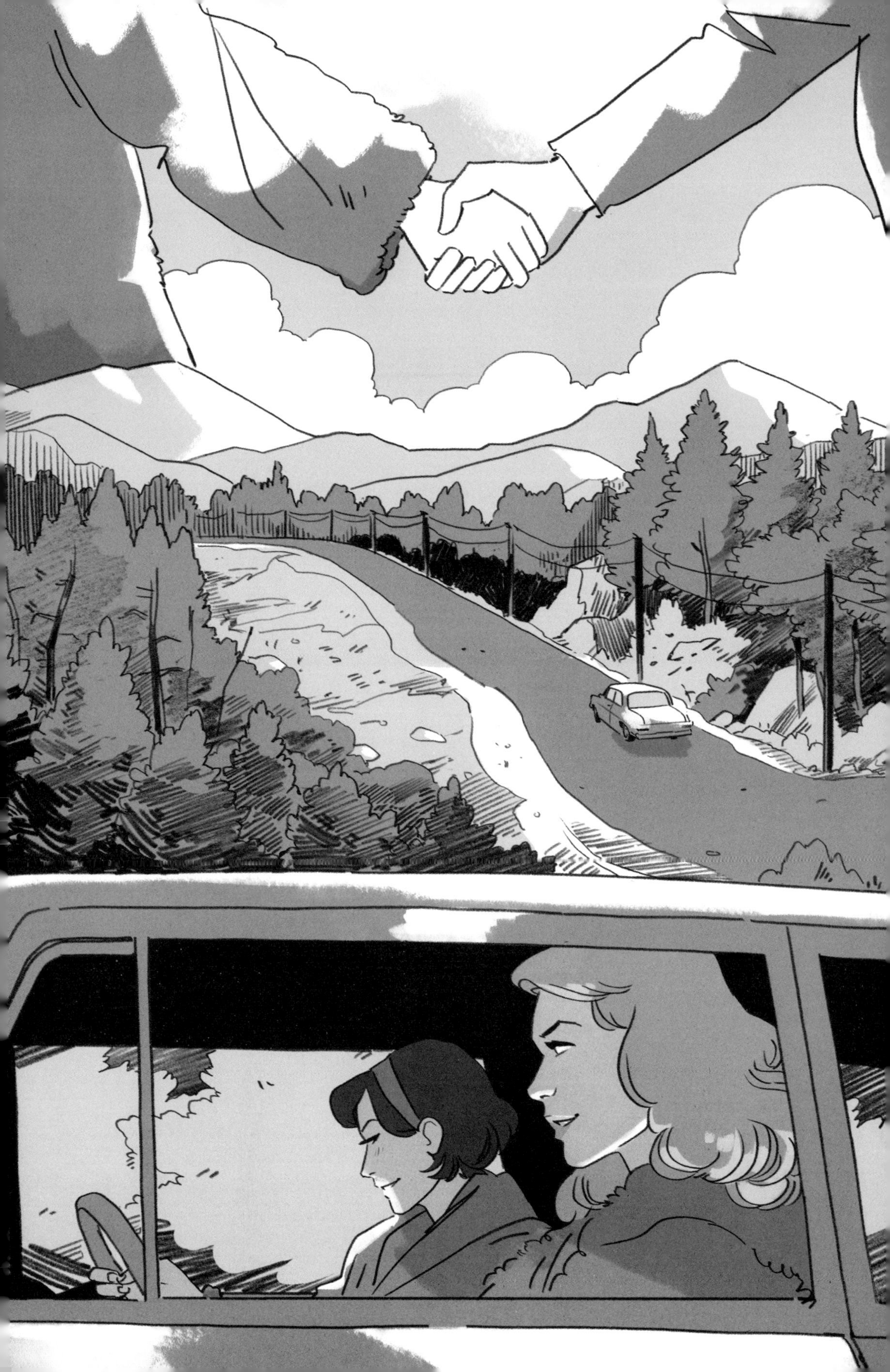

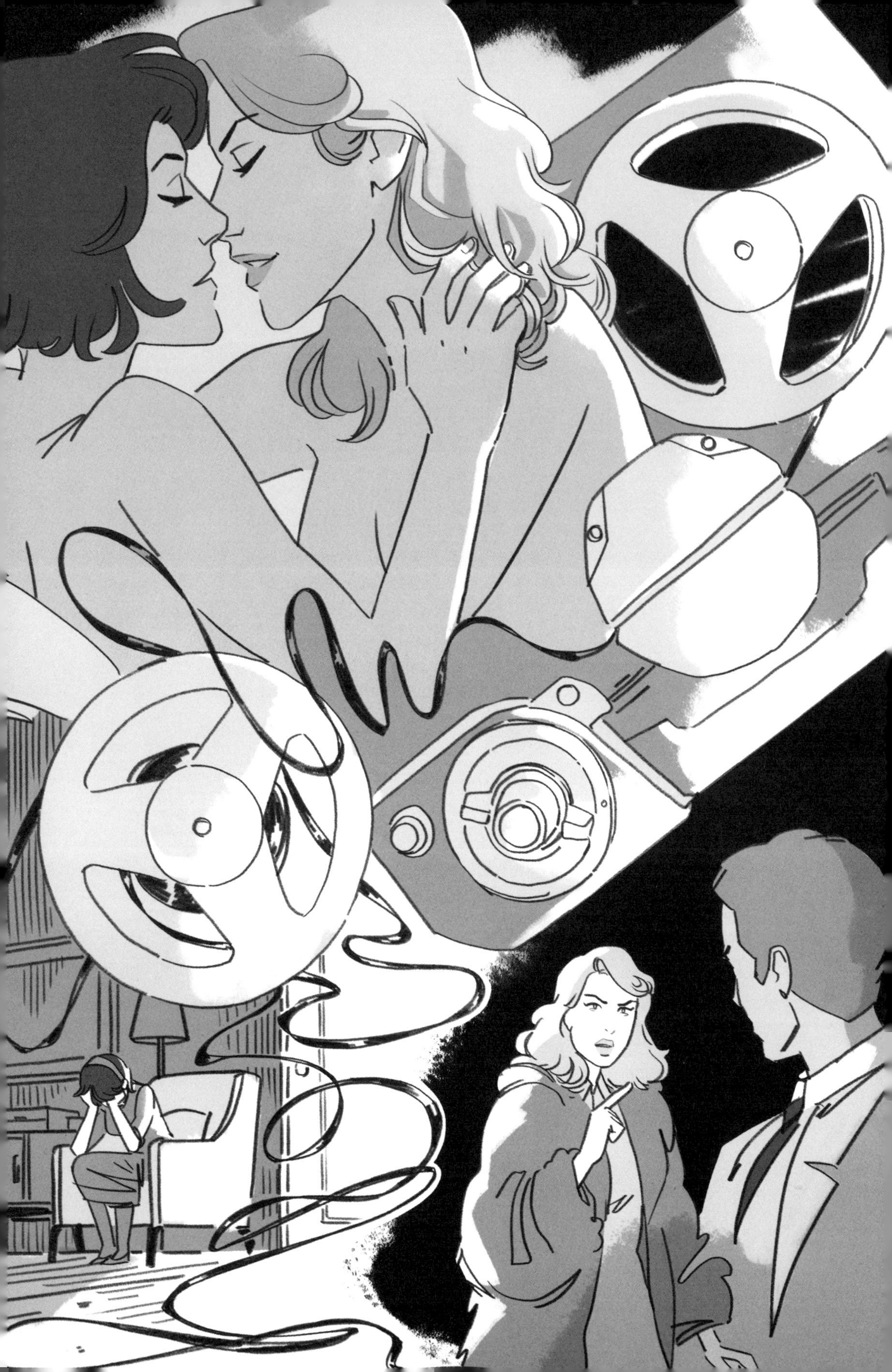

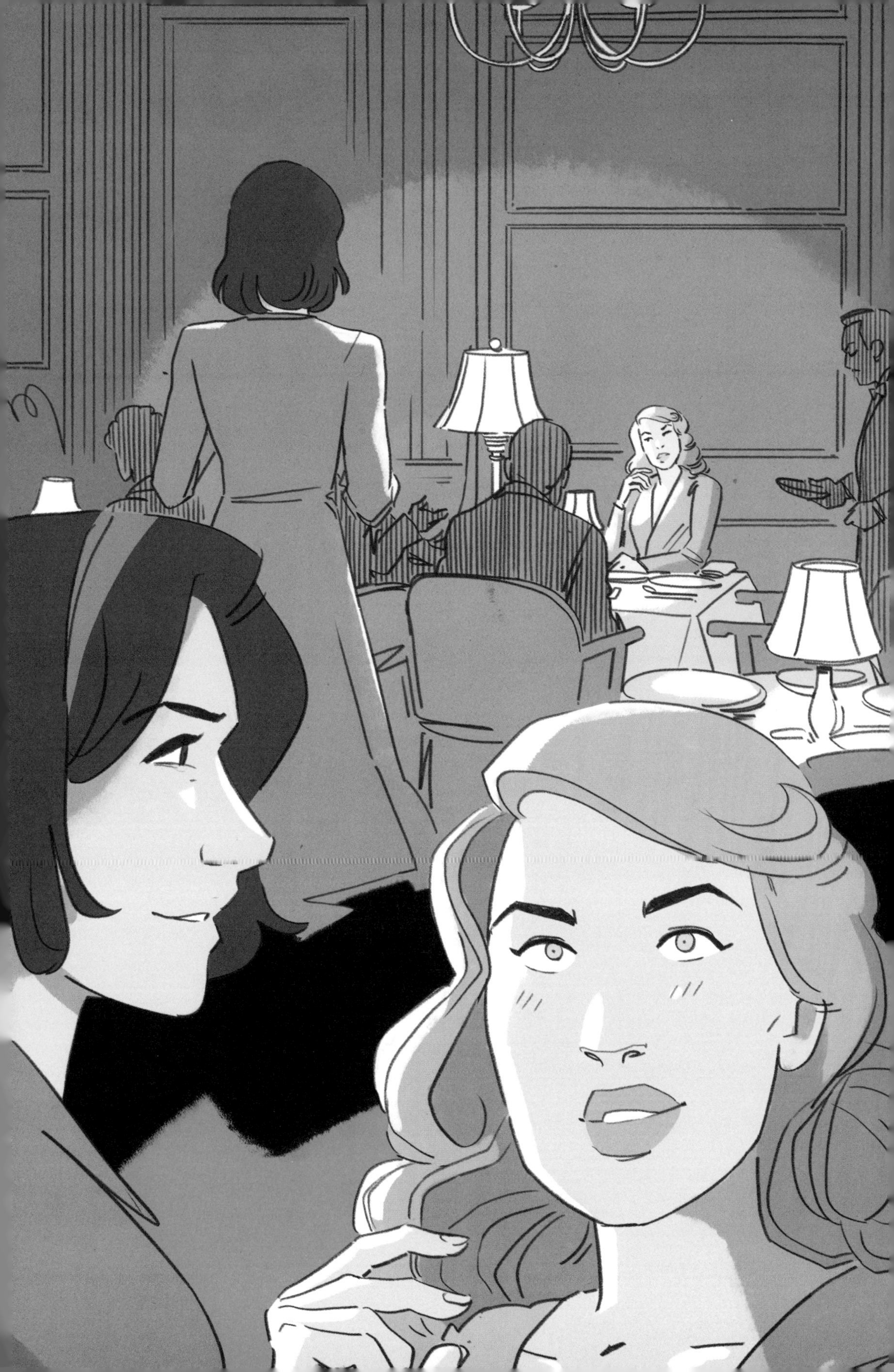

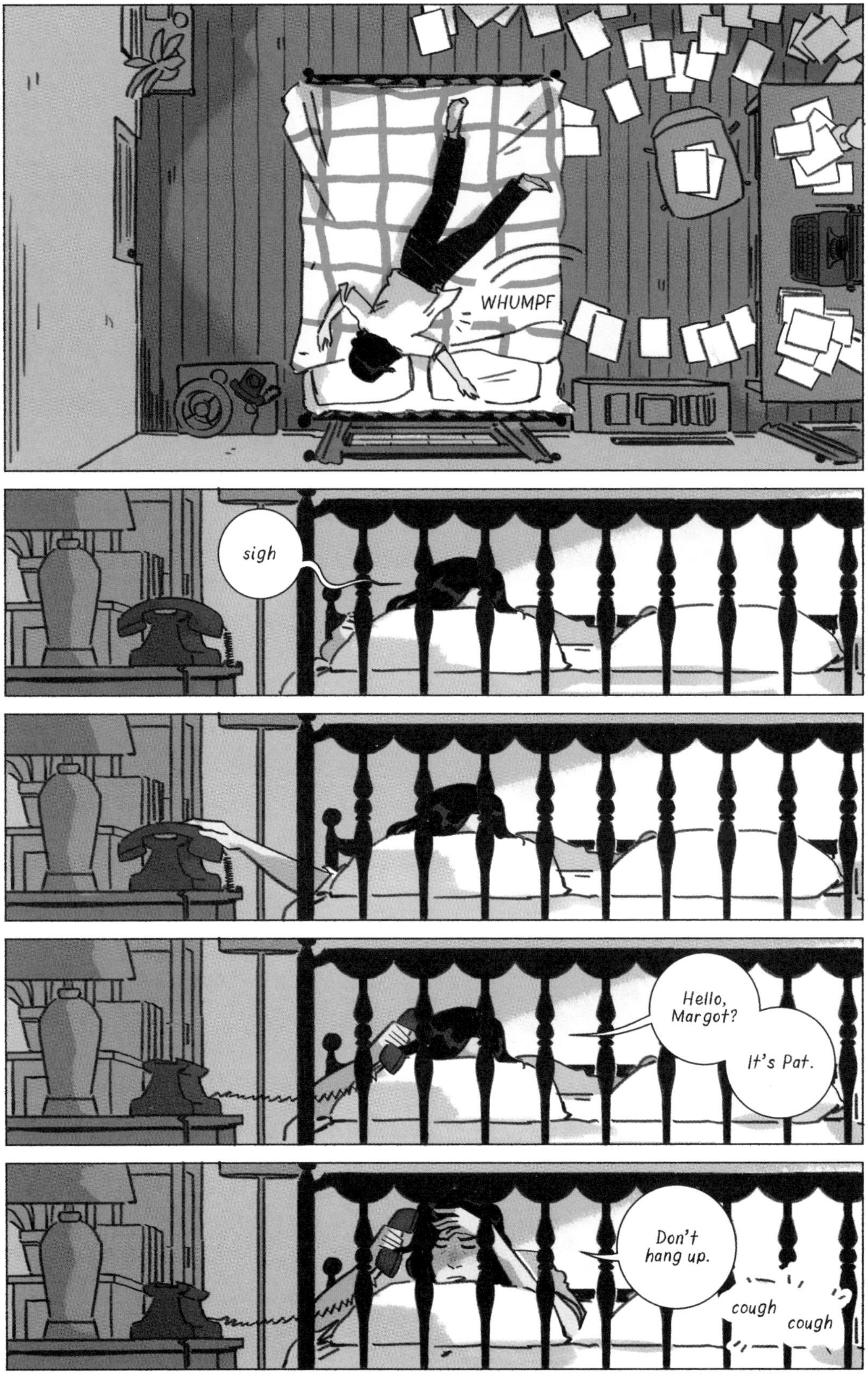
WHUMPF
sigh
Hello, Margot?
It's Pat.
Don't hang up.
cough cough

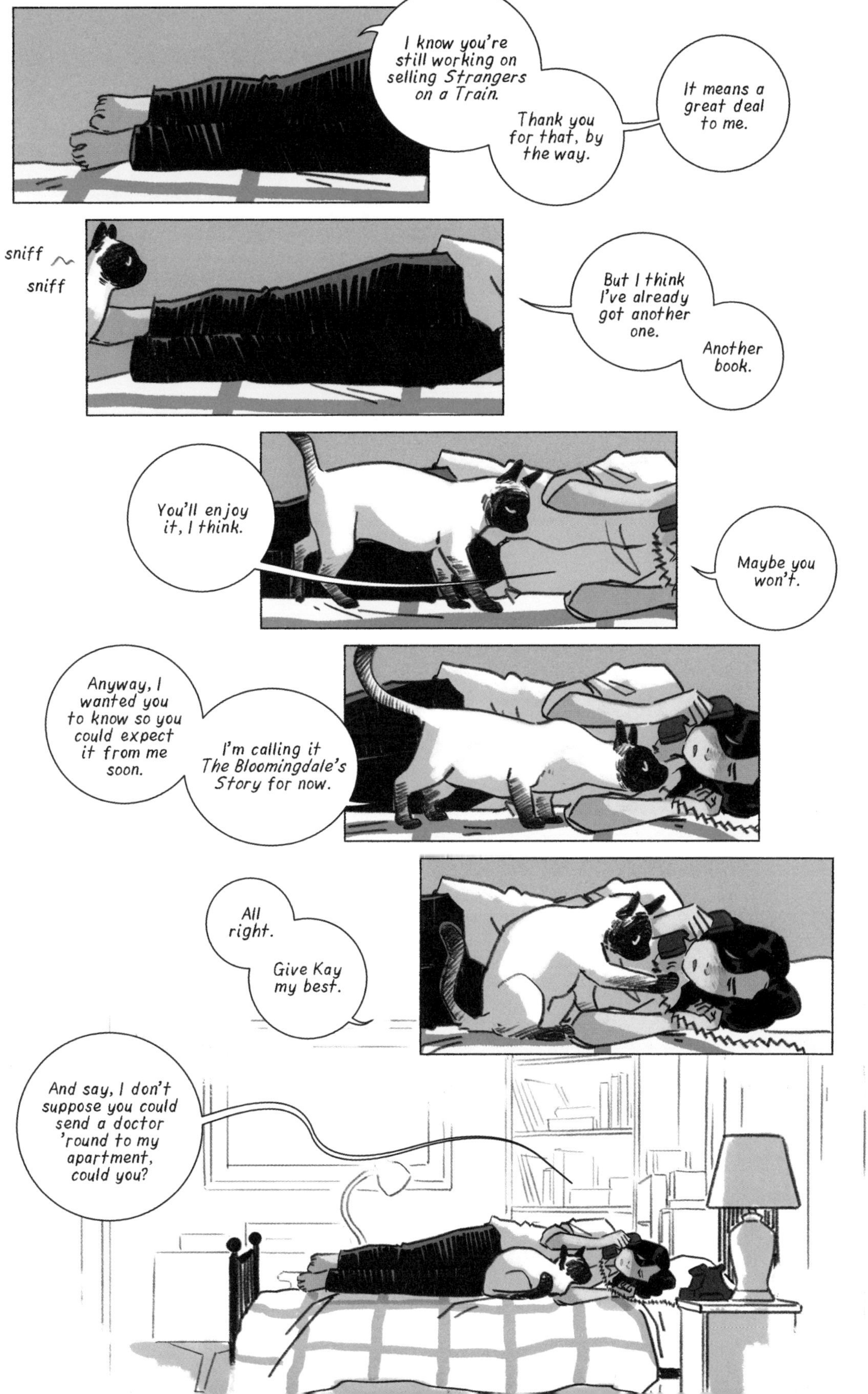
I know you're still working on selling *Strangers on a Train.*
Thank you for that, by the way.
It means a great deal to me.
sniff
sniff
But I think I've already got another one.
Another book.
You'll enjoy it, I think.
Maybe you won't.
Anyway, I wanted you to know so you could expect it from me soon.
I'm calling it *The Bloomingdale's Story* for now.
All right.
Give Kay my best.
And say, I don't suppose you could send a doctor 'round to my apartment, could you?

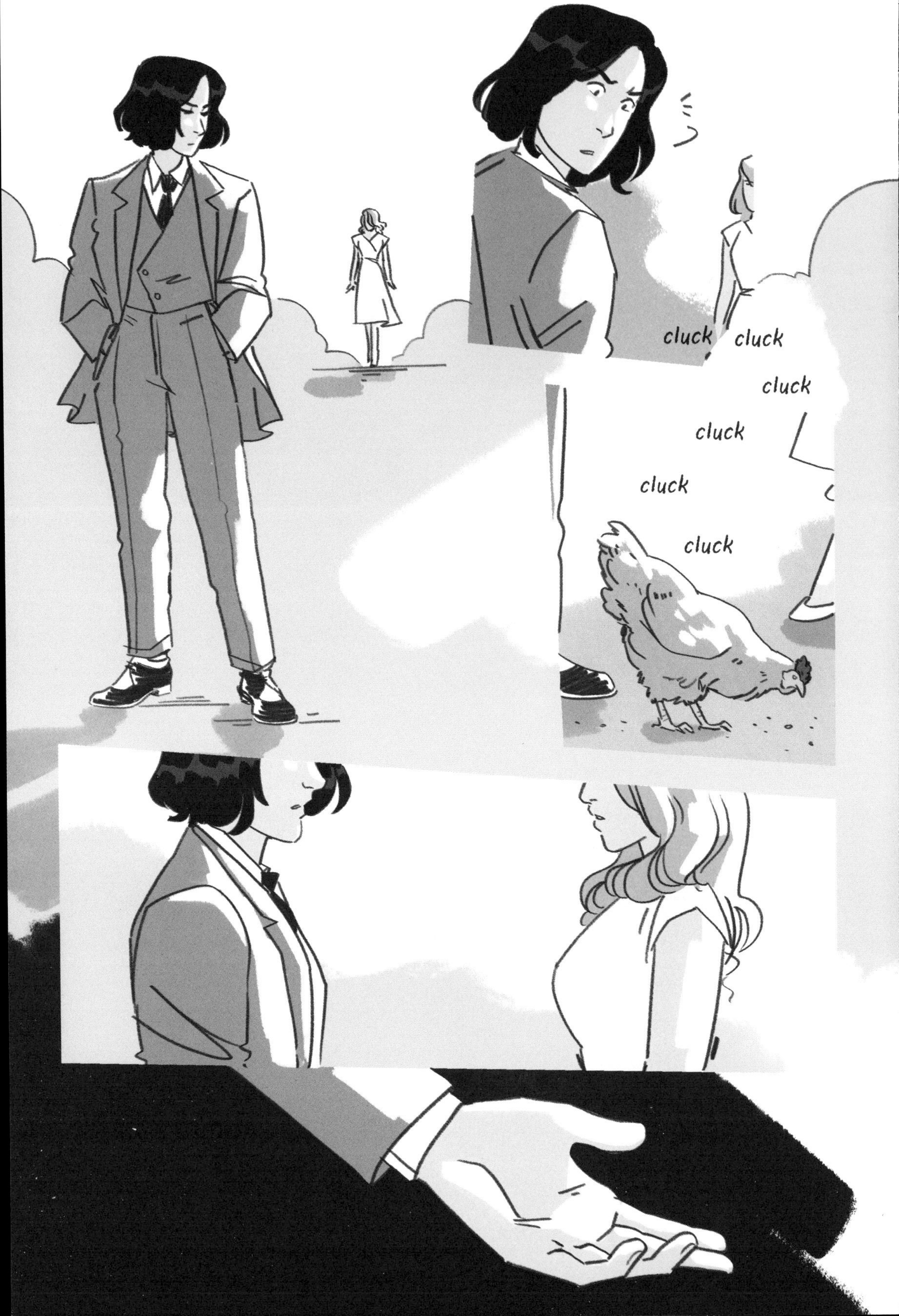
cluck
cluck
cluck
cluck
cluck
cluck

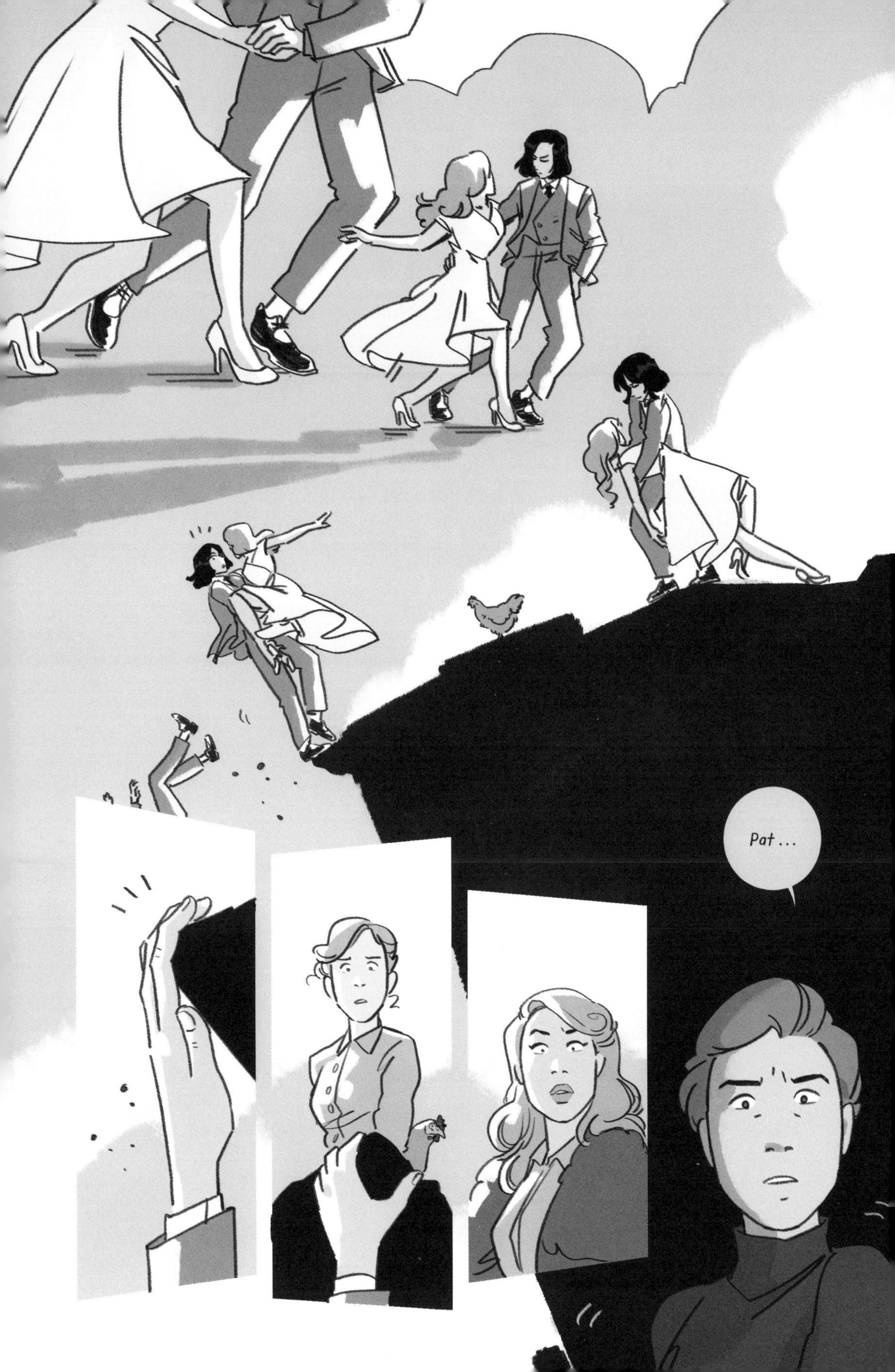
Pat...

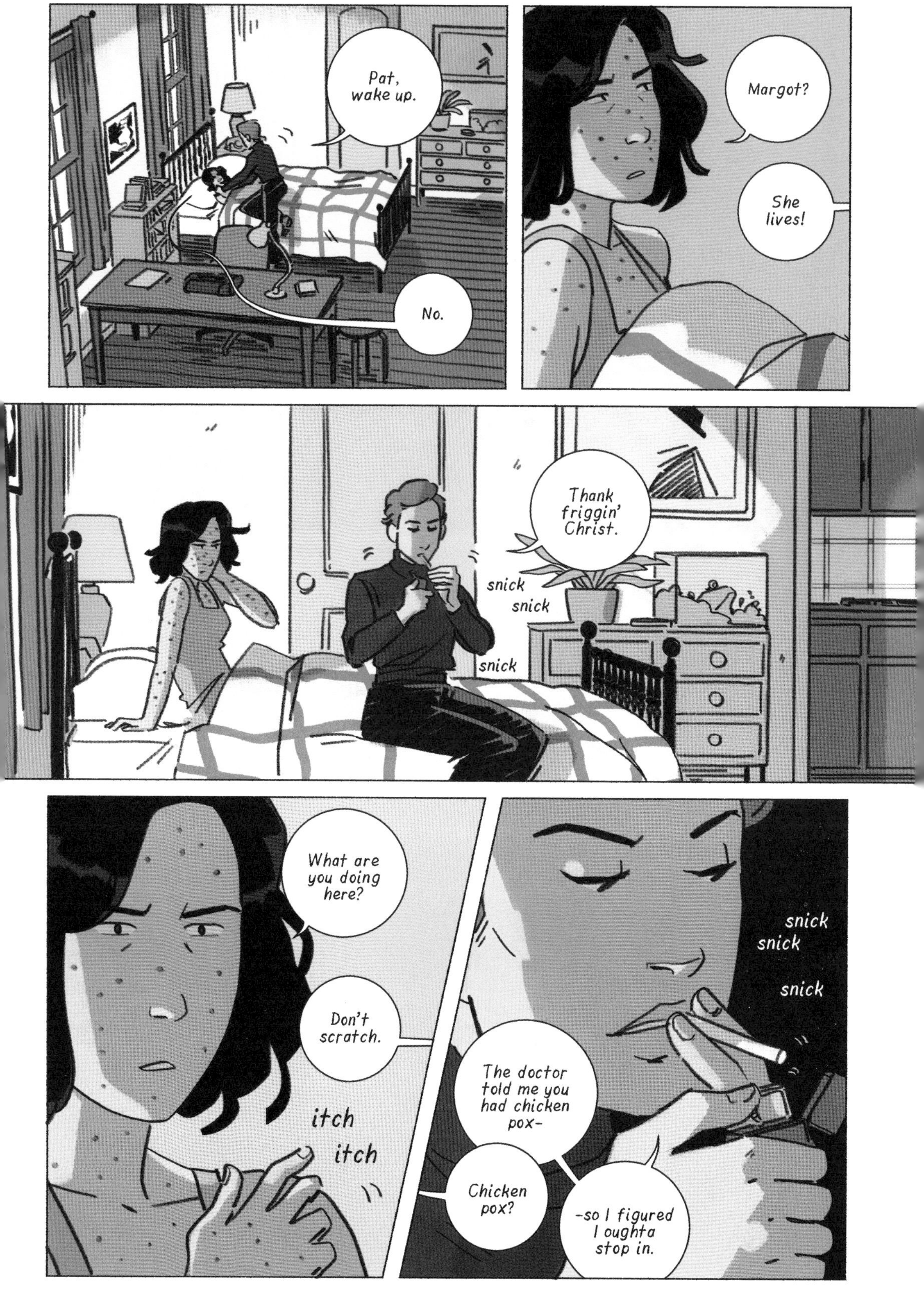
Pat, wake up.
No.
Margot?
She lives!
Thank friggin' Christ.
snick
snick
snick
What are you doing here?
Don't scratch.
itch
itch
snick
snick
snick
The doctor told me you had chicken pox-
Chicken pox?
-so I figured I oughta stop in.

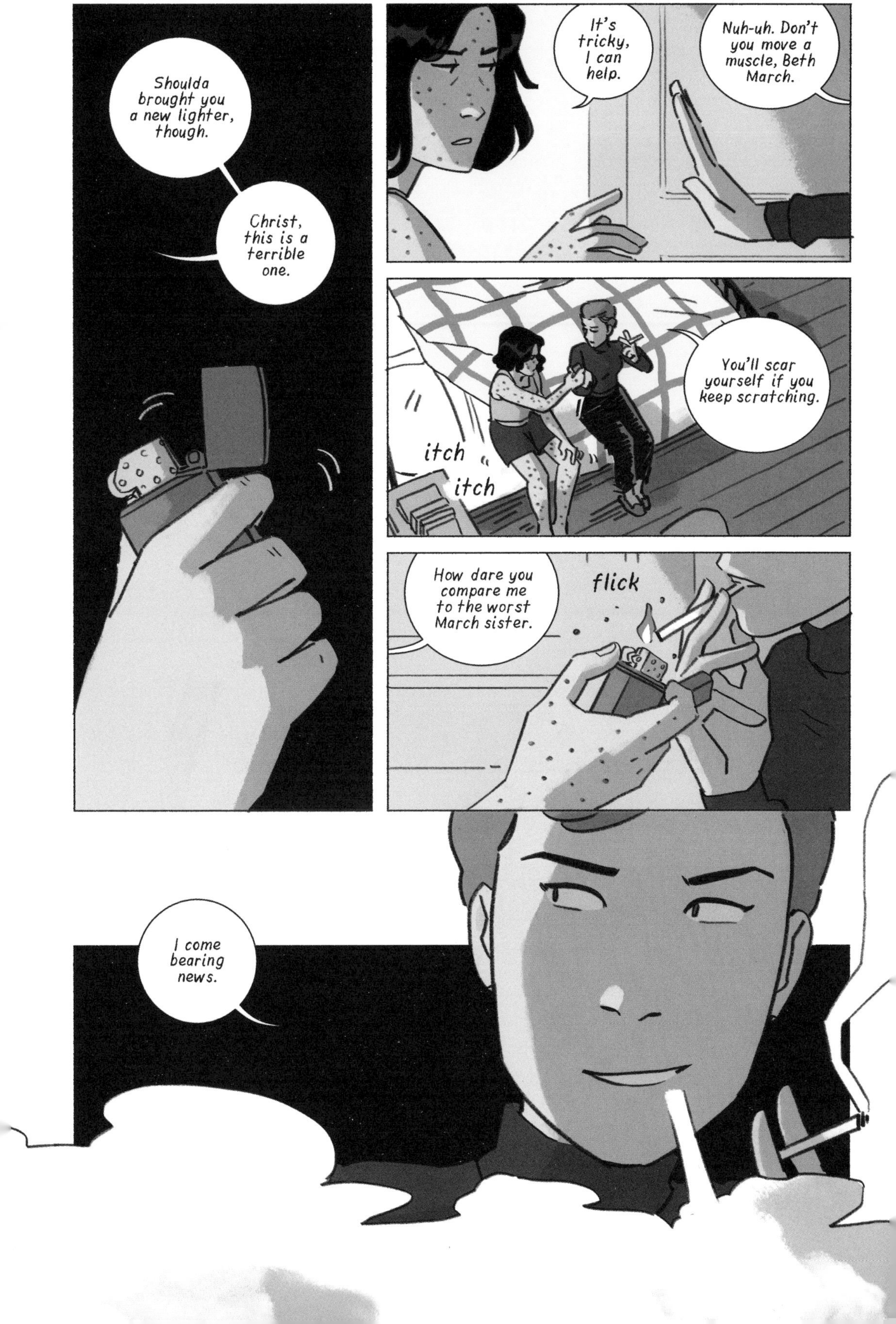
Shoulda brought you a new lighter, though.
Christ, this is a terrible one.
It's tricky, I can help.
Nuh-uh. Don't you move a muscle, Beth March.
You'll scar yourself if you keep scratching.
itch
itch
How dare you compare me to the worst March sister.
flick
I come bearing news.

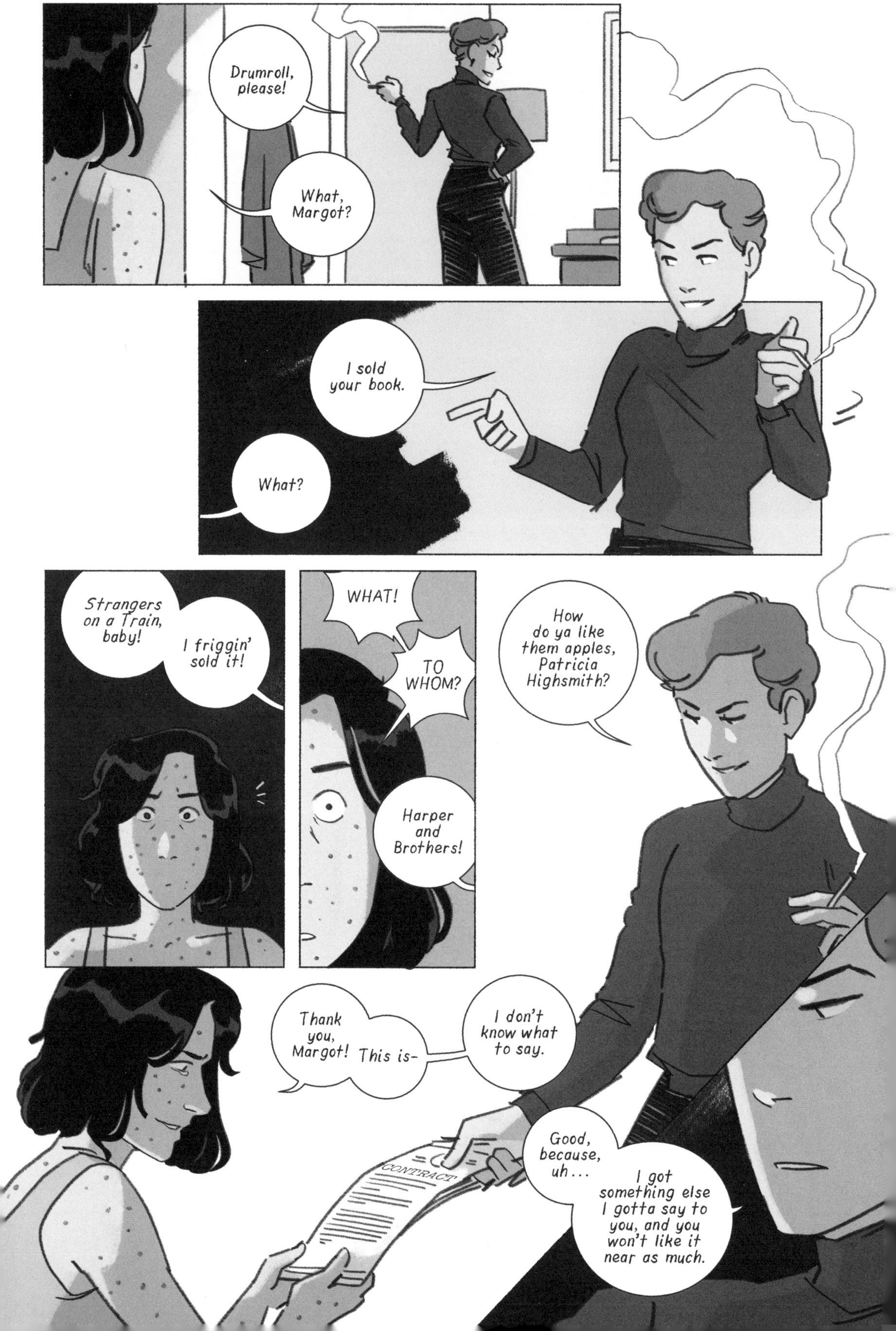

Drumroll, please!
What, Margot?
I sold your book.
What?
Strangers on a Train, baby!
I friggin' sold it!
WHAT!
TO WHOM?
Harper and Brothers!
How do ya like them apples, Patricia Highsmith?
Thank you, Margot! This is-
I don't know what to say.
CONTRACT
Good, because, uh...
I got something else I gotta say to you, and you won't like it near as much.

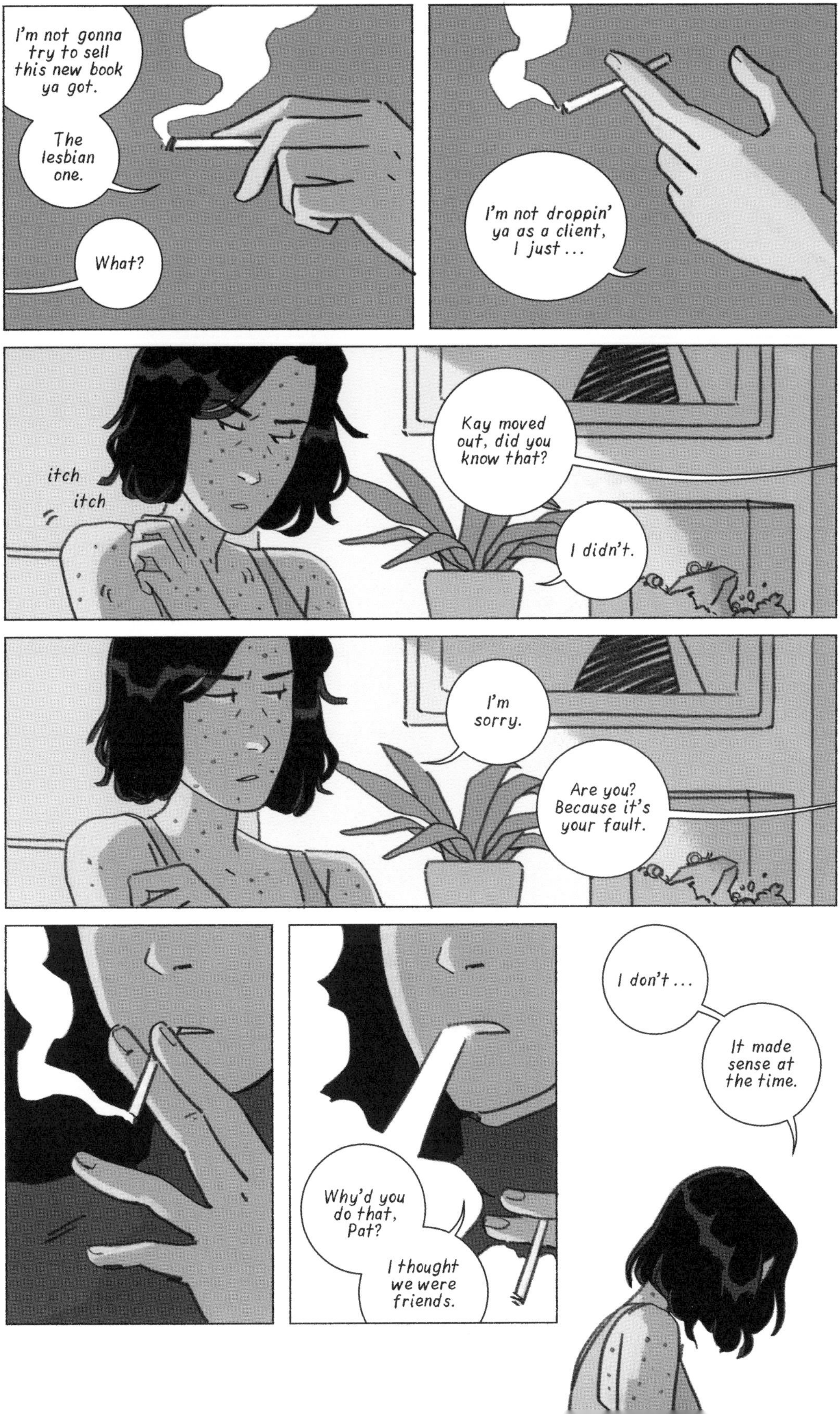
I'm not gonna try to sell this new book ya got.
The lesbian one.
What?
I'm not droppin' ya as a client, I just . . .
itch itch
Kay moved out, did you know that?
I didn't.
I'm sorry.
Are you? Because it's your fault.
Why'd you do that, Pat?
I thought we were friends.
I don't . . .
It made sense at the time.

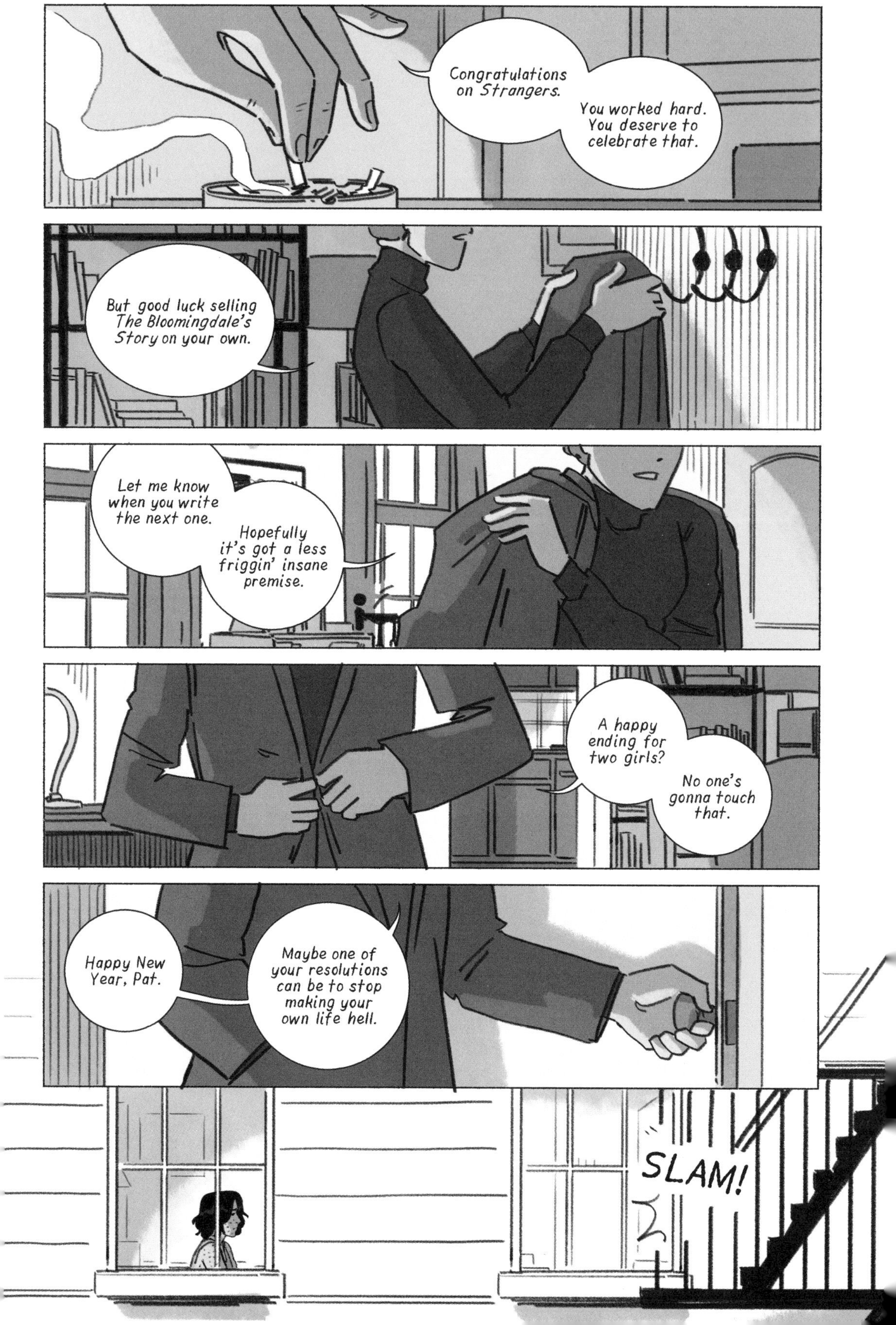

Congratulations on *Strangers.*
You worked hard. You deserve to celebrate that.
But good luck selling *The Bloomingdale's Story* on your own.
Let me know when you write the next one.
Hopefully it's got a less friggin' insane premise.
A happy ending for two girls?
No one's gonna touch that.
Happy New Year, Pat.
Maybe one of your resolutions can be to stop making your own life hell.
SLAM!

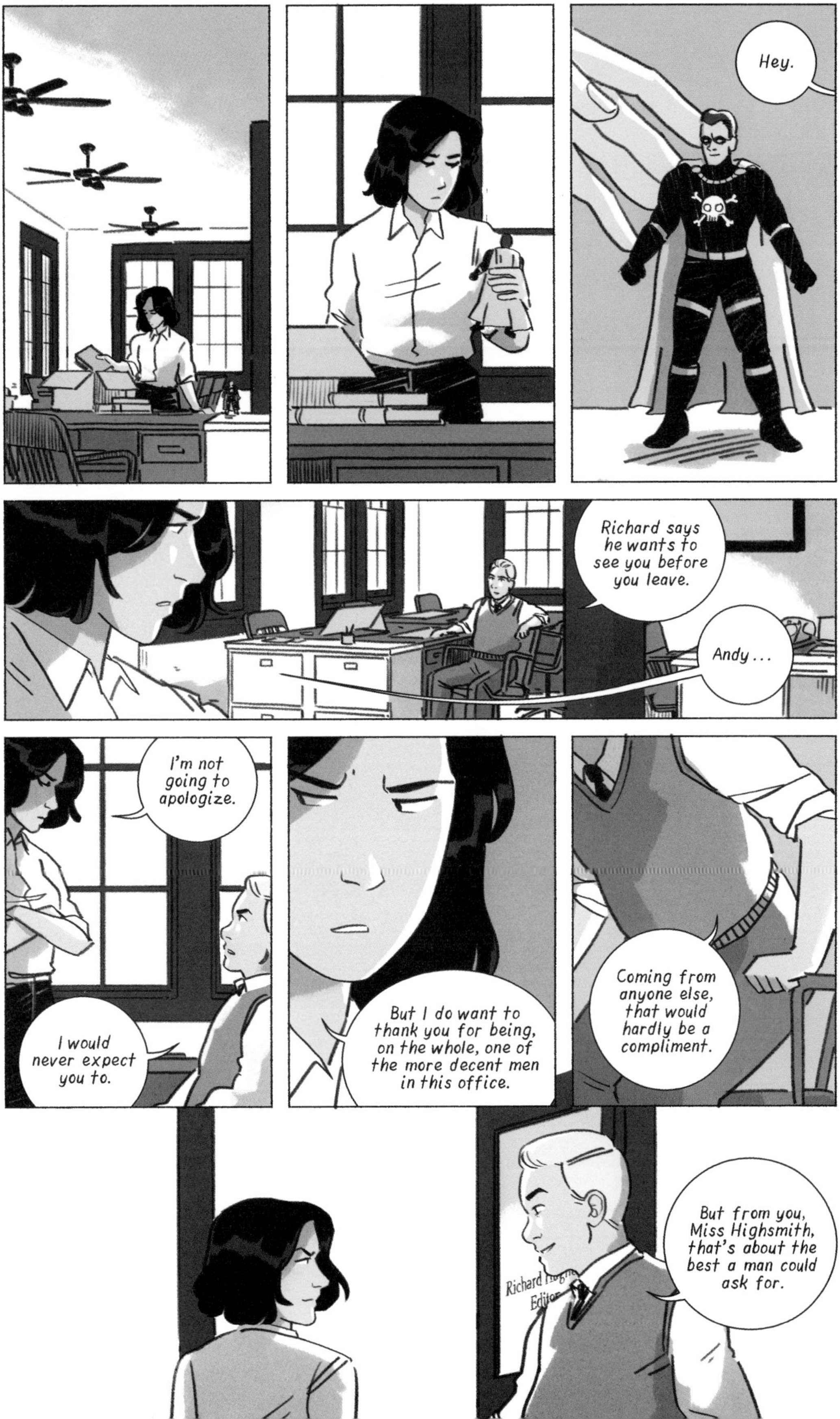
Hey.
Richard says he wants to see you before you leave.
Andy...
I'm not going to apologize.
I would never expect you to.
But I do want to thank you for being, on the whole, one of the more decent men in this office.
Coming from anyone else, that would hardly be a compliment.
But from you, Miss Highsmith, that's about the best a man could ask for.

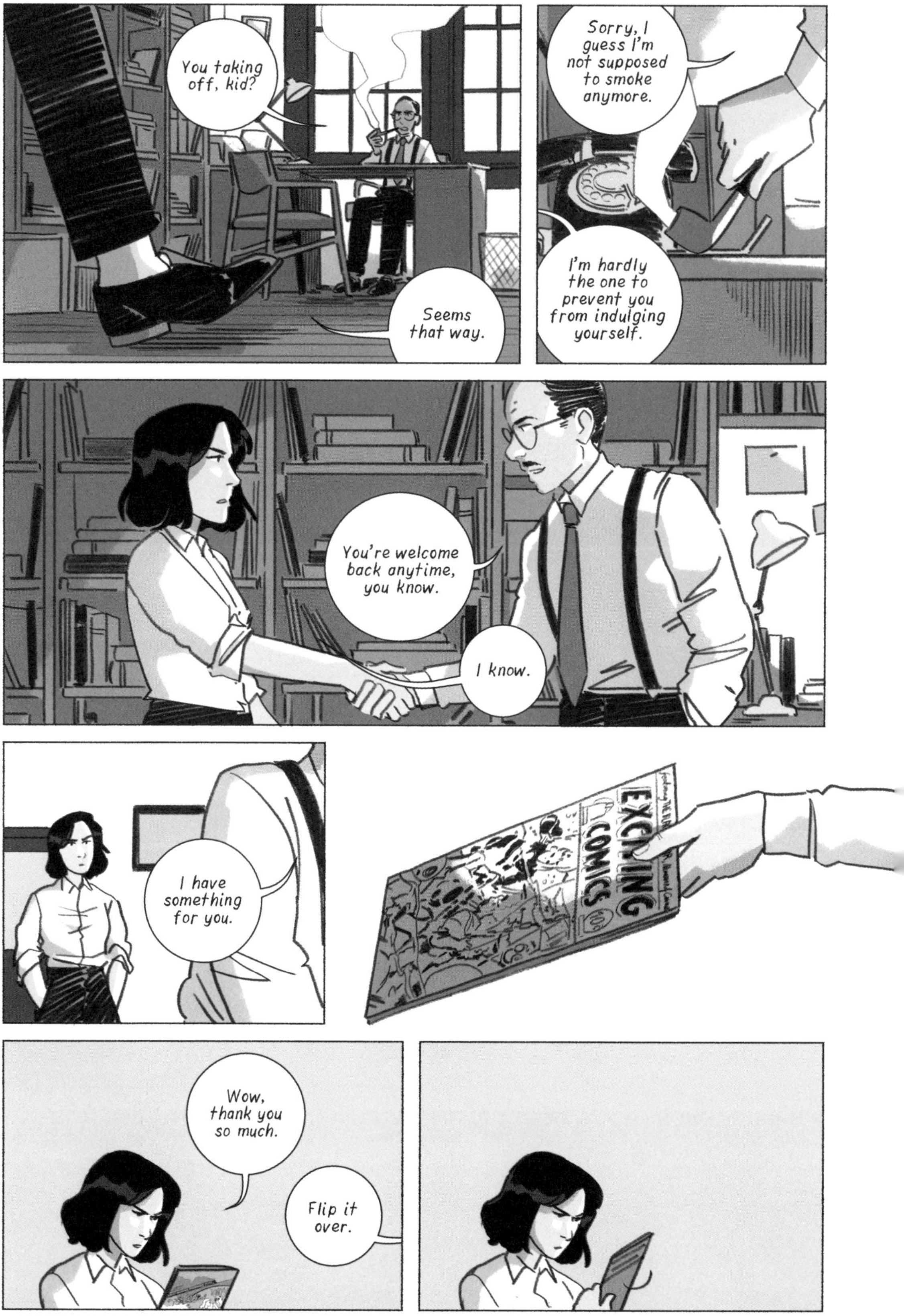
You taking off, kid?
Seems that way.
Sorry, I guess I'm not supposed to smoke anymore.
I'm hardly the one to prevent you from indulging yourself.
You're welcome back anytime, you know.
I know.
I have something for you.
Wow, thank you so much.
Flip it over.

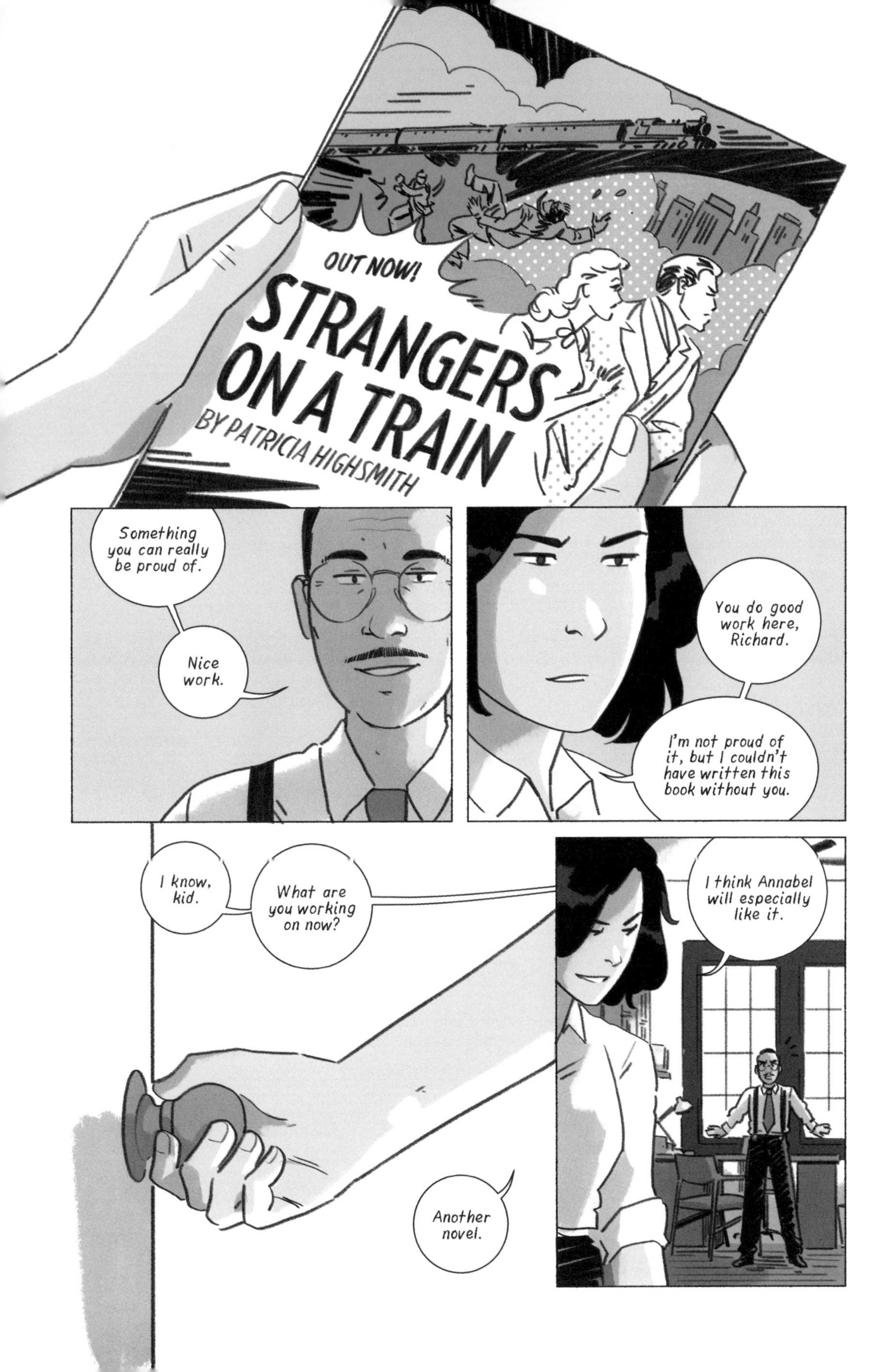

OUT NOW!
STRANGERS ON A TRAIN
BY PATRICIA HIGHSMITH
Something you can really be proud of.
Nice work.
You do good work here, Richard.
I'm not proud of it, but I couldn't have written this book without you.
I know, kid.
What are you working on now?
Another novel.
I think Annabel will especially like it.

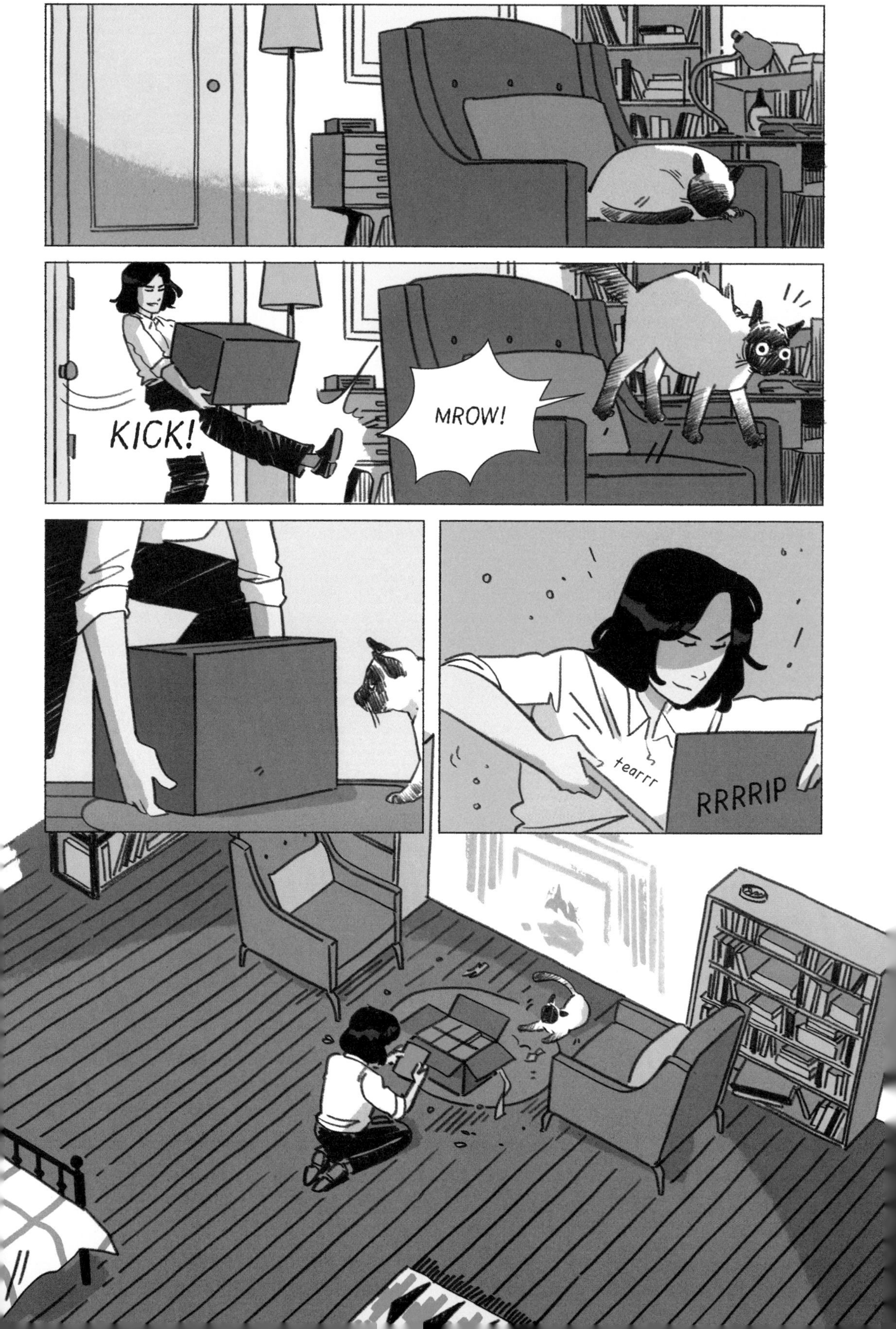
KICK!
MROW!
tearrr
RRRRIP

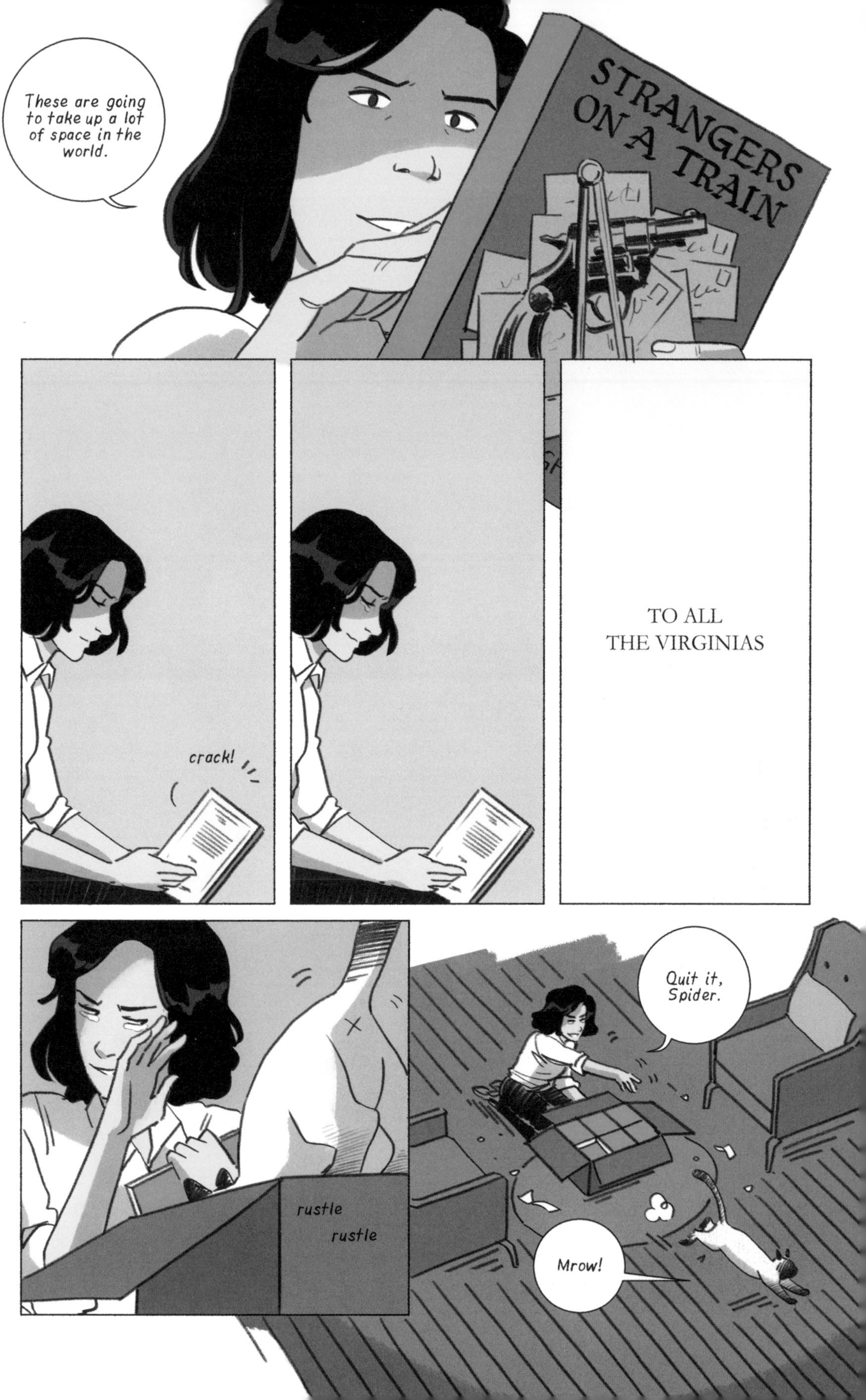
These are going to take up a lot of space in the world.
STRANGERS ON A TRAIN
crack!
TO ALL THE VIRGINIAS
rustle
rustle
Quit it, Spider.
Mrow!

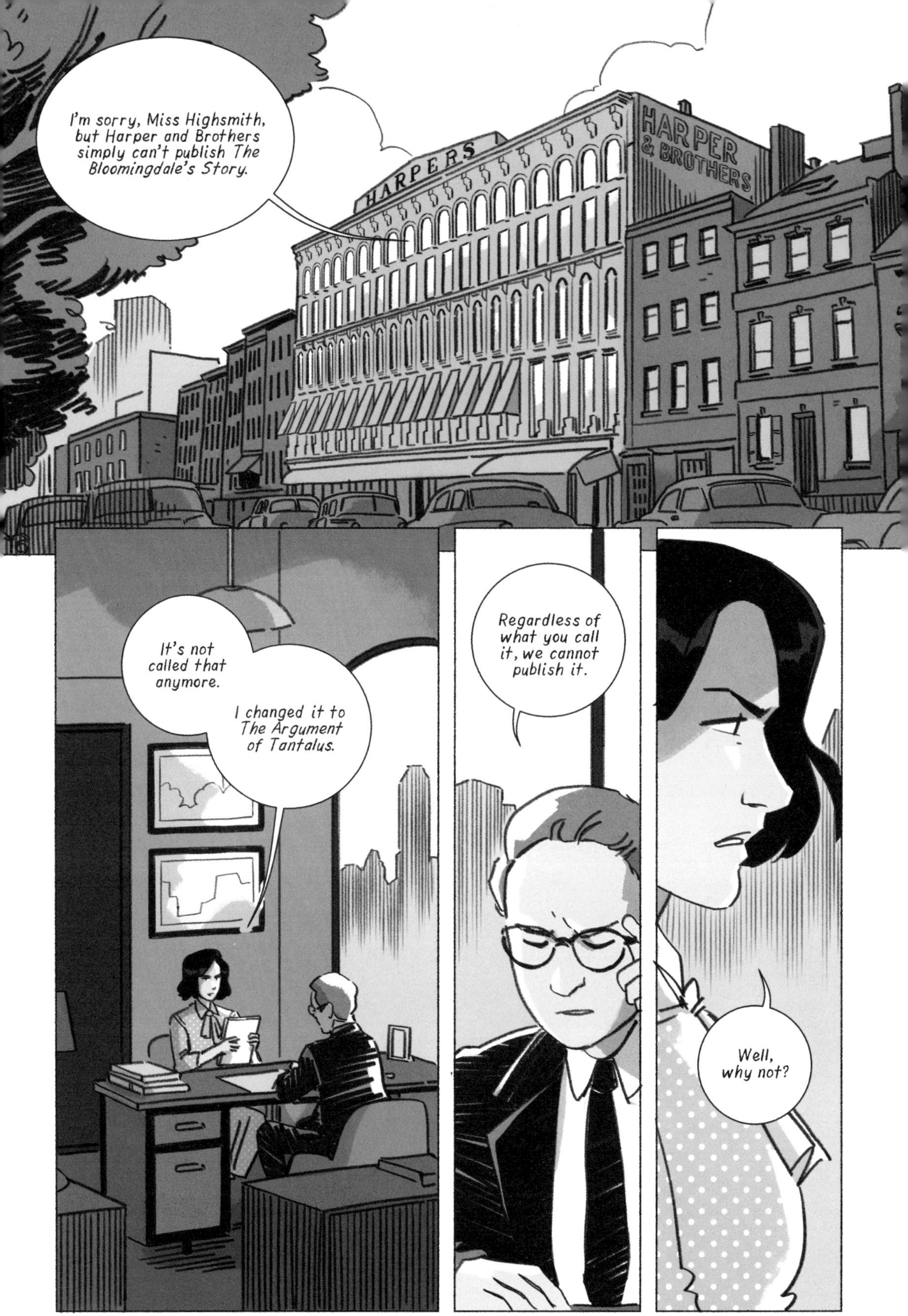
HARPERS
HARPER & BROTHERS
I'm sorry, Miss Highsmith, but Harper and Brothers simply can't publish The Bloomingdale's Story.
It's not called that anymore.
I changed it to The Argument of Tantalus.
Regardless of what you call it, we cannot publish it.
Well, why not?

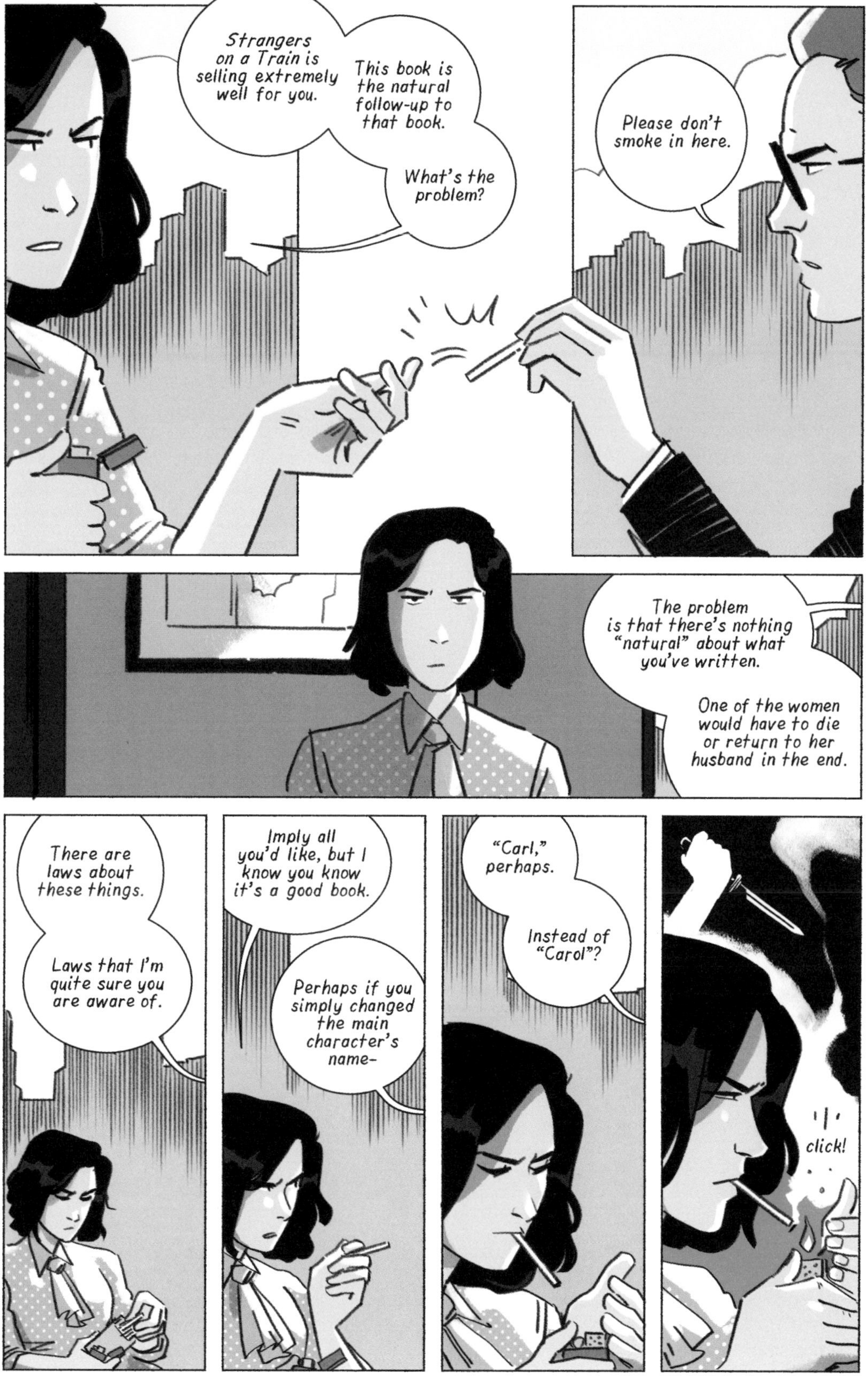
Strangers on a Train is selling extremely well for you.
This book is the natural follow-up to that book.
What's the problem?
Please don't smoke in here.
The problem is that there's nothing "natural" about what you've written.
One of the women would have to die or return to her husband in the end.
There are laws about these things.
Laws that I'm quite sure you are aware of.
Imply all you'd like, but I know you know it's a good book.
Perhaps if you simply changed the main character's name-
"Carl," perhaps.
Instead of "Carol"?
click!

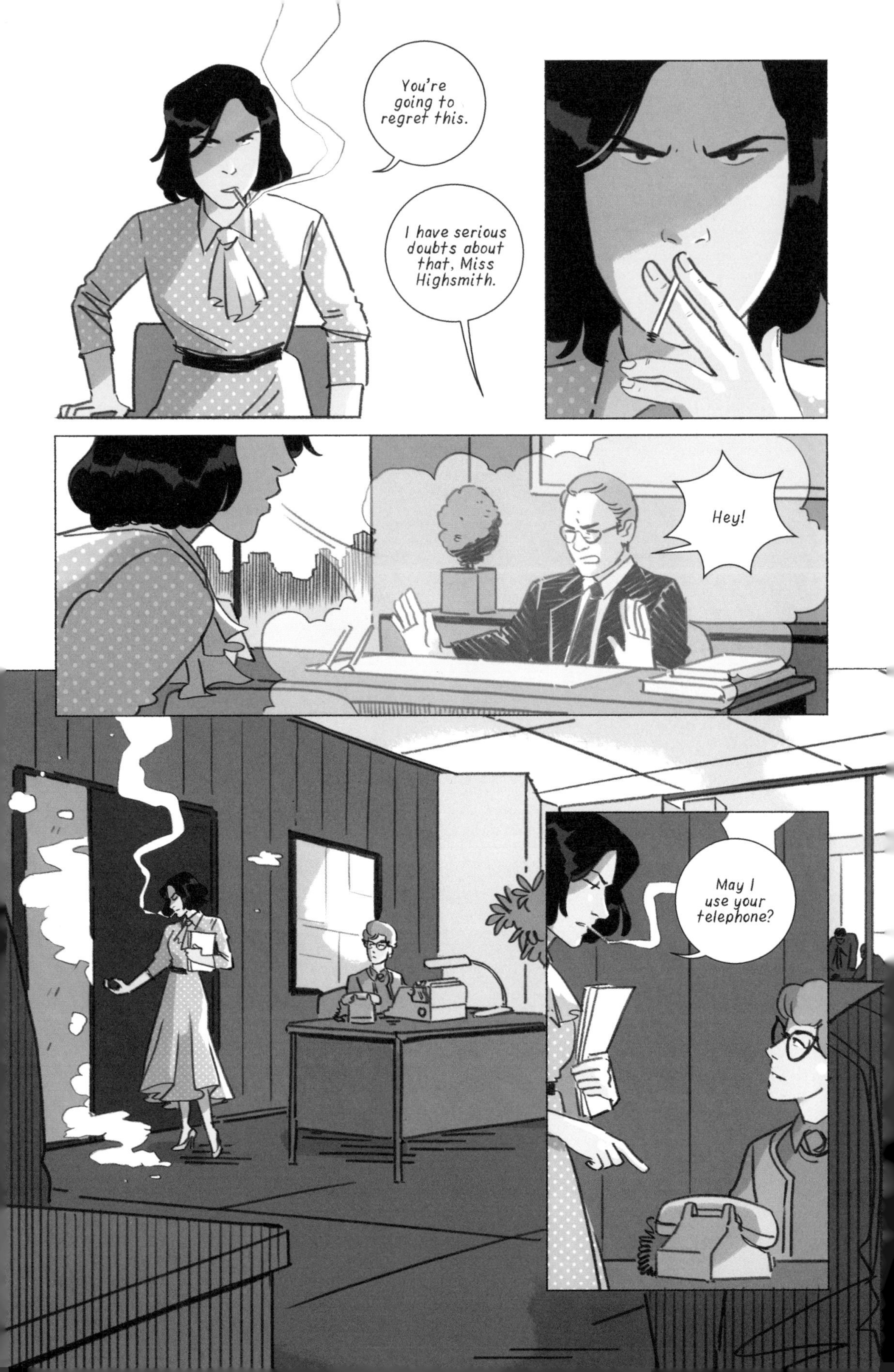

You're going to regret this.
I have serious doubts about that, Miss Highsmith.
Hey!
May I use your telephone?

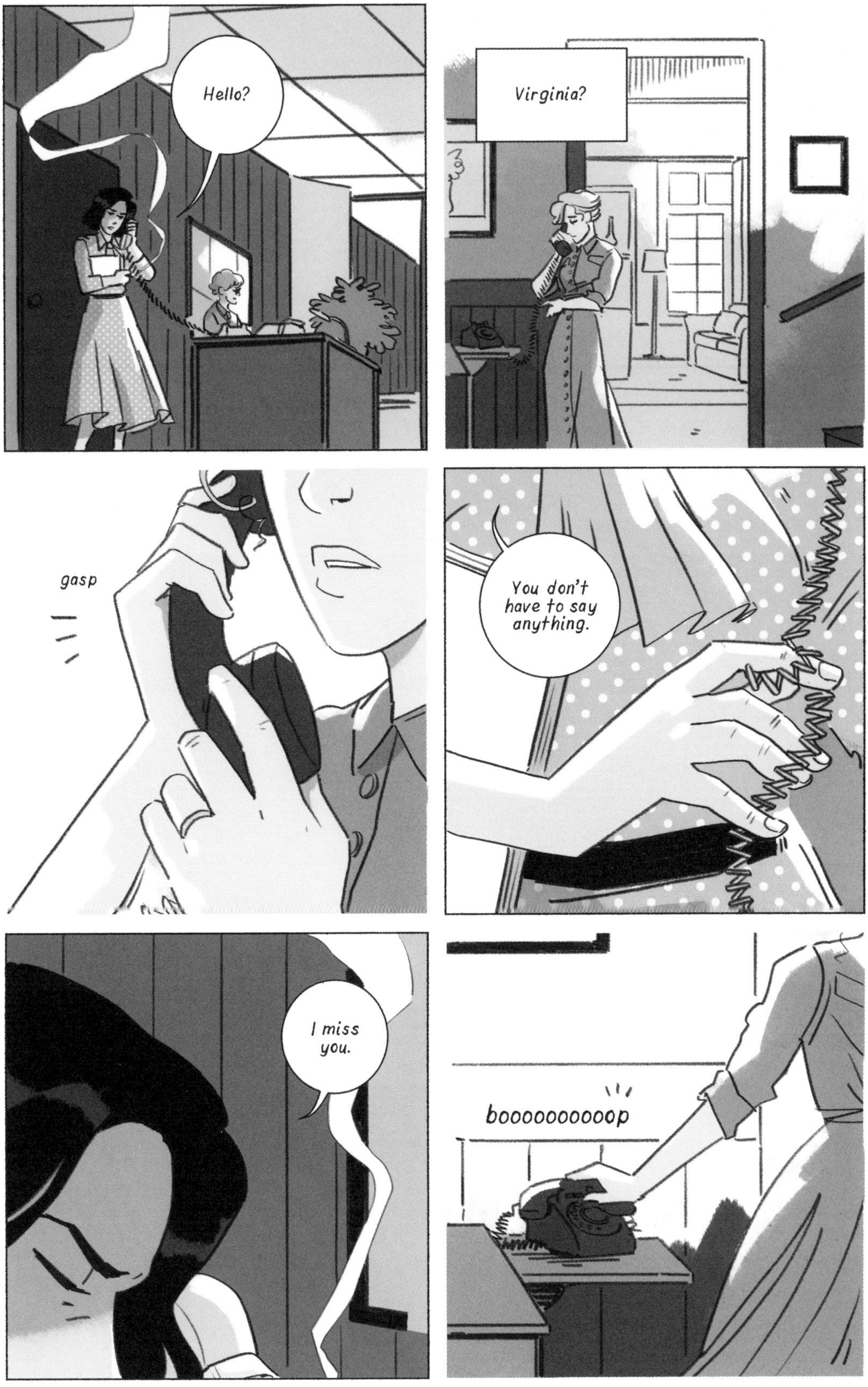
Hello?
Virginia?
gasp
You don't have to say anything.
I miss you.
booooooooooop

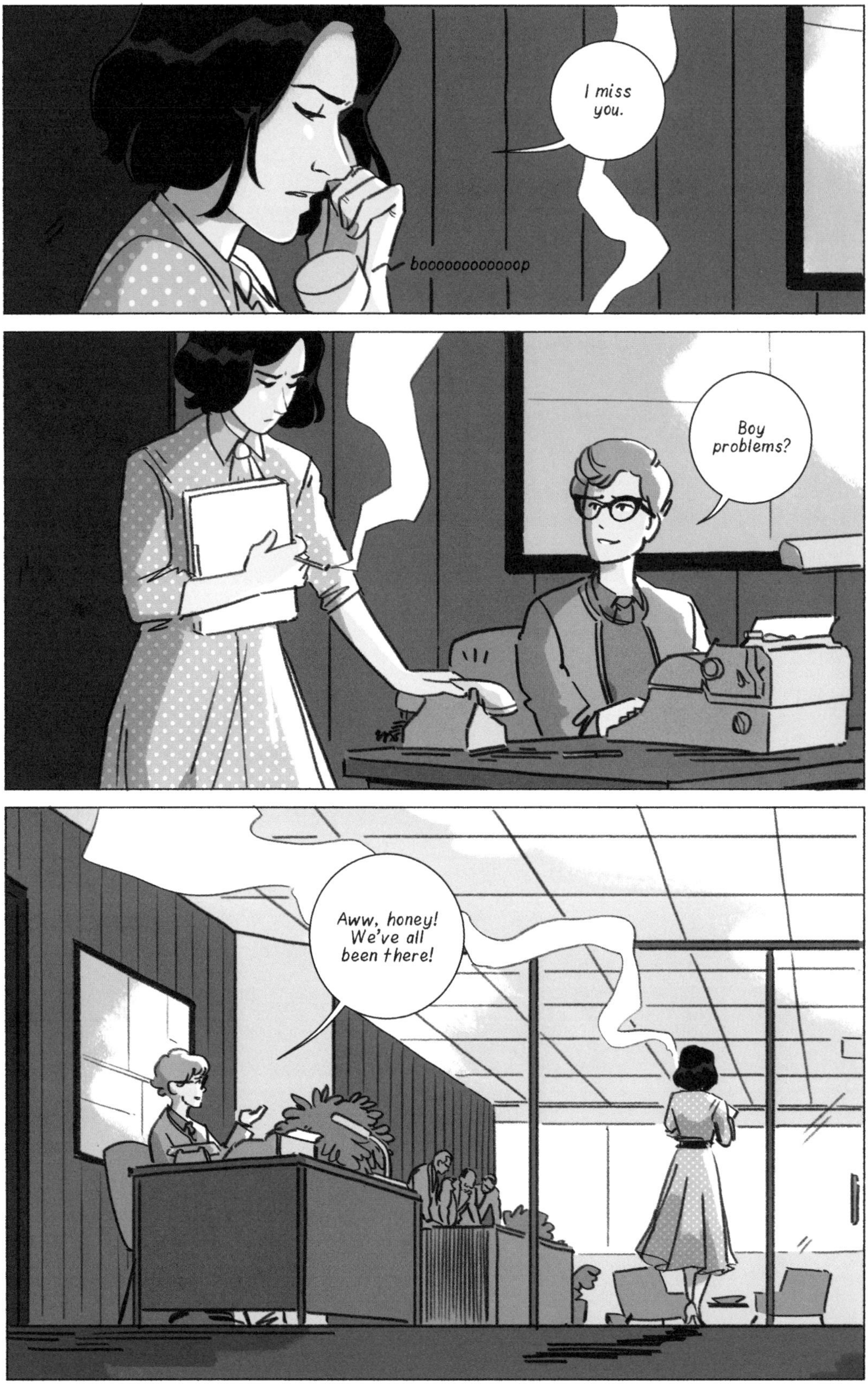
I miss you.
booooooooooooop
Boy problems?
Aww, honey! We've all been there!

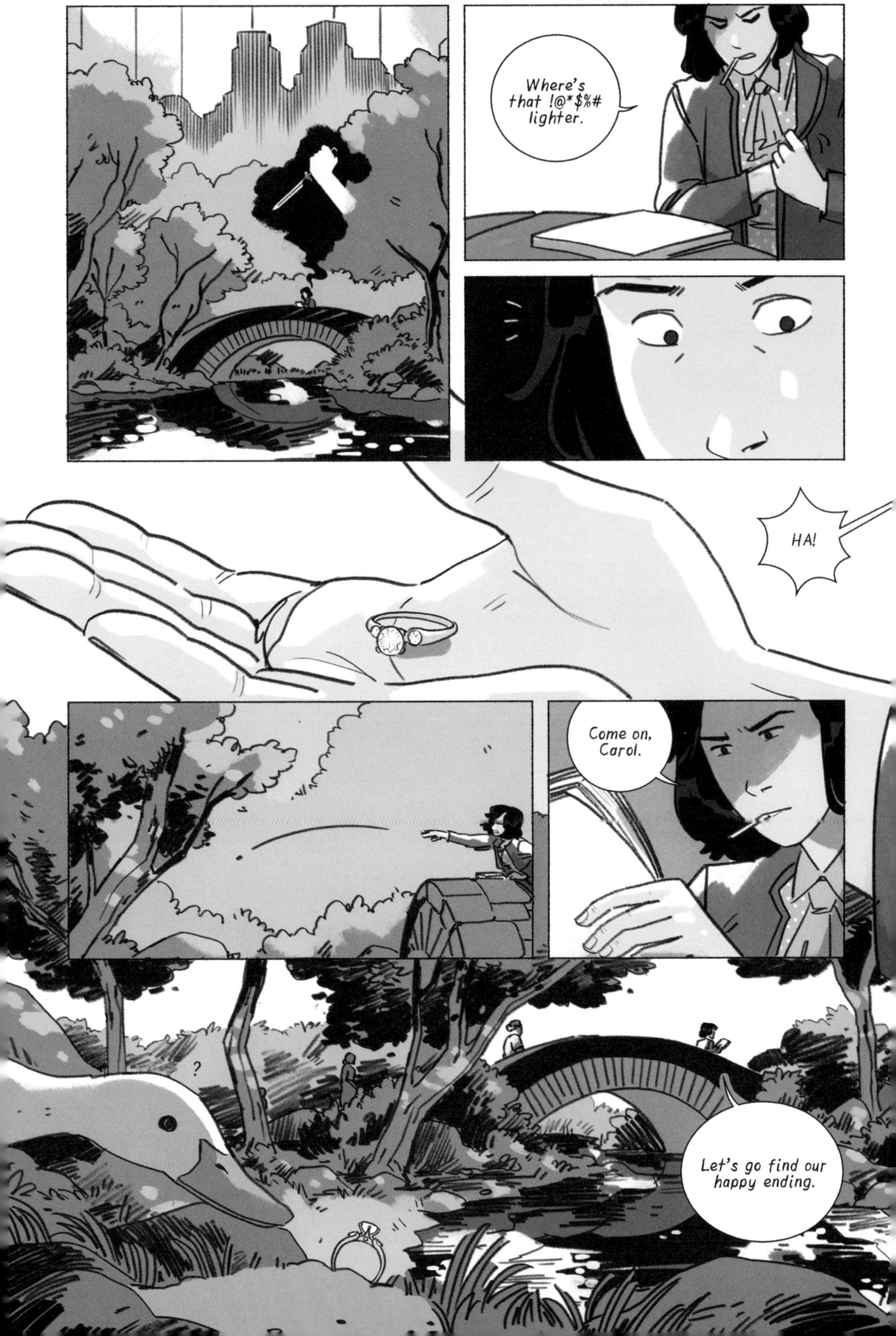

Where's that !@*$%# lighter.
HA!
Come on, Carol.
?
Let's go find our happy ending.

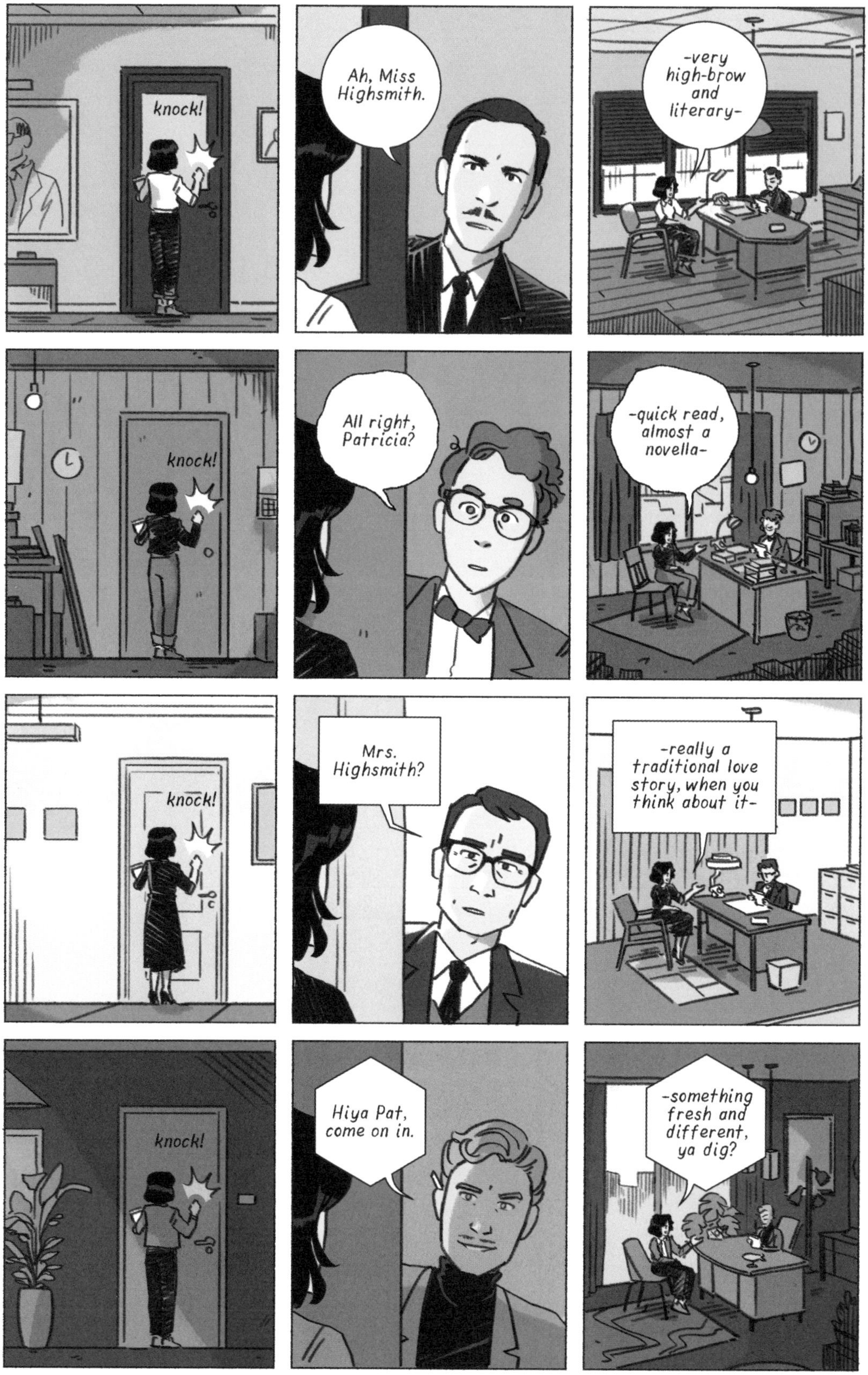
knock!
Ah, Miss Highsmith.
-very high-brow and literary-
knock!
All right, Patricia?
-quick read, almost a novella-
knock!
Mrs. Highsmith?
-really a traditional love story, when you think about it-
knock!
Hiya Pat, come on in.
-something fresh and different, ya dig?

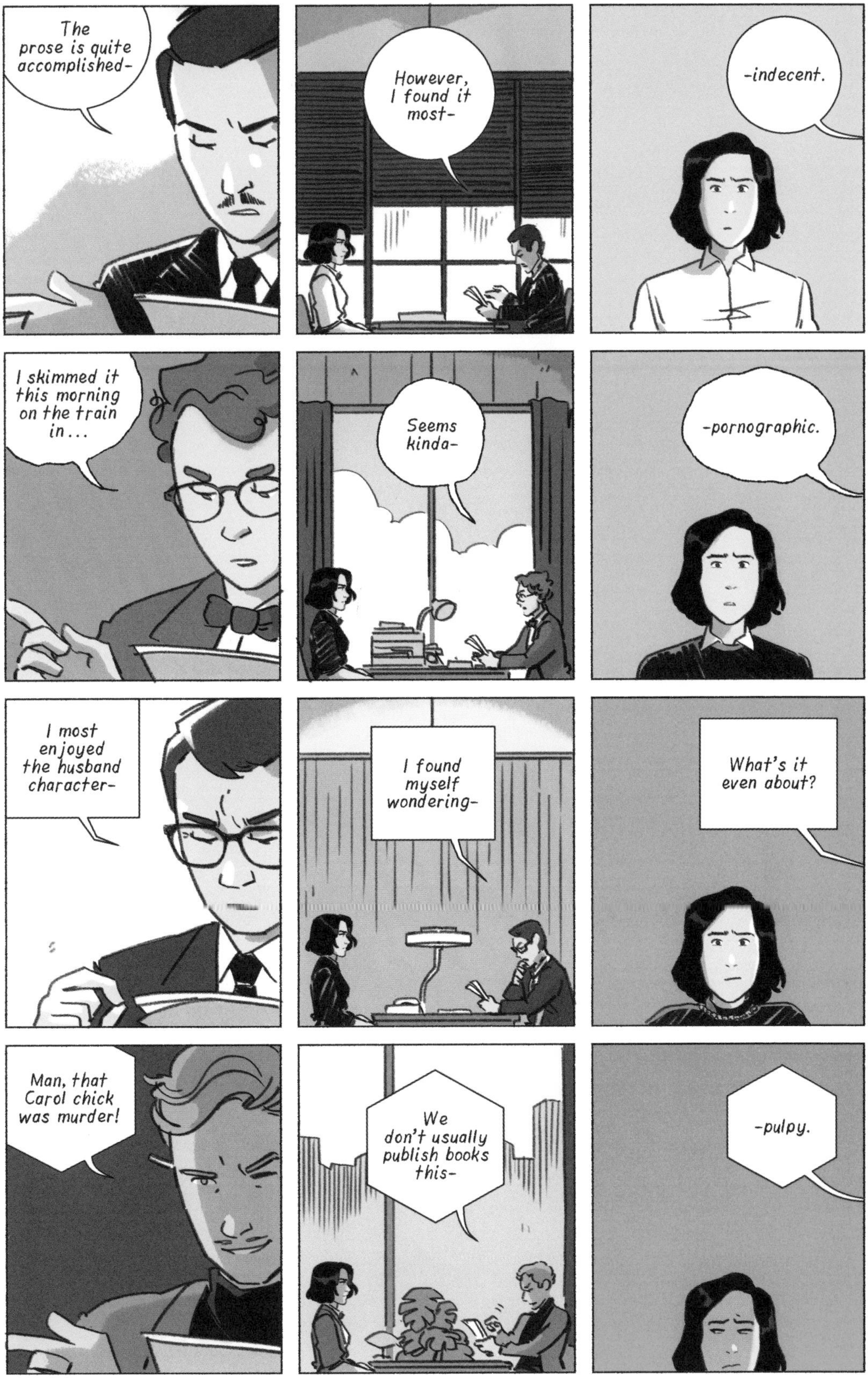
The prose is quite accomplished-
However, I found it most-
-indecent.
I skimmed it this morning on the train in...
Seems kinda-
-pornographic.
I most enjoyed the husband character-
I found myself wondering-
What's it even about?
Man, that Carol chick was murder!
We don't usually publish books this-
-pulpy.

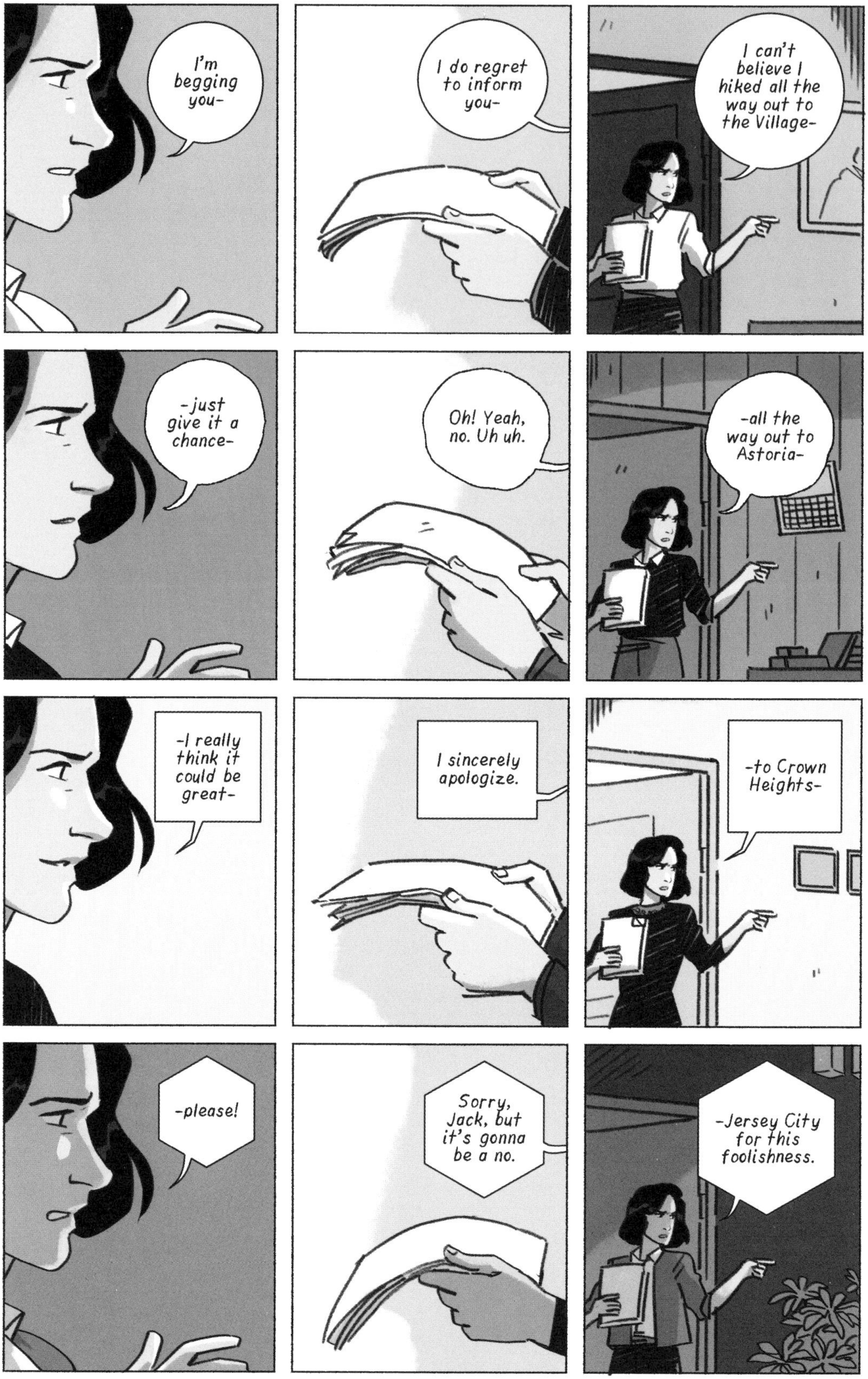
I'm begging you-
I do regret to inform you-
I can't believe I hiked all the way out to the Village-
-just give it a chance-
Oh! Yeah, no. Uh uh.
-all the way out to Astoria-
-I really think it could be great-
I sincerely apologize.
-to Crown Heights-
-please!
Sorry, Jack, but it's gonna be a no.
-Jersey City for this foolishness.

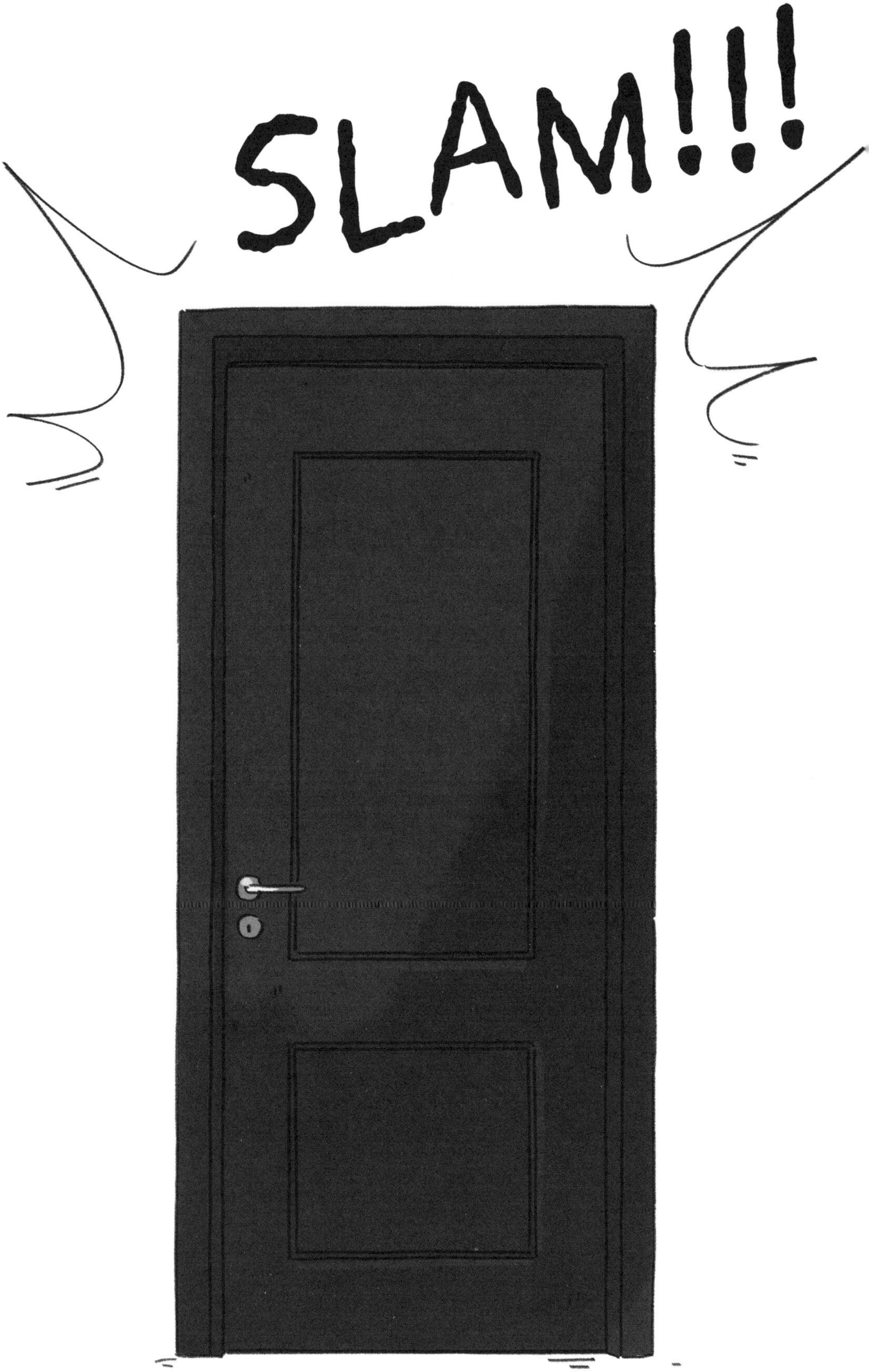
SLAM!!!

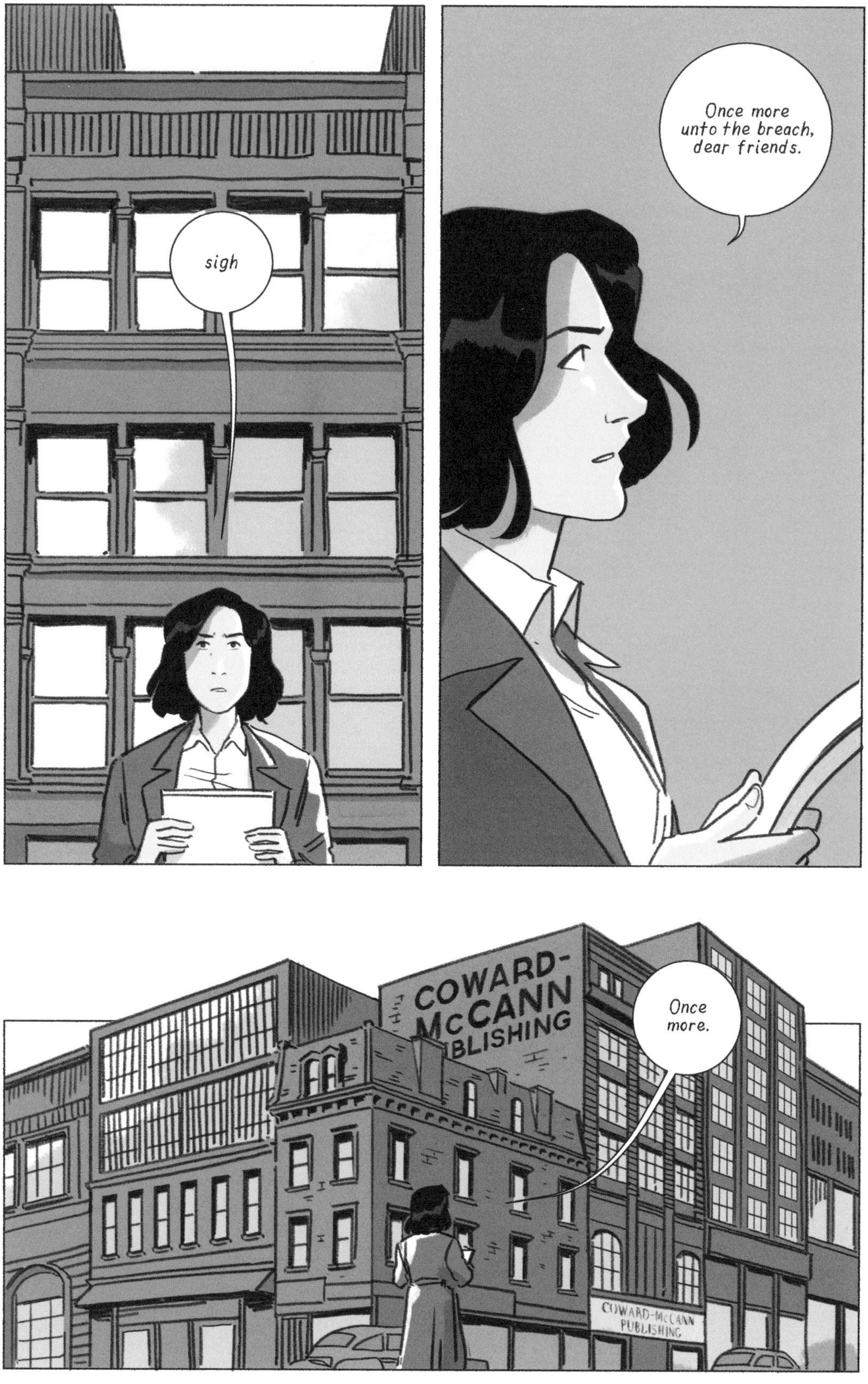
sigh
Once more unto the breach, dear friends.
COWARD-McCANN PUBLISHING
Once more.
COWARD-McCANN PUBLISHING

Oh!

Oh! I'm so sorry!

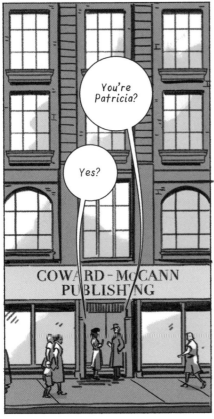

You're Patricia?

Yes?

COWARD - McCANN PUBLISHING

Wonderful! You're here for me!

Cecil Goldbeck, vice president of Coward-McCann Publishing.

I was hoping we could have our meeting over lunch.

I haven't had a bite to eat all day.

Sure!

Nothing like talking turkey over a turkey sandwich, I always say.

Well, not always, but I've said it just now.

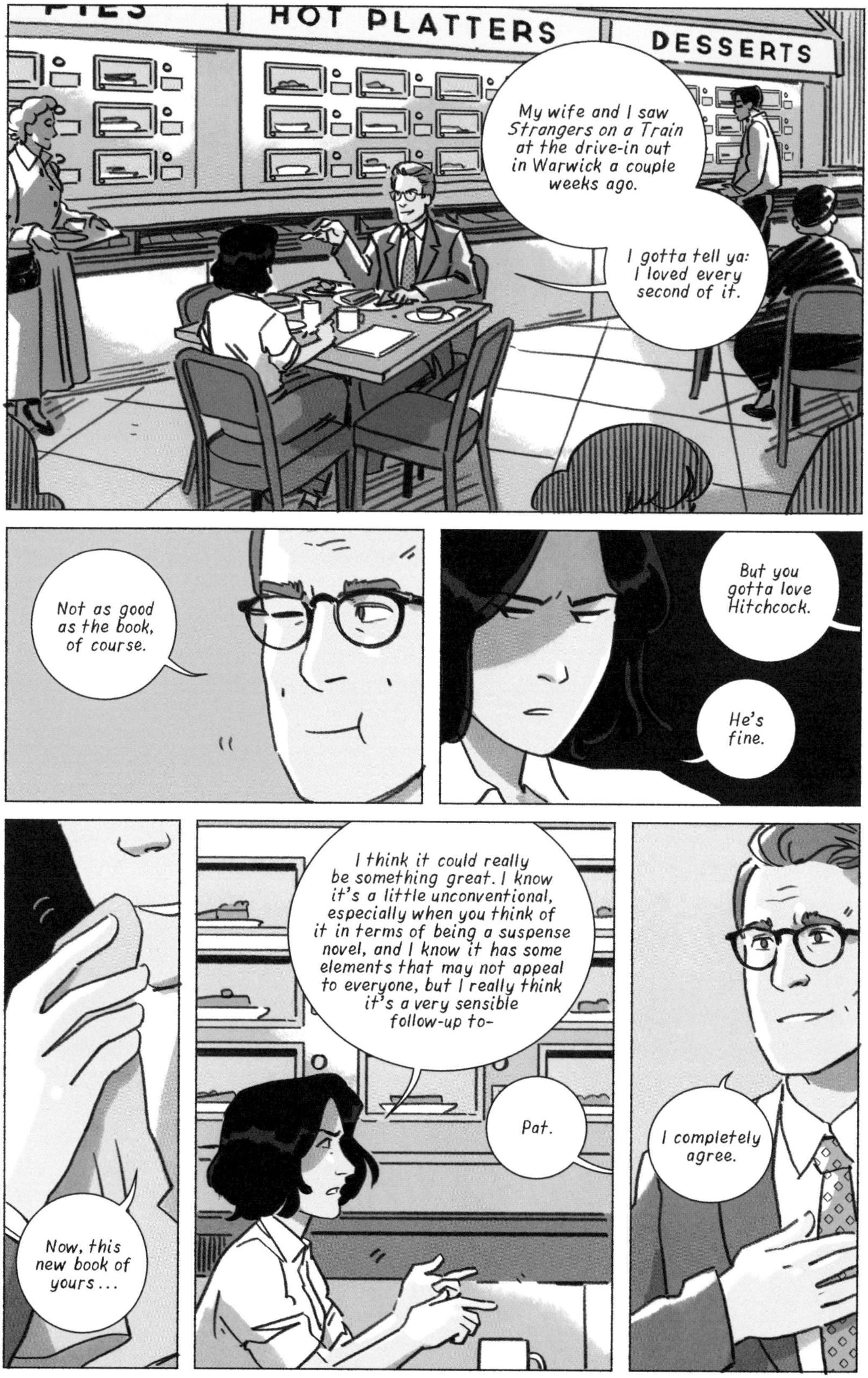
PIES
HOT PLATTERS
DESSERTS
My wife and I saw Strangers on a Train at the drive-in out in Warwick a couple weeks ago.
I gotta tell ya: I loved every second of it.
Not as good as the book, of course.
But you gotta love Hitchcock.
He's fine.
Now, this new book of yours...
I think it could really be something great. I know it's a little unconventional, especially when you think of it in terms of being a suspense novel, and I know it has some elements that may not appeal to everyone, but I really think it's a very sensible follow-up to-
Pat.
I completely agree.

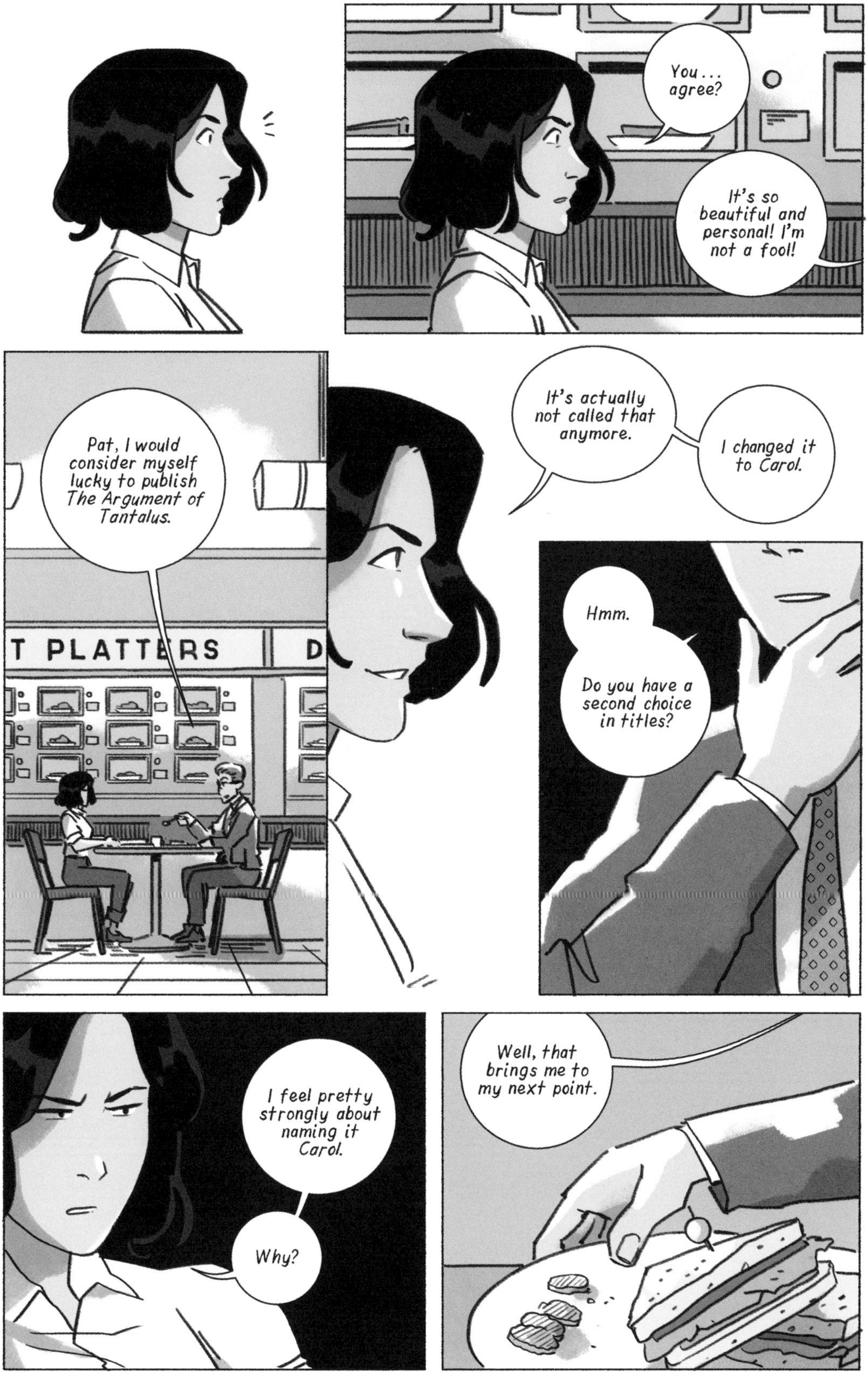
You... agree?
It's so beautiful and personal! I'm not a fool!
Pat, I would consider myself lucky to publish The Argument of Tantalus.
T PLATTERS D
It's actually not called that anymore.
I changed it to Carol.
Hmm.
Do you have a second choice in titles?
I feel pretty strongly about naming it Carol.
Why?
Well, that brings me to my next point.

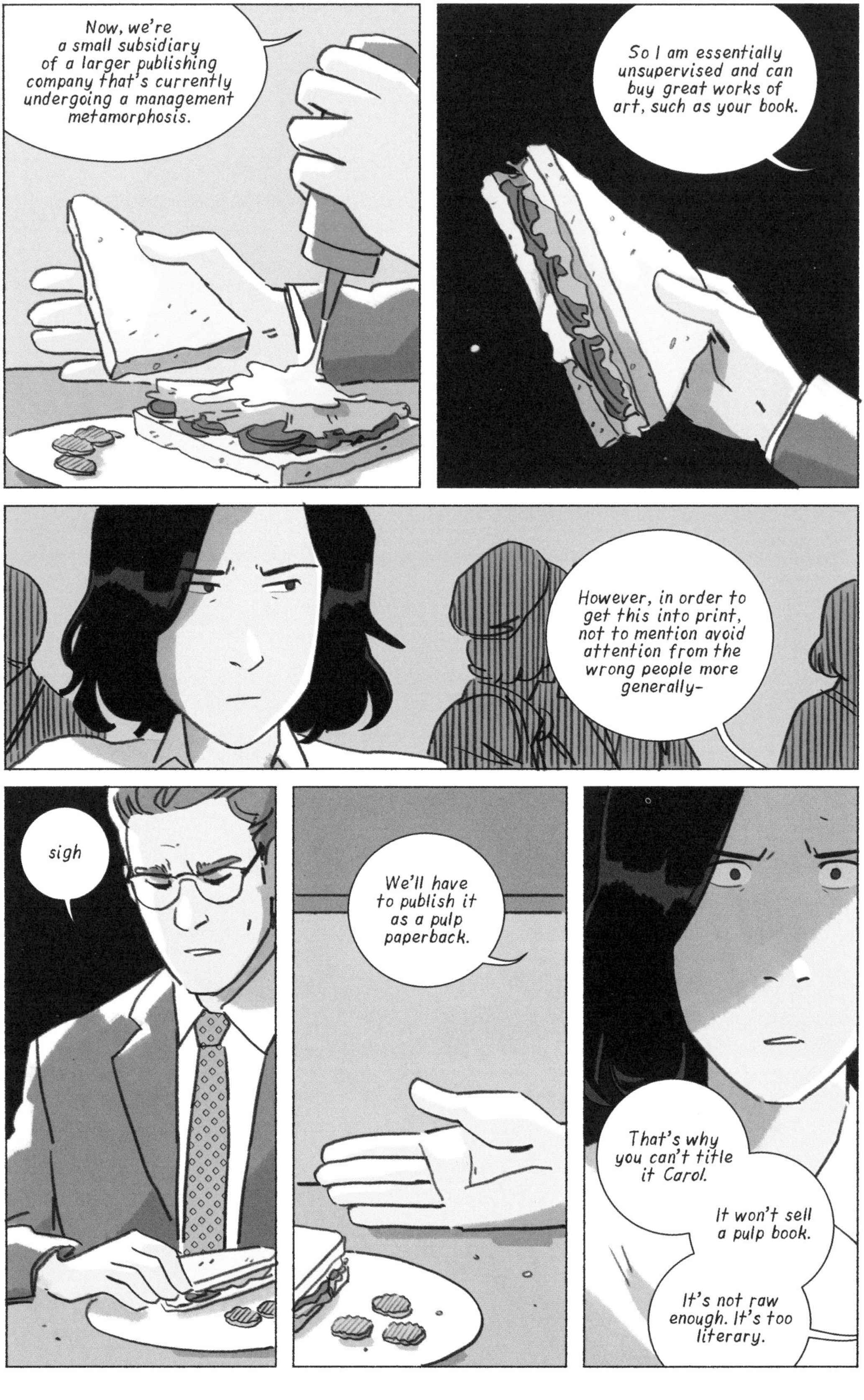
Now, we're a small subsidiary of a larger publishing company that's currently undergoing a management metamorphosis.
So I am essentially unsupervised and can buy great works of art, such as your book.
However, in order to get this into print, not to mention avoid attention from the wrong people more generally-
sigh
We'll have to publish it as a pulp paperback.
That's why you can't title it Carol.
It won't sell a pulp book.
It's not raw enough. It's too literary.

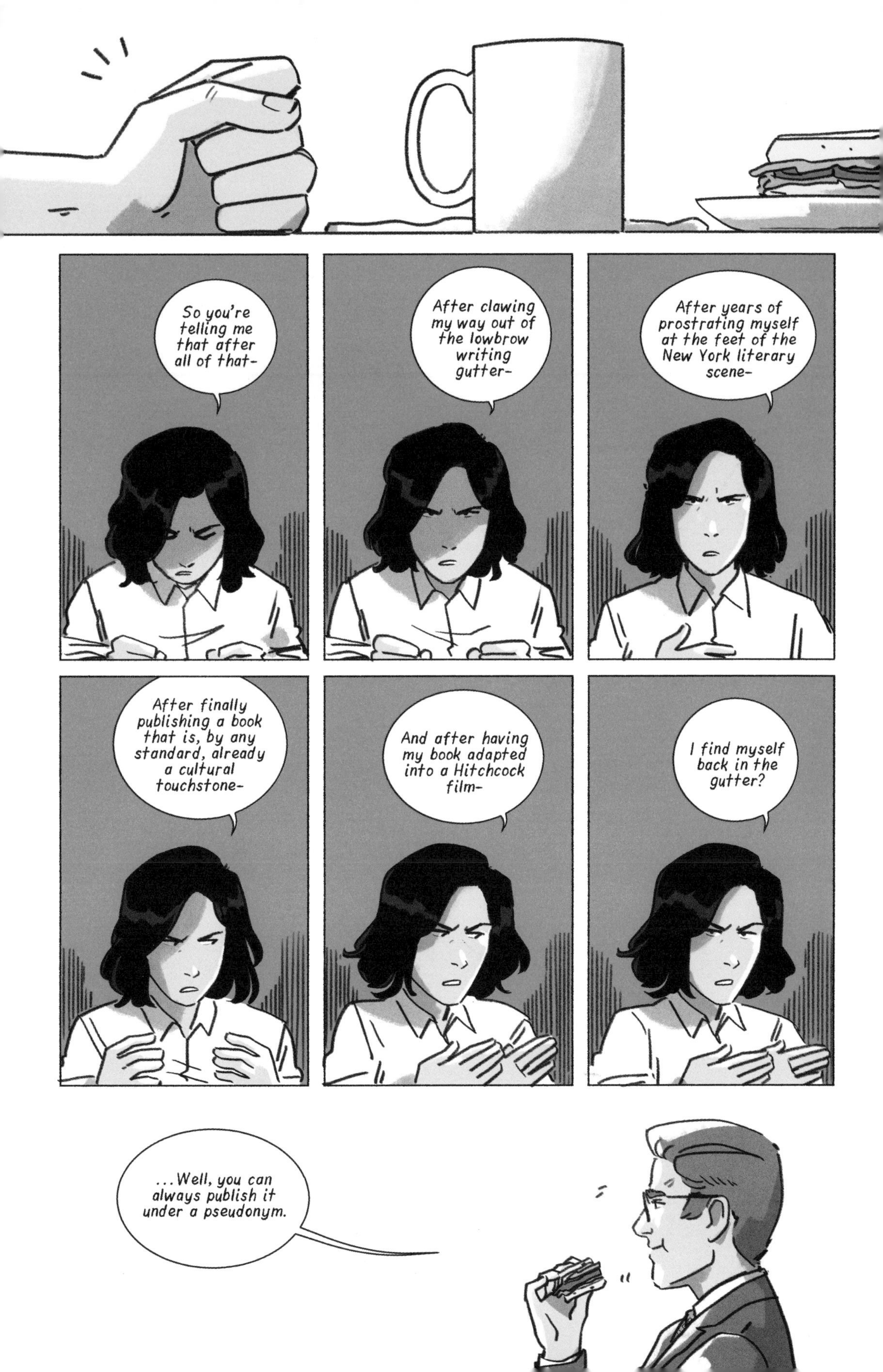
So you're telling me that after all of that-
After clawing my way out of the lowbrow writing gutter-
After years of prostrating myself at the feet of the New York literary scene-
After finally publishing a book that is, by any standard, already a cultural touchstone-
And after having my book adapted into a Hitchcock film-
I find myself back in the gutter?
...Well, you can always publish it under a pseudonym.

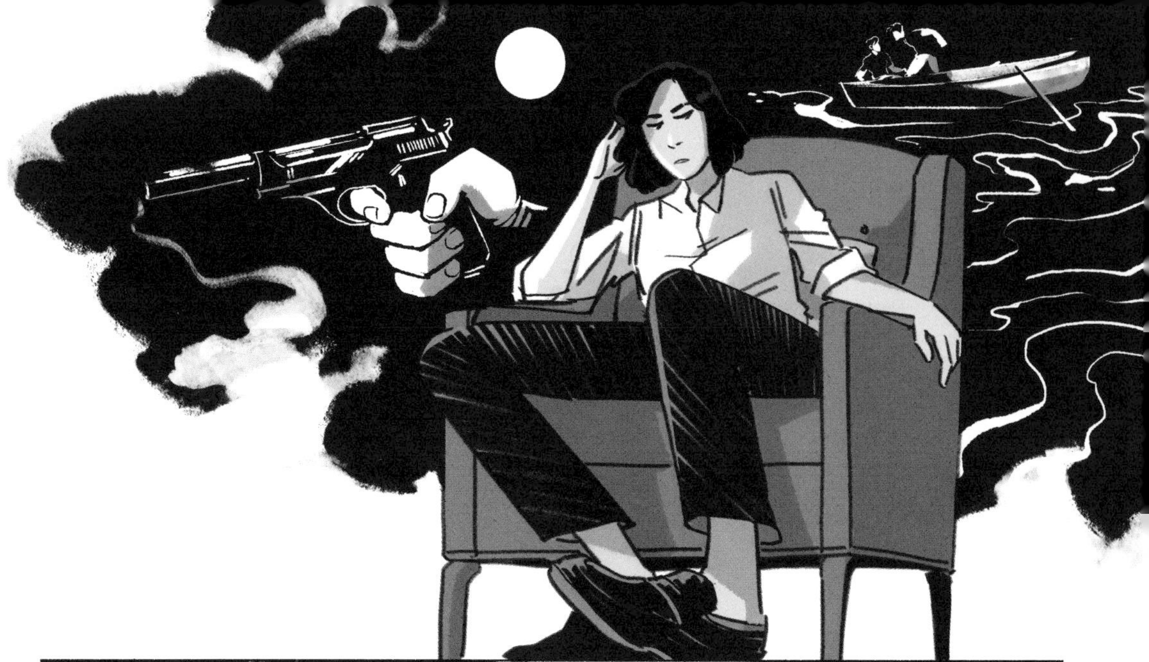

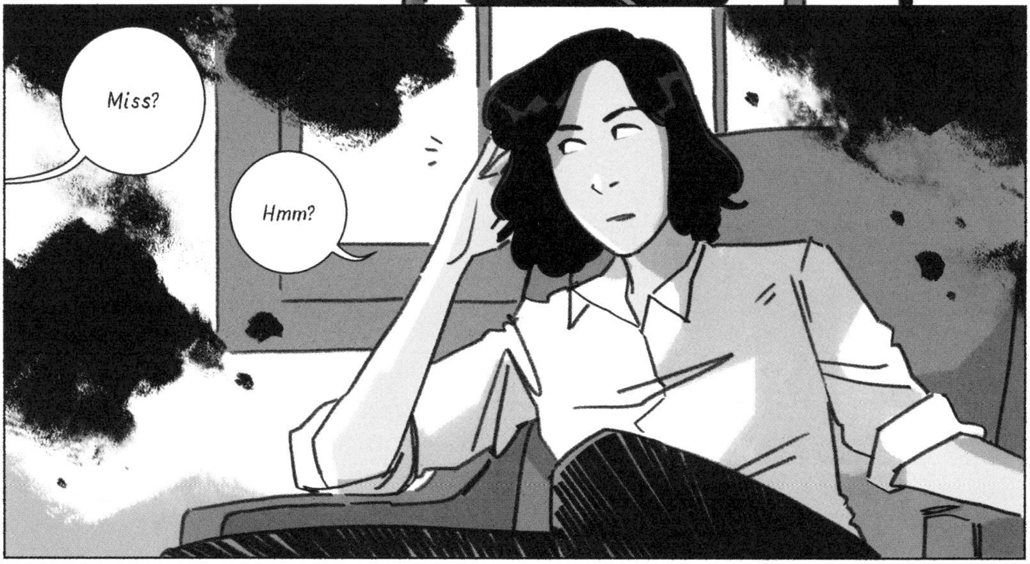
Miss?
Hmm?

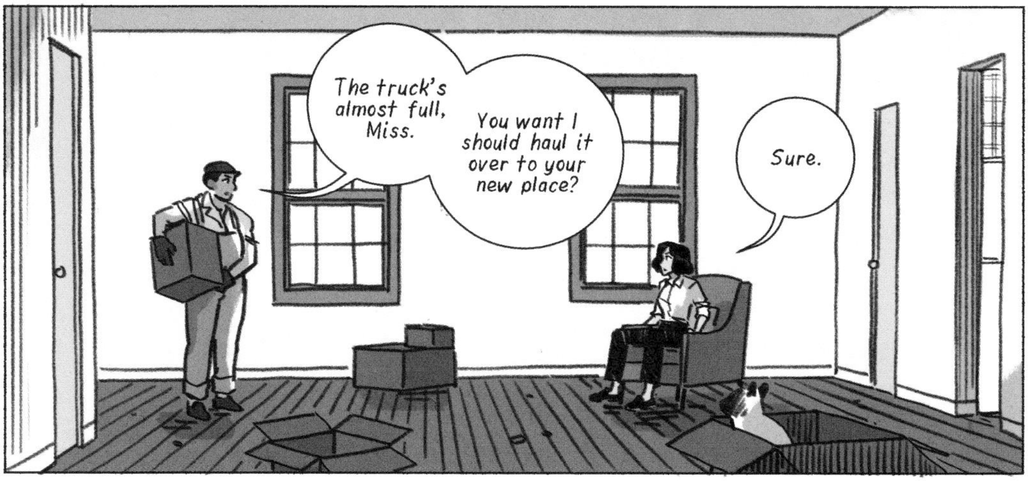
The truck's almost full, Miss.
You want I should haul it over to your new place?
Sure.

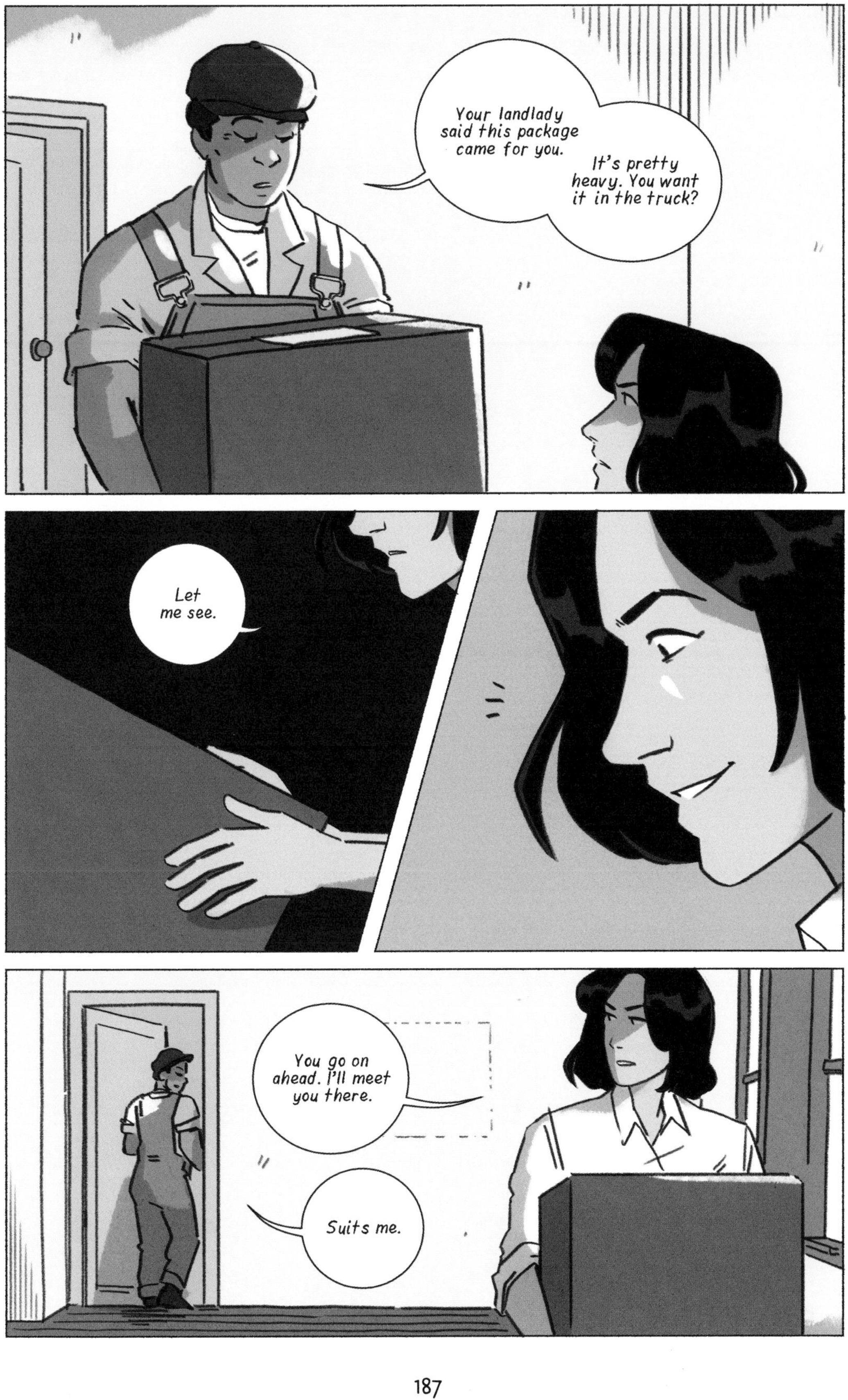
Your landlady said this package came for you.
It's pretty heavy. You want it in the truck?
Let me see.
You go on ahead. I'll meet you there.
Suits me.

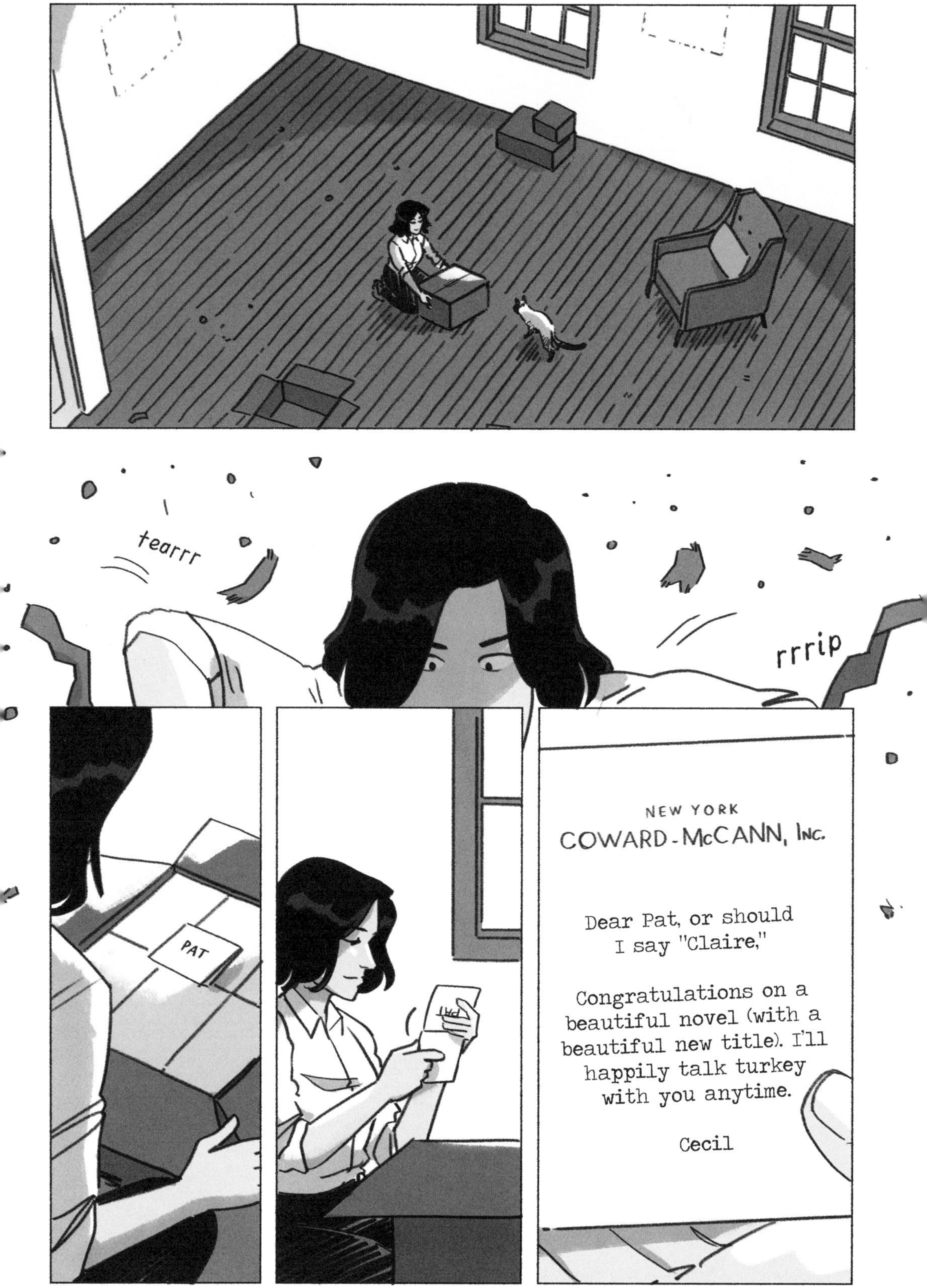
tearrr
rrrip
PAT
NEW YORK
COWARD-McCANN, INC.
Dear Pat, or should
I say "Claire,"
Congratulations on a
beautiful novel (with a
beautiful new title). I'll
happily talk turkey
with you anytime.
Cecil

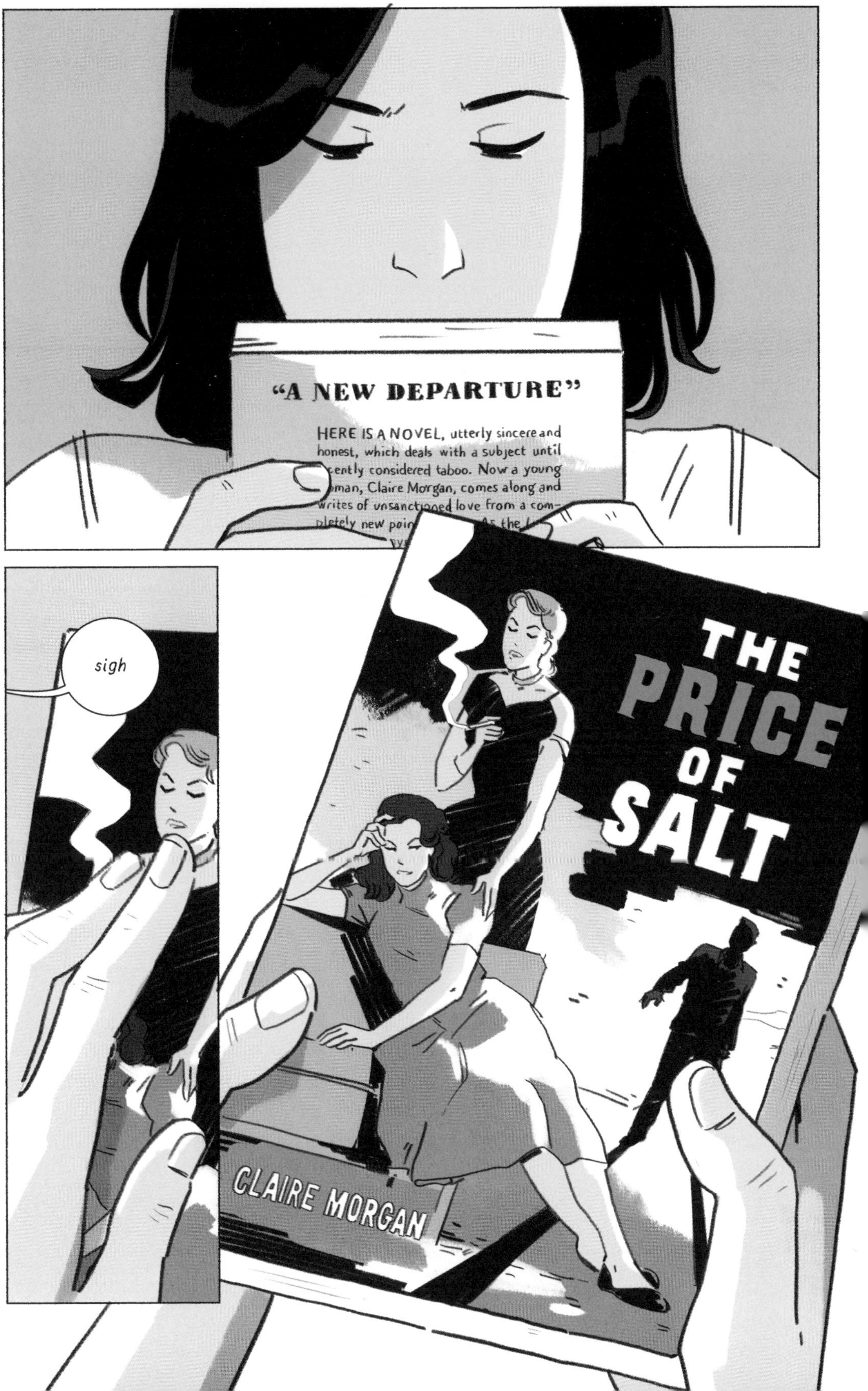
"A NEW DEPARTURE"
HERE IS A NOVEL, utterly sincere and
honest, which deals with a subject until
cently considered taboo. Now a young
oman, Claire Morgan, comes along and
writes of unsanctioned love from a completely new poin
sigh
THE PRICE OF SALT
CLAIRE MORGAN

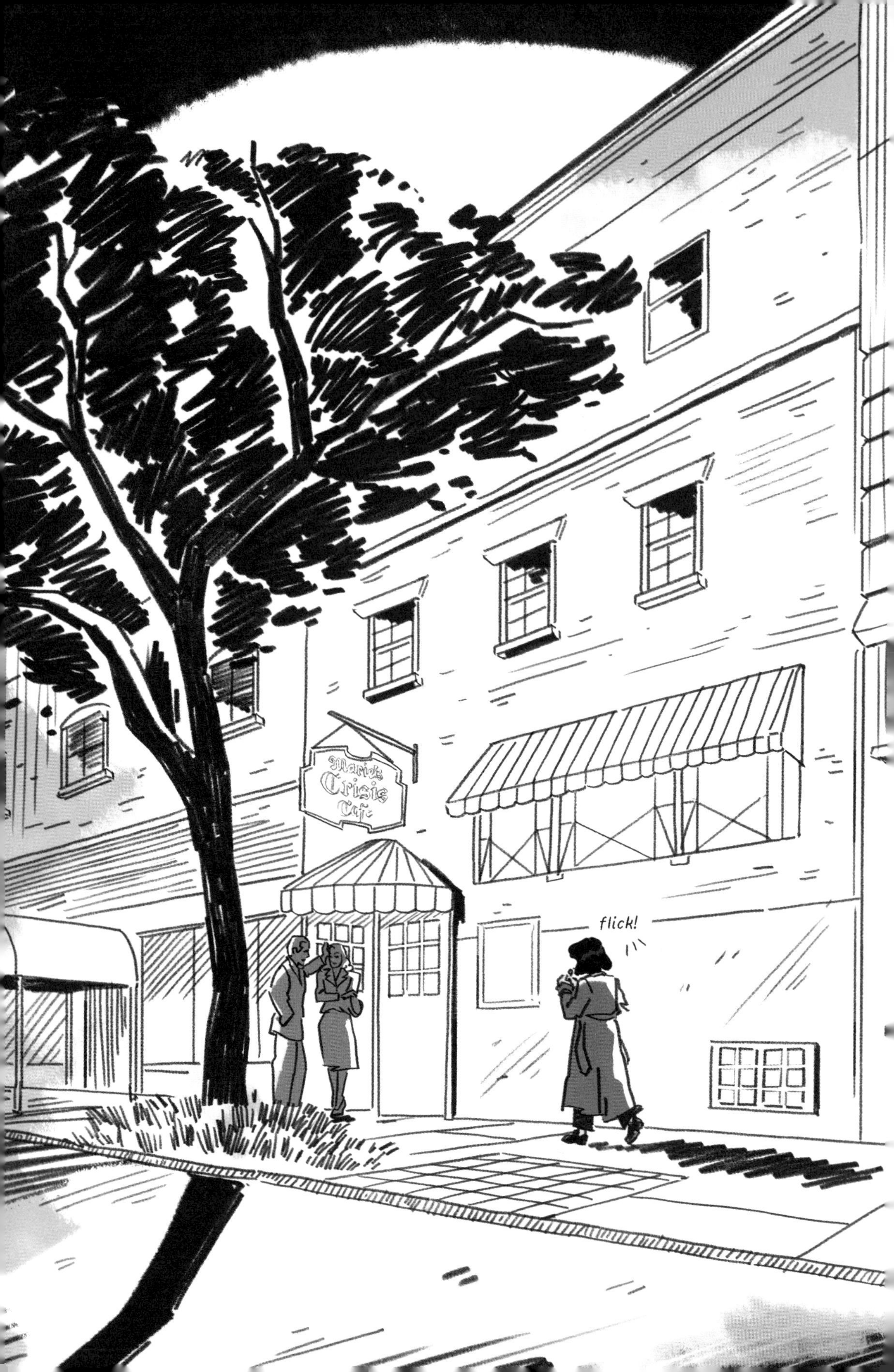
Marie's
Crisis
Cafe
flick!

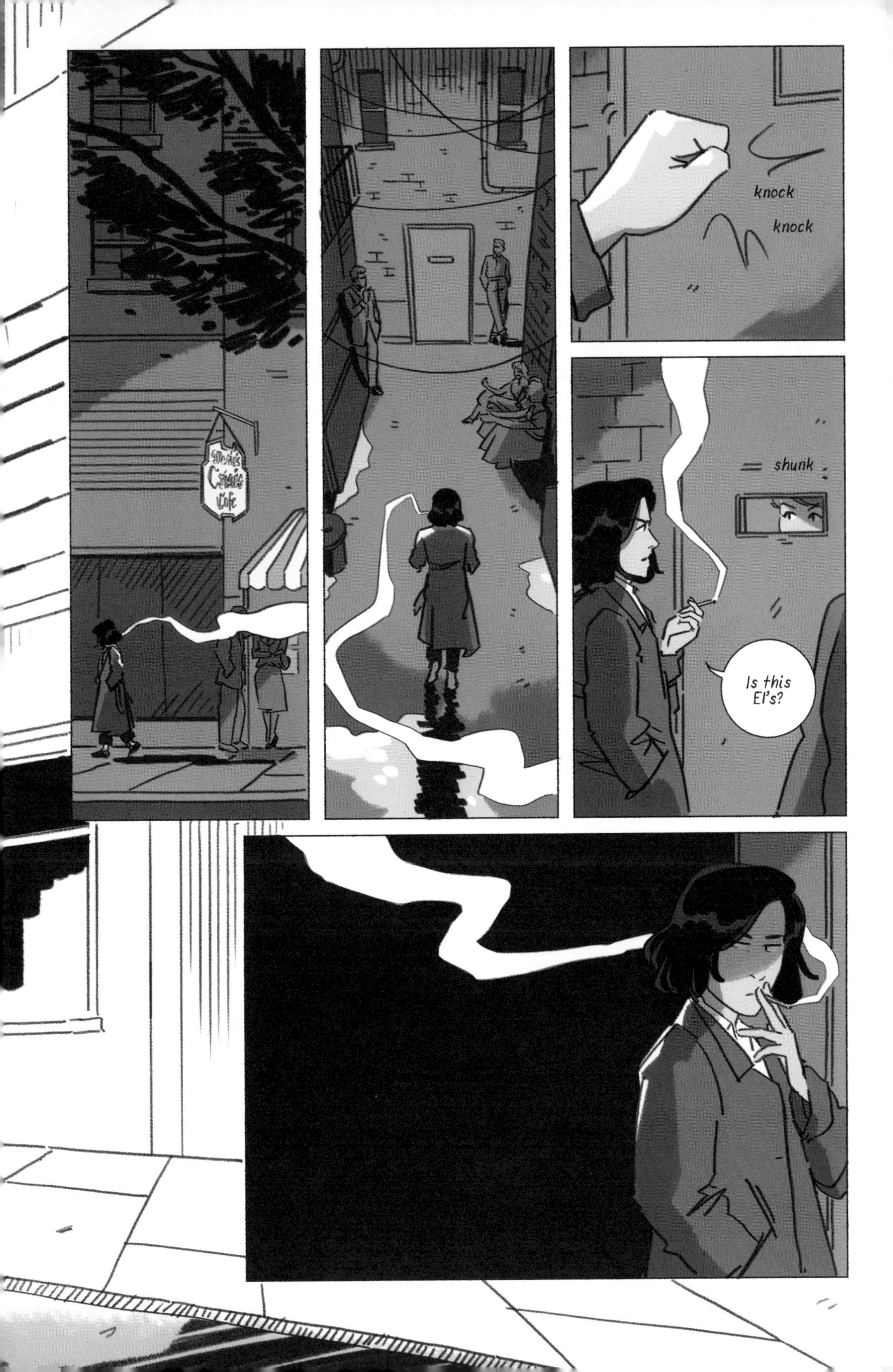
knock
knock
shunk
Is this El's?

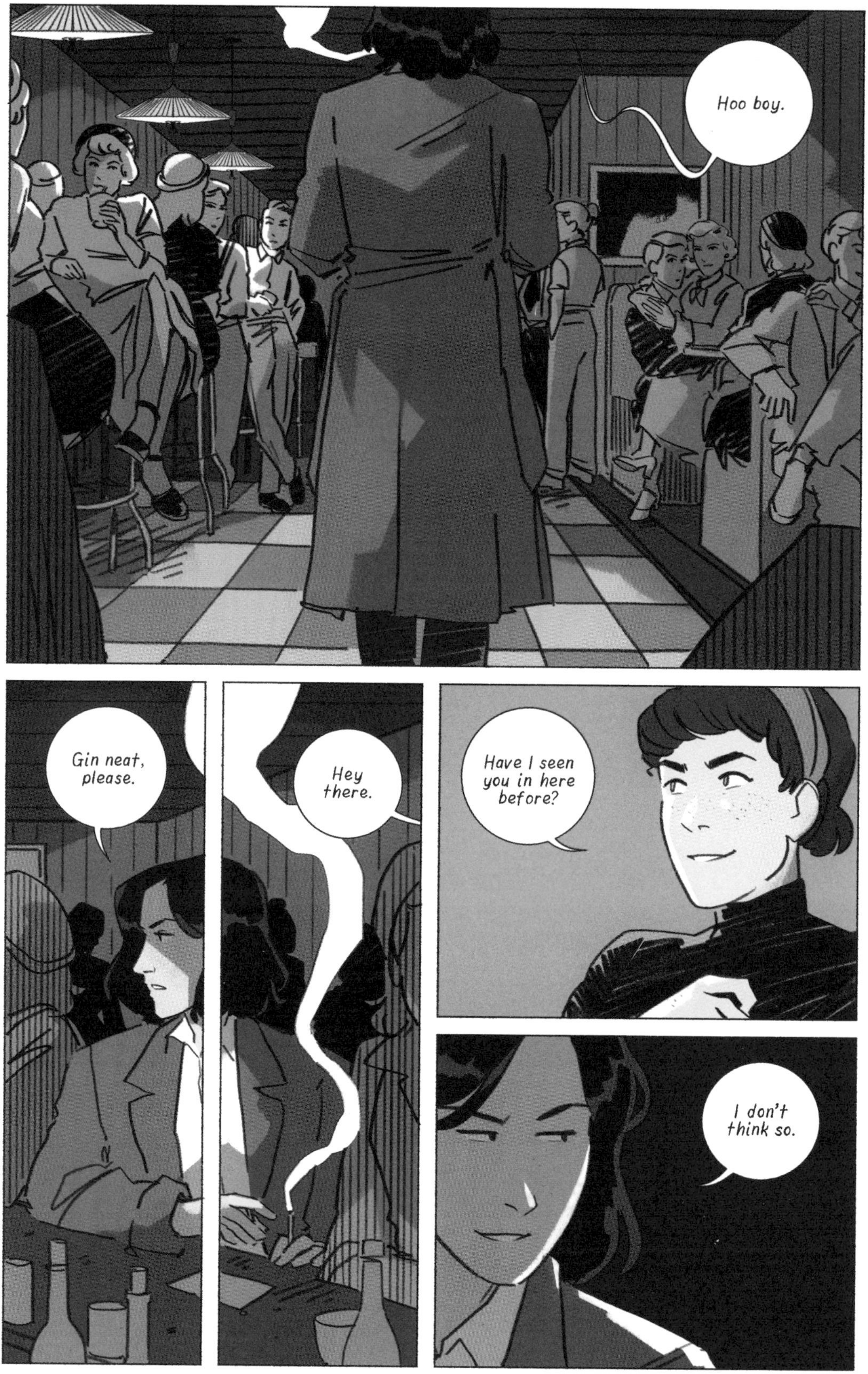
Hoo boy.
Gin neat, please.
Hey there.
Have I seen you in here before?
I don't think so.

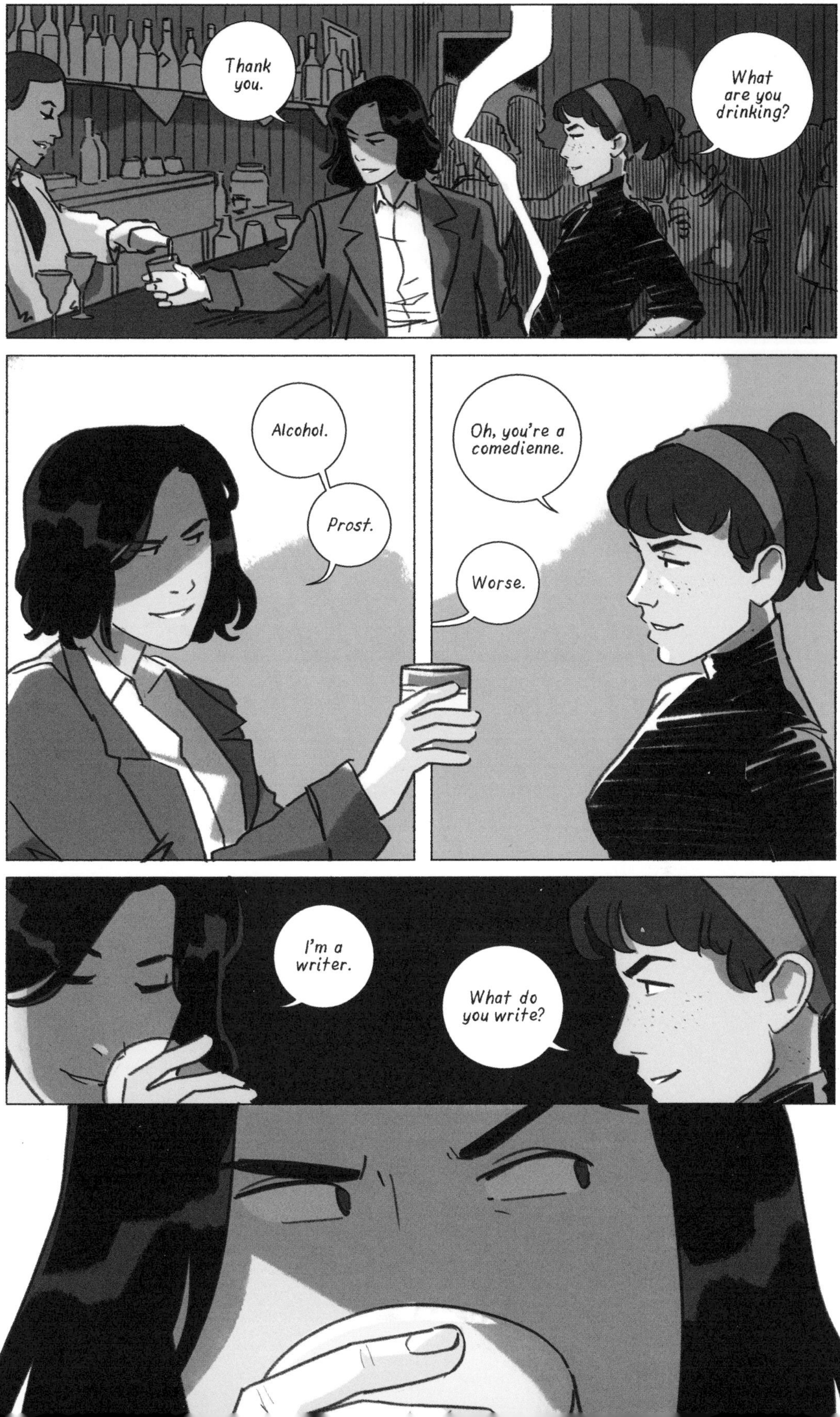
Thank you.
What are you drinking?
Alcohol.
Prost.
Oh, you're a comedienne.
Worse.
I'm a writer.
What do you write?

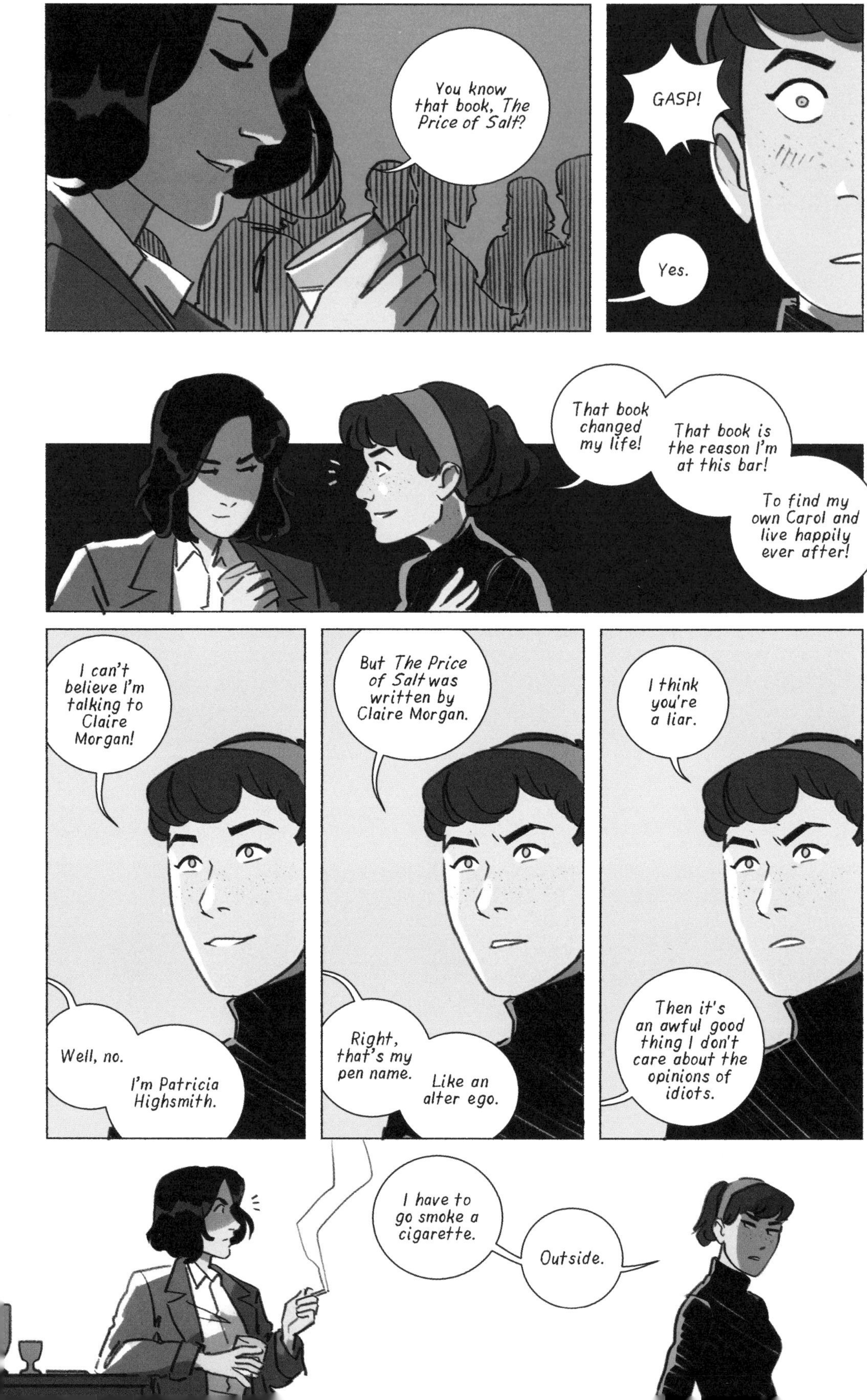
You know that book, The Price of Salt?
GASP!
Yes.
That book changed my life!
That book is the reason I'm at this bar!
To find my own Carol and live happily ever after!
I can't believe I'm talking to Claire Morgan!
Well, no.
I'm Patricia Highsmith.
But The Price of Salt was written by Claire Morgan.
Right, that's my pen name.
Like an alter ego.
I think you're a liar.
Then it's an awful good thing I don't care about the opinions of idiots.
I have to go smoke a cigarette.
Outside.

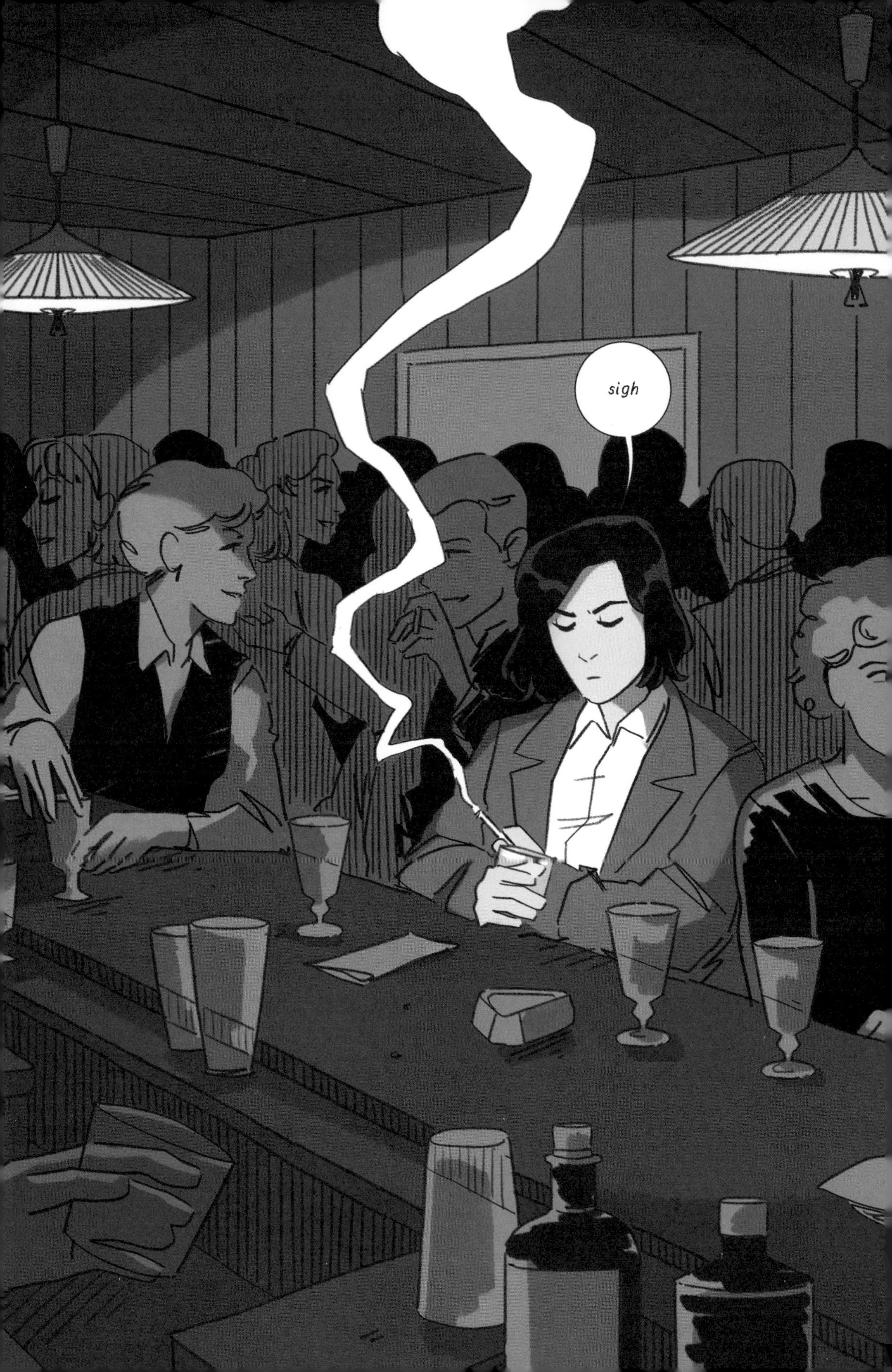
sigh

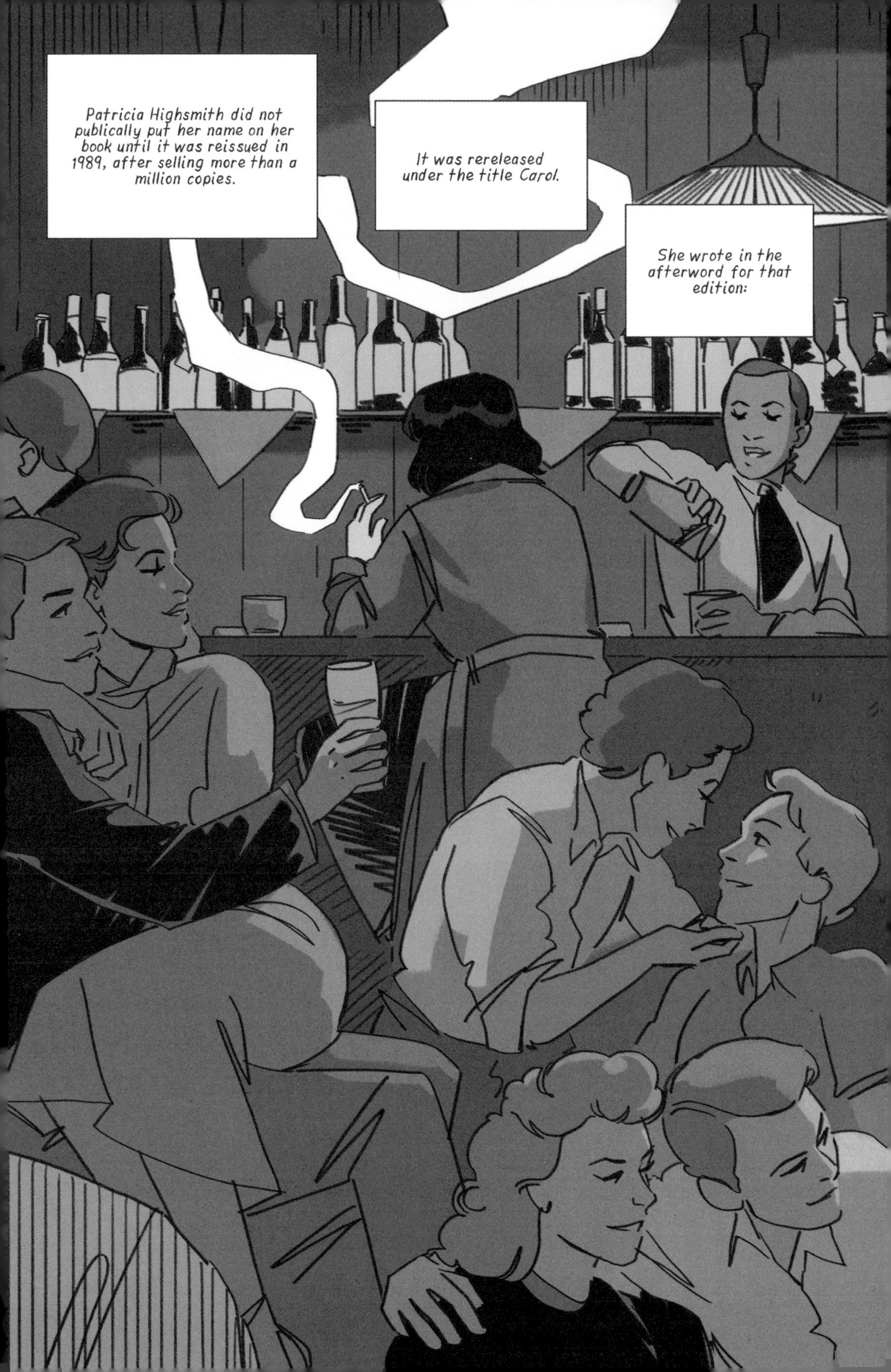
Patricia Highsmith did not publically put her name on her book until it was reissued in 1989, after selling more than a million copies.
It was rereleased under the title Carol.
She wrote in the afterword for that edition:

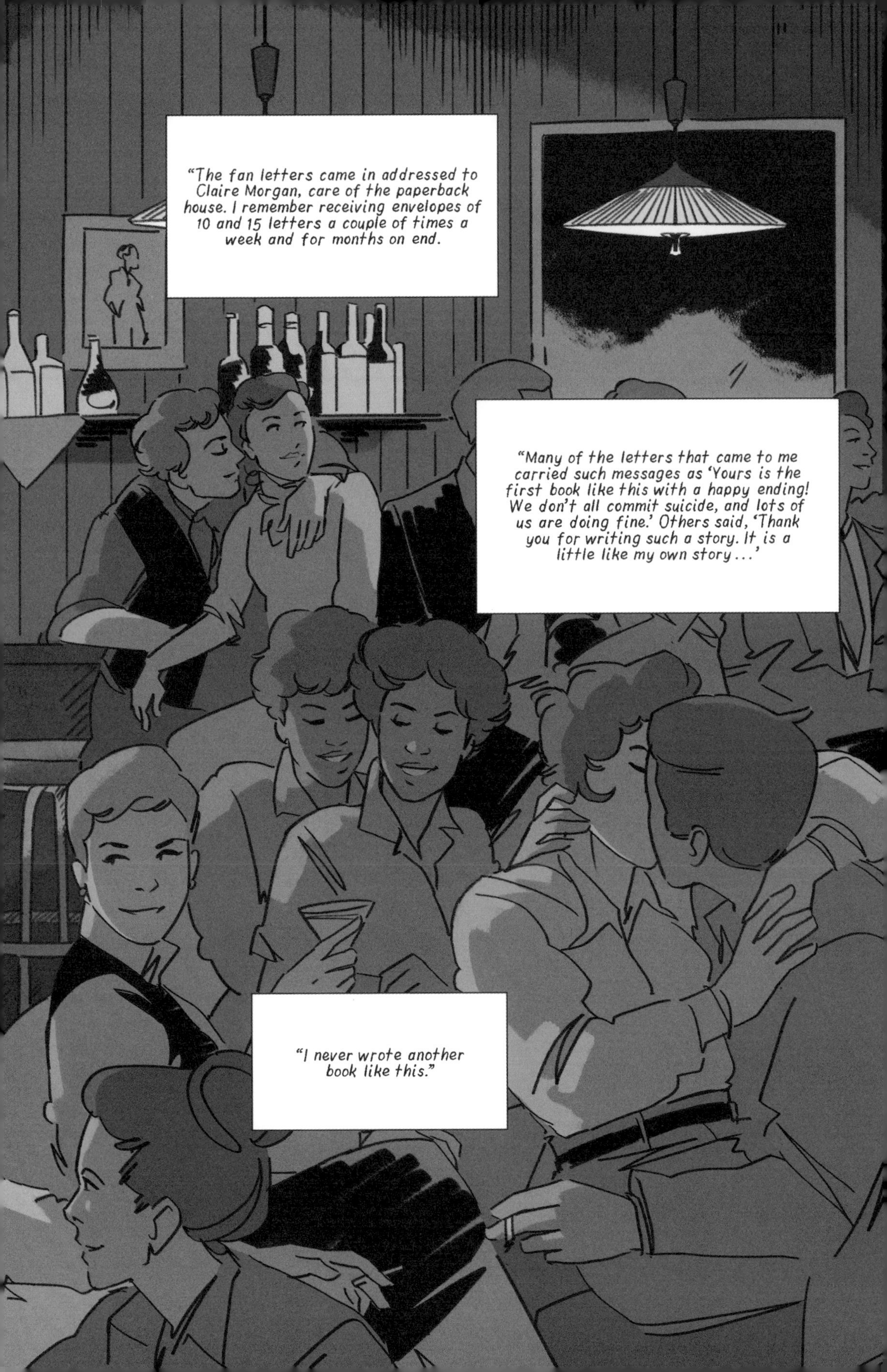
"The fan letters came in addressed to Claire Morgan, care of the paperback house. I remember receiving envelopes of 10 and 15 letters a couple of times a week and for months on end.
"Many of the letters that came to me carried such messages as 'Yours is the first book like this with a happy ending! We don't all commit suicide, and lots of us are doing fine.' Others said, 'Thank you for writing such a story. It is a little like my own story . . .'
"I never wrote another book like this."

SELECTED BIBLIOGRAPHY

Hajdu, David. *The Ten-Cent Plague: the Great Comic-Book Scare and How It Changed America.* Picador, 2009.

Highsmith, Patricia. *Carol.* Bloomsbury, 2015.

Meaker, Marijane. *Highsmith: a Romance of the 1950s.* Cleis, 2003.

Schenkar, Joan. *The Talented Miss Highsmith: the Secret Life and Serious Art of Patricia Highsmith.* Picador, 2011.

Wilson, Andrew. *Beautiful Shadow: a Life of Patricia Highsmith.* Bloomsbury, 2010.